Piers Plowman: Critical Approaches

PIERS PLOWMAN
Critical Approaches

Edited by
S. S. HUSSEY

METHUEN & CO LTD
11 NEW FETTER LANE · LONDON EC4

First published 1969 *by Methuen & Co. Ltd.*
11 *New Fetter Lane, London E.C.*4
© 1969 *Methuen & Co. Ltd.*
Printed in Great Britain by
T. & A. Constable Ltd. Edinburgh

SBN 416 12290

Distributed in the U.S.A.
by Barnes & Noble Inc.

Contents

v

Contents

Foreword

My original intention was to produce a book where half the essays would represent the best of published material on *Piers Plowman* and half original work. But the recent appearance of anthologies of criticism of medieval literature (particularly in America and including one devoted solely to *Piers Plowman*) made the first part of the plan less necessary. There would have been little point in reproducing what has been made conveniently accessible elsewhere and less in searching out articles of secondary importance. Consequently, all the papers in this collection have been written especially for it.

I have been most fortunate in my contributors, some of whom agreed to collaborate at times not specially convenient for them. Even those who had to refuse because either time or inspiration was not forthcoming were most helpful in suggesting others where these commodities might be in better supply. But a general editor has responsibilities too. The final arrangement and checking must be his, and I must answer for shortcomings of this kind. The arrangement of the papers proceeds broadly from discussion of particular sections of the poem, through consideration of especially important or difficult characters, to the poet's treatment of major aspects of his work. I have tried to ensure that previous writers on *Piers* receive fair acknowledgment, but the mass of criticism is now so large that I cannot be certain that this has always been done. I have not considered it necessary to remove conflicting views from different essays. Controversy is a marked feature of the poem itself and has often motivated its critics. Yet it is only by the presentation of various and varying views of what Langland intended that we are likely to reach the heart of what is one of the most difficult but also the most rewarding works in Middle English.

Two final expressions of thanks give me great pleasure: to Messrs. Methuen for their help in producing this book, and to Professor George Kane who long ago first aroused my interest in *Piers Plowman* and who later, both by his own scholarship and by friendly criticism, did much to cultivate it.

S. S. HUSSEY

Abbreviations

EC	*Essays in Criticism*
EETS OS	Early English Text Society, Original Series
EETS ES	Early English Text Society, Extra Series
ELH	*ELH: A Journal of English Literary History*
JEGP	*Journal of English and Germanic Philology*
MÆ	*Medium Ævum*
MED	*Middle English Dictionary*, edited H. Kurath and S. M. Kuhn
MLR	*Modern Language Review*
MP	*Modern Philology*
OED	*The Oxford English Dictionary*, edited J. A. H. Murray etc.
PL	*Patrologia Latina*, edited J. Migne
PMLA	*Publications of the Modern Language Association of America*
PQ	*Philological Quarterly*
RES	*Review of English Studies*
SP	*Studies in Philology*

Introduction

S. S. HUSSEY

Piers Plowman has the reputation of being a difficult poem. In the first place it exists not in one version but in three, conventionally called A, B and C, which seem to represent progressive revisions on the part of the author. Much of it uses allegory, a method of expression far less familiar and congenial to us than to the medieval audience. It also seems to have very little order about it; we cannot easily grasp its shape as we can that of the *Divine Comedy* or *Paradise Lost*. Into the Prologue of B and C which are busy describing the Folk on the Field, their manner of life and its justification in the eyes of man and of God, is suddenly thrust the fable of the rats who wanted to bell the cat. At the beginning of the very last passus (or section) of the poem, which relates the attack of Antichrist and his host on the barn Unity built by Piers Plowman, we meet a character called Need who justifies a life of begging and even stealing to provide him with the bare necessities of life. These insertions, and others like them, can be explained, but they are puzzling to those who expect a relatively straightforward poem where digressions, if they occur at all, are clearly labelled as such and where the author (as at the beginning of Book IX of *Paradise Lost*) takes us into his confidence and tells us clearly what he has done and what he is about to do.

Yet the primary question posed by this long poem is a simple one. Not long after the beginning of passus i, the Dreamer – the character who links the audience to the action – meets Lady Holy Church and asks her:

> Teche me to no tresore, but telle me this ilke,
> How I may saue my soule, that seynt art yholden.

The Prologue has been greatly concerned with money (*tresore*), how to get it and how to use it. Clearly this new question is more important. Lady Holy Church's answer is:

'Whan alle tresores aren tried,' quod she, 'trewthe is the best,'

and *trewthe*, 'integrity', 'loyalty', is, at the close of this passus, linked with love:

> Loue is leche of lyf, and nexte owre lorde selue,
> And also the graith gate that goth into heuene;
> Forthi I sey as I seide ere by the textis,
> Whan alle tresores ben ytryed, treuthe is the beste.

In the last passus of the poem the Dreamer, desperate and in fear of death, asks Kynde (Nature) what is really the identical question he had asked Holy Church at the beginning, and Kynde's reply is the same as hers:

> 'Conseille me, Kynde,' quod I, 'what crafte is best to lerne?'
> 'Lerne to loue,' quod Kynde, 'and leue of alle othre.'

God is Truth and God is Love – the simplest and yet the most profound answer of all.

But in any great poem it is not only the final solution that interests us. It is also the struggle to arrive at this solution, the examination and rejection of other solutions, the apprehension of new truths or of old truths seen anew, the pressure of the discussion as it veers to and fro. It is the way we are made to share in the Dreamer's search, the way we too participate in a great unfinished argument, that is, to my mind, one of the great successes of *Piers Plowman*. Had the poem been more straightforward, it might well have accomplished far less. And so many other important considerations become caught up into this argument – predestination, the state of the contemporary church, the treatment of the deserving poor, the limits of knowledge, and countless others – that, whatever the final answer, the progress of the poem cannot be simple. It is the hope that fresh examinations of a few of these questions (some of them dealing with the whole poem, others with especially difficult sections like the Pardon or puzzling characters like Piers or Conscience) may lead us to a clearer solution that has prompted this collection of essays.

For the comparative beginner in *Piers Plowman*, however, there exists another kind of difficulty which may properly be considered in an introduction. The poem has been read and quoted in every century since its composition; the sixteenth-century Protestants, for example, professed to see support for their teachings in its ecclesiastical satire, and it was one of them, Robert Crowley, who first printed the poem (in a B-text version). But *Piers Plowman* scholarship really began in 1866 when there appeared proposals for a new edition by Skeat. These consisted of an appeal for information about manuscripts and a specimen passage from the twenty-nine manuscripts which were all those known to Skeat; now over fifty are known. It is to Skeat that we owe the recognition of the A-text as a separate form of the poem and the chronology A, B, C. We are still using Skeat's Early English Text Society edition, published between 1867 and 1885, or his Parallel Texts edition which is essentially the same three texts printed on facing pages to make comparison easier. In this book, with the exception of the first essay, quotation will be from the Parallel Texts edition (omitting the mid-line caesura point and with punctuation slightly modified) but A-text readings have been checked against the text edited by Professor George Kane (London, 1960). When the Athlone Press publishes its editions of B and C and the Middle English Dictionary is complete, we shall be in a much stronger position to make an accurate and detailed study of the whole poem. Meanwhile, in the hundred years since Skeat, scholarship has not remained still. Around *Piers Plowman* there has grown up a pile of books and articles which have sometimes threatened to bury the poem they sought to elucidate. It is easy now, with the benefit of hindsight, to see that some of these investigations (such as the controversy over authorship) expended much time and ink to far less real purpose. Yet few of them have been wholly without point, and it may be useful to see how much about the poem can now be established with relative certainty.

All three versions of the poem are divided into passus (or sections). Cutting across this division is a further and larger one into visions. Several medieval poems are cast in the form of a dream, though nowhere else do we find, as here, several dreams with interludes in the 'real world' between them. Unfortunately, neither passus nor visions begin and end at the same point in all three texts. (Even more confusingly, A and B begin with a Prologue whilst the corresponding opening section of C is called passus i). Hence cross-reference between texts is a little more complicated than might be expected. For example, suppose one refers to the Pardon sent by Truth to Piers and his followers. In B, the version of the poem most often quoted by critics, this appears in passus vii, but in A the corresponding passage is in passus viii and in C in passus x. A still further and broader division of the poem can also be made. The whole first part of *Piers Plowman*, up to Piers's tearing of the Pardon and the Dreamer's reflections on this, is called the *Visio* which is simply a title used in several of the manuscripts. The *Visio* ends with the Dreamer puzzled and resolved to seek Dowel (a name which comes from the *qui bona egerunt* of the Pardon). The *Visio* is fairly closely integrated. Contemporary problems are seen in a narrative setting, but are seen from the point of view of Christianity. The rest of the poem is called the *Vita*. The word *Vita* is actually used only in manuscripts of the A-text; in B and C this long second section is usually called simply *Dowel, Dobet and Dobest*, and is divided into three unequal parts with those titles. But it is clear that a major division of the poem comes at this point in all three texts. I shall therefore call what comes before this division the *Visio*, and everything that comes after the *Vita*, even though, as has been said, these terms are 'more convenient than accurate'.[1] The *Vita* gradually gets more difficult. The Dreamer soon finds that there are two more ways of life, Dobet and Dobest, to add to Dowel. This piece of information is introduced quite casually by Thought, the first of the many allegorical characters in the first part of the *Vita*. So the Dreamer goes on seeking where these three may be found and what they mean, certain that in them lies the key to salvation. In the rest of the poem he gets various answers from people of varying degrees of trustworthiness and responsibility. The *Vita de Dowel*, the first of the three divisions of the *Vita*, does not however discuss Dowel only; it also considers Dobet and Dobest. It is usual, therefore, to italicize *Dowel* when this refers to that particular section of the poem in order to distinguish the title from Dowel, the state or manner of life understood by that name.

The A-text consists, in most manuscripts, of a Prologue and eleven passus. A twelfth passus appears fully in one A manuscript and imperfectly in two others. Its last few lines (106-117) are definitely spurious, and the preceding few (99-105) which describe the death of the Dreamer in the third person instead of the first person employed earlier in the passus, may well be spurious too. Lines 1-98 have some sort of connexion with the preceding passus A xi and may conceivably be an abortive continuation of the A-text by its author, who later had second thoughts and jettisoned this passus in the course of turning A into B. Some lines of A xii seem worthy of *Piers Plowman* proper, but this argument from style is, of course, a dangerous one. The B-text is about twice as long again as A. The *Visio* is broadly the same; there are expansions to bring out a point more clearly, but few new arguments. The B *Vita* takes up the same questions as the corresponding A *Vita*, but reaches different conclusions. It is then extended greatly beyond the scope of A to cover not only the *Vita de Dowel* but *Dobet* and *Dobest* as well. The B poet did not necessarily begin his revision of A with the Prologue. Professor Coghill believes he began with the Pardon, because that was the first part of A that really dissatisfied him. C revises almost the whole of B, except that the last two passus, covering the *Vita de Dobest*, remain virtually intact. There is a good deal of line-by-line revision in C, especially in the *Visio*. It is interesting that C is apt to revise again lines that had already been revised once in changing A into B, as if he was never quite satisfied with certain parts of his poem. Similarly, just as B's *Dowel* had been drastically changed from A's, so C's is changed yet again. The result of this last change is that C's *Dowel* is shorter (and often clearer) than B's. But C does make additions to B as well, for example an elaboration of the distinction, already there in B, between two kinds of Meed, one bad, one good. C calls these *mede* and *mercede* ('just reward'). There is also a certain amount of material transferred from the B *Vita* to the C *Visio*, especially where parts of Haukyn's confession in B appear as parts of the confessions of the sins in C. This must have been fairly easy to do because the material was very similar. The extent of these transpositions can easily be seen by glancing at Skeat's Parallel Texts edition.

It should not be thought that straightforward A, B and C texts represent the only extant 'shapes' of the poem. Some manuscripts are imperfect at the end, the result, no doubt, of the loss of the final few leaves of parchment. Others show a joining of two versions: for example, three manuscripts (Trinity College, Cambridge R.3.14; Liverpool University Library F.4.8, 'Chaderton'; and British Museum, Harley 6041) contain A Prologue to passus xi followed by a C conclusion. In medieval eyes the most desirable manuscript seems to have been not the closest to the author's original but the latest or the fullest. The scribe or compiler of a manuscript might well think it reasonable that after the A-text came to an end it should be followed by a continuation from another version. There are other cases where such contamination permeates the whole text, so that B and C material will appear suddenly in the middle of an A-text manuscript or vice versa. The clumsiness of this carpentry and the imperfect acquaintanceship it reveals with versions other than the one being copied, make it virtually certain that the scribes rather than the author were responsible.

Scribes, in fact, have a good deal to answer for in the transmission of almost every medieval text of any length. They evidently acted not simply as copyists but on their own initiative as editors, but without the modern editor's sense of responsibility towards his material. As Professor Kane has pointed out,[2] the content of *Piers Plowman* was interesting enough and of sufficient contemporary relevance to persuade the scribes of their ability to improve on the original. Frequently they appear to have tried to produce a more intelligible, a more explicit, or a more emphatic text than their exemplar. Like us, they found the poem difficult. And a work written in unrhymed lines with a greatly varying number of syllables per line made alteration that much easier. All these conscious substitutions are in addition to the mechanical errors (usually fairly easy to identify) which will naturally have arisen in the copying out of a long poem.

The editor's task begins with a complete collation of all extant manuscripts, from the most complete to the most fragmentary or corrupt. Nothing less will do. In the case of *Piers Plowman*, all manuscripts are corrupt to some extent. Most of them are copies of copies, and have suffered, to varying degrees, from the 'improvement' of scribes. Their original relationship has become obscured by contamination, 'correction' and even by chance agreement in errors, since it is demonstrable that scribal error conforms to fairly clearly defined patterns and might therefore arise independently in two manuscripts not closely connected. Certain groups of manuscripts stand out from the collation and do probably represent some degree of genetic relationship, but the number of random groupings throws serious doubt (as Kane demonstrates) on the modern editor's ability to recover the reading of the archetype by identifying and rejecting unoriginal readings. Far from the right solution of every crux by information about the relationship of the manuscripts such as might be represented by a 'family tree', the authority of the text will vary from line to line. Originality is most often determined by establishing the direction of error, by identifying the variant most likely to have given rise to the others through one or more of the types of scribal change mentioned above. Frequently the harder reading will be the original, since no one would deliberately make comprehension more difficult. In such a situation certainty is often impossible; one can only say that one interpretation of the evidence is more probable than others. Each crux is therefore unique, and the manuscript chosen as the basis for the text, while it will naturally have been selected partly because it has few obvious errors and imperfections, will ideally be no more authoritative than the other manuscripts.

The extent of authorial work on the text of *Piers Plowman*, apart, of course, from the change of A into B and B into C, is probably now no longer demonstrable. It has been suggested[3] that two B-text manuscripts (Bodleian 15563, Rawlinson Poet. 38 and Corpus Christi College, Oxford, 201) represent a stage of the B-text slightly older than that of the remaining manuscripts, and that this difference may be attributable to the author himself rather than to a contaminator. The present editor of the C-text has pointed out[4] that the C-version was apparently left unfinished; not only is *Dobest* not revised, but there are also earlier lines and longer passages whose incompleteness is not easily explained by the sort of scribal corruption evident elsewhere. If the questing and unsatisfied mind of the Dreamer is to any real extent characteristic of

B

the poet himself (a question to which I shall return), it is altogether likely that he could not bring himself finally to relinquish his poem and that he continued tinkering with it until death or some other calamity finally forced him to let go. The A, B and C texts might then represent states of the poem when either insistent demand for copies, or satisfaction for the moment with what he had written, or some unexplained temporary absence from composition allowed a crystallization of the work into one of these three shapes which were then, by the usual process of scribal transmission, removed from the poet's control. But with this suggestion speculation outruns proof. The existence of the A, B and C versions is one of the few facts in *Piers Plowman* scholarship, and unless and until new manuscripts are discovered we had better hold on to it.

Most quotations from the poem in books of criticism and histories of literature are taken from the B-text. A breaks off in the early part of *Dowel*, and C is usually held to be inferior in poetic skill to B. The poet of C does undoubtedly at times eliminate some of B's vivid images or moderates or renders more prosaic striking passages in B. He now and then becomes more moral, or at least more general, in his approach to his material. Yet, as Professor Donaldson has amply demonstrated in his book *Piers Plowman, the C-Text and its Poet* (especially chapter 3 in this connexion), everything is not on the debit side. In his changes C often seems to be motivated by clarity or accuracy, no bad qualities. It is typical of C that he omits Piers's tearing of the Pardon which, puzzling as it may be, undoubtedly provides a most effective climax in B. And the C-text is by no means without its own merits. It contains the unique 'autobiographical' opening to C vi, the compassionate view of the deserving poor in C x and the praise of patient poverty in C xiii – all passages which B might have been proud to write. In any case, C has a certain value as the author's last revision of his work: not all the changes he made are improvements, but they are unlikely to have been made without a reason. So the choice of the C-text for the most recent anthology from *Piers* (although with a basic manuscript better than Skeat's)[5] or for the exposition of the poem by Professor Vasta[6] proves a surprisingly good one. C seems to be enjoying a belated revival.

Only a few critics have questioned the order A, B, C, first established by Skeat, and these have not done so convincingly. Much more difficult is the question of what dates to assign to these three versions. On the face of it, it might seem easy to date the three from the several apparently topical references they contain. But, unfortunately, the poet does not seem very often to have removed from a later version allusions that must have been topical in an earlier. In the B Prologue, but not in A, occurs the fable of belling the cat: how all the rats thought it such a marvellous idea that they should be given warning of the cat's approach in this way, but no one rat could be found to hang the bell round the cat's neck in the first place. The poet's remark at the end of this fable:

> What this meteles bemeneth, ȝe men that be merye,
> Deuine ȝe, for I ne dar, bi dere god in heuene.

suggests that the fable has a topical (and for him potentially dangerous) application, and it almost certainly refers to events in Parliament and the court in 1376-77. It might thus help to provide a date for at least the opening of B. But there it still remains in the C-text, written some years later. Of course there is a general lesson to be learned about the nature of democracy and authority, but one wonders just how clearly the original allusion was remembered by the time of C. And just as one swallow doesn't make a summer, so we need more than one topicality to date any one version of *Piers Plowman*. It used to be thought that A could be dated 1362 on the evidence of A v 12-15. Reason is there preaching to the folk on the field:

> He preide the peple haue pite of hemselue,
> And preuede that this pestilences weore for puire synne,
> And this south-westerne wynt on a Seterday at euen
> Was aperteliche for pruide and for no poynt elles.

The chroniclers certainly mention a violent tempest of wind occurring *circa horam uesperarum* or *about euynsong tyme* on Saturday, 15 January 1362, at the very time the second great outbreak of plague in the fourteenth century was at its height, but when we examine the lines in Professor Kane's much more exact A-text, we find *the* southwest wind, not *this* south-west wind, which makes the whole reference rather less immediate. And if it was indeed as violent a storm as the following lines suggest, it would surely be remembered a few years later. That this sort of consideration applies to *Piers Plowman* can be seen from B xiii 265-271, where Haukyn is saying that the citizens of London had to go without his wafers during a famine 'not long past' in April 1370 'when Chichester was mayor'. Although there is ample evidence on other grounds for dating B 1377-79, this reference to 1370 (which is accurate) remains. To return to A. In Meed's trial before the King there are allusions which seem to be to Edward III's wars in Normandy 1359-60, but others which seem to fit a date later than that. On the whole, I incline to a date of the mid- or later 1360's for A, when the storm of 1362 and the Normandy campaign would still be remembered. In B xix, at the other end of the poem from the Rat Fable, come passages lamenting the fact that the Pope, who ought to be *keper ouer Crystene* is in fact busy fighting other Christians. This looks like a reference to the Papal schism when there were rival popes at Rome and Avignon; if it is, then the conclusion of the poem at least should be dated 1378-79. Hence B was probably written between 1376 and 1379, perhaps later in that period rather than earlier. It is most unlikely that B is as late as 1381, since there is no reference, even an obscure or allegorical one, to the Peasants' Revolt of that year.

The C-text has been dated anywhere between 1377 and 1399, but on the basis of remarkably little evidence. Skeat believed that Langland wrote *Richard the Redeless* in 1399, and therefore it followed that if he had to be kept alive until then he ought to have been writing something. We no longer believe that Langland wrote this poem, partly because of evidence unknown to Skeat. But there was another work (which Skeat had in fact himself edited) that has some bearing on the date of C. This is *The Testament of Love* by Thomas Usk, a somewhat tedious work based in its form – and often in its subject-matter too – on Boethius. Usk was, even for the Middle Ages, a great borrower of other men's phrases, and one of the books he borrowed from was *Piers Plowman*. It is difficult to be sure, because Usk usually seems to be quoting from memory, but a few of the borrowings appear to come from the C-text. If this is really the case, the C-text must have been in existence, in part at

least, by 1387, for the very good reason that Usk was beheaded on
4 March 1388.

So far I have spoken of 'the poet', but in the earlier years of this
century there was a sharp debate over whether or not it ought to be
'poets'. This began in America with J. M. Manly. Reading through
the three versions of the poem whilst convalescing from a serious
illness, he was struck by the differences between them rather than
by the similarities. He thought he could distinguish the work of
five separate writers in *Piers Plowman*. Leaving out a certain John
But who signed his name to the concluding lines which he added to
A xii, the others were A1 (responsible for Prologue-viii), A2
(ix-some point in xii), B and C. A more detailed part of Manly's
view is known as the 'lost leaf' theory. He suggested that there
were two lacunae in the confession of the sins in the A-text, caused
by the loss of the two leaves of one sheet of vellum from the archetype. B (a different man, remember) is supposed to have noticed
A's omissions, but to have made a 'bungling attempt' to rectify
them. Had B been the same man as A, he would surely have done
a better job than this; he would, of course, have made the obvious
correction and replaced the contents of the missing leaves of A. In
fact, as was quickly pointed out by Manly's opponents, there is not
a shred of manuscript evidence for this. The 'lost leaf' theory was
to be part only of the wider differences between the four writers
(excluding But):

> There are differences in diction, in metre, in sentence structure, in
> methods of organizing material, in number and kind of rhetorical
> devices, in power of visualising objects and scenes presented, in topics
> of interest to the author and in views on social, theological and various
> miscellaneous questions.

Manly and his supporters never demonstrated in detail the alleged
differences of this quotation which comes from volume II of the
Cambridge History of English Literature, an authoritative work and
a rather unsuitable place to publish what was still only a theory.
There is less reason to dwell on the authorship controversy here
because the whole question has recently been comprehensively
reviewed and the case for single authorship overwhelmingly

demonstrated.[7] Nowadays only a few American scholars really believe in multiple authorship, and in the notes to a book by one of their number, A1 and A2 are considered to be the same man,[8] so that we are now down to A, B and C. Of course there are many revisions and alterations in B and C, but B and C show an extremely close knowledge of the poem they are revising, often developing ideas latent in earlier versions. Most probably, therefore, they are one and the same poet.

The authorship question, however, has to be faced for another reason. Unless you believe in single authorship, you cannot use details from all three versions of the poem to build up a picture of the poet and his manner of life. You cannot do this either unless you agree that the Dreamer in *Piers Plowman* reflects the life and thoughts of the poet himself. Although we should beware of attributing to the poet every view expressed by his often irascible and ill-informed Dreamer, the general principle seems sound from other medieval examples. The Eagle in Chaucer's *House of Fame*, for instance, calls the man he carries in his beak 'Geoffrey' and reproaches him for leading just the sort of all-work-and-no-play existence Chaucer may have been leading at the Custom House when he was writing that poem. In any case, the identification of Dreamer and poet in *Piers Plowman* seems to be made by B xix 1:

Thus I awaked and wrote what I had dremed

and B xix 478:

And I awakned therewith and wrote as me mette.

But it is important to realize that the sort of picture produced of the man who wrote *Piers Plowman* is a composite of two kinds of evidence: external (from remarks made about the writer by scribes or others in the colophons of the manuscripts, or from other scraps of information outside the poem) and internal (from the poem proper). We need the second badly in this case because the poet seems to have played no part in the important events of his time. There is Chaucer, at the age of fourteen or so, being fitted out with a new pair of breeches by Elizabeth, Countess of Ulster, in whose husband's service he was, and there are sufficient records of Chaucer the courtier and civil servant to suggest that later pairs of breeches were better and better quality. But practically nothing about Langland. There is a note added to one C-text manuscript stating that the poet's father was called Stacy (Eustace) de Rokayle; this does not necessarily mean that he was illegitimate, since hereditary surnames were not fully in vogue in the fourteenth century. The rest is silence. He seems to have been known only as the poet who wrote, or (as the Middle Ages put it) 'made', *Piers Plowman*. We are therefore forced back on internal evidence. His name was probably William Langland, on the basis of B xv 148:

'I have lyued in londe,' quod I, 'my name is Longe Wille.'

Wille Longe-lond: William Langland; laughable to us, but with no title page to most manuscripts a poet had to introduce himself by some such method. References to 'Wille' are scattered throughout the poem, and also crop up in colophons to manuscripts of every class. Whilst some of these may be to the common noun *wille*, meaning 'desire' or 'wilfulness' as opposed to knowledge or wisdom, others seem to be clear allusions to the Dreamer and so to the poet. It is often stated that Langland was born in 1332 and died in the 1390's, but this is far from certain. Two lines in B xi might be interpreted to mean that the Dreamer was forty-five years old. If Dreamer equals poet, and if 1377 is the date of the B-text, then 1377 minus 45 equals 1332. He was probably born near Ledbury, about eight miles from the Malvern Hills which form the setting, such as it is, for the first two visions. There was a hamlet called Longlands in the neighbourhood from which he may have taken his name. He seems to have been put to school in his youth (internal evidence) – some critics believe to a monastic school since the monks are treated less harshly in the poem than the friars, though they do not get off scot free – but he fell on bad times when his father and friends died. In recent studies of the poem the older opinion that Langland picked up scraps of learning by talking to men better educated than himself has been replaced by the view that he attended some institution of higher education, if not a university perhaps an advanced school run by an order or by a cathedral. It is still difficult, however, to detect in *Piers Plowman* any recognized medieval system of learning, and we ought to bear in mind the circulation of a large number of anthologies on a multitude of subjects; then as now, to cite a few quotations from some of the 'doctors' does not necessarily mean having read deeply in their works. From internal evidence he had a wife Kit and a daughter Calote, and at some stage of his life he moved to London and lived on Cornhill. But his death in the 1390's is only a guess based on the supposed date of the C-text. Work in Edinburgh on the dialect of Middle English manuscripts has unearthed the interesting fact that the C-text seems to have circulated especially in the area of the Malvern Hills, as opposed to the more cosmopolitan circulation of B.[9] Does this mean that Langland went back to Malvern, like Shakespeare to Stratford, with the difference that Langland went on writing? It is a remarkable concentration of C manuscripts, even when we remember that their dialect is that of their scribes and not necessarily that of their author.

Langland's occupation is not very clear, and he himself seems to have had serious misgivings about the value to God of what he did. There are more seemingly personal details in the C-text, especially the first hundred lines of C vi, which are not in A or B. The most important passage is C vi 44-52; I quote it in the text of the York anthology which uses a better manuscript than Skeat:

> And so I leve yn London and uppe lond bothe;
> The lomes that I labore with and lyflode deserve
> Ys *pater-noster* and my prymer, *placebo* and *dirige*,
> And my sauter some tyme and my sevene psalmes.
> This I segge for here soules of such as me helpeth,
> And tho that fynden me my fode vouchen-saf, I trowe,
> To be welcome when I come, other-while in a monthe,
> Now with hym, now with here; on this wise I begge
> Withoute bagge or botel but my wombe one.

On the basis of these lines there has been built up a picture of Langland as a clerk in minor orders (not a full priest, that is) going about singing masses for the souls of the dead. Probably a truer picture is that he had been in minor orders and that he had withdrawn from the direct service of the Church (because of his marriage or for some other reason? we can only speculate). In effect at the time of his poem he was a pious layman with a more or less regular itinerary ('London and uppe lond bothe'), with prayers for the living as well as for the dead ('soules of suche as me helpeth' – in the present tense), and with occasional odd clerical jobs elsewhere. This obviously resembles begging, and Langland hated able-bodied beggars. He, or the Dreamer at least, says he is too weak and sometimes too lazy to do manual work, and he seeks to make a distinction between his own occupation and begging, but it is not a very clear one, to us at any rate. This is about as far as we can get. Where probable internal evidence and reliable external evidence reinforce one another, or where internal evidence can be supported by what we know of fourteenth-century conditions, we may be reasonably certain that the poet's starting point was his own experience, whether the poem as we have it exaggerates or minimizes that experience.

Most critics agree that *Piers Plowman* represents a search for salvation. This, at any rate, is what the Dreamer asked Holy Church to show him right back in passus i:

> Teche me to no tresore, but telle me this ilke,
> How I may saue my soule, that seynt art yholden.

But it is only in the last thirty years or so that critics have tried to show that the poem does not drift, but proceeds according to a definite plan. Earlier writers were content to accept some degree of confusion:

> The scheme of the poem defies analysis. There is indeed no skill of artistry about it. All the effects are gained, it would seem, at haphazard, and without being sought. Langland does not select, or contrive, or arrange.[10]

And although W. P. Ker in 1912 asserted that the poem 'moves harmoniously in its large spaces',[11] the spaces seemed to most readers to be well railed off from each other and large enough to contain a good deal of rough and stony ground inside. The typical view was that Langland was unfortunate in his choice of the alliterative metre, lacked any architectonic gift, but was a good poet occasionally. *Piers Plowman*, like *Beowulf*, did not fit neatly into a satisfying Aristotelian plan with beginning, middle and end, so its greatest admirers were compelled, paradoxically, to apologise for it. After all, were not real dreams, as well as imagined ones, often incoherent?

The critical pendulum later (as pendulums will) swung back in the other direction. Until quite recently criticism became too ready to see coherence everywhere in *Piers Plowman* and to find a set of beautifully interlocking parts. But first, to concentrate on the 'large spaces'. In manuscripts of all classes, after the Pardon has been torn up by Piers and the Dreamer has tried to make out the significance of this (at the end of A viii, B vii, C x), there occurs some phrase like:

> Explicit hic Visio Willelmi de Petro le Plou3man. Eciam incipit Vita de Dowel, Dobet et Dobest secundum wyt et resoun.

This is clearly a major division in the poem, and, equally clearly, the *Visio* is easier to interpret than the *Vita*. Its subject-matter is more down-to-earth, its allegory more easily interpretable, and a straightforward historical approach often pays dividends: for instance, economic conditions after the Black Death are reflected in the attitudes of Piers's helpers on the half-acre in B vi and in his uncertain attitude towards them. The *Visio* is a happy hunting-ground for social historians. But the *Vita* is more difficult, especially the *Vita de Dowel* (B ix-xiv) and the first part of the *Vita de Dobet* (B xv and xvi). Perhaps this is because the transition between two ideas which have been growing in prominence since the tearing of the Pardon at the end of the *Visio* is not satisfactorily made in detail. These ideas are first, complete abandonment to the will of God ('voluntary poverty', *ne solliciti sitis, fiat voluntas tua, pacientes vincunt* – all key ideas in the central part of the poem) and second, charity (love). When discussion gives place to Biblical narrative, of the Crucifixion and the Harrowing of Hell, *Dobet* becomes much easier. The *Vita de Dobest* returns to the question posed in the *Visio*, the relationship between society and God's plan revealed in history. How should the Christian stand in relation to the kingdom of God? What is the contemporary (that is, the fourteenth century) church doing to advance God's kingdom? There may well be, behind the last two passus of the poem especially, an apocalyptic view of history, where the pattern of events is used as a criticism of or divine warning for contemporary society. It was popularly believed that Christ's second coming would be preceded by Antichrist, who does, in fact, attack Piers's barn in the *Vita de Dobest*.[12]

When we try to find a more detailed plan than this, we come

upon several pointers but few solutions. The passus divisions do not correspond in the three versions. The passus themselves vary enormously in length and do not always begin and end at important stages in the argument, although they sometimes do. More promising is the fact that *Piers Plowman* consists of a number of visions. This in itself is remarkable. Most dream poems in Middle English contain only one dream. Chaucer, for example, gets off to sleep eventually, after a period of bedside reading, and wakes up near the end of his poem. But not only are there eight visions in the B-text, but two more dreams within dreams, something peculiar to Langland among medieval poets, plus interludes between the visions, in the real world as it were. Yet these interludes do not provide a setting against which the dream-characters can meet and talk, nor is there – except at the beginning and end of the poem – any such setting in the dream itself, as there is in *Pearl*, for example. In *Piers Plowman* the interludes between the visions are often short; the Dreamer wakes up, and three or four lines later is asleep again. Where they are longer they ponder on important lessons (such as the meaning of Piers's Pardon) or reflect on what has been learned at the end of a long vision (for example, the summary at B xiii 1-20 following the disappearance of Imaginative). Semi-autobiographical material sometimes appears in these interludes: the Dreamer wanders like a beggar or itinerant preacher and is unwilling to pay the proper respect to rich and important men.

We can now take a closer look at the visions themselves as a structural device. I shall use the B-text; the divisions are not quite so tidily made in C although they mostly correspond. The first dream begins at line 11 of the Prologue and ends at v 3 when Meed has been finally discredited and the King decides to rule in future according to Conscience and Reason. By v 8 the Dreamer is asleep again, and stays asleep through the confession of the Sins and the ploughing of the half-acre until the noise of Piers and the priest arguing over the meaning of the Pardon wakes him up at vii 139. This is the effective end of the *Visio*. These first two visions have unity of place (the Malvern Hills) and of time (the Dreamer falls asleep in the morning and wakes up from the second vision with the sun setting); moreover, the field full of folk is the scene against which both visions take place. Unfortunately, this sets a standard of artistic unity never to be repeated in the poem. After an interlude when the Dreamer ponders on the reliability of dreams and the relative importance of Dowel and pardons, and has an inconclusive encounter with two friars whom he questions about Dowel, he falls asleep for his third vision, at the beginning of *Dowel*, at viii 67. This is a long vision not ending until xiii 1 by which time the Dreamer has stumbled but has been set on the right road again by Imaginative. Within this long third dream occurs the first of the two 'dreams within dreams'. In these the text has the Dreamer fall asleep without having woken up from the vision in progress; he wakes from this inner dream to meet different characters, but still allegorical ones because he is still in the main dream. The purpose of this first 'inner dream' (xi 4-396) may well be to let the Dreamer experience for himself the usefulness of learning and reason which he had formerly treated with contempt; he is certainly much more patient when Imaginative clinches the argument for him in the part of the main vision which follows. Vision number four begins at xiii 21 and closes at the very end of the following passus (xiv 332) with the reformation of Haukyn. The fifth vision begins at xv 11 and ends at the last line of passus xvii before the Crucifixion. It too contains a dream within a dream (xvi 20-167) explaining the Tree of Charity to the Dreamer (this inner dream is dropped in C and the material integrated with the main vision). The following vision, the sixth, is largely narrative, covering the Crucifixion, the debate of the four daughters of God and the Harrowing of Hell (B xviii 4-425). Vision seven begins at xix 5 with a long account of Christ's life, but now carried beyond the Crucifixion to the time of Pentecost when the Holy Ghost is given to Christ's followers, 'Piers and his fellows'. Piers builds his barn, Unity Holychurch, and it is defended against Antichrist and his army. The final vision, the eighth, begins at xx 50 and ends at the very last line of the poem; it tells of the attack of Antichrist and Pride in detail, and how the attackers finally gain entry to the barn. At least in B, Langland seems to have intended each vision to cover an important stage in the development of his poem.

Is there any more detailed plan than this? After all, the visions are sometimes long ones, extending over two or three passus. The clue appears to lie in the meaning of Dowel, Dobet and Dobest. The *Vita de Dowel* consists of the Dreamer questioning everyone he meets about what Dowel, Dobet and Dobest mean. Naturally, since he asks very different characters, the Dreamer gets different answers, but that has not deterred those searching for a plan from trying to equate Dowel, Dobet and Dobest, a triad found only in *Piers Plowman*, with one of the other medieval triads, found much more commonly, which are used to explain progress towards perfection. The favourite choice from among these is the active, contemplative and mixed (or episcopal) lives, and the standard exposition of this view is the lecture 'The Pardon of Piers Plowman', delivered to the British Academy in 1945 by Nevill Coghill. Not only, says Professor Coghill, do Dowel, Dobet and Dobest represent respectively the active, contemplative and mixed lives, but these are made incarnate in Piers who lives each life in turn, beginning as a simple ploughman (active), changing to contemplative ('clerkly' as Coghill sometimes calls it) after he tears up the Pardon, and remaining in that state later in *Dobet* when he is the man in whose armour Christ gives battle to the Devil at the Crucifixion. Finally, in *Dobest*, when Christ delegates power to Piers and his followers, Piers becomes a kind of ideal pope and embodies the mixed life. It is an attractive theory and has become widespread. Here are two statements of it:

> The allegorical level, for example, is concerned with the church, and the basic classification of persons in the poem under Dowel, Dobet and Dobest rests on the traditional division of persons in the church as active, contemplative, and prelatical. More exactly, Dowel, Dobet and Dobest represent the ideals which persons in these states should follow. Actual persons either exemplify these ideals or their corruption.

> Do-wel is the active life, the life of the good layman; Do-bet is the contemplative life, the life of the man of a religious order; Do-best is the life of the highest human responsibility made possible by the unity of activity and contemplation, the life of the Bishop.[13]

But in recent years this view has been losing ground.[14] In the first place, active, contemplative and mixed lives are apt to be defined (rather than just mentioned, as the first two often are in

Piers Plowman) in works addressed to recluses and attempting to chart the mystic's progress towards God; *Piers Plowman* is simply the wrong kind of poem. And in these books contemplative life is absolutely the highest of these three states; the bishop (or similar person with both religious and secular responsibilities) would wish to be contemplative, but the needs of his flock prevent him; applied to *Piers Plowman* this would produce an odd triad: Dowel, Dobest, Dobet. In any case, the equation of Dowel with active life rests upon too narrow a definition of the latter which in fact was not limited to manual labour but included much of what these critics would assign to Dobet. We need a far clearer understanding of the terms 'action' and 'contemplation', as Father Dunning shows in an essay later in this book. Whatever Dowel, Dobet and Dobest signified to Langland and his audience, the triad is abandoned as casually as it had been introduced by Thought in B viii 76-79. It never occurs after the *Vita de Dowel*, except for an extended example at B xix 104 ff, where it is stated that Christ lived all three lives in turn.

There is, in fact, another combination of three: purgative, illuminative, and unitive states, which has also been suggested as an explanation of Dowel, Dobet and Dobest. The first consists of the expulsion or purgation of error and sin, the second of the deeper knowledge (or illumination) and more exact imitation of God, and the third in the achievement of union with God, begun imperfectly in this life and completed in heaven. Now Piers's barn which he builds towards the end of the poem is called Unity, but this is defined as *holicherche on Englisshe* (B xix 325) which seems to indicate a non-technical use of the term. And this triad, purgative, illuminative and unitive, is an even more mystical one than active, contemplative and mixed, and so that much less likely as an explanation of Dowel, Dobet and Dobest. *Piers Plowman* is not only the Dreamer's search for salvation – although it is primarily that – but it is also a poem concerned with Christian perfection. It is more social than mystical. It is worthwhile also to remember that Dowel, Dobet and Dobest is not the only triad mentioned in *Piers Plowman*. The titles of the contributions to this volume by Miss Kean and Mr Burrow show that other organizing groups are at work in the poem.

Dowel, Dobet and Dobest can hardly be called characters in the poem. But the fortunes of Piers on the one hand and of the Dreamer on the other offer possible means of charting the poem's own progress. There are two approaches to the meaning of Piers, who, we should remember, gives the poem its title. The first is Coghill's: that Piers in the *Visio* is a figure of this world, a simple ploughman, the good man who performs his duties faithfully and lives according to the principles of Truth. When he tears the Pardon he says he will not be so anxious (*bisy*) about the things of this world and will trust in God absolutely. Thus Piers takes up the life of Dobet and when he returns to the poem in B xvi after a long absence, he is teacher, healer, and the man in whose armour Christ can give battle to the Devil. Finally at B xix 177, when Christ delegates power to Piers and his fellows, he becomes Christ's vicar on earth, a kind of ideal pope, Dobest. This interpretation of Piers can be made independently of the equation of Dowel, Dobet and Dobest with active, contemplative and mixed lives. It assumes that Piers is Langland's own creation and that what he means must be puzzled out from the poem itself. The second approach to the understanding of Piers assumes that he is not Langland's own creation, and that the poet did not therefore need to explain Piers's character fully because its outline would be already familiar to his readers. Piers always seems to appear suddenly; the very first time we meet him he 'puts forth his head' and says he knows where Truth is to be found. He is appealed to as an authority by Conscience (B xiii 123) and by Anima (B xv 190). At B xvi 18 the Dreamer swoons *al for pure ioye* on hearing Piers's name. As one critic says, Piers always seems to appear or to be mentioned when the way seems darkest.[15] If Piers was a clearly recognized symbol or if certain facets of his make-up were already known, these sudden appearances would be easier to understand. Miss Raw's essay below is a sophisticated and persuasive example of this second approach.

Much more down to earth is the figure of the Dreamer who spends much of his time following in Piers's wake. The very figure of a search, with its false starts, hesitation and changes of direction, is no bad analogy for the uncertain progress of the poem, and gives the author a chance to introduce new characters whilst retaining

some sort of continuity. In the A-text the Dreamer is too much of
an observer to be realized as a character; only in the *Dowel* section
does he begin to develop the argumentative nature characteristic
of the B continuation. It is in the C-text, especially in the long
opening passage to C vi, that we are given information about his
personality and way of life which is fuller than the hints given in
the B-text (for example, B xiii 1-11). A good deal of work has been
done in recent years on the *personae* of medieval dreamers who
are apt both to share certain features with the poet himself and
also to ask the characters they meet rather obvious leading questions. Dr Mills's essay here begins by examining some of these
approaches to the function of the Dreamer. The Dreamer of *Piers
Plowman* certainly seems the most curious and at the same time
the most argumentative of all his fellows. Imaginative (B xii 217)
calls him one who 'sekest after the whyes'. He tells Anima – whose
multiplicity of titles puzzles him – that he wants to know 'Alle the
sciences vnder sonne and alle the sotyle craftes' (B xv 48). At
B xi 336 his intellectual curiosity leads him into an eighteen line
discussion of the habits of birds. But generally, as Clergy complains (A xii 6) he is, like so many of us, 'lef to lerne, but loth for to
stodie'.

These two figures, Piers and the Dreamer, are, it seems to me,
of much greater assistance than Dowel, Dobet and Dobest in
following such plan as the poem possesses. For one thing, *Piers
Plowman* begins and ends in a similar way: in B xix (*Dobest*) Piers
once again becomes a ploughman, as he had been on his first
appearance, but this time his team consists of the four evangelists
and his field is no longer the half-acre of B vi, but the whole world.
He has become the ploughman of men's souls, and the harvest he
hopes for is salvation. In the fourteenth century the ploughman
was also the type of the poor and the exploited, so in this way
Piers represents all labourers. This might help to explain the
curious fact that Piers Plowman, the hero of what is in many ways
a very conservative poem, came to be one of the rallying cries of
those who instigated the Peasants' Revolt. Piers, although he
changes significance in the poem, is both the model for all Christians and also, as one of themselves, the norm.[16] As with the
Dreamer, Langland has involved his readers in the progress of his

poem. Piers is a fitting character to lead both fellow-characters and audience towards the kingdom of God. In B xx, the sins which attack Piers's barn, Unity Holychurch, are those of which the folk on the field in the Prologue and also Meed's followers in the *Visio* had been guilty. Meed is not mentioned by name in *Dobest*, but the power of money for which she stands is evident in the success Pride and Antichrist have in corrupting several people who might otherwise have followed Conscience (and Conscience was Meed's opponent in the debate before the King back in B iii). The cure for the sins of these people is temperance and moderation in accordance with the law of love. Kynde's speech at the end of the poem (B xx 207-210) harks back to that of Holy Church in passus i (B i 20-25, 35). That speech was made to the Dreamer after he had observed the field full of folk in the Prologue. These people, erring mankind, are always, in one form or another, at the back of the argument in *Piers Plowman*. After Meed has been discredited Reason preaches at B v 10 to the *felde ful of folke* and it is they who confess their sins and set out on the pilgrimage to Truth. Haukyn in B xiii and xiv is a kind of synthesizing character: his confession shows him to be guilty at one time or another of all the deadly sins, and only gradually is he led to desire eternal values rather than temporal ones. In the same way certain subjects recur in this long poem. They never fail to interest Langland and often inspire some of his best poetry. The Crucifixion; charity (in the modern sense 'almsgiving'); the friars (it is a friar, masquerading as a surgeon for the spiritually sick, who gains entrance to the barn Unity and hastens its downfall); minstrels of various kinds; the deserving poor (especially in the C-text) – all these crop up time and again and by their reappearance help to give coherence to a rather untidy poem. Recurrent imagery, such as that of food, clothing or jousting, has something of the same effect.

Recently there have been attempts to investigate the effect of sermon literature on *Piers Plowman*. Owst, the pioneer of this approach, overstated his case,[17] but the sheer number of sermons composed, preached, and presumably listened to in medieval England is undeniable. Like *Piers Plowman* they contain repetitions, cross-references, surprising transitions, several *exempla*

C

(illustrative stories) and often a good deal of satire: in general they demonstrate the primacy of religious teaching over tight artistic organization. Certainly there is a good deal of subject-matter in common, and the content of these sermons will often illuminate the darker corners of *Piers Plowman* better than will the writings of the scholastics or the mystics. Certainly, again, some of the characters in *Piers Plowman* are seen 'preaching' (e.g. Reason at B v 11 to 'all the realm', as a result of which the Sins confess; and Scripture at B xi 103)[18] and there are occasional references to the *teme* or text (e.g. B vii 135, B xiii 74). But I cannot see that the sermons provide more than an apt analogy to *Piers Plowman*. Their content, like some of the shared imagery, shows simply that they must often have been addressed to a similar audience; we cannot yet be sure that the manuals of preaching, or indeed any particular group of sermons, directly influenced the construction of the poem.

What sort of audience was this? *Piers Plowman* survives in many more manuscripts than most alliterative poems. It has been suggested that its audience was in the main fifteenth-century prosperous literate laymen who could afford manuscripts but whose tastes remained didactic and conservative, men perhaps rather like Chaucer's Franklin.[19] The poem would also appeal to parish priests and to the host of those in minor orders. All such men might welcome a less esoteric style than that affected by some contemporary alliterative poetry. The poetry they wanted would have to be above all intelligible. The alliterative technique of the poem is, on the whole, much freer than in most others, and the freedom seems to have grown from A through B, so that by C Langland is writing alliterative poetry much as Shakespeare, in his later plays, is writing blank verse – as second nature, so that idea transcends form. The diction of *Piers Plowman* is also usually more prosaic and less diffuse than that of several Middle English alliterative poems, particularly the romances where descriptions are apt to become over rhetorical and splendidly decorative. Its syntax, too, is generally less tortured than theirs. With only a few big exceptions, the style of *Piers Plowman* remains remarkably stable throughout. Instead of changing his diction, Langland will speed up his action or suddenly change tone from bitter satire to sincere sympathy. He can be long-winded, but it is almost always because of a difficulty in saying exactly what he wants to say rather than from any desire to write impressively for its own sake.[20]

It would seem to follow that it is mistaken to apply the fourfold method of scriptural interpretation to a poem as individual as this.[21] A good deal of *Piers Plowman* is quite literal: the second vision of the *Vita de Dobet* for instance, telling the story of Christ's Crucifixion and the Harrowing of Hell. There is no hidden meaning here. Yet it is obvious that Langland often thought in allegory. Chaucer's pilgrimage starts from a specific place, the Tabard Inn, and moves along the road to Canterbury towards the shrine of St Thomas à Becket, a real-life saint. Langland's pilgrimage is much more an affair of the spirit: to seek St Truth or salvation. Its background, in the *Visio* at least, is the tower on a toft (Heaven) and the deep dale with its dungeon (Hell) beneath and the fair field full of folk (the world) between – a much more cosmic setting. Chaucer speaks of a monk, a friar and a cook, but Langland of monks, friars and cooks. What part, asks Langland, are they meant to play in a Christian society? What good (or bad) are they doing? He even, at B Prologue 46-49, questions the purpose of pilgrimages. And so the portraits in Langland's Prologue are shorter and less detailed than in Chaucer's; there is no running sore on Langland's cook's shin or yellow hair hanging down his pardoner's back. It is true that the portraits of the seven deadly sins in B v come gloriously alive, but the sins themselves are often composite figures: Wrath is now the friary gardener, now the cook in the nuns' kitchen, or again grumbling at the plain food in a monastery. Sloth sees himself sometimes as a priest, sometimes as a layman. And this is quite proper with personifications like these. But not, surely, four senses for *all* the allegory and symbolism in *Piers Plowman*. Dante, who is often quoted in this connexion, remarks of the second (allegorical) sense that it is 'true that the theologians take this sense other than the poets do'. Walter Hilton, who was actually speaking about scriptural exegesis, says that 'It is expounded and declared letterly, morally, mystically (i.e. allegorically) and heavenly (i.e. anagogically) *if the matter suffer it*.[22]

Langland's discussion of his reasons for writing poetry is a very brief one. Imaginative accuses the Dreamer of playing about, writing poetry, when he might be employing himself much more profitably:

> And thow medlest the with makynges, and myȝtest go sey
>   thi sauter,
> And bidde for hem that ȝiueth the bred; for there ar bokes
>   ynowe
> To telle men what Dowel is, Dobet and Dobest bothe,
> And prechoures to preue what it is of many a peyre freres.
>
>   B xii 16-19

The Dreamer admits this, but confesses to a guilty fascination with poetry to *solacen* himself. This suggests that, to him, subject-matter was more important than manner. So we would hardly expect – although there is some word-play in the poem – to find the careful preoccupation with words that we find in many modern poets. Nor is there any deliberate cultivation of literary devices to conceal a want of inspiration, as can sometimes happen in poets like Dryden or Tennyson. As far as we can tell, Langland does not follow a conscious process of construction on fashionable models, like Chaucer in his early poetry. The final impression is that *Piers Plowman* is not really very like anything else in Middle English. It shares some of the characteristics of several different types of writing.[23] We can use some of these – the dream and its Dreamer, the search, the correspondences between Dowel, Dobet and Dobest and other triads, Piers himself and his reflection of the divine image – to assist us in finding a way through the complexities of the poem. It is to be hoped that the essays in this book, by their patient examination of some of the more important questions the poem raises, will help to make the way clearer. But Truth, as both Langland and Donne knew, whilst easy to see, is less easy of apprehension; the way is strait and the approach is circuitous:

>   On a huge hill,
> Cragged, and steep, Truth stands, and hee that will
> Reach her, about must, and about must goe;
> And what th' hills suddennes resists, winne so.[24]

Some Aspects of the Process of Revision in *Piers Plowman*[1]

G. H. RUSSELL

Piers Plowman, if the emphasis of modern scholarship and criticism is to be believed, offers few problems which are easy of solution. It is, then, surprising that, with minimal dissent, the division of surviving manuscripts into groups testifying to three identifiable versions of the poem has been so easily accepted.[2] A great deal of this ready acceptance must have been made on trust, but it can be said that a close study of the extant manuscripts does confirm this view.

It is true that, on occasions, there is revealed evidence of a kind that might seem to raise doubts. There exist manuscripts which, in whole or in part, appear to offer a shape of the poem which does not correspond to what we may properly call the traditional division into A-, B- and C-versions. We have, for example, one of the Huntington Library manuscripts of the poem which is traditionally and correctly listed as a 'B manuscript'. Yet a study of the text which it supplies makes clear that here we have a manuscript which does not fit into the traditional classifications. In shape it is neither an A-, nor a B-, nor a C-version manuscript. Clearly there is at least a possibility that we have here yet another 'version' of the poem, yet another genuinely independent attempt on the theme.

However, a close study of the manuscript and the text which it attests reveals that it is, apparently, an editorial construct. An editor, with access to manuscripts of all three versions of the poem, seems to have produced his own conflated version of the poem. The nature of the process is such that we cannot properly grant to it the status of a 'version' of the poem, in the sense that we traditionally use the word in this context.[3] Again, a manuscript in the Bodleian Library (Bodley 851) which is traditionally classed as a C-version manuscript proves, on a similar scrutiny, to testify to the demonstrated C-version shape only in its second half. The earlier part of the manuscript is found to offer a text which is markedly different from that offered by any other manuscript of the A, B or C tradition. The latter part of the manuscript, by contrast, proves to be a text of the C-version which has not been subjected to revision. The shape of the first part of the poem, once more, is not, I believe, of the kind that was authorially produced. It appears to be the characteristic product of the editor or editing scribe: and there seems to be little reason to dissent from Skeat's description 'mere rubbish'.

These examples, which might be multiplied, are perhaps fairly obvious: there are less clear cases. If, for example, we begin to read the poem as it appears in what was formerly known as the 'Ilchester manuscript'[4], we may be tempted to believe that, so great is the amount of variation that we encounter in the Prologue, we are reading yet another 'version' of the poem. To take an example, here is the text of the C-version Prologue as supplied by Skeat's text:[5]

> What cheste, ⁊ meschaunce . to [þe] children of israel,
> Ful on hem þat free were . þorwe two false preestes.
> For þe synne of ophni . and of finées hus brother,
> Þei were disconfit in bataille . and losten *Archa dei*;
> And, for hure syre sauh hem syngen . and soffrede hem don ille,
> And noȝt chasted hem *þer*-of . and wolde noȝt rebukie hem,
> A-non, as it was ytold hym . þat þe children of israel
> Weren disconfit in bataille . and *Archa dei* ylore,
> And hus sones slayen . anon he ful for sorwe
> Fro h*us* chaire þare he sat . and brak hus necke a-tweyne.
> And al was for veniaunce . þat he but noȝt hus children;
> And for þey were preestes . and men of holychurche,
> God was wel þe wroþer . and tok þe ra*þere* veniaunce.

As against this, here is the version of the Ilchester manuscript (f. 5[b]):

> What cheste and meschaunce fel vpon þe children
> Of Israel þat fre were for tuo false prestes
> For þe synne of Offyn and Fynees his bro*þer*

Þat beten were in bataile and losten archa d*omi*ni
And for þair sire soeffrede þe sennes þat þey wrogh[ten?]
And chastised not his children of her euel chekkes
He stombled dou*n* fro his stool in stede *per* he sat
And brak his nekke bon in tuo for so þe book telles
For þay wer*e* p*r*estes vnpure peres of holy chirche
Wronge*s* on þe wrecches wroken was þe harder
Forþy ȝou p*r*elates I p*r*eche and peres of holy chirche
Þat soeffre me*n* do sacrifice and sory mawmetȝ
And ȝe her gyo*ur*s vnder god schulde don he*m* go þerfro
Bep war I warne ȝow witterly for god wol wroken
⁊ sende sorwe on ȝour self sadlier to falle
Þan fel on Offyn or Fynees or on her fader awther
For ȝo*ur* sory soffr*ance* and for ȝour awen synne.

These are, I believe, recognizably forms of the same original,
which has been introduced into the Prologue by the C-reviser who
would have found it, in a shorter form, at B xiii. The first form is
demonstrably corrupt. The sense that it offers is dubious: the
shape of many of the lines is, at best, suspect. Those of the second
form are superior, but by no means unexceptionable, and we have
to decide whether they represent an attempt (presumably scribal)
to repair a ruined (or unfinished) original or whether they represent a superior survival of an original which has been deformed in
the version preserved by the other manuscripts.

There is no space to offer argumentation on the question in this
paper. I believe that the Ilchester text is, at this point, a superior
text and is a reflection of a better state of the poem and not a
merely editorial attempt at repair. I believe that the application of
normal editorial methods could produce from Ilchester's text a
shape of the lines which is very much closer to the original than
could be produced from the majority text.

Whether this is true or not is not, at this stage, the central issue.
What is really important is the realization, as we read further in the
manuscript, that it is not, in fact, offering a different version of the
poem. The general shape is nearly identical with that of the other
C manuscripts and we are left to conjecture just how this superior,
even though still imperfect, form of this part of the prologue is
attested in only this one manuscript. There is, I believe, no question of its being a part of a fourth 'version'.

While, in spite of these and similar reservations, we need have little difficulty in subscribing to the traditional division of the poem into its three stages of revision, we should, at the same time, realize that the representation of these three versions is by no means unequivocally clear. At many points, in many manuscripts, the picture is blurred by omissions, additions, alterations and conscious or unconscious changes of many kinds. As a consequence we have constantly to face the problem of discriminating between a process of authoritative (and putatively authorial) revision and a process of non-authoritative (and putatively editorial or scribal) revision. The distinction is one of crucial importance: it distinguishes between those successive, autonomous acts of creation which produced what we recognize as the three 'versions' of the poem, and those attempts to improve and modify the poem which are apparently posterior to, and independent of, those acts of creation and which, whatever their quality, form no part of the authorial process. They are attempts to modify and improve an already existing poem: they consequently represent an editorial process which is distinct from the creative activity of the author. It is a process which is familiar enough to students of early texts, but the centrally important moral, social and political concerns of *Piers Plowman* seem to have made it unusually vulnerable to the attentions of the self-appointed editors.

Skeat's great edition, then, distinguished three separate versions of the poem which he labelled A, B and C in presumptive chronological order, and subsequent study has confirmed Skeat's findings. It seems clear that the poem first came into existence in that short form that we know as the A-version, attested by a substantial group of manuscripts.[6] This first attempt of the author on his complex task seems to have ended in dissatisfaction, even in something approaching despair, and this first attempt was brought to an end in a manner that reflects this dissatisfaction.

If the accepted theory is correct, another attempt was made on the same material. For there exists a second large group of manuscripts which testify to a form of the poem which appears, in the first ten passus, to be very similar to that offered in what we have identified as the A-group.[7] And yet a close study reveals that the shape of the poem as it appears here is, in fact, very different.

These earlier passus, while similar in general shape, are decisively and, one feels, magisterially modified. And as the poem progresses, this process of modification becomes more and more elaborate. To the changed form of the earlier part is added a massive amplification, again of arresting quality. As a consequence, we now have a poem that is so transformed that we cannot properly see it as the product of any kind of merely editorial or scribal modification of its predecessor. It is not a variant form of the earlier shape: it is a revision of it. That is, the complexity and the magnitude of the alterations to the original are of such a kind that one cannot reasonably conclude that there is here a question of what could properly be called editorial activity. What we are offered is a new poem, the product of a genuinely creative activity which is, then, not external to the poem, not the product of a process of tampering, but which is directed to its restatement. This new poem we properly call the B-version.

Further study of the extant manuscripts of the poem reveals that there is a third group of them which offers us yet another shape, again altered from, and expanded over, that which we have identified as the B-version. The process of change is not dissimilar to that which transmuted the A-version into the B-version. Once more there is a base of common material, but beyond this, a detailed and substantial revision which an attentive reading reveals to be so thoroughgoing as to constitute a new and, at times, radically altered version of the poem. This group, that is, testifies to the existence of a shape of the poem which, in general, preserves the lineaments of the first version as modified by its reviser, but which has been subjected to persistent (though not constant) alteration, sometimes of major dimensions. Once more the nature of the process is such that our experience of the mode of operation of the editing scribe or editor can scarcely allow us to see here an example of his work. One's judgment must be that here, as with the preceding group, we have a deliberate and conscious attempt to change the original which can only have come from the hand of one who set out to make over anew the material of the first revision throughout the greater part of its length, and who thought of himself as producing a new, even if essentially similar, poem.

It has, then, been traditional to accept the view of Skeat, and it has not been seriously challenged. And yet we need to recall that the manuscript situation is not quite as tidy as it might appear. We have already cited the cases of manuscripts Hm 114 and Bodley 851. To these, and their like, we might add a number of manuscripts which offer conjoint versions – versions in which, for example, an A- or B-version beginning is followed by a C conclusion.[8] In these cases the possibility of their offering a further set of genuine revisions hardly arises. They are clearly the result of a purely mechanical process of joining together already existing versions, with, at best, a minimum of linking material to ease the transition. The normal situation which seems to have produced such versions was the realization that there existed versions of the poem which were very much longer and more elaborate than the A-version and a consequent decision to add the additional material to the end of the A-version manuscripts. In some manuscripts, it is true, the process is rather more complicated, but they remain constructs whose components are fairly easily distinguished. Lack of space prevents any study of these examples in this paper, but we may simply note that a number of manuscripts of all versions display evidence of 'contamination'. That is, while they remain basically A-, B- or C-version manuscripts, there has been imported into their texts a number of readings which are identifiable as coming from one of the other versions. This again is a common enough phenomenon and seems to call for no particular comment.[9]

If, then, we retain our belief in a twofold revision of the poem, two further problems present themselves. The first is the problem of chronology; the second that of authorship. And both questions are, in their different ways, highly complex.

As we know, Skeat's original identification of the versions represented the earliest stage as being that which we now know as the A-version. This consists of a prologue and eleven (or twelve) passus, a total length of some two and a half thousand lines. Skeat's B-version is a much longer poem. It consists of a prologue and twenty passus, giving a total of some seven thousand two hundred lines. The C-version, as we have noted, is similarly expanded. Its length is a little greater than that of the B-version and the process of revision is less striking, though not necessarily less thorough, than that which obtained in the A-B transition. And yet, we need to remember that the differential between the two versions is not simply quantitative. For all the significant similarity of structure and length, the differences between the two versions and the intensity of revision are very considerable.

The argument for accepting Skeat's order for the three versions is, of course, one which demands the kind of demonstration which a short essay cannot offer. Professor Kane has already set out the case for the priority of the A-version over B and C, and in the forthcoming edition, the case for the priority of B over C will be set forth.[10]

In essence, both cases rest upon a reading of the evidence which concludes that the existing shape of the B- or C-versions is most convincingly explained by their being revisions of the shapes of the A- and B-versions respectively, and that this, and not its converse, is the most reasonable explanation of the relationship of the manuscripts. The most convincing evidence is supplied by those lines or passages which can be reasonably explained only on the assumption that they are modifications or revision of material which already existed in another form, and that the reverse explanation is not reasonably tenable. In this context, it is fortunate that the text offered by all extant B-version manuscripts is relatively inferior and that the text which the C-reviser used as his working copy was a scribally produced manuscript which contained corruptions and that, seemingly, he had no access to his autograph or its equivalent. A part of the process of revision in the C-version is in fact, as we shall see, repair work upon this defective working text. There are many passages in which we detect an effort to correct a B original which we know to be corrupt in the extant manuscripts and which seems also to have been corrupt in the reviser's manuscript. In these cases, that the C form is more reasonably derived from the B form and that it is, consequently, posterior to it, seems a more convincing explanation of these cases than the converse.

Some years ago, the question of the authorship of the successive revisions was the most contentious issue in the whole of *Piers Plowman* scholarship, and we know that a great deal of the energies of post-Manly scholarship was devoted – wastefully one might think – to the resolution of this issue. Happily this enthusiasm for controversy has waned. While there is doubtless no unanimity upon the question, it seems that there is now a substantial majority view and that, in any case, the issue is not regarded by most scholars and critics as being of central concern to those seeking to approach the poem.

There are, however, some people who cannot set the problem aside and who must, in fact, take a decision on the question. In particular, those who are concerned with textual relations between the versions, especially editors, must accept either the theory of single authorship or one or other of the theories of multiple authorship. The decision taken will, of course, profoundly influence the nature of the editorial process and, as a consequence, the nature of the text which is its product.

For the purposes of this essay the assumption of single authorship is made. Professor Kane's exhaustive monograph on the subject has seemed as nearly conclusive as can be expected in a discussion of this kind. His conclusion that the three versions are the work of one man, and that this man was probably named William Langland is, at very least, a reasonable reading of the evidence.[11]

Similarly anyone who will write about the phenomenon of revision in the poem must make an assumption about the authorship of the successive revisions. It is clearly essential to form an opinion on the question of whether we are dealing with the work of one man who returned to his original on two separate occasions or whether we are dealing with two, three or more men who made separate attempts upon the material. If our assumption is the former, we can legitimately postulate that the successive processes of revision will be undertaken with a unique understanding of the sense and structure of the original which is being revised, and even that, with the final revision, the reviser may recall, may even have access to, texts of both the earlier versions which are markedly superior to those which survive. He will certainly have an unrivalled understanding of the earlier forms of the poem. If we make the latter assumption – that is, that we are dealing with three or more different poets – our attitude and consequently our procedure will necessarily be quite different. We will not, and cannot, assume that B's interpretation of A, or C's interpretation of B, have any particular authority. A revision undertaken in these circumstances will produce in successive versions three poems which bear a more or less close resemblance to one another, but which will be distinguished by their representing three totally separate attempts upon similar material and which need bear no closer relationship to one another than any three poems on the same general topic. Above all, in the process of revision, there will be real danger of major misunderstandings since the revisers will not necessarily have any more authoritative access to the poem under revision than will any other reader. We would, in fact, expect poets, who are, by definition, characterized by uniqueness of vision, to offer radically different readings of the centralities of a poem as complex and inaccessible as *Piers Plowman*.

Even if we assume single authorship of all three versions and see them, in all the complexity of their manuscript transmission, as being in essence one man's attempt, spread over a number of years, on a great and demanding theme, we are still by no means clear of difficulties of all kinds. And these difficulties appear to be integral to the method of revision illustrated in the poem, which may well be typical of medieval methods.

It is difficult for a modern reader to free himself of the assumptions which would be made, and the practices which would be followed, if revisions of this kind were undertaken under the modern publishing system. He finds it difficult to imagine an author who would not retain a fair copy of his text, or who would not have ready access to the authorized text of all published editions, or who would not undertake his revisions in an orderly, probably continuous, fashion acceptable to his publisher, or who, finally, would not regard even the *minutiae* of his text as sacrosanct and ensure their preservation. All such considerations would be central to the concerns and practices of any modern author revising his work or for an editor undertaking revision of the work of another.

But the evidence offered by the extant manuscripts of *Piers Plowman* strongly suggests that few, if any, of these conditions obtained during the process of the poem's revision. Indeed the circumstances of medieval publishing would seem to make it very unlikely that they could normally obtain, at least in a work that quickly became widely disseminated and was not produced by a man with ready access to, and control over, the materials and facilities for transcription and reproduction.

It may then, be useful to attempt to reconstruct what can reasonably be deduced of Langland's circumstances and resultant practice. The A-version is, of course, not in question here. By our definition it has not been subject to a process of authorial revision: it is Langland's first attempt to render his theme, and variations occurring in the extant manuscripts are assumed to be scribal or editorial in origin.[12] The B-version, putatively Langland's first revision, is, as we have seen, a large-scale reworking of existing A material and offers an addition to this of a very substantial amount of new material. Indeed, so great is the degree of revision that it is less easy to draw conclusions about the AB transition than it is about the BC transition, since the latter relationship is much closer than the former.

Pending the appearance of the text supplied by the new edition of the B-version which, predictably, will be very different from that offered in Skeat's existing edition, it would be fruitless, and indeed presumptuous on my part, to discuss in any detail the process of revision which transmuted the A-version into the B-version. The detailed analysis will be given in the forthcoming B edition by editors with access to all the evidence, but even our present state of knowledge allows some generalizations.

Obviously, the revision of B over A was a radical process. A study of the convenient, even if inadequate, three-text edition of Skeat[13] makes it clear that the process was twofold – an adaptation, characterized by painstaking revision, of the material which appeared in A and a massive process of augmentation which appears as expansion of existing material, as addition to this material and, especially, as large-scale development of the latter part of the A-version into a major sector of the new poem which more than doubles its length and adds to it some of its most significant material.

The state of the existing printed text makes conjecture hazardous, but even a study of this seems to demonstrate that the range of revision is enormous – from mere verbal changes involving one or two words in a line or minor alterations of order within a line, through small additions of material of two or three lines, through larger pieces of alteration and addition to great stretches of material which are either completely new or which have been so thoroughly dismantled and rebuilt that little remains of the original.

The revision from B to C is less obviously spectacular. But the process which produced the revision is no less radical and significant. While it is, certainly, quantitatively less striking, it offers, through the greater part of the C-version, evidence of an alert and scrupulous scrutiny of that which had been written and a desire, whether mistaken or not, to modify the original. And yet, with occasional exceptions, the process is not one of substantial accretion or of major rearrangement.[14] It is as though the general shape of the poem has been accepted by the reviser, but the detail of the poem still warrants the sharpest scrutiny.

This BC transition, then, although still representing a profound and important modification, offers a much more useful body of material for the study of the process of revision than does the product of the AB transition. This, along with my diffidence about discussing a problem which I do not know at first hand, leads me to use the BC revision for the purpose of detailed discussion.

It is generally agreed that the extant B manuscripts and, presumptively, their archetypal tradition, do not supply a faithful version of the original shape of the first revision.[15] The extent of the unreliability of the B tradition will doubtless be demonstrated in the new edition, but even a superficial study of Skeat's text reminds us of two things: that the B manuscripts are frequently in conflict with the A and C manuscripts when all three versions contain what appears to be common material, and that they offer a remarkable degree of unanimity of attestation. The evidence certainly suggests that the transmitted B-version is seriously deformed and that this deformation is archetypal, that is that the corruption was already present in the manuscript from which all extant B manuscripts descend.[16]

Whenever they are testifying to material which seems not to have been subjected to heavy revision, the C manuscripts, and presumptively their exclusively common ancestor, appear to offer a generally superior text. But it is certainly not a text which is of any unusually high quality, and there are many places in which it is demonstrably inferior to its B counterpart. As we shall see, this judgment can be tested under unusually interesting circumstances in the last two passus of the poem.[17]

But whatever the quality of the text transmitted in the archetypal C tradition, it is nevertheless true that the reviser of C had as his working copy a manuscript of the B-version which was superior to any of the extant B manuscripts, and, it seems, superior to their exclusive common ancestor.[18] And yet that manuscript was certainly not the author's fair copy of B: it was, demonstrably, a scribally transmitted copy which already contained substantial corruption. Nor did the reviser, seemingly, have access to his fair copy, or an accurate recall of its details, since there are a good number of places where an apparently corrupt reading has been accepted from the B-version, as transmitted, into the C-version, presumably because the reviser was unaware of the existence of the corruption or because, on occasions at least, he was indifferent to the precise shape of the line provided that its basic shape and sense had not been altered. Nor, we may add, is there any evidence that he had access to a fair copy of the A-version which, distant as it was from the completed B-version, would, nevertheless, have provided him with an important check on the reliability of his working copy.

As the C-reviser, then, addressed himself to his task of revising the B-version he had, first, to face the disadvantage of not having before him a fair copy of either the A- or the B-version. This, in contexts where the restoration of the original reading or an effective substitute was judged to be of importance, laid upon him the necessity of making more or less minor alterations throughout the process of revision.

But it would seem unlikely that this task of correction was the reviser's first concern. Clearly there must have been other, substantial, grounds for undertaking the huge task of the revision of a work, already once revised, the very bulk of which suggests that it must already have occupied a great deal of time and demanded a great deal of effort. But whatever these grounds were, we must assume that they arose from dissatisfaction of some kind with what had already been written, and not simply a concern to correct the errors of existing circulating copies, though doubtless this was a subsidiary consideration. The revision of A to B had already revealed responses to dissatisfactions of various kinds – the desire for greater precision and point, the desire to explore at greater depth, the desire to attain more meaningful structures, the desire to bring to the poem that wider dimension and that deepened significance that is represented by the extensive revision towards the end of A and the massive addition which followed that revision.

All these, and other, motives had produced a new poem. But still there was dissatisfaction: in part, no doubt, the dissatisfaction of an artist who seems to have cared passionately for what he had written and who seeks a more meaningful exploration and projection of his cosmic theme: in part, perhaps a dissatisfaction with areas of the poem which were open to misinterpretation and which may even have attracted the attention of hostile critics. For we recall that this poem was circulating at a time when ecclesiastical and political critics were sensitive to what might appear subversive. A maladroit formulation of a doctrine might easily cause trouble.

On occasions, a great deal has been made of the allegedly greater caution and conservatism of C. Their existence has, indeed, been cited as one of the difficulties standing in the way of the acceptance of the theory of single authorship for B and C. There are, I believe, contexts in which there does seem to be a greater circumspection and a desire for a prudent modification of what has been written. But, as Donaldson has demonstrated, the case for C's conservatism has at times been grossly overstated and misrepresented, often for tendentious purposes.[19]

But even if we may wish to admit this element of greater caution and circumspection, we should be careful not to assume that the reviser necessarily sat down to revise his poem by means of an orderly and thoroughgoing review which began with the opening lines of the Prologue and was designed to continue through to the end of the final passus. The evidence of the text does not seem to me to indicate that the process of revision was of this orderly and systematic kind. One might even suggest that it was sporadic; that it had certain points of departure which were, presumably, points of dissatisfaction and that, while the revising activity might be intense at these points and might continue through relatively long

D

passages, quite large stretches of the poem were left to stand and
may, indeed, never have received close scrutiny since the need for
revision did not represent itself to the reviser. This is to say that it
seems to me at best doubtful if the C revision was undertaken – as
I believe the B revision was undertaken – to offer a radical and
large-scale rewriting of the whole poem: rather it was designed to
be a limited operation to meet specific problems. This is, of course,
not to say that the process which began in this way confined itself
to these limited objectives: once more the evidence of the text
suggests otherwise, and there are notable examples of the poet's
having moved from repair work to substantial alteration and
reorganization.

If we are to reduce these general observations to detail, we might
begin with the simplest of examples, that is the cases presented
when the C-reviser found in his working copy a reading which he
judged to be unacceptable, either as a consequence of his poet's
instinct for the perception of the inferior or of his memory, now
not totally secure, that he had, in fact, written differently.

By way of introduction to this kind of revision, we may remind
ourselves of the faulty nature of this text which the reviser was
using. From a relatively large number of examples we may cite
passages in which the B-version seems clearly to have deformed the
A-reading but in which the reviser has either not adverted to the
fact of corruption, or has not bothered to make an alteration.[20] I
assume that in all these cases the AB difference is not the result of
authorial revision, but is a consequence of scribal alteration or
error.[21]

Some simple examples of this process are:

A v 106	mat/mad	BC megre
A v 106	loke	BC wayte
A vii 89	frendes	BC douȝtres
A ix 36	watris	BC wederes
A x 22	sixe	BC fyue
A x 199	ysamme	BC togideres.

To these might be added many more examples of the same kind.
One of these, which is more extensive, will perhaps serve. At
A iv 74 ff, we read:

'God wot', quaþ wysdom, 'þat were not þe beste.
And he amendis mowe make let maynprise hym haue,
And be borugh for his bale & b[ig]gen hym bote;
Amende þat mysdede, & eueremore þe betere.'

In the B-version there is no evidence of any attempt to rewrite the passage, which runs without significant variation until B iv 90 where we read:

And so amende þat is mysdo . and euermore þe bettere.

A's spare *þat mysdede* has been altered, without contextual warning, to the longer form *þat is mysdo*, and it is now preceded by an explicit linking phrase to make clear that which, in the sparer A form, has been left implicit. Both variants – the longer and the more explicit – are characteristic of scribal activity. And yet, with one slight variant, the C-version (C v 86) has no difficulty in accepting the B form.

One can, I believe, multiply these examples.[22] Readers will interpret this phenomenon in various ways. Whatever the interpretation of various cases, the general proposition seems not in question. For our purposes, however, it is of interest only because it leads us to the first, and simplest, kind of revision that we find in the poem.

Once more this centres upon what appears to be corruption in the reviser's manuscript. Whereas in the previous set of examples the reviser, for whatever reason, allowed the scribal reading to stand, in the cases that follow, the shape of the C-version suggests two things to us: first that, once again, the reviser's manuscript contained a corruption; second, that, in these cases, the reviser recognized the fact of corruption and elected to alter his new version so that a more satisfactory reading was supplied. We cannot say whether it is simply a question of recognition or non-recognition of error which distinguishes the cases or whether there has been recognition in both cases and action in only one. But certainly the effect is very different, for, as we shall see, this recognition of error and decision to revise often has an important bearing upon the intensity of the whole process of revision in certain contexts.

Two examples of this phenomenon may be examined at this point:

At A vii 209-210 appear the following lines:

> Þat nedy ben or nakid, & nouȝt han to spende
> Wiþ mete or [wiþ] mone let make hem [fare þe betere]

In B (vi 226) we have this reading:

> That nedy ben, and nauȝty . helpe hem with þi godis

In C (ix 233-234) we read:

> In meschief oþer in mal-ese . and þow mowe hem helpe
> Loke by þy lyf . let hem nouht for-fare.

To this point, the three versions are fairly close together. The break comes with B's line. If we compare it with A, we become aware that the initial warning of its unoriginality, which its defective alliterative pattern gives us, seems to be borne out by the nature of the B line itself. Its opening is clearly a reflex of the corresponding part of the A line: its conclusion is an extraordinarily lame dilution of the remainder of the two A lines, which offers a faulty alliterative pattern and disastrously reduced sense. If, then, we turn to C, we find that the single B line has been replaced by two lines, but that these are rewritings which no longer reflect the A form, except perhaps in the appearance of *for-fare* which may reflect A's *fare* which had disappeared in the B rendering.

The rewriting is almost total and one's guess is that the C-reviser is responding to B's formal irregularity and enfeeblement of sense. He repairs the alliteration in his revision and he restores some part of the vigour of the A lines. But two conclusions seem to follow from the process: first, he does not appear to have had access to his A form, though he may have had a distant memory which his use of *for-fare* reflects; second, we may legitimately postulate that the shape of the B line which he had before him was similar to the existing B line, since C retains an unmistakable reflex of *helpe hem with þi godis* in his *and þow mowe hem helpe* which is not suggested at any point in the A line.

Again at A xi 308 we read:

> Þanne arn þise [k]ete clerkis þat conne many bokis

which appears in B (x 457) in the following form:

> Þan ar þis cunnynge clerkes . þat conne many bokes

while C (xii 291) offers this shape:

> Cominliche þan clerkes . most knowynge and connynge.

If we compare B with A it is not hard to see what has happened. The word *kete* is a difficult word, and indeed a number of A scribes found it so. So, it seems, did the scribe of the B archetype (or the tradition which he was following). In its place he wrote, desperately perhaps, *cunnynge* which was presumably suggested by *conne* later in the line and which offered a kind of sense, reduced though it was. Seemingly the C-reviser found unacceptable the shape of the line as B transmitted it to him. He accordingly rewrote it in a form which had, for him, greater point. But in doing this he seems, by his retention of *connynge* which, as we have seen, did not appear in A, to demonstrate that the form in which he encountered the line was that of the present B-version, not that of A.[23]

In these examples, we have confined ourselves to short passages which illustrate the reviser's response to a single corruption. But the importance of this phenomenon extends beyond these patching and repairing operations. It is noticeable that once the reviser's attention has been caught by what he judges to be a corruption in his manuscript and has stopped to effect repairs, he is likely to linger over the passage and its context and to subject them to a close scrutiny which often issues in quite detailed, even finicky, revision extending over a number of lines. In a number of cases, then, we have revisions which, in other contexts, would not have appeared because the reviser's attention was not directed to the passage and its organization. An example will illustrate the nature of the process:

At B iv 19 ff we read:

> 'And sette my sadel vppon suffre- . til-I-se-my-tyme,
> And lete warrok it wel . with witty-wordes gerthes,
> And hange on hym þe heuy brydel . to holde his hed lowe,
> For he wil make wehe . tweye er he be there.'
>   Thanne conscience vppon his caple . kaireth forth faste,
> And resoun with hym ritte . rownynge togideres,
> Which maistries Mede . maketh on þis erthe.
>   One waryn wisdom . And witty his fere
> Folwed hem faste . [for þei] haued to done

> In þe cheker and at þe chauncerie . to be discharged of þinges;
> And riden fast, for resoun . shulde rede hem þe beste,
> For to saue hem, for siluer . fro shame and fram harmes.

Against this we may set C v 20 ff:

> 'And sette my sadel vppon soffre- . til-ich-see-my-tyme,
> Let warroke hym wel . *with* a-vyse-[þe]-by-fore,
> For it is þe wone of wil . to wynse and to kyke;
> Let peitrel hym and pole hym . with peyntede wittes.'
> Thenne conscience on hus capel . comsed to prykie,
> And reson *with* hym ry3t . rounyng to-geders
> Which a maister mede was . a-mong poure and riche.
> Then waryn wysman . and wyly-man his felawe
> Fayn were to folwen hem . and fast ryden after,
> To take red at reson . þat recorde sholde
> By-fore þe kyng and conscience . yf þei couthen pleyne
> On wily-man and wittiman . and waryn wrynge-lawe.

Reference to the corresponding A passage (A iv 18 ff) shows us that the second of B's lines is malformed and of weakened sense. C seems to have realized this and he alters it decisively, but not in the direction of A, which he cannot recall. Again characteristically, he then writes a new line to replace B 21 and alters B 22 which again is textually doubtful. From this point the revision is persistent and scrupulous: scarcely a line is left untouched. If we look further on in the same passus, to B 37 ff, we can see a similar process operating. This is not the heavy revision of a poet wishing to change the direction of his poem: it is rather the reconsideration and alteration of small matters, and it is not always happily contrived. It is from passages of this kind, and there are many of them, that C inherits its often well-deserved reputation for fussiness.

This kind of revision, then, is the simplest and most readily explicable type displayed in the poem. It is – in its genesis at best – imposed upon the reviser: the result, according to his judgment, will be a small or large-scale alteration of the text. It is this type of revision, one is tempted to think, which gives to the C-version its reputation for greater prolixity and specificity. There is, indeed, some case here, though we do need to recall that Skeat's base manuscript for C (Hm 138) contains a good deal of scribal meddling leading to a kind of prosaicization which does not always appear in better manuscripts like Hm 143 and T.C.C. R.3.14, which seem, on balance, likely to offer a text of the poem closer to that of the archetypal tradition.

But there are, obviously, other kinds of revision which are not of this order. They do not arise from the need to repair mechanical errors or the results of scribal meddling; they are the consequences of an authorial decision, independent of the facts of transmission, to modify the poem and, as such, they constitute the most important sector of the process of revision and are of central concern to the reason.

The range of such revisions is very wide. Some of them are small, the alteration of a word, the shift in the shape of a line, the deletion or addition of a short passage of two or three lines and the like. Others of them are massive – the addition of passages of a hundred or more lines, the shifting of one or more substantial passages from one part of the poem to another, the detailed and exhaustive modification of long passages so that their whole significance is altered and the context, and, through this, perhaps the whole poem, decisively changed.

Changes of this kind, whether small or large, are different in nature from their predecessors. In sum they reflect the author's new and, in the case of the C-revision, final reading of his theme. The significance of such large-scale alterations is increased if we recall that there is no evidence that decisively suggests that the reviser necessarily undertook a painstaking, line-by-line revision of his text. The evidence rather suggests that the process was a selective one centred upon particular passages and particular lines of thought. Consequently considerable stretches of the poem are, in a real sense, left untouched except where, almost adventitiously, the reviser's attention is caught by a corrupt reading of his working copy or where, following on from this, he elected to undertake detailed, though not necessarily very significant, revision.

It is obviously difficult, in a short paper of this kind, to illustrate this kind of large scale revision which, although of the greatest significance for the interpretation of the poem, is textually of rather less interest, and perhaps its full study belongs elsewhere. Nevertheless we can recall several examples. We have, for example, the extensive study of the nature of meed in terms of grammatical analogies at C iv 317-409; we have the large addition of the 'auto-biographical' passage at C vi 1-108; we have the large-scale transpositions of material from B passus x and xiii which appear in C passus vi, vii and viii, which result in a substantial modification of the portraits of the Seven Deadly Sins; we have the very significant alteration of the pardon scene in C passus x, a passus which is very considerably altered by the C-reviser; we have the very substantial alteration to C passus xvi 233 ff which results from the earlier changes made in passus vii and viii, and, as a final example, we have the very considerable amount of reduction and addition of material which characterizes C passus xviii.

These cases, in general, offer examples of material moved bodily to another part of the poem, added to the poem or removed from it. To these we may add an example of a revision of the poem which manifests itself at various points over a greater part of its length as a consequence of the rehandling of a theme which is recurrent through the poem. The theme is that of the Salvation of the Heathen with which I have dealt elsewhere.[24] There is no need to repeat the details of the argument here, but the case is a useful reminder of a different kind of revision. If this thesis is correct, it appears that the C-reviser took pains to see that, as between the B- and C-versions, a quite different line of thought was developed and that, since this line of thought ran through the greater part of the poem, numerous alterations were made at various points. This projection of what seems to be a new attitude to one of the notoriously difficult problems confronting medieval Christian thinking manifests itself in omissions, additions and transpositions. There can be little doubt, I believe, that this strand of thought was followed through with care by the C-reviser and that he was prepared patiently to refashion parts of his poem to accommodate the new view.

A detailed examination of the motives underlying such revisions is beyond the scope of this essay, since any adequate discussion of their nature would take us deep into the interpretation of the poem in its three forms. But some general observations may be in order.

The first is that it seems clear that, to the end, the poem was still evolving. This means that it continues to exhibit, in its final form, some signs of indecision and what look suspiciously like raw ends left untended. I believe this to be true of the *Visio* in particular, where both the Prologue as it stands, and the account of Meed seem to call for further attention and where the revised portraits of some of the Seven Deadly Sins are not fully convincing.

Another point of remark of a rather different, though related, kind may be made. It is that appearances suggest that the revision of C, in addition to being sporadic, is unfinished. This is suggested by one major piece of evidence. A study of the two final passus of the two versions (B xix, xx: C xxii, xxiii) strongly suggests that they have not been subjected to authorial revision at all. It is true that if one sets alongside one another the two versions of the passus as they are printed by Skeat, there appear frequent differences which bear the appearance of revisions. But it seems extremely unlikely that we are here dealing with the operations of a revising author. It is much more likely that these apparent revisions are the consequence of scribally introduced variations. The two versions show variation in some one hundred places: of these at least one half suggest that the B-version has been scribally corrupted and there are about one-third where C appears to be the offender. The remaining cases are harder to decide, but I believe that none of them can be unequivocally demonstrated to be authorial in origin. This pattern is, I think, so markedly at variance with what we observe in earlier passus that it seems impossible to argue that the process of revision is still in operation. Indeed it might be held that something of the same thing might be said of the preceding passus (B xviii, C xxi). There is, I believe, some evidence to suggest that this passus shows signs of the tapering off of the process. Its first two-thirds appear to have been subjected to a fairly searching review; its last third seems, by comparison, to have been very lightly touched.

It is true that the appearance of the two last passus is susceptible to other explanations. We have already observed the rather sporadic and, at times, adventitious nature of the revising process. It may be that we have here a large-scale illustration of what we observe elsewhere – a satisfaction with what exists and a refusal to admit the necessity of alteration. But one must also say that, if this is the case, the resulting situation is quite unlike that obtaining in any other part of the poem, and that there is no parallel for the suspension of the revising process over such a stretch of text. Indeed, this explanation is so unlikely that we scarcely need entertain it.

On the other hand, the absence of revision from the final two passus can be explained in another way that is far more convincing and, perhaps, impossible to disprove. It is that the archetypal text of C may be a conjoint text and that it was made up of twenty-one passus (or a prologue and twenty passus) in the revised, C form, but that, for some reason, it lacked or had lost the revised form of the last two passus and that the resulting gap was repaired by borrowing the corresponding passus of the B-version.

We can demonstrate something of this kind to have happened elsewhere. There are, of course, a large number of manuscripts which graft a C conclusion to an A beginning; there are a number of manuscripts which, by some kind of accident, have lost material which, putatively at least, they once contained. This happens in the middle sections of manuscripts but is, of course, most common at the beginning and at the end. Indeed, there is a group of manuscripts (Bodley 814, BM Additional 10574 and Caligula A xi) which represent a line of descent of the text in which the opening part of the poem to B ii 20 are in the form of the C-version and the remainder in that of the B-version. It seems certain in this case that a missing block of text at the beginning of the poem was supplied from a manuscript which came to hand and that that manuscript chanced to be a C-version manuscript. If this happened with one group of manuscripts, there is no reason to deny that it could happen elsewhere and that the exclusive common ancestor of the C manuscripts was a defective manuscript subsequently repaired from B.

Our choice between the possibilities can scarcely be unequivocally demonstrated. Perhaps our reading of passus xxi will be crucially important. If, as I believe, this demonstrates a slowing-down to the point of disappearance of the process of revision, the case for asserting its absence in xxii and xxiii is strengthened. One might venture to go a little further and postulate that the unfinished C-version was put in a publishable form by an editor or literary executor. For if the process of revision was not completed, it seems very unlikely that its author was able to oversee the production of a final fair copy.

It is, perhaps, proper to end with a question-mark. As these notes may serve to indicate, the problems surrounding the process of revision in *Piers Plowman* are complex and often intractable. That this should be so is no surprise since we are dealing with the life-work of one of the most complex and elusive writers of the English Middle Ages, and that he or his work would easily respond to simple processes of analysis seems unthinkable.

The Tearing of the Pardon

ROSEMARY WOOLF

Piers Plowman is one of the most difficult poems ever written: it is a work that constantly challenges but evades interpretation; and in it there is no scene that is more important or more elusive than that in which Piers tears the Pardon. Modern critics have been unanimous on one point only, that the scene has a dramatic resonance that extends far beyond the limits of passus vii and therefore that it is central to the whole meaning of the poem; on all other points their disagreement with one another ranges from the partial to the complete.

The course of the action, which begins in passus v, is on the surface deceptively simple. After the repentance of society expressed in the confessions of the Seven Deadly Sins, Piers Plowman sets himself to organize a just, ordered and ideal society, in which each member will conscientiously carry out the duties appropriate to his rank or profession. Thereupon God sends a 'pardon' to Piers; but, when the contents of the 'pardon' are revealed, it turns out to be Verse 41 of the Athanasian Creed, 'Et qui bona egerunt ibunt in vitam eternam; Qui vero mala, in ignem eternam'. A priest then tells Piers that this is not a pardon and Piers in 'pure tene' tears up the document. This summary, however, deceives, for it conceals both the problems and the dramatic intensity of the sequence. The difficulties are roughly as follows: how the words in the document are to be reconciled with the description of it as a pardon; whether the priest speaks as a representative of Christianity or as a corrupt priest only too ready to sneer at good works; what Piers himself at this stage of the poem symbolizes; and whether his tearing of the document is a trivial action belonging chiefly to the literal level of the story or whether it is an action of serious allegorical meaning.

The diversity of modern opinion on all these issues may be illustrated by a brief summary of three substantial analyses of the scene. Professor Coghill, who, in his British Academy lecture for 1945,[1] was the first scholar to attach adequate weight to the scene, supposed the pardon to be the pardon bought on Calvary, the text from the Creed to be 'a catch-phrase about Salvation', the priest to be 'the villain of the piece' and, by implication, the tearing of the pardon to be insignificant. The apparently disconcerting emphasis upon 'qui bona egerunt' he explains in terms of the allegorical reference of Piers: Piers in this part of the poem signifies 'Do-Well, or in Latin *qui bona egerunt*; it is his very name, and the pardon is truly his', and his followers, who have made confession and are seeking to carry out his commands, justly share in it.

Professor Lawlor's more recent interpretation of the scene is almost the exact reverse of this.[2] The pardon he takes to be a sign of admonition rather than forgiveness; the priest is a figure of the same order as Clergy or Scripture in the later passus, 'what they say is true, but fails to meet their interlocutor's real need'; whilst Piers himself is the best man that the corrupt society of this world can produce, and yet even he fails to meet the conditions of the pardon. Piers therefore throws himself on the mercy of God, finding only despair in the justice of the pardon: his recognition of the need for mercy is dramatically symbolized by his tearing of the pardon. What Professor Coghill understands as a scene of Redemption, Professor Lawlor takes to be a scene of judgment and condemnation.

Midway between these poles is Professor Frank's interpretation.[3] Like Professor Coghill he believes the pardon to be a true pardon, and reconciles this with its character of judgment by maintaining that the society depicted by Langland has by and large done good works and therefore can be aptly rewarded with this text: there is no question in this instance of God's justice being at odds with His mercy. Like Professor Lawlor, however, he has laid stress upon the tearing of the pardon. According to his view, in the scene between Piers and the priest, Langland's intention is to attack the system of indulgences, and the tearing of the pardon therefore symbolizes the rejection of papal pardons: 'the pardon contains a message which is by implication an attack on pardons', and Piers trusts to the message whilst rejecting the form.

It is in accord with the peculiar power of the poem that the two theories that in content are most irreconcilable seem truer to the text than the moderate one, which does not do justice to the stature of the scene. The dubiousness of indulgences was undoubtedly in Langland's mind as he wrote, and the Dreamer explicitly draws this moral. But excessive trust in pardons was a sermon commonplace of the time, and it is a meaning too banal to warrant the dramatic tension that Langland has contrived. It is surely a reflection on the limited understanding of the Dreamer that he can only extract so slight a significance from the majestic enigma of his vision. Professor Frank's interpretation has the further disadvantage that it finds two solutions to one mystery. The paradoxical relationship between the pardon and its contents leads to the aesthetically satisfying action of the tearing, and a disjunctive explanation is therefore insufficient.

The solutions proposed by Professor Coghill and Professor Lawlor do not divide the mystery into two but do not fully account for all its elements. Professor Coghill's explanation of why, contrary to immediate appearances, the pardon is a pardon (because it is sent to Piers, the personification of *qui bona egerunt*) is subtle and moving, but it leaves the tearing of the pardon unexplained. By contrast, Professor Lawlor's explanation of the tearing of the pardon satisfyingly accounts for the dramatic power of this episode, but leaves the earlier element in the puzzle unresolved, namely why a judgment – and one that is shown to be entirely damnatory – should have been called a pardon. This cannot be ignored as though it were a random piece of mystification.

At the heart of many interpretations of the Pardon scene there lies a misstatement of the problem. The question asked is, 'Was it a valid pardon?' and to so tendentious a question there can only be one answer, yes, for the pardon that the priest demands to read is said to have been sent by Truth, who is God, and it contains a text drawn from one of the authoritative creeds of the Church. That the text itself is the word of God is incontestable: not only does it come from the Athanasian creed, but the creed itself at this point is closely echoing the words of Christ in *Matthew* xxv. What Christ spoke can indeed be presented as a message from God. The correct form of the question, however, is, 'Can this text be described as a pardon?' for, if it cannot, the true conclusion is, not that Truth has lied, but that the poet for his own purposes has misled us: it is the poet in his own voice, not God as a character in the poem, who describes the document as a pardon: it is the Dreamer and Piers and his followers who believe the document to be a pardon and, if it is not, we can say that Langland in writing the first lines of passus vii ('Treuthe herde telle herof . . . And purchaced hym a par-doun') gave himself the licence to deceive, deliberately allowing us to hear in them the omniscient narrative voice of the poet, when in fact he is only reporting a misconception of his created characters. But it would be an elaborate deception and one that would require a substantial justification.

That Langland intended a shock and a mystery, of which an elaborate deception would form an essential part, is suggested by the very careful construction of the passus. There is first of all the very marked delay between the mention of the pardon in the third line of the passus and the revelation of its content more than one hundred lines later. The intervening space is taken up by the narrator's homiletic exposition of the glosses upon the text of the pardon, which (in accordance with medieval scribal custom) are imagined to be written in the margins of the document.[4] These glosses (like, for instance, the glosses on decretals) show how a general statement relates to precise circumstances, in this instance how the pardon applies to various types of society. The narrative order here is markedly odd, for the exposition of the pardon is given before the text of the pardon itself. The material itself, how-ever, is reassuringly familiar, for by implication it is at least semi-satirical, and Langland uses the fiction of the glosses to revert to his favourite themes of the avarice of lawyers and merchants or the fraudulence of the lazy poor.

As so often in the poem Langland in this passage only fitfully remembers the literal level of his allegory,[5] and indeed the idea of the glosses provides only a narrow base for the discursive warning to the followers of Lady Meed on how they must amend their lives before they may profit from the pardon. It is therefore easy to read the passage as a typical and rather repetitious disquisition on the kind of subject that so often diverted Langland from the steady development of his theme. It is, however, more likely that Langland was here manipulating his own digressive tendencies, for the effect of the digression is to build up suspense, a suspense that is fulfilled in the dramatic emphasis upon the words of the pardon. Piers for the first time opens the document, so that the priest may read it, and the Dreamer as it were peers over his shoulder ('And I bihynde hem bothe bihelde al the bulle'). This is a most extraordinary treatment of the Dreamer: normally he is either a detached observer of the vision or he is present in the dream in life-like contact with the other characters. Here, however, the reader sees him in physical relationship with the other characters but they are unaware of this, as though he were a ghost in his own dream. The effect is to bring the words of the pardon into startling focus: the poet manifestly intends us to be surprised.

We are not only surprised but also bewildered, and so too is the Dreamer at the end of the scene. He lies awake at night pondering what kind of a pardon it was and debating within himself the value of dreams. This passage on dream theory may seem unremarkable, for Chaucer, who makes it an almost invariable element of his dream-visions, has accustomed us to the acceptance of this as a traditional element. But this is the only point in the poem in which Langland wonders about the nature of dreams, and the placing of the passage is therefore very important. Moreover, it is significant that out of a fund of traditional dream material he draws out the two great enigmatic dreams of the Old Testament, the dreams of Joseph and Nebuchadnezzar,[6] dreams that have to be expounded with divine inspiration before they are understood. Langland never overtly expounds the dream of the pardon, but the many critics who assume that the exposition lies hidden in the tenor of the rest of the poem have surely rightly unfolded Langland's method of working.

The kind of dream that Langland uses in passus vii is that which Macrobius described as follows: 'By an enigmatic dream we mean one that conceals with strange shapes and veils with ambiguity the true meaning of the information being offered, and requires an interpretation for its understanding.'[7] There are two parts to our attempt to unravel this enigmatic dream, the first to define exactly the nature of the problem, the second then to penetrate beneath the strange shapes to the inner meaning. The surest way of approaching the first part is to try to reconstruct how a medieval audience would have understood it. It is certain that they would have been puzzled by the scene in a way not intended: the omission of the tearing of the pardon in the C-text strongly suggests that this action caused bewilderment, for over and over again one finds that the rugged mysteries of the B-text have been smoothed out in the C-text. But, though they were puzzled, this does not mean that their confusion was identical with ours, and a consideration of the literary and semi-theological background to the scene suggests that whilst they were probably no abler (indeed, probably less able) than us in discovering a solution, they were probably able to formulate the problem more clearly.

The best point at which to begin this reconstruction of a medieval audience's reactions to the scene is at the long pause, already noticed, between the announcement of the pardon and the revelation of its content. For this pause, which is filled with material of only moderate interest, offers an opportunity to the reader to pursue his own thoughts and to anticipate, at least semi-consciously from the progress of the poem and his knowledge of traditional allegorical procedures, what the pardon will be in both form and significance.

The term 'pardon' nowadays is largely familiar as an abstract noun synonymous with forgiveness or, if used to mean an act of forgiveness, the nature of the act remains unclear. In the Middle Ages, however, it had a precise and generally known sense of a document conferring a royal pardon.[8] The latter would be for some offence committed, and the recipient would keep it in his possession to guarantee his future immunity from officers of the law in regard to his crime. Walter Hilton in the *Scale of Perfection* begins an allegorical example as follows:

> For if a man had forfeited his life against a king of this earth, it were not enough to him as for a full security for to have only forgiveness of the king, but if he have a charter the which may be his token and his warrant against all other men.[9]

In the *Scale* this is used to show the need for confession and absolution as opposed to private contrition, an application that is unusual and lacking in the pointed aptness normally characteristic of medieval allegorization. But the narrative manner suggests that this is one of the many instances in which Hilton draws upon what is familiar in everyday life in order to illustrate a devotional point, and it therefore confirms, what one would anyway expect, that a pardon was the kind of legal document that people knew of and understood in the Middle Ages.

Whilst on the one hand a pardon might be known from common experience, on the other hand it might be known as a literary image, one of the many signifying the redemption. To prove this it is necessary to make a brief excursus on the development of the theme. The invariable element is that of a legal document written in Christ's blood, a document sometimes called a charter, sometimes a pardon. As we shall see, there was confusion between the two, for though to a lawyer they would seem completely distinct, from the literary point of view their field of reference was identical, and their significance the same: a charter would confer heaven on man, a pardon would give him release from hell.

The earliest extant allusion to this image is in the allegory of the lover-knight in the *Ancrene Wisse*, in which the Christ-knight is said to bring his beloved letters patent (charters were written in this form) 'and wrat wiðð his ahne blod saluz to his leofmon'.[10] In this allegory the letters patent are the gospels (in contrast to the Old Testament in the form of letters close): this probably represents a primitive stage in the literary development of the image, as later the charter itself was invented as a literary form. Of this, however, there is no evidence until the beginning of the fourteenth century, when in his punning lyric 'Þou wommon boute uere',[11] William Herebert describes how Love has written the charter of the Redemption, using as an inkhorn the wound in Christ's side. A similar reference occurs in Chaucer's 'ABC':

> And with his precious blood he wrot the bille
> Upon the crois, as general acquitaunce,
> To every penitent in ful creaunce.[12]

Chaucer's use of this conceit is noteworthy as it does not occur in his French source.

The Charter to which William Herebert and Chaucer refer is probably that described in the poem known as 'The Charter of Christ'.[13] There is no extant text of this before 1350, but since manuscripts only provide a *terminus post quem*, the work itself may well date from the first quarter of the fourteenth century. According to the allegory in this poem the charter was made by Christ on the Cross and it endowed man with the kingdom of heaven. Every detail of the appearance of the document and materials used was interpreted allegorically: the parchment was Christ's skin, the pen the lance or nails, the letters His many wounds, and the seal His wounded heart. The actual conferment of heaven begins with a familiar charter opening and proceeds in legal language, including a translation of the crucial phrase, *habendum et tenendum*:

> *Sciant presentes et futuri & cetera.*
> wytt yhe þat bene & sall be-tyde,
> I Ihesu crist with blody syde,
> Þat was born in bethleem
> And offerd in-to Ierusalem,
> Þe kyng[es] son of heven oboufe,
> With my fader will and lufe,
> Made a sesyng when I was born
> To þe mankynd þat was forlorn.
> With my chartre here present,
> I mak now confirmament
> Þat I have graunted & given
> To þe mankynd with me to lyfen
> In my rewme of heven blys
> To have & hald withouten mys,
> In a condicioune if þou be kynde
> And my luf-dedes haue in mynde,
> ffre to haue & fre to hald
> With all þe purtenaunce to wald
> Myne erytage þat es so fre.[14]

This poem soon became popular, and it survives in a large number of manuscripts, though many belong to the fifteenth century. Amongst the fourteenth-century manuscripts to include it is the Vernon Manuscript.

Another current version of the allegory was that embodied in *The Pore Caitiff*, a didactic and devotional treatise written in the last quarter of the fourteenth century, and very popular, as the number of surviving manuscripts indicates. In this version the idea of the charter becomes blended with that of a pardon, for the document is said to be 'þe chartre of his [man's] eritage & þe bulle of his euerlastinge pardoun':[15] some manuscripts, taking their rubric from this sentence, describe what follows as 'a notable chartour of pardon'. This chapter often circulated separately in manuscripts and when it was printed as an independent work in the sixteenth century it was given the title *A General Free Pardon or Charter of Hevyn Blys*. The substance of this passage is the allegorical conceits and it does not contain the formal conferment of heaven. The author seems to have been confused and to have had in mind three kinds of documents, charters, pardons and wills, for there are allusions to all three. It is, however, unlikely that the author would have introduced the notion of a pardon if he had not had a source in which the conceits were associated with this form of document instead of a charter that was a grant of land. The blending or confusion may have been facilitated by a verbal connection in that a pardon was frequently referred to as a charter of pardon, *carta perdonationis*.

Both 'The Charter of Christ' and *The Pore Caitiff* may be called popular literature, popular in the sense that they were intended for a less than learned audience, and popular in the sense that the ideas that they contain may well have been floating commonplaces. There is, however, one very important fourteenth-century description of a pardon that would be known only to the educated. It occurs in the *Pèlerinage de l'âme*, a long French allegorical poem, written by Guillaume de Guilleville between 1340-50. This poem is the middle one of a trio, the others being the *Pèlerinage de la vie humaine* and the *Pèlerinage de Jesus-Crist*. These poems circulated in English manuscripts from the last quarter of the fourteenth century: Chaucer knew the first (and therefore probably the others), for his 'ABC' is a translation from it. More important is the fact that Langland probably knew Guillaume's trilogy, for it contains so many possible sources for individual allegories in *Piers Plowman*, and even for the outline structure of the wandering pilgrim, that it would be a strong coincidence if Langland had gathered the allegories that he has in common with Guillaume from other scattered sources. This work therefore will not only have guided the response of some of the most educated of Langland's audience, but also gives a precise significance to the word 'pardon', which was in all probability known to the poet himself.

In the *Pèlerinage de l'âme* the soul of the pilgrim after death is transported to heaven where it is led to the particular or individual (as opposed to the general) judgment (that an individual judgment awaited every soul was an accepted belief). A debate ensues between the Four Daughters of God, Justice, Righteousness, Mercy and Peace, concerning its fate. Satan and Conscience accuse it whilst the wretched soul asks for mercy. Pity urges that no pilgrim has ever kept to the right road and therefore none can be saved except through Christ and the Blessed Virgin, but Justice insists that Christ did not die for those who persist in their sins but only for those who have amended their lives. At this point St Benedict proposes the weighing of the soul, the good deeds to be put in one scale, the evil in the other. Though apparently proposed impartially, this is a solution that favours the cause of Justice, for the scale with the good deeds flies up, whilst the other sinks down heavily laden. Thereupon Mercy turns to Christ and the Blessed Virgin for help, and returns with a letter. In the later prose translation of the *Pèlerinage* and in the translation of this particular part ascribed to Hoccleve, this letter is called a 'chartre of pardon'. But, though Guillaume does not himself describe the letter in this way, he manifestly intends a legal document, for he gives it the formal opening characteristic of letters patent:

> Je Jhesus, haut seigneur du ciel,
> A nostre lieutenant Michiel
> Et a tous les coassistens
> Qui la sont pour nos jugemens
> Salut.[16]

Furthermore, from its contents the document is plainly a conditional pardon: all those who make confession and ask for mercy shall escape the due penalty of hell:

> D'especial grace accorde
> Que d'enfer soient relaschies
> Ceux qui en la fin leur pechies
> Aront dit en confession.[17]

With this letter goes a casket filled to overflowing from the Treasury of Merit,[18] and thus a suitable symbolic object to be placed in the scales, and by this means the scale of the pilgrim's good deeds weighs heavy, whilst that of evil deeds flies up as though it contained scarcely any weight. Though the decision to combine the two allegories of the charter of pardon and the Psychostasis has here necessitated the intermediary symbol of the Casket of Merit, the poetic attention given to the charter far exceeds that given to the casket, the latter becoming, a little awkwardly, a subordinate symbol of the Redemption.

The evidence assembled in this digression on the charter-pardon image shows that by the end of the fourteenth century the intended audience of *Piers Plowman* would certainly be familiar with the idea of a legal document symbolizing and conferring the benefits of the Redemption, and probably knew that this document could be either a pardon or a charter. Their expectation that the contents of Piers's pardon, when revealed, would be a remittal from the pains of hell expressed in legal formulae and written in the blood of Christ, would be sharpened by the fact that this kind of allegorical episode would be consonant with the allegorical methods already used in the poem. In the early passus of *Piers Plowman* Langland made use of precisely and minutely worked allegories, such as the road of the Ten Commandments at the end of passus v. More particularly he had shown himself interested in the literary potentialities of legal formulae. Of this kind is the last will and testament made by Piers at the beginning of passus vi, a legal form more often used for moral, satirical and devotional purposes,[19] but here serving rather as a model disposition for a virtuous Christian; and, more strikingly, the allegorical charter of Favel in passus ii: indeed a medieval reader with a literary turn of mind might well have thought that the poet's intention was to set against the charter of the seven deadly sins the charter of the Redemption.

Before we consider the audience's probable understanding of the unexpected contents of the 'pardon', it is necessary to assess the spiritual state of the pilgrims up to this point. The pardon episode in the *Pèlerinage de l'âme* is again helpful here, because it too is set in a narrative context, and it is specifically said to be for pilgrims (*les pelerins*), pilgrims who have come to judgment and do not merit heaven through their own good deeds. In the later translation of their charter of pardon ascribed to Hoccleve, the situation of the sinful pilgrims is described even more emphatically than in Guillaume's French original:

> Ther be pilgrymes (as thei certifie)
>   That to meward hire weies had [i]take,
> Wich have mysgon, and erred folily
>   Be steryng of the foule bestis blake,
>   That some of hem hire iourney had forsake,
>   And efte hire iourney have a-geyn begunne,
>   But sudei[n]gly hath failed him the sonne.
>
> Some have be lettid be foule temptacioun
>   And steryng of hire fleschly wrechidnesse;
> So, be disease and tribulacioun
>   Thei have [i]falle in-to huge hevynesse;
>   And some also to this worldes besynesse
>   So greuously hire hertes ouersette,
>   So þat thei have of hire iourney be lette.[20]

This description of the pilgrims who so desperately need the bestowal of mercy leads one to ask the question of whether Langland's pilgrims are in any better spiritual state: in other words, do they need a charter of pardon if they are to be saved or would their scale of good deeds weigh heavily enough without the merits of Christ?

The story of Langland's pilgrims begins in passus v with the strangely self-contradictory allegory of the seven deadly sins who go to confession and express contrition, a contrition that is belied by the tone of their confessions and in particular by the revelatory continuous present tense in which most of the confession is couched. There would seem to be two ideas in this passus that clash with one another. One is that of a society in which all ranks and orders are riddled with the seven deadly sins, and the form of confessions is little more than a convenient mode for the satirist: one should no more ask how the personification of a sin can repent than one should ask why Chaucer's Pardoner so revealed his wickedness to his travelling companions. The other idea is that of the field full of folk who, though guilty of all the seven deadly sins, are moved by the sermon of Reason to go to confession and then moved by Repentance's preaching of the Redemption to amend their lives, that is, according to the first allegory to set out on the pilgrimage to Truth, and, according to the allegory that supplants it, to serve Piers well in his half-acre.[21] The problem is the relation of the two ideas, and whether the impression of continuousness that is given by the confessions of the sins casts an ominous shadow over the pilgrims' resolve of amendment. The solution to the problem is revealed in passus vi.

A commentary upon the Athanasian Creed provides guidance in the interpretation of this passus: it defines *qui bona egerunt* as those who have persevered in virtue.[22] The function of perseverance is clearly described by St Thomas, 'Sustinere autem difficultatem quae provenit ex diuturnitate boni operis, dat laudem perseverantiae'.[23] In this virtue is crystallized what is known from common experience, that the difficulty lies, not in the performance of isolated acts of virtue, but in the continuous practice of virtue day in day out without backsliding. In passus vi of *Piers Plowman* Langland shows dramatically and with psychological probability that it is this virtue of perseverance that the pilgrims lack. The first defection occurs at the end of passus v, where some pilgrims turn back instantly after the arduous journey to Truth has been described and its goal in the house guarded by the seven virtues:

'Now, bi Cryst,' quod a cutpurs, 'I have no kynne there!'
'Ne I,' quod an apewarde, 'be auȝte that I knowe!'
'Wite god,' quod a wafrestre, 'wist I this for sothe,
Shulde I neuere ferthere a fote for no freres prechynge.'

. . . .

'By seynt Poule,' quod a pardonere, 'perauenture I be nouȝte
   knowe there,
I wil go fecche my box with my breuettes and a bulle with
   bisshopes lettres!'
'By Cryst,' quod a comune womman, 'thi companye wil I folwe,
Thow shalt sey I am thi sustre.' I ne wot where thei bicome.

This is the rabble, lay and religious, satirically dismissed: thieves, low entertainers, prostitutes and pardoners are allowed to show their contempt for the journey in the colloquialism of their speech.

But even though this is the rabble, the company of a thousand pilgrims seems the less secure for their departure.

The main body of the pilgrims, however, do not relapse so instantly but submit themselves to Piers's advice and agree to work in his half-acre, and Piers is shown to be attempting to build a just and well-ordered society, one which in the reader's eye will counter-balance the corrupt society depicted in the previous passus:

> Now is Perkyn and his pilgrymes to the plowe faren;
> To erie this halue-acre holpyn hym manye.
> Dikeres and delueres digged vp the balkes;
> Therewith was Perkyn apayed and preysed hem faste.
> Other werkeman there were that wrou3ten ful 3erne,
> Eche man in his manere made hymself to done,
> And some to plese Perkyn piked vp the wedes.
>
> (B vi 107-113)

However this ideal order lasts for only three lines of the poem, for, when Piers goes amongst his labourers to see how each is working, he finds those who helped 'erie his half-acre with "how! trollilolli!"' and *wastours* who are feigning illness. From here on the order of the just society, symbolized by conscientious labouring on Piers's farm, disintegrates. The wasters are once more made to work through the compulsion of hunger, but with the harvest they take again to idling, and with the harvest too the people do as 'Glotoun tau3te'. Gluttony's contrition and Reason's advice to Waster (v, 24-25) have come to nothing.

In the first part of passus vi Langland temporarily broke the bounds of his allegory to show ladies sewing altar-cloths and knights protecting the poor; but in the later part of the passus he returns to sustained allegory so that all sins and all society are represented by the greedy and idle workmen. In the field of reference of the allegory there is perhaps a hint of the parable of the labourers in the vineyard,[24] but here there is no one who 'stod þe long day stable'. Furthermore, in accordance with medieval thought, and in particular with Langland's thought as revealed in passus xiv, to indicate the sinfulness of the whole of society through the sinfulness of the poor is especially pointed, for if the poor are not virtuous there is no hope for the rich. In passus xiv it is the poor man with the pack of good deeds on his back who strides into heaven ahead of the rich who are too heavily cumbered by their possessions to move at his speed. And in this passus too Langland movingly expresses the traditional medieval view that the poor through their endurance of hardship have purgatory here on earth and could therefore deserve their heaven immediately. In medieval descriptions of the Last Judgment the poor are often given a special place: sometimes they are amongst the accusers of the rich, sometimes they sit by Christ Himself as assessors, thus escaping the Judgment altogether. Langland has therefore chosen a most telling allegory, for he has symbolized the failure of the whole of society by the failure of the one part whom we might have expected to endure in virtue.

The seriousness of the labourers' relapse into sin is driven home by the ominous note on which passus vi ends:

> Ac I warne ȝow, werkemen, wynneth while ȝe mowe,
> For Hunger hiderward hasteth hym faste,
> He shal awake with water wastoures to chaste.
> Ar fyue ȝere be fulfilled suche famyn shal aryse,
> Thorwgh flodes and thourgh foule wederes frutes shul faille,
> And so sayde Saturne and sent ȝow to warne:
> Whan ȝe se the sonne amys and two monkes hedes,
> And a mayde haue the maistrie and multiplie bi eight,
> Thanne shal Deth withdrawe and Derthe be iustice,
> And Dawe the dyker deye for hunger,
> But if god of his goodnesse graunt vs a trewe.

Langland here is not the bewildered dreamer, but the prophet-poet exhorting his characters to repent whilst there is yet time. The last five lines – added in the B-text – though inferior poetically are most important to the sense, for they draw on the strange contemporary prophecies of the coming of the Anti-Christ, whose arrival would herald the end of the world and the Day of Judgment.[25] It is therefore a sinister warning to the people in Piers's half-acre, whose intention of amendment had lasted so short a time. Despite the weirdness of the esoteric imagery, the warning is the same as that of the famous and more awe-inspiring opening of the *De contemptu mundi* of Bernard of Cluny:

> Hora novissima, tempora pessima sunt, vigilemus.
> Ecce minaciter imminet arbiter, ille supremus.[26]

In sharp contrast, passus vii opens in an apparently sunnier way, 'Treuthe herde telle herof . . . And purchased hym a pardoun'; though coming straight after the dark, apocalyptic conclusion of passus vi, it may sound a little bland, and certainly the word 'herof' is slyly ambiguous, for it could refer either to the attempt at amendment or the relapse. Nevertheless, the pardon undoubtedly sounds reassuring, for the thousand pilgrims, who made confession and who at least momentarily sought amendment of life, might at their death hope to have Guillaume's charter of pardon added to their pitifully light scale of good deeds. The shock to the medieval audience must therefore have been intense when they found that the time for mercy was apparently past, and that the pilgrims are to be confronted with the sentence of the Last Judgment, the day of wrath that had been foreseen at the end of passus vi.

It is beyond all shadow of doubt that Verse 41 of the Athanasian Creed refers solely and emphatically to the Last Judgment: it has to be read with the preceding verse:

At whose [Christ's] coming all men shall rise again with
their bodies, and shall give account for their own works.
And they that have done good shall go into life everlasting:
and they that have done evil into everlasting fire.

The second verse is of course based on the Last Judgment parable of the sheep and the goats in *Matthew* xxv, and on the rare occasions when it is quoted in medieval literature, as in *The Castell of Perseverance* and an anonymous sermon on Psalm cxxix, 3 ('Si iniquitates obseruaueris, Domine, Domine, quis sustinebit'),[27] it is in the context of the Judgment. Moreover, though the text itself seems to be quoted rarely, its content in the form of direct address is the common substance of Advent sermons and plays of the Last Judgment in the mystery cycles.

The Athanasian Creed is the only one of the three creeds to be so explicit about the Last Judgment, and its emphasis upon good and evil deeds may perhaps support the recent view that it was composed in a semi-Pelagian milieu. Admittedly even this distribution of reward to the good was held to have been made possible by the Crucifixion alone (so that even this verdict could be said to have been 'purchased' [vii, 2] by Christ), for before the Redemption the patriarchs and prophets of the Old Testament awaited their release in the Limbo of the Fathers, which was the outermost part of hell. But stated so baldly, and in such a position, this judgment has a discomforting, if not a heretical, ring.

In their treatment of the Redemption and the Judgment medieval theologians and preachers had to reconcile two apparent paradoxes. The first that, according to St Thomas (whose views may be taken as the orthodox teaching of the Middle Ages), every good deed was initiated by grace, sustained by grace, and in the end, despite its deficiencies, held to be good through grace. Nevertheless co-operation with grace was necessary, and this co-operation between man and the movement of grace is especially elusive to the understanding, being indeed potentially misleading to the un-theologically-minded Christian. For, whatever the truth, the average man feels that, when he has acted rightly, the initiative and effort were his own, and to learn that they were not might well prove an encouragement to acquiescence in one's own worst impulses. The solution to this in popular didactic literature was to divide the paradox into its parts, sometimes, as we shall see, showing that man is saved through Christ's mercy, sometimes, as in the Last Judgment plays, showing that his salvation depended upon good works.[28]

The second paradox is a related one, namely the relationship of God's justice to His mercy. It was a traditional view that God's mercy would be supreme until the moment of the Last Judgment, but then no longer, for at the end of time all would be ordered in accordance with His justice. This had been the view of St Augustine, who expressed it in a much-quoted comment on Psalm c, 1 ('Misericordiam et iudicium cantabo'), saying '. . . modo tempus esse misericordiae, futurum autem tempus judicii'.[29] Such a distinction was of course repugnant to the scholastic theologians, such as Peter Lombard in the *Sentences* and the authors of subsequent commentaries upon this work, but they made it philosophically acceptable along the lines of the comment on the same psalm in the *Glossa Ordinaria*: 'Semper haec simul in eo sunt: sed per tempora secundum effectus distinguuntur, misericordia nunc, judicium in futuro.'[30] There was here a distinction easy to embody in popular literature: Christ's mercy was displayed at the personal judgment, His justice at the Day of Doom.

In order to appreciate the medieval understanding of the Last Judgment it is worth pursuing these theological paradoxes a little further, not in theology, but in the works of didactic and devotional edification. It was of course always the method of this kind of literature to simplify in order to present the unimaginable vividly to the imagination. In drama, art, and narrative the apparently contradictory cannot be presented simultaneously. Therefore, for instance, the simultaneous triumph and suffering of the Redemption are portrayed successively: the suffering in the Crucifixion, the triumph in the Harrowing of Hell. So also mercy and justice could be displayed successively: the good deeds that would be all-determining at the Last Judgment are, when inadequate, shown to be super-abundantly augmented at the particular judgment. This was done at the cost of narrative discrepancy, as for instance, in *The Castell of Perseverance*. In this play the hero, *Humanum Genus*, after various moral vicissitudes, is in his old age tempted out of the Castle of Perseverance, by Avarice:

> How, Mankynde! I am a-tenyde
>   for þou art þere so in þat holde.
> Cum & speke with þi best frende,
>   Syr Coueytyse! þou knowyst me of olde.
> What, deuyl schalt þou þer lenger lende
>   with grete penaunce in þat castel colde?[31]

Humanum Genus then abandons perseverance in virtue until struck down by Death. His soul is transported to the weighing, which is to be done by Righteousness ('þanne wey I his goode dedys and his synne'). In the debate between the Four Daughters of God, Justice maintains that he must be damned for he has not performed the seven works of mercy and the gospel says that such cannot enter heaven. But Mercy pleads the pains of the Passion, and at her prayer God receives the soul into heaven. At this point God, in a speech that is preceded by the text from the Athanasian Creed, foretells how at the Last Judgment He will divide the sheep from the goats. In terms of narrative this is pure contradiction: *Humanum Genus*, deficient in good deeds, is received at God's right hand, for sin is quenched by mercy as is a single spark by the sea, and yet God foretells how in the future He will reject all those lacking good deeds.

A similar discrepancy, though not within a single work, is found in the versions of the exemplum of the man with four friends.[32] In most allegories of this the condemned man is abandoned by all his friends save the fourth (the last and least valued), and the faithful friend is Christ; but in the play of *Everyman*, which has this exemplum for its plot, the last and only faithful friend is Good Deeds. Contradictions of this kind reflect both the apparent antithesis in God between His justice and His mercy and also the dual needs of man, who must exert all his efforts towards virtue, whilst recognizing that it is through the mercy of Christ alone that he can hope to be saved.

The Castell of Perseverance was written later than *Piers Plowman*, but its themes are ancient and traditional, and it provides a compact illustration of the two issues that concern us: the one, the failure in perseverance being met by God's mercy, the other, the adamantine justice of the Day of Judgment. This play is also interestingly linked to the scene of the Pardon in the *Pèlerinage de l'âme*, for it is in these two works alone that the popular allegory of the Four Daughters of God[33] is applied exclusively to the judgment of the soul. This debate is much more commonly applied to the doctrine of the Redemption formulated by St Anselm: Justice demands that man should die, Mercy that God should show compassion; the Sisters are reconciled by God the Son proposing the Incarnation. According to St Anselm's theory God found in the Incarnation a unique way of harmonizing justice with mercy: the significance of the allegory is therefore the nature of the Redemption. In the *Pèlerinage* and *The Castell*, however, its aim is to demonstrate how sinners may be saved, how the Redemption will work for each man, however sinful he may have been. But, though the use of the debate in the *Pèlerinage* is uncommon, the complementary theme of the weighing of the soul occurs frequently in both exempla and in art. Invariably in the Psychostasis (as this theme is technically called) the weight of the scale of good deeds is increased by some symbolic object: sometimes it is a rosary (this has been shown to be characteristic of English iconography) or sometimes the Virgin puts in the hem of her dress or actually depresses the scale with her hand. The significance of the Psychostasis is always, not merit rewarded, but mercy prevailing.

Moreover, not only was the Day of Judgment a day of strict justice, according to the theologians, but also in the devotional tradition of liturgy, sermon and hymn it was a day of terror, the day on which even the just will tremble. Two verses from Zephaniah provided the starting point for meditative expansions of this subject: 'Iuxta est dies Domini magnus, iuxta est et velox nimis; vox diei Domini amara, tribulabitur ibi fortis. Dies irae dies illa, dies tribulationis et angustiae, dies calamitatis et miseriae . . .'.[34] These words are echoed in the moving responsory, *Libera me, Domine*, which was part of the Mass for the Dead, and in the opening of the famous hymn, *Dies irae*, which was probably sung on the first Sunday in Advent.[35] In both of these and elsewhere is found the idea that on that day of wrath the just man will tremble, for even he will scarcely be saved:[36] 'vix justus salvabitur';[37] 'quid sum miser tunc dicturus . . . dum vix iustus sit securus';[38] 'et si iustus vix evadit,/impius ubi parebit?'.[39]

It is certain, therefore, that the appropriate response to the thought of the Day of Judgment was that of fear, and it was not a theme that could be used to demonstrate the rewards of the virtuous. The rich and complex body of Christian thought was matched in the Middle Ages by an equally rich and abundant store of themes and images, and they could not be mixed. Langland was an eccentric writer, but he never confused traditions in this way. The company of pilgrims, therefore, even if they had been more perseverant in virtue, could not have come to the sentence of the Last Judgment with equanimity or trust in their own good deeds. It is inconceivable that Langland would have used a Last Judgment text in a way that would seem reassuring to his characters and complacent to his audience.

An investigation of the literary and theological background of the pilgrims and their pardon shows very clearly how the scene should be read up to the moment of the tearing. Society corrupted by the seven deadly sins makes a fleeting attempt at amendment. Nevertheless (or therefore), a 'pardon' is sent by God, a pardon that should be a promise of forgiveness and a symbol of the Redemption; but the content of the 'pardon' turns out to be a threat and a symbol of the Day of Judgment. Langland can thus be seen to have created two pairs of intolerables; a society

pessimistically conceived and darkened with the devices and exag-
gerations of the homiletic satirist is juxtaposed to a text that in its
isolation presents an equally partial truth, and this juxtaposition
means damnation; yet this sentence of damnation for more than a
hundred lines is deceptively alluded to as a pardon.

From here on the viewpoint of the medieval audience, in so
far as it can be reconstructed, is no longer helpful. The priest's
exclamation 'I can no pardoun fynde' would have expressed their
own feelings, but beyond this we know only that some people were
so bewildered by the next action, the tearing of the pardon, that
Langland omitted it in the C-text. Nevertheless a paraphrase of
the scene in terms of the probable medieval understanding of it
serves to define the issues so sharply that only one solution remains.
For if it is accepted that the document which Piers held and the
priest looked at was not a pardon but a condemnation, then there
is only one way of justifying Langland's description of it as a
pardon and the lengthy deception in which he describes the glosses
upon it: the document was not a pardon when it was received, but
it was a pardon after Piers had torn it. The suggestion that the
tearing of the document symbolizes the mercy and forgiveness
shown in the Redemption may seem startling, but even at first
sight has a certain propriety. A sentence of death, when torn up,
might appropriately be called a reprieve. To call it a reprieve in
advance would be normally impermissible but could be justified in
terms of poetic anticipation and illuminating paradox.

This proposed interpretation prompts two closely related
questions: What does Piers signify? and, Can a parallel be found in
other parts of the poem for so strange an allegorical method? Up
to now there has been one point on which all critics have been
agreed, namely, that whatever divine affinities Piers may reveal
later in the poem, at this stage he represents no more than the
simple, virtuous Christian, in other words that he is scarcely an
allegorical figure, the literal level of the story containing almost the
entire meaning (Professor Coghill's theory that Piers here represents Do-Wel gives depth to this view but does not radically change
it). But, though in passus vi there is a very strong literal level to the
allegory – Piers has a wife and children and land to plough – and,
in contrast to this, when Piers much later re-enters the narrative,

the literal level is almost entirely stripped away so that he becomes a mysterious figure unlocalized in time or place, there is nevertheless some suggestion in passus vi that Piers has dignity and powers that are not those of the virtuous active layman, for he speaks and acts with an authority whose source is not revealed.

Piers orders and preaches to the company of pilgrims, which contains all ranks of society from knights to beggars, and this they accept reasonably and courteously. When, for instance, he has instructed the knight to act justly towards his tenants and to protect the poor, he goes on to remind him of the levelling power of death:

> For in charnel atte chirche cherles ben yuel to knowe,
> Or a kniȝte fram a knaue there; knowe this in thin herte.

And the knight replies:

> 'I assente, bi seynt Iame', seyde the kniȝte thanne,
> 'Forto worche bi thi wordes the while my lyf dureth.'
>
> B vi 50 ff

To understand this episode as one in which the little man of simple virtue admonishes the mighty is possible, but is probably anachronistic and certainly diminishes the power of the scene. Piers's treatment of the lower ranks of society could be explained in terms of social realism for he might be thought of as a just though severe overseer, but yet more strikingly exceeds this simple interpretation, since he has powers that are not those of an ordinary farm-bailiff. For the seasons of the year with their consequent famine and fullness are at his command: in anger he summons Hunger to force the lazy to work, and then in compassion for the people's misery dismisses Hunger again. The simple meaning of this passage could have been presented naturalistically through the normal passing of the seasons, and unless there was some further significance, there was no need to give Piers command over natural forces. It would be unwise to ask at this point what Piers signifies: like the Green Knight he seems to be a dispenser of justice without any explanation being given for this authority, and if an explanation were given, the powerful but indefinable effect of awe in both poems would be dispelled.

In the figure of Piers in passus vi, however, there are no more

F

than almost imperceptible intimations of divine power, and it is only when we look back at this passus in the light of the later parts of the poem that they become more readily discernible. But, if Piers seems Christ-like in his tearing of the Pardon, then it can certainly be held that there are adumbrations of this in the preceding passus. It is, however, in the much later scene of the Tree of Charity in passus xvi that Piers's divine prerogatives shine out unmistakably, and this episode is particularly relevant to the Pardon scene, for it has the same mysterious and dramatic intensity, and for the same reason in that in both Piers acts violently and strangely. In the passage beginning at line 75 of the B-text, Piers at the request of the dreamer shakes the tree so that the fruit may drop off, and the apples, which symbolize all mankind, and in particular the patriarchs and prophets who lived under the Old Dispensation – Adam, Abraham, Isaiah and others – all drop from the tree and the devil gathers them up: at this, Piers seizes one of the props of the tree, which symbolizes the Second Person of the Trinity, and hurls it after the devil, and the Annunciation begins. Just as Piers's tearing of the Pardon is cut out from the C-text, so also in the C-text here his rôle disappears, and it is Old Age who shakes the tree and Libera-Voluntas-Dei who throws the prop. In the C-text therefore the meaning of the action is plain but commonplace: men die of old age, God in His utter free-will chose to redeem man. Not only is the meaning of the two individual actions made commonplace but also the fact that they are performed by different figures much diminishes the force of the whole. The meaning of the B-text cannot be so readily translated into non-allegorical terms, but it is clear that what God has done Piers does. God has decreed that all men shall die, for He said 'in the day that thou eatest thereof thou shalt surely die', and it is God who appoints to each man the hour of his death. In *Everyman*, for instance, God summons Death and sends him to Everyman[40] and in the Play of Herod in the *Ludus Coventriae* Death announces himself as God's messenger.[41] So Piers shakes the tree. But the God who ordained death also ordained the Redemption, and therefore Piers hurls the prop.

In this episode, as in the Pardon scene, the literal and allegorical levels are interwoven in a bewildering and unpredictable way.

Rosamund Tuve has pointed out that most medieval allegorical narratives are only allegorical intermittently and that they therefore cannot be read as continuous and consistent allegories.[42] But in the best passages of *Piers Plowman* the transitions from literal to allegorical are so swift and startling that, even with Rosamund Tuve's warning, it is not easy to identify them. In the two scenes that we are discussing Piers does something of most august significance in response to some trivial action which belongs solely to the literal level: the priest asks to see the pardon and then dismisses its worth in the condescending manner and contemptuous tone of a trained theologian dealing with an ignorant layman, so Piers tears the Pardon; correspondingly the Dreamer, standing by the fruit tree, asks casually for an apple, so Piers shakes the tree. Moreover, just as the action is stimulated by a simple comment or request, so also in both instances Piers seems to be motivated by fairly trivial emotions: on the first occasion he is dismayed and humiliated by the priest's words, on the second occasion he is cross that a sneak-thief should steal his fruit; in feelings he is no more than a disappointed, simple man, or an angry farmer. It is, however, noticeable that both times Piers acts out of *pure tene*. This could be a verbal coincidence (Langland has a device of animating his allegorical figures by attributing extremes of emotion to them, particularly anger: only a moment before Piers had stared at the Dreamer *egrelich*), and he was not a meticulous writer. It is, however, likely that this verbal echo that resounds between two such carefully worked scenes was not merely the fortunate chance of careless writing.

The triviality of the stimulus for the action and of Piers's emotional response are matched by the triviality of the symbolic actions on a literal level: nothing could be more ordinary than to tear a letter or throw a stick. Again it is characteristic of Langland to choose the most everyday of human actions to bear the most sublime significances. However, although these actions are commonplace, it would be reasonable to expect to find in them some propriety between their nature and the thing signified. But since what is signified has no corporeal pattern, the parallelism has to be sought between these actions and more traditional imagery. For the hurling of the staff this is easy, for in its violence and movement it suggests the great leap that Christ made when He descended from heaven to earth. For the tearing of the pardon the analogies are more involved. In the act of tearing there may well be, as one critic has already suggested, an allusion to the rending of the veil of the temple. But the crucial point here is probably not the precise action of tearing but the more general idea of a document destroyed. In some ways very close is the image in *Colossians* ii, 13-14 of the 'chirographum peccatorum nostrorum, quod erat contrarium nobis', which Christ annulled by nailing it to the Cross. The *Legenda aurea* explains the *chirographum* as a debt incurred by Eve,[43] increasing with interest throughout the ages until cancelled by Christ; Ludolf the Carthusian more illuminatingly describes it as 'chirographum peccatorum nostrorum et mortis'.[44] The contents of the *chirographum*, however, is different from that of the pardon, but it resembles it in being a document containing a sentence of damnation that was destroyed by the Redemption.

Theologically, however, a closer parallel is to be found in the traditional allegory of Church and Synagogue. In this, when represented iconographically, Church on the right side of the Cross holds a chalice into which flows the blood from Christ's side, whilst on the left side stands Synagogue from whose hands fall the tables of the law.[45] This analogy is helpful because it shows that there was nothing doctrinally repugnant in demonstrating in artistic form the dispossession of the Old Law under the New Dispensation. That the Ten Commandments fall from the hands of Synagogue does not mean that they are not binding on the Christian: the Ten Commandments were, for instance, an important element in medieval penitential treatises, such as *Handlynge Synne* and the *Parson's Tale*. Similarly the text from the Athanasian Creed can be torn up without its validity in other contexts being questioned. Their destruction in individual scenes is but a striking way of demonstrating that with the Redemption it is mercy and not the Law that is at the heart of the matter.

If this is a true interpretation of the tearing of the pardon, Langland did not deceive his audience with his implied promise that the back-sliding pilgrims would through God's mercy be saved. But he executed the promise, not in the conventional and traditional way that the term 'pardon' had suggested, but in a unique allegory, which can more illuminatingly be called myth. For it is often a characteristic of myth that trivial actions have cosmic consequences: to tear a letter, to throw a stick, to open a box, to eat an apple, are all equally commonplace. It is also of the nature of myth that there are no clear allegorical equivalences: allegory is not necessary when one is dealing with the absolute sources of power. Furthermore, myth has a far closer and more mysterious relationship to what is signified than does allegory. If Piers's document had contained, not two lines of condemnation, but a long charter of pardon, this would have been an allegorical equivalent to a statement that men though sinful are saved through Christ. But by the brilliant invention of a myth, Langland makes the Redemption happen precisely in the social world that he has created, not far away on Calvary, not in the mysterious garden of the Tree of Charity, but in the field full of folk. But the myth though located in time is also timeless in that the nexus of the seven deadly sins and the tearing of the pardon is always present in the world.

The further profit of rejecting the conventional allegory of the charter of pardon is that this allegory by its roundness and definiteness would have brought the poem to a close: there would have been nothing more to say. Structurally, however, Langland has only come to the end of his prelude, and therefore his method is to state a main element of his theme at first enigmatically, and then repeating it with a gradually increasing explicitness, until it is boldly and majestically revealed in its full grandeur in passus xviii on the Harrowing of Hell. Langland's concern in the whole poem is with the relationship between the world and its Redemption in every facet. In passus vii he brings the two into a momentary, striking conjunction. But, because this conjunction is startling and mysterious, it poses the problem rather than solves it, and therefore the poet and his audience, the Dreamer and Piers, are not contented, and the search continues with greater intensity of enquiry and determination.

Justice, Kingship and the Good Life in the Second Part of *Piers Plowman*

P. M. KEAN

The second part of *Piers Plowman* is not only a great deal longer than the first, it is also a great deal more complex. Not only is the allegory, for the most part, of a more fluid and indeterminate kind, but the ideas which it embodies are not, as a rule, as clearcut as they are in the *Visio*. This is partly because Langland is handling a much greater bulk of material in the *Vita*,[1] but also, I think, because he is treating it in a different way. In the *Visio* he seems to be working in close control of his plan and subject matter. In the *Vita*, although I believe that here, too, he keeps more closely to a plan than has sometimes been admitted, his inspiration seems of a different kind, and the intensity – often an anguished intensity – with which he pursues a train of thought which seems to arise spontaneously, and sometimes even unexpectedly, out of the main development, suggests that he is involved in his work in a rather different way. In fact, in the *Vita* he often seems to be possessed by his message in a way which would rank him with writers whose work comes to them in a form over which they have little conscious control – a Boehme or even a Blake – rather than with a Dante or a Chaucer. In the *Visio* he still has much in common with other great intellectual poets of the Middle Ages.

It follows that, while in the case of the *Visio* it is not too difficult to trace out the argument on any given topic, as I have tried to do for the theme of justice and kingship,[2] it becomes much more

difficult to do the same thing in the case of the *Vita* where some
ideas, indeed, never seem to emerge into full light, but remain
as a kind of necessary substratum which we cannot leave out
of account, but which is very difficult to disengage in a clearcut
form.[3]

In the *Visio*, I have suggested, Langland explores the idea of
justice in the Aristotelian sense of 'virtue entire'. For this he uses
the term *lewté*, and was not alone in the fourteenth century in
doing so. This virtue, however, is not absolute, but is exercised 'in
relation to our neighbour', and is, therefore, inevitably linked to the
idea of law because:

> practically the majority of the acts commanded by the law are those
> which are prescribed from the point of view of virtue taken as a
> whole; for the law bids us practise every virtue and forbids us to
> practise any vice.[4]

Virtue in this sense, is, thus, dependent on the existence of a
properly conducted state. This, as St Thomas Aquinas explains in
his representative treatise, *de Regimine Principum*, is for man, who
is essentially a social animal, a necessary prerequisite to the life of
virtue – to what he calls 'living well', and Langland 'doing well'.[5]
Justice thus becomes, for all practical purposes, dependent on the
person of the ruler, who is at once the source of all law in the state,
and above law.[6] Law and *Lewté*, however, are part of a triad whose
third member is love. The reason for this is that, for Langland,
no moral action is conceivable without charity, which is, for him,
the supreme and all-inclusive virtue. This is emphasized in many
passages, some of which we shall presently have occasion to quote.
Moreover it is especially through charity, which he always links
closely to mercy, that God acts on man to render the Good Life
effective for salvation. This is contained in Holy Church's sermon
in passus i, in which she speaks of love at length (140 ff), and calls
it, among other things, 'leder of the lordes folke of heuene' (157),
and a modifier of the law against sin, punning on 'mercy' and
'merciment'.[7]

The *Visio* deals at length with the prerequisite to the Good Life,
that is with the good state, dependent on the good ruler. The Good
Life itself, however, the fact of living virtuously, must necessarily
follow; and it is this which is demanded by the Pardon:

Dowel, and haue wel, and god shal haue thi sowle.

B vii 113[8]

The Pardon is a logical conclusion to the political preoccupations of the *Visio*; and, at the same time, it announces the subject of the second part of the poem. It is freely offered to all who labour honestly and faithfully to help provide the prerequisites of the Good Life, but it does not provide immediate reward. Its promise is, rather, the ultimate reward of salvation to those who go on to live the Good Life itself. In this sense it is, of course, as the priest says, no pardon. Nor is it – and Langland makes the point at the beginning of the next section – a simple recipe for success to sinful man living his life in the world. It is to his analysis of the difficulty by the exploration of the formula 'dowel' that we must now turn.

II

Much of the discussion of the Good State in the *Visio* turned on equivalences of a positive, measurable kind – for example on the pair true labour-just hire. The Good Life, however, cannot be discussed in terms of such simple equations. It at once involves us in imponderables – on the one side human desert, on the other divine reward, a pair which have no possible means of striking an arithmetically satisfactory balance. At the beginning of passus viii the Dreamer points this out. He says that no human being can pretend to be without sin, using the text *Species in die cadit iustus*, and concluding that Dowel is not compatible with the state of man: 'Dowel and Do-yuel mow nouȝt dwelle togideres.' The Friars reply to this by distinguishing between deadly and venial sin (30 ff). Man can only commit deadly sin with the consent of freewill (49-50). Dowel, the Good Life, considered here as something systematized, teaches him to use his freedom of will correctly. Dowel is also, (46) 'Charite the champioun, chief help aȝein synne'. For Langland, as we have seen, no moral achievement is possible without charity; moreover Holy Church has already explained how charity, in its two aspects, man's love of God and God's love of man, works for salvation.

This discussion takes place while the Dreamer is awake. He is dissatisfied with it, and says that he will go where he can learn

better. When he falls asleep, it is Thought – 'A moche man . . .
and lyke to myselue' (70) – who gives him a commentary on what
has been said, and, in doing so, provides him with a full and complex definition of the Good Life.[9] We shall have to pause over this
definition, because, as I believe, it is not superseded in the *Vita*,
although it is at times both summarized and elaborated. In fact, I
think that if we take it as a guide we can see sense and consistency
in what R. W. Frank has called the 'maddening refrain'[10] of
'Dowel and Dobet and Dobest the thridde'.

Thought introduces the triad into the poem in these words – its
three parts are, he says, 'three faire vertues' (79). Virtue, here,
means, I think, 'a force for good in the life of mankind' (*OED*
virtue sb. II, 9 c.) Dowel is defined:

> Whoso is trewe of his tonge and of his two handes,
> And thorugh his laboure or thorugh his londe his lyflode wynneth,
> And is trusti of his tailende, taketh but his owne,
> And is nouʒt dronkenlew ne dedeignous, Dowel hym folweth.
>
> > viii 80-83

This, as is appropriate to Thought = comprehension, is put in
terms of ideas with which we are already familiar. It is, in fact, a
patchwork of phrases from the *Visio*. We are reminded of 'Trewe-
tonge, a tidy man' and of 'Tomme-Trewe-tonge', in iii 320 and
iv 17. The whole passage repeats i 88-90:

> Who-so is trewe of his tonge and telleth none other,
> And doth the werkis therwith, and wilneth no man ille,
> He is a god bi the gospel. . . .

Drunkenness is dealt with in i 25 ff. 'Taketh but his owne' echoes
'eche man to knowe his owne' in Prol. 122. Labour for 'lyflode' is
recommended in vi 236 and 253-254.

We could, in fact, sum up Thought's definition of Dowel in
Aristotelian terms as consisting in acts commanded by law, which
bids us practise every virtue, and we are further reminded of the
association in the *Visio* of the good labourer described by Thought
with law.[11] The next definition, that of Dobet, includes Dowel –
'doth ryʒt thus' (84) – but it goes further and enlarges the concept
of the Good Life by including activities which would come under

the heading of 'virtue entire', that is goodness directed to one's neighbour or *lewté*:[12]

> Dobet doth ry3t thus, ac he doth moche more;
> He is as low as a lombe and loueliche of speche,
> And helpeth alle men after that hem nedeth;
> The bagges and the bigurdeles he hath tobroken hem alle,
> That the erl Auarous helde, and his heires;
> And thus with Mammonaes moneie he hath made hym frendes,
> And is ronne into Religioun and hath rendred the bible,
> And precheth to the poeple seynt Poules wordes,
>   *Libenter suffertis insipientes, cum sitis ipsi sapientes,*
> 'And suffreth the vnwise with 3ow for to libbe',
> And with gladde wille doth hem gode, for so god 3ow hoteth.
>
>   viii 84-93

Dowel was concerned with physical *lyflode*. Dobet helps the people to spiritual food. In phrases, once again, reminiscent of the *Visio*, he is said to have, in effect, made a conquest of Meed. The line 'He is as low as a lombe and loueliche of speche' is used of Truth, Piers's master, at v 560, and the line that follows repeats the teaching of Truth concerning Piers's 'blody bretheren':

> Treuthe tau3te me ones to louye hem vchone,
> And to helpen hem of alle thinge, ay as hem nedeth.
>
>   vi 211-212

The reference to the 'erl Auarous and his heires' recalls the dignities involved in Meed's marriage settlement – the 'erldome of enuye . . . counte of coueitise . . . vsure and auarice', (ii 83 ff). It also reminds us of references like that to the avarice of 'curatoures' (i 193) or to the 'clerken coueitise' (iv 119), which fails to clothe the poor.

The definition of Dobet, in fact, involves active charity towards others. If we look back to the lines which are actually quoted from the *Visio* we shall see that it also carries the implications of another act of charity – that of Christ in the atonement. The reference at vi 210, to Piers's 'blody bretheren', points forward not only to this passage, but to that on Christ's blood-relationship to man, where the same phrase is used (xi 193-195; cf. xviii 392-393); while the reference to Truth = God as a humble lamb clearly indicates the Lamb of God who takes away the sins of the world. These deeper implications are left in the background for the moment; but, as we shall see, they are taken up again in the final treatment of the triad.

The definition of Dobest is short:

> Dobest is aboue bothe, and bereth a bisschopes crosse,
> Is hoked on that one ende, to halie men fro helle.
> A pyke is on that potente to pulte adown the wikked,
> That wayten any wikkednesse Dowel to tene.

viii 94-97

Dobest is not said to include Dowel and Dobet, as Dobet was said to include Dowel. It is, on the contrary, different in kind to the other two, and exists on a different plane – it is 'aboue bothe'. This difference is underlined in what follows. The internal organization of the triad is outlined, and the possibility is envisaged of Dowel and Dobet acting against Dobest (100). To prevent this a mysterious king is crowned, to whom we must presently return. For the moment it is only necessary to note that his existence serves to emphasize the gulf between the first two members of the triad and the third. The same discrepancy is implied later, when Study says:

> 'now def mot he worthe . . .
> But if he lyue in the lyf that longeth to Dowel;
> For I dar ben his bolde borgh that Dobet wil he neuere,
> Theigh Dobest drawe on hym, day after other.'

x 130-133

Here Dowel and Dobet are to be lived or acted by man, but Dobest is something which acts on him. The way in which it acts is obvious from Thought's words. Dobest has power to defeat sin, a power which is symbolized by the bishop's crozier.

The bishop is elsewhere associated with Dobest, and it has been suggested that, in this context, he stands for the mixed life, while Dowel stands for the active, Dobet for the contemplative life.[13] I do not think, however, that Langland does, in fact, show any interest in this particular classification in *Piers Plowman*. The bishop here, I think, stands rather for a way in which man actually has power over sin – that is, the Dreamer's objection at the beginning of *Dowel* is answered – through the mediation of the Church, which stands between purely human well-doing (Dowel and Dobet) and the goodness of God which man cannot reach unaided. An element is thus introduced into the discussion of the Good Life which is not wholly under human control, and it is in expressing this that it becomes necessary to emphasize that Dobest is different in kind from Dowel and Dobet.

It is clear from this passage and many others (e.g. the emphasis on the sacrament of confession in the conversion of Hawkyn the Active man; the importance of the figure of Holy Church in passus i; the fact that the main work of Grace at the end of the poem is to superintend the building of the Church) that Langland places great emphasis on the position of the Church as intermediary. In this, as in other respects, he would seem to be wholly orthodox. Man's ability to bridge the gap which stands in the way of his salvation can, however, be viewed in another way. As the Friars pointed out, it is his possession of free-will, which is natural to him because he was created in the image of God, that enables him to avoid deadly sin. Salvation, in fact, depends on the internal organization of the human soul (explored in the Vision of the Tree of Charity), as well as on the external, but also divinely appointed, organization of the Church. Dobest can therefore, as we shall see, sometimes be thought of in terms of the individual soul rather than of the Church. The ease with which Langland passes from one viewpoint to another can be seen if we compare the allegory of the Castle of Kynde in passus ix, where the soul, a 'lemman' loved by God, is guarded by the Good Life, and especially Dobest, thought of as an internal arrangement, with the passage at the end of passus x, where Christ's treasure – 'the which is mannes soule to saue' – is guarded by 'clerkes of holikirke' (473).

If Dowel and Dobet can, as we have seen, be equated with Law and *Lewté*, it is obvious that Dobest can be equated with the third member of that triad – that is with Love. Holy Church called love the 'leder of the lordes folke of heuene' (i 157), and the intermediary between the King and his people. Love, too, modifies the law 'Vpon man for his mysdedes' (159-160). We must, however, make a proviso here. For Langland, as we have said, love is a *sine qua non* of all effective moral action. Therefore, while in a sense it belongs especially to Dobest, without which no moral action can achieve its purpose, yet, in a more general sense it belongs to all three elements of the triad. Study, for example, says:

'Loke thow loue lelly ʒif the lyketh Dowel;
For Dobet and Dobest ben of Loues kynne.'
x 187-188

There are no reminiscences of the *Visio* in the phrasing of Thought's definition of Dobest. The links are all forward ones, and it is not until passus xvi in the B-text that we actually meet with decisive action against sin described in similar terms. Here, in the Vision within the vision of the Tree of Charity, the three props which support the tree are used by Piers and by *Liberum-Arbitrium* to 'palle down' (xvi 30, 51) the would-be stealers of the fruit, the world, the flesh and the devil.[14]

Thought has thus produced definitions of Dowel, Dobet and Dobest, which sum up much that has already been said in the *Visio* and which also, in the case of Dobest, points forward to future developments. Dowel is to do what is commanded, and not to do what is forbidden – that is to obey the law (whether of God or man is not here specified); and Thought expresses this with the help of terms which recall what was said concerning the basic bodily necessities in the *Visio*. Dobet is to do this and also to help one's neighbour. This help is described in terms which were applied, in the main, to the clergy in the *Visio*; and the most important help that Thought envisages is clearly spiritual. Dobest differs from the other two in that it involves something which is not available to man without the intervention of God's grace and the mediation of the Church. Dobest, clearly, has no meaning apart from Dowel, since it is the force (*vertue*) through which the Good Life can be rendered fully effective and can reach its end of salvation and the heavenly reward. On the other hand, Dowel can sometimes be used alone to stand for the Good Life as a whole, thought of simply as what St Thomas Aquinas calls *operatio secundum virtutem*.[15]

It must, of course, be pointed out that, when he associates grace with Dobest, Langland is not necessarily associating it with one stage of the Good Life rather than another. Dowel, Dobet and Dobest are not stages. They are an analysis of the Good Life, and it is in the course of his analysis that Langland deals with grace under Dobest. Since he constantly equates grace with charity, or with mercy – between which he makes little distinction – it seems probable that, just as charity pervades the Good Life and can be spoken of in relation to all three elements of the triad, although it belongs especially to Dobest, so grace also pervades it. It would, however, be impossible, I think, to extract a theology of grace from Langland's poem. He does not write of it technically, preferring to speak in general terms of God's goodness and love.

It remains to be seen whether the other definitions of Dowel, Dobet and Dobest which the Dreamer is given do, in fact, agree with that of Thought, or whether R. W. Frank is right in saying that 'no two characters agree in their explanation'.[16] We can, I think, separate the use of the triad into two main groups. First there are the major definitions, in which Langland has in mind the Good Life in its widest sense. Secondly there are the passages in which he is thinking of narrower aspects of this life. For example, when Hawkyn's coat is to be cleansed, the Good Life is reduced to a single process at a single moment – the use of the sacrament provided by the Church for the remission of sins. Therefore, the triad stands here, and here only, for the three parts of Confession. Similarly, while Wit is in close agreement with Thought in his important summing up at the end of his speech, in passing he uses a classification which is appropriate in the context, but which does not belong to the consideration of the Good Life in a general sense.[17] Or, again, at ix 107 Wit introduces the theme of marriage – 'Trewe wedded libbing folk in this worlde is Dowel'. This theme, I believe, has important implications for Langland, but it is not central to the discussion of the Good Life in a general sense, and Dowel, therefore, has a narrower sense here.

The passages with which we shall be mainly concerned are, therefore, Wit's conclusion and some generalizing within his speech; Clergy's lengthy exposition at x 230-260; the group of definitions given in passus xiii; and the final application of the triad to the life of Christ in passus xix. All these are concerned with the Good Life in a wide sense.

III

Thought sends the Dreamer to Wit to learn 'How Dowel, Dobet and Dobest don amonges the peple'. Wit is the right character to provide this information since, if we turn again to passus xv and the definitions of Isidore of Seville, we shall find that:

> . . . whan I fele that folke telleth my firste name is *Sensus*,
> And that is wytte and wisdome, the welle of alle craftes.
>
> xv 29-30

Wit, in fact, is the faculty through which information from the world outside is taken into the mind.

Wit's exposition is a long one, and parts of it are difficult. If we start at the end, however, we find that his conclusion is very similar to Thought's:

> Dowel, my frende, is to don as lawe techeth,
> To loue thi frende and thi foo, leue me, that is Dobet.
> To ȝiuen and to ȝemen bothe ȝonge and olde,
> To helen and to helpen is Dobest of alle.
> And Dowel is to drede god, and Dobet to suffre,
> And so cometh Dobest of bothe and bryngeth adoun the mody,
> And that is wikked Wille, that many werke shendeth,
> And dryueth away Dowel, thorugh dedliche synnes.
>
> ix 199-206

Dowel is here explicitly equated with law. Dobet = helping others, and Dobest helping to the point of actually healing (i.e. curing sin). Wit is here summing up, and giving an explanation in general terms. Earlier in his speech he had given a more particular set of definitions. He has, after all, been asked to show the triad in action among the people. He begins, therefore, with the situation of the individual soul. This is expressed by means of the allegory of the castle of the body, composed by creative Nature out of the four elements (ix 1-4). Dowel is 'duke of this marches' and is opposed to 'a proude pryker of Fraunce, *prynceps huius mundi*'(8). There is a suggestion here of the Holy War – 'duke' in Middle English generally implies military activity, and clearly does so in this context. In fact this is no more than to say that Dowel opposes Do-evil, virtues against vices. Dobet is the daughter of Dowel and serves the lady of the castle, Anima, as her damsel. Here the allegory is perhaps somewhat intractable, but we have the idea of service, normally associated with Dobet, and of a more intimate relation to Anima. Dobest, once more, is 'aboue bothe' and, as was the case in

Thought's definition, he is associated with the bishop – he is 'a bisschopes pere', and has ultimate authority over them all (14-16). After this Langland abandons the triad and the rest of the allegory is worked out in terms of 'Inwitte'. Although this is not an allegory which lends itself easily to an exposition of Dowel, Dobet and Dobest – it is much more meaningful in terms of the faculties – there is nothing here which contradicts what has gone before.

The next character to be encountered by the Dreamer, Dame Study, does not give a systematic exposition of the triad, although what she does say is significant.[18] It is Clergy who gives the next important set of definitions at x 230 ff. Dowel, he says, is Faith, that is the *fides catholica*, as set out in the Creed:

> . . . . on holycherche to bileue,
> With alle the artikles of the feithe that falleth to be knowe.
>
> x 230-231

This, of course, means that law is now fully and exclusively defined as the law of God, as taught by the Church.

If Dowel is, in this sense, faith, Dobet is works:

> . . . . man, bi thi miȝte, for mercies sake,
> Loke thow worche it in werke that thi worde sheweth.
>
> x 251-252

If we needed any reminder that for Langland good works always mean service to others we should have it in the words 'for mercies sake'. We must also note the use of the word suffer in this passage (repeating Wit at ix 203) – 'Thanne is Dobet to suffre . . . Al that the boke bit' (249-250). Suffering is the action proper to *patientia*, later to appear as a character in the poem. It means here, and elsewhere in the fourteenth century, a willing co-operation with what is imposed by the will of God: it does not merely imply passive endurance.[19]

Dobest, finally, is according to Clergy, 'to be bolde to blame the gylty' – that is, it is directly concerned with the overcoming of sin. Clergy, however, adds the warning that one should attack one's own sins before worrying about those of one's neighbours (256 ff). Here, therefore, the emphasis is on Dobest as it concerns the individual, rather than on the Church.

These definitions, obviously, agree closely with those of

Thought, and with Wit's summing up. The C-text makes the correspondence even closer. It omits the separate definitions of Dobet and Dobest, and concludes after the passage in which Dowel is described as belief in God's law:

> Thus Byleyue and Leaute and Loue is the thridde,
> That maketh men to Dowel, Dobet and Dobest.
>
> C xii 161-162

Here the two triads are brought together, and the substitution of Belief for Law as the first member of the first triad emphasizes the fact that Law has ceased to have any political significance and now means God's law, as taught by the Church. The equation of the two triads, Law, *Lewté* and Love and Dowel, Dobet and Dobest, goes furthest in the C-text, but it is also present by implication in this passage in B, and elsewhere in that text. In B xii 30 ff, for example, Dowel (used alone for the Good Life in general) is described in terms of marriage as living 'as lewté techeth' (33), as loving, (34) and as living 'as lawe wole' (35). In xi 84 ff *Lewté* makes a brief appearance as a character, and speaks of Law (89 ff). He does not, however, mention Love, since the Dreamer is still in a state of alienation from the Good Life. In passus xiv, after the conversion of Hawkyn, the poet, in his own person, utters a dignified and beautiful conclusion on the meaning of the Good Life for the rich. They should 'lyuen as lawe techeth – done lewté to alle'; if they do they shall 'han dowble hyre for her trauaille,/Here forȝyuenesse of her synnes, and heuene blisse after'. (153-154). The two triads are also brought together in the final summing up on the themes of Kingship and the Good Life in relation to the life of Christ in passus xix.

Clergy's explanation is the last authoritative statement concerning the triad for some time. Before the subject is taken up again we have the Visions of Fortune and of Nature, and a period in which, as the Dreamer says:

> . . . . of Dowel ne Dobet no deyntee me ne thouȝte;
> I had no lykynge, leue me if the leste, of hem auȝte to knowe.
>
> xi 47-48

When the discussion is reopened it is to take a decisive new step both in the plan of the poem and in the elucidation of the Good

G

Life. This takes place at the house of Clergy, where the Dreamer dines in the company of Conscience and Patience, and also of a learned doctor of divinity. We are given three separate definitions of the triad. The first is that of the doctor, who is shown by his actions to be both selfish and gluttonous:

> 'Dowel?' quod this doctour – and toke the cuppe and dranke –
> 'Do non yeul to thine euenecrystene, nou3t by thi powere.'
>
> xiii 103-104

This is not absolutely out of keeping with earlier statements, but it is a limited definition – doing no evil is only a part of Dowel. The definitions of the complete triad which are at last drawn from the doctor are not much better:

> 'Dowel' quod this doctour, 'do as clerkes techeth,
> And Dobet is he that techeth, and trauailleth to teche other,
> And Dobest doth hymself so, as he seith and precheth.'
>
> 115-117

For one thing, this is slanted towards the doctor's own position in life – he is a teacher and, if the identification with Friar William Jordan O.P. is correct, he belongs to the order of teachers par excellence. For another thing, neither the first nor the last proposition is complete. 'As clerkes techeth' is not necessarily the same as the *fides catholica*, as the fourteenth century, an age of controversy, heterodoxy and even heresy, was well aware. And, although, supposing the teaching to be correct, to do as one teaches is clearly a good thing, this is not the Dobest to which we have become accustomed – the power over sin which arises because in it man and God find a meeting place.

The fallacies and evasions of the learned glutton are followed by a speech of Clergy – that is of the learning which the doctor abuses. Clergy has not the same confidence as his follower. First he says that he cannot at present define Dowel:

> 'I haue seuene sones,' he seyde, 'seruen in a castel,
> There the lorde of Lyf wonyeth, to leren hym what is Dowel;
> Til I se tho seuene and myself acorden,
> I am vnhardy,' quod he, 'to any wy3t to preue it.'
>
> 119-122

This, and the ensuing discussion down to line 171 is deliberately expressed in obscure and even riddling terms. This is dramatically required at this point in the poem because the doctor, barren learning without virtue, is not to understand the truths expressed by Clergy Conscience and Patience. But we are not only to part with false learning. Even true learning. Clergy is, for a time at least, to be left behind as the poem moves on to explore a new range of ideas. In the speech just quoted Clergy states that he cannot convey knowledge of the Good Life to men – 'to any wyȝt to preue it' – until something has happened. What this is we will in a moment try to determine. He does, however, offer a saying of Piers the Plowman, which is obscure both to him and to Conscience. The full explanation must await the coming of Piers himself (123-132). In the meantime, Patience *can* give a definition of the triad. This is expressed in terms which seem nonsensical to the doctor but which determine Conscience to join Patience in a pilgrimage with the object of learning more (180-182). This involves separation from Clergy; but, it is implied, the separation will not be permanent (198-205; the farewell to false learning, 198, is not qualified). Clergy also points out that Patience alone, without the guidance of learning in the form of the Bible, and in particular of the Old Testament (185), will not always be enough. That is, learning of the right kind has its true place in the pursuit of the Good Life.

This is the context of the definitions of the triad which we now have to consider. First, however, we must return to Clergy's disclaimer. The seven liberal arts, his seven sons, are, he says, serving in a castle to teach its lord, the lord of life, what Dowel is, and he cannot pronounce on it until they are brought into agreement with him. At first sight this suggests a reference back to the castle allegory of the opening of passus ix; but there is a significant difference. There, the castle contained a lady, Anima. She is certainly equated with life (ix 53 and xv 23), but this life is the vital being of the individual. Now, the castle has a lord; and the phrase 'lord of life' is used elsewhere with much wider implications. It could, in fact, only mean Christ in this poem.[20] The allegory here, then, does not refer to the ordinary case of the combination of a human body and soul, but to the special one of the incarnation. Clergy, in effect, is saying that true learning, like all other human activities and experiences, is not the same after the incarnation as before it.[21] At the moment he has only the Old Testament to offer the pilgrims. While they must go forward to the New, he still warns them that the Old, with its prophetic knowledge of Christ's coming, cannot be dispensed with. The knowledge of the New Testament is associated with two things. First with Patience, true submission to and co-operation with God's will; with the further implication here of this will manifested in the working out of the pattern of history, as it moves towards the incarnation. Secondly with Piers the Plowman, the figure who is associated with all the direct revelations from God which alter the human course of events in the poem; and who is thus pre-eminently the servant of Truth = God, retaining, though with a different emphasis as the message changes, the basic rôle in which he was introduced in the *Visio*.

Although, with the separation of Clergy and Patience, Langland is clearly dealing with an historical order of events, and with the Old and New Testaments as records of different historical epochs, I do not think that he ties the plan of his poem to the course of history.[22] In fact his whole conception of Dowel, Dobet and Dobest presupposes the incarnation and redemption as having already happened – as indeed does the development of his ideas in the *Visio*. It is rather that the unfolding of the argument has now reached the point at which the problem of the Good Life cannot be taken further without a direct account of the part played by God in human salvation. This has always been implied in the definitions of Dobest, but the discussion has, up to now, been mainly concerned with what man can do – or, as in the case of the Vision of Fortune, not do. We are now moving towards the direct accounts of the life and passion of Christ, of the descent of the Holy Ghost, and the founding of the Church, which form the main part of *Dobet* and *Dobest*. These events are always present in the poem by implication, but they are not always equally present in the argument. The importance of the new subject matter is announced by the use of two devices which are normally associated with imminent and far-reaching change in the poem – and also with depth of feeling. One is prophecy: Patience's speech is cast in prophetic terms;[23] the other is the symbol of pilgrimage (used to initiate the movement which culminates in the Pardon in the *Visio*, and again at the end of the poem when Conscience finally sets out to look for Piers the Plowman).

Clergy next says that Piers the Plowman has called in question all learning and science, and goes on to quote his definition of the triad:

> For one Pieres the Ploughman hath inpugned vs alle,
> And sette alle sciences at a soppe saue loue one,
> And no tixte ne taketh to meyntene his cause,
> But *dilige deum* and *domine, quis habitabit*, etc.
> And seith that Dowel and Dobet aren two infinites,
> Whiche infinites, with a feith, fynden oute Dobest,
> Which shal saue mannes soule; thus seith Piers the Ploughman.
>
> xiii 123-129

The texts with which Piers supports his argument are, first, *Matthew* 22, 37 and secondly Psalm 14 (Vulgate). In *Matthew* 22 Christ replies to the lawyer-pharisee who tempts him. The answer is in terms of the two commandments to love God and to love one's neighbour – 'on these two commandments dependeth the whole law and the prophets'. As Christ confounded the learned pharisees, therefore, so Piers 'sette al sciences at a soppe' – and, incidentally, confounds the learned doctor. The use of this text reasserts the primacy of love as above all moral action, and suggests the result of the involvement of Clergy's sons with the Lord of Life.

Psalm 14 concerns the reward of the man who 'walketh up-rightly and worketh righteousness'. *Matthew* 22 gives the law; this text shows *lewté*, or the just man. Piers, therefore, explains the Good Life first in terms of Love, Law and *Lewté*. We are then given a more abstract definition in terms of Dowel, Dobet and Dobest, and the wording becomes more obscure. We need to know the meaning of 'infinite'; how an 'infinite' can 'find out' Dobest, and what is the precise significance of the phrase 'with a feith'.

It would, perhaps, be possible to attribute the sense 'something boundless, unlimited' to *infinite* in the fourteenth century. Chaucer uses the word in a closely related sense (*O.E.D.* Infinity 1). If this is the meaning, however, the sense seems to me obscure, and I hardly know how to paraphrase it. We should have to say that the Good Life, as implied by the terms Dowel and Dobet, is unlimited in potentiality, a potentiality which, through the working of faith is realized in Dobest, the power which renders the activities of Dowel and Dobet effective for salvation. This, however, is to introduce an idea which is not necessarily contained in that of infinitude – the idea of potentiality. Rather than strain the sense in this way, it seems to me better to understand *infinite* in a more limited and technical sense, well known in Latin, though not elsewhere re-corded in English in the fourteenth century. This is the sense in which *infinitus* was used in scholastic logic (*OED* Infinite a. and sb. A8). This was Boethius's translation of Greek *áoristos*, Aristotle's name for the negative terms *non-B*, *non-homo*, etc., the *ónómata áórista – nomina infinita*, 'indefinite nouns'. Dowel and Dobet, then, are indefinites until, through the working of faith, they find definition in Dobest, that is achieve their object and, instead of undefined possibility, gain actual realization.

Light is thrown on the 'feith' by an earlier passage:

> For what euere clerkis carpe of Crystenedome or elles,
> Cryst to a comune woman seyde, in comune, at a feste,
> That *fides sua* shulde sauen hir, and saluen hir of alle synnes,
> Thanne is byleue a lele helpe, aboue logyke or lawe.
>
> xi 210-213

This feast, too, takes place at the house of a pharisee, and, once more, false learning is being refuted. Moreover, there is the same play that there is in Piers's definition on Love, Law and *Lewté*. Law is to be replaced by a belief (elsewhere equated with another sense of law) which will prove a *lele* help, and which is further equated with love in the context from which Langland is quoting – 'Her sins which are many are forgiven, for she loved much: but to whom little is forgiven, that same loveth little.' (*Luke* 7, 36 ff.)

Patience, unlike Clergy and Conscience, *can* speak of the Good Life, though still in riddling terms, which are contemptuously dismissed by the doctor. As we read them we have to remember that Patience is associated with the New Testament and its teach-ing. For Langland the idea of Patience (which the *Gawain*-poet, for example, can associate with the Old Testament figure of Jonah) is primarily that of patient poverty, the chief characteristic and moral lesson of the life of Christ. It is also intimately linked to the idea of Charity, both because Christ represents perfect charity, and because of St Paul's words in I *Cor.* 13, 4: *Charitas patiens est.*[24]

Patience picks up the words of the learned doctor and gives a definition of the triad in terms of learning and teaching – but with a difference.

> '*Disce,*' quod he, '*doce, dilige inimicos.*
> *Disce* and Dowel; *doce* and Dobet;
> *Dilige* and Dobest.'
>
> xiii 136-138

These three are further equated, in line 140, 'with wordes and with werkes . . . and wille of thyne herte' – that is with faith, belief in the law, which is handed down in words and affirmed in words; works in the service of others, here especially in teaching; and will, not here 'wikked will' but the free-will which gives man power over sin. This, in fact, fits in with the other major definitions of the triad. Patience goes on to speak in an obscurely prophetic vein in praise of love (150 ff) whose primacy is again emphasized by its equation with all three members of the triad (140 ff). Love will lead to a millennium of peace and goodwill on earth. It is to this that the doctor particularly objects:

> Al the witt of this worlde and wiȝte mennes strengthe
> Can nouȝt confourmen a pees bytwene the pope and his enemys,
> Ne bitwene two Cristene kynges can no wyȝte pees make.
>
> 173-175

The doctor is no doubt correct in stating that the millennium cannot be achieved by 'power and policy' ('witt of this world and wiȝte mennes strengthe'). In the *Visio*, indeed, Langland, like other political thinkers of his day, saw such a millennium as the outcome of the perfecting of the state, but also as the elimination of the state as such.[25] Nevertheless, as we shall see, the doctor's words are picked up again later and used in a context, in relation to Christ the Conqueror, which gives a new dimension to the political argument.[26]

After the cleansing of Hawkyn's coat in passus xiv 16-25, the triad Dowel, Dobet and Dobest is dropped from the poem until passus xix. The reason for this is, I think, obvious. As we have said, the speeches of Clergy and Patience and the use of the symbol of pilgrimage have prepared the way for an important change, and have pointed out its nature: Langland is preparing to deal with the life and passion of Christ. Since the triad has, on the whole, been used to represent the difficulty man meets with in leading the Good Life, and to point the way, through Dobest, by which this difficulty can be overcome, it would serve no useful purpose in the description of Christ's life, which is the Good Life in its most total and perfect form. Nevertheless, Langland does return once to the triad to show just how that life constitutes the great *exemplum* of all that has been taught concerning man's struggle towards goodness.

This passage is part of Conscience's explanation of the meaning of the life of Christ. He deals first with the sense in which Jesus is knight, king and conqueror (xix 26 ff) and then explains the sense in which He can be said to Dowel, Dobet and Dobest (104 ff). Dowel is equated with the miracle of the conversion of water to wine, in which the wine is understood as law. This is the normal association of Dowel, but there is a difference:

> And lawe lakked tho, for men loued nouȝt her enemys.
> And Cryst conseilleth thus, and comaundeth bothe,
> Bothe to lered and to lewed to louye owre enemys.
>
> 108-110

This takes us back to Piers Plowman's definition of the Good Life (xiii 124-126), in which the commands love God and love your neighbour are paramount; and to Patience's, which adds love of one's enemies. The law, in fact, under the auspices of Christ the King, has become the royal law of St James –

> Si tamen legem perficitis regalem secundum Scripturas:
> Diliges proximum tuum sicut teipsum: bene facitis.[27]

Now, elsewhere, this kind of active charity belonged to Dobet, so that Dowel has, as it were, been raised to a higher power by the transforming fact of the incarnation – just as the water has been transformed to wine.

Next, the healing miracles are mentioned and equated with Dobet:

> Thus he conforted carful and cauȝte a gretter name,
> The whiche was Dobet, where that he went.

For defe thorw his doynges to here, and dombe speke he made,
And alle he heled and halp that hym of grace asked.

124-127

In a sense this agrees with the earlier definitions of Dobet as
serving and helping others; but, once again, we are in the presence
of a higher power, of the healing which, in the case of ordinary
mankind, is associated with Dobest.

Dobest itself follows the resurrection and the appearance to the
apostles:

And whan this dede was done, Dobest he tauȝte,
And ȝaf Pieres power, and pardoun he graunted
To alle manere men, mercy and forȝyfnes,
Hym myȝte men to assoille, of alle manere synnes.

177-180

This is Dobest as we know it – the power over sin which resides
primarily in the Church on earth. But here, too, there is something
added through the fact that we see, not merely man's efforts to
reach the ground on which he can co-operate with God towards his
own salvation, but God's act, through which the whole process is
rendered possible and effective. We can thus see that, in relation to
the life of Christ, each member of the triad is transformed and, as
it were, raised above the corresponding aspect of the Good Life
as it applies to ordinary mankind.

Taking Thought's definitions as a standard and a starting point,
it is, I believe, possible to see a fundamental consistency in Langland's use of the triad. He uses it, however, in one other way,
which we must also examine before leaving the subject. This is as
headings or titles for the three parts of the *Vita*. If we take these
headings in the most natural way, as descriptive of the content of
the respective sections, we can, I think, see that they too fall in with
Thought's plan. The main subject of *Dowel* is Belief/Law – it
deals with the application of the powers of the mind to various
sources of information about the Christian faith, and contains the
debate on true and false learning. The main subject of *Dobet* is
the life and Passion of Christ, that is the supreme example of
charity active in the world, serving and helping. *Dobest* is concerned with the founding and life of the Church, that is with the

setting up on earth of power over sin. The three sections thus fit in well with the plan of the triad as Thought expounds it, and the difficulty which has always been felt in reconciling them with a plan consisting in stages of achievement in the Good Life is removed.

IV

At the starting point of the long discussion of Dowel, Dobet and Dobest, Thought, as well as setting the tone, as we have seen, for all subsequent general and inclusive definitions, spoke of another factor making a fourth with the triad. Thought called this factor the King (probably taking a hint from St James's 'royal law' of Dowel); and it is to the ideas which Langland associates with the King, in relation to the Good Life, that we must now turn. Thought says:

> And Dowel and Dobet amonges hem ordeigned
> To croune one to be kynge, to reule hem bothe;
> That ʒif Dowel or Dobet did aʒein Dobest,
> Thanne shal the kynge come and casten hem in yrens,
> And but if Dobest bede for hem thei to be there for euere,
>   Thus Dowel and Dobet, and Dobest the thridde,
> Crouned one to be kynge, to kepen hem alle,
> And to reule the Reume bi her thre wittes,
> And none other-wise but as thei thre assented.

viii 98-106

There is an apparent contradiction here (eliminated, as usual with passages which could lead to misunderstanding, in the C-text).[28] First it is Dowel and Dobet only who crown the King to keep themselves in order and to protect Dobest from themselves. Then, in 103 ff, all three members of the triad crown the King. This is, I think, comprehensible if we remember that Dobest is of a different kind, and implies a different plane of action, from Dowel and Dobet. Even those who wish to lead the Good Life cannot avoid sin without the working together of their own freedom of will and God's grace, which process Langland typifies by Dobest. There is an apparent illogicality, because, as the Dreamer said to the Friars, those who sin Do Evil, not Well, so that, in fact, the King would seem to be needed to prevent the activity of Do-evil, not of Dowel and Dobet. Langland, I think, expresses himself in this somewhat puzzling way because his basic idea is that, owing to the lack of parity between the first and second terms of the triad and the third, it has an inherent instability. The fourth term, the King, is thought of as remedying this instability, just as the political king keeps the state together, by providing a source of authority and imposing it on the three orders of society.

Thought's words concerning the King are, like the first two parts of his speech, the definitions of Dowel and Dobet, made up of numerous reminiscences of the *Visio*. Lines 98-99 recall the B Prologue, 112 ff, on the election of the King. The King's postulated action in the event of harm being done to Dobest recalls the case of Wrong versus Peace, in which the King calls on a constable to cast Wrong into irons, and swears:

> But Resoun haue reuthe on hym, he shal reste in my stokkes,
> And that as longe as he lyueth, but lowenesse hym borwe.
>
> iv 108-109

Finally, just as at the end of passus iv the King swears to have 'leute in lawe' by ruling the realm in accordance with Reason and Conscience, so here the Good Life is to be ruled by the King in accordance with the triad. There is also a forward link to passus xix, to the crowning of Conscience as King, after Grace has enabled men to live 'lelly'.

The *Visio*, with its political preoccupations, thus provides the model for the figurative King of the *Vita*. It also, of course, provides a model for the idea of a King in close relation to a triad, since in the *Visio* the King is always closely related to Law, *Lewté* and Love. This particular relationship is most fully exploited in a passage in the C-text, presumably written after the completion of the B-version, and therefore to some extent reflecting ideas which Langland developed through his equation in the *Vita* of the triad Law, *Lewté* and Love with the other triad, Dowel, Dobet and Dobest. This is the passage using the terms of grammar inserted into Conscience's speech in condemnation of Meed in passus iv 335 ff.

Conscience's argument in C runs as follows: true meed is distinguished from false meed in the same way that the direct relationship is distinguished from the indirect in grammar (here he puns

on the meanings rect = right, true; indirect = false, corrupt, both
well evidenced for the fourteenth century, see *OED* Indirect a.,
1 b. and 3 a; Rect a, but Langland's use here is not well distinguished). Direct meed, in lines 350-353, is the inalienable right of
the true labourer who is worthy of his hire. This labourer is further
explained as the Christian who hopes to gain salvation, the
ultimate goal towards which the medieval state is orientated and
towards which it is the function of the King to lead his people.[29]
But, Conscience continues, the same 'direct relation' obtains
between the King and his people:

> Ac relacion rect is a ryhtful custome,
> As, a kyng to cleyme the comune at his wille
> To folwe hym, to fynde hym and fecche at hem hus consail,
> That here loue thus to him thorw al the londe a-corde.
> So comune cleymeth of a kyng thre kynne thynges,
> Lawe, loue and leaute, and hym lord antecedent.

C iv 377-382

This relationship is a reflection of man's relation to God. Man:

> Seketh and suweth hus substantif sauacion,
> That ys god, the grounde of al, a graciouse antecedent.
> And man ys relatif rect yf he be ryht trewe.

355-357

There is, of course, a difference. The relation of King and Commons is such that neither has any existence outside it – it consists
in the political situation, without which neither term has any
meaning. Milton was later to express the same idea:

> We know that King and Subject are relatives, and relatives have no
> longer being than in the relation.

The Tenure of Kings and Magistrates, 1649.

Man is in this sense relative to God, without whom he would have
neither meaning nor existence, but God is not conditioned by the
relationship. He, therefore, is not a relative in relation to man, but
an antecedent. There is, however, a sense in which the King is also
an antecedent. This is in relation to the triad Love, Law and
Lewté, which, in so far as it expresses the Good State, can have
neither meaning nor stability without the Good Ruler. The King,

therefore, could also be called 'grounde of al, a graciouse antecedent', as far as this triad is concerned.

We do not need to ask what the King of the *Visio* is. He is,
simply, the Good Ruler; and, although Langland certainly glances
from time to time from the outer to the inner commonwealth, the
King is in no consistent sense any inner faculty. But the *Vita* is,
in the main, concerned with the inner commonwealth, and we have
therefore to ask the question, what does the King of Thought's
speech actually stand for? Is he, for example, Reason, or Conscience
(who is later in fact crowned king by Grace), or free-will, which
the Friars emphasized as having power over sin? Or is he the image
of God in which man was created, whose restoration forms the
basis of human salvation? Or Charity, 'the greatest of these'? The
very fact that, once one tries to identify Thought's King, the list of
possibilities becomes a long one, suggests that Langland was not
here thinking in such precise terms. He does, in fact, name all
these things at different points of his poem, and most of them
appear as characters in their own right. If the King was to be
identified with one of them there is, therefore, no reason why the
fact should not have been made clear. It is, I think, rather that the
King appears here because Langland has the political analogy
ready to hand, since he had developed it throughout the *Visio*. It is
noticeable that ideas which had been important and which are
given a systematic development in the *Visio* tend to reappear in the
Vita as mere phrases, motifs or detached figures. The King, for
example, is a recurring motif in the *Vita* but his appearances are
isolated, and are not linked into a consistent presentation of a
personality, as was the case in the *Visio*. In fact in the *Vita* it
would be true to say that the King is a recurring image, while in the
Visio he is a character in the action.

But these phrases, motifs and figures of the *Vita* are charged and
illuminated by what has already been established through their
more emphatic and extended use in the *Visio*, and they thus provide a powerful means of expressing the poet's ideas, either by
direct reference or by a kind of analogy. The King, therefore, is
to the inner commonwealth what the earlier King was to the
outer – the source of law and order and the means for their
enforcement. I do not think that the King in Thought's speech

means either more or less than this – that is that, in a potentially unstable situation the prerequisites of stability exist. If Langland is thinking of human activity in the Good Life in more specific terms he speaks of this order and stability as depending on something specific – on Reason, Conscience or Freewill, for example, according to circumstances. The King stands here, I believe, for the possibility of order in itself, thought of in terms of the political analogy. This is, however, certainly a point at which Langland's ideas are far from clear – where, as I have suggested, we must postulate a kind of substratum of thought without which the poem is unintelligible, but which fails to reach the surface in its entirety.

The idea of triads owning a King as a fourth, although it is not always given explicit expression, seems to run persistently through Langland's thought. We have, first, the scheme (which is no invention of his) of the secular state, consisting of Commons, Knighthood and Clergy with the King at their head. We then have Law, *Lewté* and Love, with the King as lord antecedent. Dowel, Dobet and Dobest also have their King, elected and crowned by them in Thought's speech, and, in the application of the triad to the life of Christ in passus xix, consisting in Christ himself, as King and Conqueror. Moreover, we can, I think, detect a similar tripartite scheme in relation to a King in the treatment of the epiphanies of Piers the Plowman. He is seen first as the true labourer, servant of Truth (Dowel); secondly as the leader and organizer of the Field (Dobet); thirdly as the Guardian of the Tree with power to defeat evil, and as the organizer of the Church, with the power to offer the second pardon (Dobest). In all these manifestations he serves Truth = God, finally manifest as Christ the King. The tendency to think of the triad as needing a fourth for its most perfect expression is also exemplified in Piers's statement in passus xiii, where the faith (= love) of the Samaritan woman is added to it.

It is, of course, possible that Langland was acquainted with numerical theory which often – on the basis of Pythagoreanism – made four a more perfect number than three; or that he saw his triad as a triangle, completed by a fourth point to make a square. It seems to me, however, that if these ideas had been at all near the forefront of his mind he would have expressed himself more fully

in terms of number. In fact, apart from an occasional 'the thridde'
to complete the line, he makes very little play even with the nume-
ral three. I do not think, either, that we are dealing with a quater-
nity used to express the idea of wholeness. This is, of course, very
often to be met with in alchemical works. Of these Jung says:

> Natural symbols of totality, such as occur in our dreams and visions,
> and in the East, take the form of mandalas, are quaternities, or
> multiples of four, or else squared circles.[30]

It may well be that Langland feels the influence of some such
'natural symbol', but I think that the addition of a fourth to his
triads arises immediately from the structure of his thought. His
two triads, Law, *Lewté* and Love, and Dowel, Dobet and Dobest,
both stand, essentially, for processes, not for states. They are thus
necessarily incomplete, regarded from the point of view of achievement, and it is this incompleteness which gives rise to the fourth
term. The alchemical conception, which, of course, generally
relates to the four elements, and the natural cycle of change, is
summed up in the very influential axiom of Maria Prophetissa:
'One becomes two, two becomes three, and out of the third comes
one as a fourth.'[31] This refers to the emergency of plurality from
the monad, and its return to it, and is, therefore, basically a quite
different idea.

Before turning to Langland's final and most important use of the
image of the King in the Vita, in passus xix, we must consider two
earlier passages: the *exemplum* of the Emperor Trajan, the Good
Ruler who is saved from Hell through Law, *Lewté* and Love, and
secondly, Scripture's prophetic invocation of a future King in
passus x. In spite of his contempt for books –

'Ʒee! baw for bokes!' quod one, was broken out of helle –

xi 135

the story of Trajan is actually an *exemplum* confirming Scripture's
use of the text *Misericordia eius super omnia opera eius*. Langland
uses it as an example both of the greatest possible extension of
God's mercy, and of a pattern of salvation which falls within a
scheme he has already established. Trajan, and this is emphasized,
was not saved because a good Pope prayed for him, but because,
as far as he was able, he had lived the Good Life:

> . . . al the clergye vnder Cryste ne miȝte me cracche fro helle,
> But onliche loue and leaute and my lawful domes.
>
> 139-140

The same idea is expressed in lines 145-147. Langland does not, of course, mean that the Pope's prayer was not instrumental in bringing about Trajan's salvation; it is the immediate cause, but the final one, without which the prayer would never even have been uttered, is the fact that the pagan Emperor, by the light of Reason and Nature, lived the Good Life. Langland does not use the triad Dowel, Dobet and Dobest here. The reason, I think, is obvious. He associates them exclusively with the Christian life, since for him Dobest, as we have seen, is equated with the mediation of the Church. This, in fact, is the part which Gregory acts – as Dobest, the bishop's peer, he 'wilned me were graunted/Grace' (143-144) and thus brings it about that the Good Life, as Trajan lived it, becomes effective for salvation. Law, *Lewté* and Love is, too, an appropriate formula for the Good Life in Trajan's case, since for him this was the life of the Good Ruler, the King who achieved *Lewté* in Law – something which, as he explains, cannot be had without love:

> Loue and leute is a lele science;
> For that is the boke blessed of blisse and of ioye: –
> God wrouȝt it and wrot hit with his on fynger,
> And toke it Moyses vpon the mount, alle men to lere.
> 'Lawe withouten loue,' quod *Troianus*, 'leye there a bene!'
>
> xi 161-165

The whole passage plays on the words Love, *Lewté/lelly*, and law/learning, and they are attributed in their various senses at times to Trajan and at times to St Gregory, so that the Good King and the Good Pope are brought into comparison and contrast as the supreme examples of the Just Life and of the Christian Good Life in which Dobest is brought into operation.[32] In lines 145-146, for example:

> And I saued, as ȝe may se, withoute syngyng of masses,
> By loue and by lernynge of my lyuyng in treuthe,

the learning (in a sense other than that in which learning is condemned in this passage) is Gregory's; while at 140 and 146 love is both the love which Trajan feels, which makes it possible to say that he lived the Good Life, and the love, leading to effective action for good, with which Gregory regards him.

The main point of the *exemplum* is, of course, that it is a supreme instance of the love and mercy which mitigates the rigours of the law for mankind, and which leads the lord's people towards heaven. We are reminded of Holy Church's sermon in passus i, and of Piers the Plowman's in passus vi, to say nothing of Study's at x 186. It is, too, an important instance of the interrelation of the ideas which Langland associates with the Good Life, expressed, on the one hand by Law, *Lewté* and Love, and on the other by Dowel, Dobet and Dobest – even though the second triad is not actually used. It also exemplifies the importance for the Good Life of the secular ruler, on the one hand, and the Church, with its power over sin, on the other.

In passus x, in a famous passage, Scripture describes the coming of a king who will bring about the reform of a church whose clergy have come to 'leten hem as lordes, her londe lith so brode', (B x 316 = C vi 168). This king will also settle the vexed question of the friars[33] by making them accept a part in an endowment which, it is implied, the rest of the Church has put to bad use (323-325); and he will give an incurable wound to the Abbot of Abingdon and all his issue (C to the Abbot of England and 'the abbesse hys nece').[34] Skeat, in his note on the passage, appears to have taken the king literally, and equated the idea with Wycliffe's attitude to royal authority over the Church.

There are two reasons which make this interpretation unlikely. First, I do not think that there is any sign in Langland's poem, here, or elsewhere, of the repudiation of the hierarchy of the Church which is an essential part of Wycliffe's theory of the power of the king.[35] Langland certainly criticizes the papacy in a number of passages, but there is no indication that he differs from its many other orthodox critics, and wishes for anything but its reform. He would like to see papal elections better conducted (Prologue 100 ff); he would like to see the monetary affairs of the church in better order, but does not seem to visualize any fundamental change in the system, like disendowment (in the passage we are considering); he would like to see the end of papal wars (xiii 174).

H

But there is no indication that he wanted anything but such re-forms. Secondly, the King of this passage is not an historical King, of England or anywhere else. His reign is to be understood in an apocalyptic sense. It will be preceded by that of Antichrist, for whom Cain here stands:[36]

> Ac ar that kynge come, Cayme shal awake.
> Ac Dowel shal dyngen hym adoune and destruyen his myȝte.
>
> 329-330

Moreover the text quoted concerning this King is *Isaiah*, 14, 4-6, which describes the destruction of the wicked king of Babylon. The 'dominus' who comes to save the people in this passage is God, so that the idea in passus x seems to be that a time will come when God himself will take charge of His Church on Earth. The clergy who have sinned by acting like secular lords will then find that they have to submit, like secular lords, to royal power. They will, too, since they have sinned, find themselves among the wicked whom God, as an avenging King, will destroy among the forces of Antichrist.[37] The King here, it seems to me, is thus partly God, the triumphant Christ of the second coming and of the Last Judgment, and partly the principle of order and rule which must be invoked if the misrule in the Church is to be cured. In this sense Scripture's King bears some relation to Thought's fourth member added to the triad of Dowel, Dobet and Dobest.

The Dreamer thinks that he has at last grasped something

> 'Thanne is Dowel and Dobet,' quod I, '*dominus* and kniȝthode,'
>
> 331

but Scripture's reply is that kingship and knighthood, in the normal sense, are no help towards heaven (332-334). The Dreamer is, in fact, as usual, in error, and the exchange helps to point up the unusual sense in which the terms have been used in the previous passage. For ordinary man, royal power, both in the literal sense, and in the sense in which a king is added to the triad of the Good Life, cannot in itself ensure salvation, though both the political king and the king of the triad are an important factor towards it. But in the person of the incarnate Christ, which is to become Langland's main subject, the royal power and the Good Life are fused and inseparable. This passage is, therefore, an important preparation for what is to come, when, in passus xix, the life and acts of Christ are discussed in terms of, precisely, the *dominus* and kniȝthode rejected by Scripture.

Morton W. Bloomfield rightly points out (quoting Conrad Pepler), that Langland shows little devotion to the humanity of Christ as it was seen by much fourteenth-century piety. 'The poet', he says, 'concentrates on the kingship of Jesus, the Pantocrator, and on the transformation of society into the Kingdom of God'.[38] It is, however, important to remember, that for Langland the idea of kingship has been developed in a consistent, individualistic way, and has become an integral part of the imagery of the poem. It has also, as we have seen, come to play a special part in the idea of the Good Life as expressed by the triad Dowel, Dobet and Dobest, and it is within this context that the idea of the kingship of Christ on earth is developed. For Langland, it must be emphasized, it is Christ within history, walking on the soil of Palestine, who is the King in relation to the Good Life. Christ's kingship, in fact, is not restricted to the appearance of the Christ in majesty of Dobest (xix 6 ff). This is clear from the passage beginning at xix 71, in which the offerings of the three Kings are described. These are 'Resoun and riȝtwisnesse and reuth' (79). They are further explained in 82 ff:

> That o kynge cam with resoun, keuered vnder sense.
> The secounde kynge sitthe sothliche offred
> Riȝtwisnesse vnder red golde, resouns felawe.
> Golde is likned to leute that last shal euere,
> And resoun to riche golde, to riȝte and to treuthe.

Here, in the first two gifts we have the same ideas which we find associated with law and *lewté* (named in line 85) in the *Visio* and elsewhere. The third gift is mercy – 'For mirre is mercy to mene' – and mercy, as we know from, for example, Holy Church's sermon in passus i, is closely associated with the mediation of love between mankind and the rigours of the law. Here, then, we have all the associations of the triad which belongs especially to the Good Ruler.[39] Langland goes on, however:

> Ac for alle thise preciouse presentz owre lorde prynce Iesus
> Was neyther kynge nor conquerour til he gan to wexe
> In the manere of a man.

92-94

The kingship of Jesus, in fact, is inherent in his acts as a man. Further, as a conqueror, these acts are of a varied kind:

> As it bicometh a conquerour to konne many sleightes,
> And many wyles and witte that wil ben a leder;
> And so did Iesu in his dayes, who so had tyme to telle it.
> Sum tyme he suffred, and sum tyme he hydde hym,
> And sum tyme he fauȝte faste, and fleigh otherwhile.
> And some tyme he gaf good and graunted hele bothe,
> Lyf and lyme as hym lyste he wrought.
> As kynde is of a conquerour, so comsed Iesu,
> Tyl he had alle hem that he for bledde.
>
> xix 95-103

Langland seems to imply here that the separate actions of Jesus's life take their significance from the inner perfection which directs them, and from the total purpose which lies behind them. He thus emphasizes a fundamental difference between the Good Life as it is lived by Christ and by an ordinary man, and does not propose any detailed *imitatio Christi*. The use of *wyles and witte*, for example – 'worldly wisdom and policy' – is necessary to achieve the great conquest, but would not be recommended in all circumstances. We are reminded of the 'witt of this world' which the learned doctor in passus x thinks inadequate to bring peace on earth, and of the rather dubious characters of the *Visio*, 'Wisdome and sire Waryn the witty' (iv 67 ff). St Bonaventura makes precisely this point in a work Langland may have known, since it was a central text of the debate on poverty, and poverty is one of Langland's major themes. This is the *Apologia Pauperum*,[40] where St Bonaventura distinguishes between the internal and external perfection of Christ:

> Actus autem Christi sunt multiformes et varii, et quamvis in comparatione ad Christi personam omnes sint perfecti, tamen secundum naturam proprii generis quidam sunt excellentes, quidam mediocres, quidam condescensivi, sicut in praecedentibus aliqualiter patuit et subsequenter magis patebit.

> For Christ's actions are manifold and various, and although considered in relation to the person of Christ they are all perfect, yet, considered according to their own particular natures, some are excellent, some indifferent, while some can only be judged according

to the outcome; for example when, as was said above, He suffered in
a certain limited way in order that he might later suffer more.

II, 10 242, a

St Bonaventura specifically mentions the generically imperfect
act of fleeing death (sum tyme he hydde hym . . . and fleigh other-
while), resorted to by both Christ and St Paul. He explains that in
special circumstances this act could become perfect if, for example,
it meant suffering more gloriously for God in the end.[41]

It is thus clear that Langland relates Christ's kingship to all the
acts of his earthly life. It is also clear that, although he regards this
as the Good Life in the fullest possible sense, it is yet a life which is
not open to imitation in every detail. In fact, as we have seen, each
member of the triad Dowel, Dobet and Dobest, when it is seen in
terms of the life of Christ, takes on a completeness and significance
which places it beyond the reach of ordinary man. This attitude is
well summed up in Leff's words on St Bonaventura: 'There could
be no direct comparison between the actions of Christ and other
men. They flowed from different sources: one from perfect charity,
the other from imperfection. In this sense Christ was inimitable.'
(p. 85). This is not, of course, to say that for either Langland or St
Bonaventura, there were not other senses in which the life of Christ
was imitable. Nevertheless, there is no doubt that, for both, in the
last resort, the Good Life is irrevocably different in kind when it
is lived by Christ incarnate. In Langland's case the difference is
expressed both in terms of his triad, and through his favourite
image of the King.

In the first place, the active co-operation of God and man towards human salvation, which is only possible through Dobest
for an ordinary man, is perpetually and perfectly present in all
aspects of the Good Life as it is led by Christ. This is why all the
members of the triad are, as it were, raised to a higher power in
relation to Christ in passus xix. Secondly, as King and Conqueror,
Christ is in his own person that fourth stabilizing element which
helps to complete the triad and render it fully effective for salvation. This is not to say that there are not other important aspects of
the Kingship of Christ, but as Langland presents it, in passus xix,
relating it first to the triad Law, *Lewté* and Love, which he always
associates with the Good Ruler, the stabilizing force in the good

state, and then to Dowel, Dobet and Dobest, the triad expressive
of the Good Life which also needs its stabilizing King if Dowel is
to become the 'royal law' of St James, we cannot doubt that this
idea was in his mind. In the life of man the 'King' is present so long
as order and stability are maintained – and only so long. But in the
life of Christ the King, order and stability in the Good Life are, of
necessity, always present and always perfect.

B xix ends with the founding of the Church, and with the rapid
return of the elements of disorder. Among these are the bad king,
who once more raises the old problem of the *Visio*: since the king
is the 'hed of lawe' (466), his exactions, however oppressive, must
be in accord with '*spiritus iusticie*, for I iugge ʒow alle' (471).
Conscience can only give the answer which had already been given
in the *Visio*:

> 'In condicioun,' quod Conscience, 'that thow konne defende
> And rule thi rewme in resoun riʒt wel, and in treuth,
> Take thow may in resoun as thi lawe asketh.
> *Omnia tua sunt ad defendendum, set non ad depredandum.*'

xix 474-476

This grim reminder, far from showing us a Wycliffian King capable
of reforming the Church, brings us back to the troubled present of
the *Visio*; and, with a pointed contrast to the kingship of Christ,
the passus ends. The historical pattern is clearly present, and of
importance, but it is a condition of Langland's thought about the
problems of the Good Life, and is not used schematically to further
the plan of his poem.

V

By examining Langland's handling of the themes of Kingship
and the Good Life in the *Vita* we can, I think, gain insight into the
fundamental consistency of his thought – a consistency which is
not destroyed by the occasional obscurities and failures of an idea
to surface in the poem. Many questions, of course, remain unanswered. The most important is probably that of how far in the
Vita Langland is concerned with the reform of Church and State,
how far with the inner reformation of the individual. For Langland, it must be remembered, the two problems cannot be altogether separated. No medieval thinker would be likely to see the

individual as standing apart from the political community, or as separate from the corporate life of the Church.

Nevertheless, the age in which he was writing was a troubled one, and the first ominous signs of changing attitudes were certainly apparent. Langland's poem clearly reflects – perhaps more clearly than more obviously controversial works – the prevailing climate of doubt and anxiety. Yet it is surprising how little he actually has to say on the main controversial topics of the day – on, for example, the relation of Church and State; the relation of the sacramental life of the Church (which he seems to take for granted) to the individual; the significance of the Bible (which he uses in the traditional way and never translates).[42] His apocalypticism seems to be restricted to a few references, and, as I have pointed out, when he does bring Antichrist on the scene it is in a general, not a particular sense. Indeed the typical apocalyptic imagery and *personae* are notable for their almost complete absence from the poem. Even when he writes of poverty, which he does treat as controversial, he uses only a few standard arguments, and, by his very opposition to the Friars, he cannot link the topic to apocalypticism. His sympathy with the poor and simple is a constant feature of his work, but even here, where he would seem to be most closely involved in the external world, his position is by no means easy to define. This can be seen in the famous passage in which he claims that simple labourers 'Percen with a *paternoster* the paleys of heuene', while 'clerkes of holikirke' may curse the time when they learnt more than the creed. At first glance we seem to be within reach of reformation by a return to primitive simplicity, or by the substitution of true goodness for a corrupt priesthood. We might even think ourselves in the presence of Wycliffe's tenet that every good man was a priest in his own right. This is, however, clearly not the case. Langland does not suggest any transference of power or activity from the priests to the poor men. On the contrary, the priests are at greater risk from the very fact that they 'kepen Crystes tresore,/The which is mannes soule to saue' (x 473-474; C is even more emphatic: 'kepen sholde and saue/Lewede men in good byleyue, and lene hem at here neede'. xii 302-303). Moreover, the 'lewed Iottes' of line 460 cannot be taken entirely at their face value, but must be read within the whole context of the nexus of ideas which Langland has built up around the figure of the true labourer who is worthy of his hire, as well as within that of the debate on true and false learning which has been the main subject of *Dowel*. This passage, therefore, is hardly a suggestion for radical reform of the church, but rather a comment on the different kinds of difficulty encountered by the different types of individuals living the Good Life.

This, in fact, seems to me the one fundamental subject to which Langland always returns in the *Vita*, and round which the whole poem is built. The Good Life is, of necessity, lived by individuals – but, equally by necessity, individuals cannot be thought of apart from a social and ecclesiastical frame. In the same way, though the individual problem is, in a sense, independent of time and place, it cannot be given definition apart from the historical context – and this means both the present, with all its problems, and the divinely organized and appointed progression culminating in God's final intervention at the end of the world.

All this means that Langland's concept of the Good Life and its problems has a breadth and richness which is unique. We have neither the exclusive concentration on the inner transformation of the soul which we find in the writings of the avowed mystics, nor the restriction to the historical and social perspective of the political theorist or controversialist. The Christian dilemma and the Christian solution are, in fact, put before us on a canvas whose width leaves few aspects unexplored; if the result is at times chaotic, there is a compensating sense that problems are being examined within the complex world in which they really occur, and not in artificially induced isolation.

Words, Works and Will: Theme and Structure in *Piers Plowman*

J. A. BURROW

The purpose of this essay is twofold. First, I shall illustrate Langland's preoccupation, as moralist and satirist, with the twin themes of hypocrisy and formalism. Second, I shall argue that this preoccupation affects Langland's view of the poem he is writing and of himself as its author. He has a sense of what, morally and poetically, may be false or, as we say, 'bogus' in his creation. This sense manifests itself chiefly in certain peculiarities in the structure and progress of *Piers Plowman* which I shall discuss in the later part of the essay. I shall refer to the B-version of the poem throughout, and most frequently to the second and third of the visions in that version.

In the course of passus xv the Dreamer, Will, asks Anima what Charity is. Anima replies with a rhapsodic description of the virtue, which prompts the Dreamer to exclaim: 'By Cryst, I wolde that I knewe hym.' But Anima replies that it is impossible to know him without the help of Piers Plowman. This surprises the Dreamer. Surely, he asks, learned churchmen know him? To which Anima replies as follows:

> Clerkes haue no knowyng . . . but by werkes and bi wordes.
> Ac Piers the Plowman parceyueth more depper
> What is the wille and wherfore that many wyȝte suffreth,
> *Et vidit Deus cogitaciones eorum.*
> For there ar ful proude-herted men paciente of tonge,
> And boxome as of berynge to burgeys and to lordes,
> And to pore peple han peper in the nose,

And as a lyoun he loketh there men lakketh his werkes.
For there ar beggeres and bidderes, bedemen as it were,
Loketh as lambren and semen lyf-holy,
Ac it is more to haue here mete with such an esy manere
Than for penaunce and parfitnesse, the pouerte that such taketh.
Therefore by coloure ne by clergye knowe shaltow hym neuere,
Noyther thorw wordes ne werkes, but thorw wille one.
And that knoweth no clerke ne creature in erthe
But Piers the Plowman, *Petrus, id est, Christus.*

xv 192-206.

The question raised by Will, as Anima understands him, is one
which concerned Langland both as a moralist and as a satirist: Is
it possible for us to know – really know – the moral condition of
another person? Anima's answer, which is a pessimistic one, turns
on a triad of words much favoured by the poet, *will, words* and
works (an alliterating set corresponding to the *thought, word* and
deed of the Confiteor). He says that men in this life, even learned
ones, can judge others only by observing what they do (*works*)
and say (*words*); and that such inferences cannot be safe, since
vicious people find it very easy to simulate virtues such as humility
and patience. The only safe knowledge is direct and non-inferential
knowledge of another's thought or *will*, such as Christ demonstrated while he was on earth (e.g. *Matthew* ix, 4, 'And Jesus knowing
their thoughts said, Wherefore think ye evil in your hearts?').

Anima seems to suggest that this uncanny power may still be
available to men, through the agency of Piers Plowman; but elsewhere in his poem Langland attributes the power only to God or
Christ:

For Crist knoweth thi conscience and thi kynde wille.

iii 67, and compare x 431-435, xi 179-183, xvi 229

So in practice, it would seem, human beings have to rest content
with such uncertain knowledge as can be derived from ordinary
observation. The ideal of Truth, as expounded by Holy Church
in passus i, requires that words, works and will should be har-
monized in the service of God:

Whoso is trewe of his tonge and telleth none other,
And doth the werkis therwith and wilneth no man ille,
He is a god bi the gospel, agrounde and aloft.

i 88-90, and compare iii 237-238, xiii 140-141

In such cases, as in the more common ones where a wicked will finds expression in wicked words and deeds, appearance and reality coincide. But Langland's world is one where things are more often not what they seem. The advice which Clergy gives to Will is not generally followed:

> Loke thow worche it in werke that thi worde sheweth;
> Suche as thow semest in syȝte be in assay yfounde;
> *Appare quod es, vel esto quod appares;*
> And lat no body be bi thi beryng bygyled,
> But be suche in thi soule as thow semest withoute.
>
> x 252-255

Men speak a great deal about virtue, in sermons and in conversation; but their works bear little relation to their fine words. Thus in passus xiii we see a learned friar, who four days earlier had preached in St Paul's on the theme of penance, gorging himself at the high table before the eyes of the indignant Will:

> 'Thei prechen that penaunce is profitable to the soule,
> And what myschief and malese Cryst for man tholed;
> Ac this Goddes gloton,' quod I, 'with his gret chekes,
> Hath no pyte on vs pore; he performeth yuel;
> That he precheth he preueth nouȝt.'
>
> xiii 75-79

But there are also those whose fine words are less blatantly exposed by their deeds – those hypocrites or 'faitours' who manage to preserve every appearance of the real thing. Such men are like counterfeit money:

> As in Lussheborwes is a lyther alay, and ȝet loketh he lyke a sterlynge,
> The merke of that mone is good, ac the metal is fieble;
> And so it fareth by some folke now; thei han a faire speche,
> Croune and crystendome, the kynges merke of heuene,
> Ac the metal, that is mannes soule, with synne is foule alayed.
>
> xv 342-346, and compare xv 108-114

Many people in the Middle Ages believed that the Church, having passed through an age of persecutors and then an age of heretics, was now in a third and more dangerous age – the age of the hypocrites or 'false brethren' (the 'falsi fratres' of II *Corinthians* xi, 26). These enemies of the Church are to all appearances good members of it, 'as in Lussheborwes is a lyther alay, and ȝet loketh he lyke a sterlynge'. They display neither the open hostility of the persecutors nor the false doctrine of the heretics; and so they are able to inflict upon the Church what one writer calls an 'intestina et insanabilis plaga', an internal and incurable wound. It is in the last passus of his poem that Langland portrays this state of affairs. The fortified barn of Holy Church is under siege. Hypocrisy hurts many Christians in a skirmish round the gate of the peel, and the wounded men cry out for a surgeon who will not hurt them. Friar Flatterer is summoned, and is announced by his companion as 'Sire *Penetrans-Domos*' – an allusion to St Paul's description, in his second letter to Timothy (iii, 5-6), of those who 'having a form of godliness, but denying the power thereof . . . creep into houses and lead captive silly women laden with sins'. The friar corrupts Contrition with easy and venal absolution; and the Seven Deadly Sins, the enemies of the Church outside the gate, redouble their assaults. It is at this point, with Conscience setting out in search of Piers Plowman, that the poem ends. As passus xiii 69 shows, Langland (following what Skeat calls a 'venerable' pun on *frater*) looked for the *falsi fratres* of St Paul among the friars; and that is why in the Dobest section it is a friar who, with Hypocrisy, inflicts the internal, and perhaps incurable, wound on the Church. The friars, by granting their 'pleasant' absolutions, encourage confession without contrition, and so reduce an essential sacrament to a set of meaningless words and actions, a mere formality.

The theme of formalism in Langland's poem is intertwined with the theme of hypocrisy. Because people cannot directly perceive the inner world of the spirit and the will, they are inclined to forget about it, and become preoccupied with forms of words and external observances which in themselves have no value. They betray the spirit and cling to the letter, like the Jews who, as the Middle Ages believed, 'kept straitly the law in bodily observances and not in ghostly understanding'. Thus they become, metaphorically speaking, idolators:

> *Confundantur omnes qui adorant sculptilia; et alibi:*
> *Vt quid diligitis vanitatem, et queritis mendacium?*
> xv 79

So the whole body of the Church, its teaching, sacraments and institutions, stands in permanent danger of being transformed into mere body – a Pharisaic travesty of the real thing, running on fine words and 'bodily observances'.

The chief representatives of such formalism in *Piers Plowman* are the palmer and the priest in the second of the two dreams which constitute the *Visio*. In this dream, as I argued in an earlier essay, Langland attempts to portray a process of inner, spiritual conversion in terms of a four-part external action: sermon, confession, pilgrimage and pardon.[1] Piers Plowman, who makes his first appearance in the poem half-way through this dream, guides the people on the true inner 'pilgrimage' (the life of Truth in the half-acre – not a pilgrimage at all in the literal sense) and receives on their behalf the true 'pardon' (God's promise of salvation to the faithful). But at each stage Piers is confronted with an indignant exponent of the literal institution in its most 'bodily' form – first the palmer, who has never heard of a pilgrimage to *Truth*, and then the priest, who cannot recognize *Truth's* pardon. The portrait of the palmer conveys particularly well the strength of Langland's feeling in such matters:

> This folke frayned hym firste fro whennes he come.
> 'Fram Synay,' he seyde, 'and fram owre lordes sepulcre;
> In Bethleem and in Babiloyne I have ben in bothe,
> In Ermonye, in Alisaundre, in many other places.
> 3e may se bi my signes, that sitten on myn hatte,
> That I haue walked ful wyde, in wete and in drye,
> And souȝte gode seyntes for my soules helth.'
> 'Knowestow ouȝte a corseint that men calle Treuthe?
> Coudestow auȝte wissen vs the weye where that wy dwelleth?'
> 'Nay, so me God helpe!' seide the gome thanne,
> 'I seygh neuere palmere with pike ne with scrippe
> Axen after hym er til now in this place'.

> v 532-543

The alliterative line has a tendency to lack point in its second half; but in this brilliant passage Langland makes a virtue of that weakness. He expresses the palmer's preoccupation with external matters by second half lines which add fussy and pointless little physical details: '. . . that sitten on myn hatte', '. . . in wete and in drye', '. . . with pike ne with scrippe'.

Piers Plowman (whatever his exact significance) is in part defined, throughout the poem, by his opposition to such formalism. It is he who can see directly to the will, without inference from words and works; so it is proper that he should appear inattentive to those external matters which preoccupy the palmer and the priest. He can afford to interrupt the pilgrimage, and even to tear the pardon up. Later we see him as guardian of the tree of Charity, which grows in the inner garden of man's heart, a garden farmed by Liberum Arbitrium (Free Will); and by the end of the poem, he seems to stand for that inner virtue which has gone out of the contemporary Church. His unobtrusive departure from the barn of Holy Church, somewhere towards the end of passus xix, leaves the Church open to the hypocrisy and formalism of the 'false brethren'. It is remarkable that this departure is never actually described. The effect is that the reader, once he comes to the end of the poem where Conscience sets out to seek Piers 'as wyde as al the worlde lasteth', feels that the inner virtue which Piers represents has drained out of the Church somehow mysteriously and inexplicably.[2]

These ideas about hypocrisy and formalism are among the commonplaces (if the more interesting commonplaces) of the Christian tradition. They have their roots in the Bible (in *Isaiah* and in Christ's sayings against the Pharisees, for example), and they appear frequently in medieval moral, satirical and religious writings. To say that they occupy a prominent place in *Piers Plowman* is not to define any peculiar characteristic of that work. But Langland not only brings these ideas to bear *in* his poem; he brings them to bear *on* it, too, and on himself at the same time. We come closer here to his very individual genius.

Langland's name was William; and he puts himself into his poem, as dreamer and poet, under the name of Will. This name suggests an object, rather than an agent or source, of moral judgment. The agent is Reason or Wit. When Thought introduces Will to Wit in passus viii he points this contrast between them:

> Where Dowel, Dobet and Dobest ben in londe,
> Here is Wille wolde ywyte, if Witte couthe teche hym,
> And whether he be man or no man this man fayne wolde aspye,
> And worchen as thei thre wolde, this is his entente.
>
> viii 123-126

Will is indeed keen to learn; but he is no paragon of virtue. He repents his sins together with the folk of the field in passus v, but in passus xi he is misled by Covetise-of-Eyes and lives a worldly life for forty-five years without thought of Dowel. His old age, as described in passus xx, is ugly, painful and humiliating (182-197). But such unflattering self-portraits are quite common in medieval poetry: the poet says, in effect, 'See, I am a sinner too, and not ashamed to say so.' What is uncommon in Langland is that he goes on from here to ask himself an awkward question: 'Who am I, then, to be writing a poem such as this?' That challenge is presented by Imaginative to Will at the beginning of passus xii. Imaginative, referring to Will's wasted forty-five years, tells him it is high time he began to amend. But Will, he says, is too busy writing poetry about the good life to begin living it:

> 'And thow medlest the with makynges, and myȝtest go sey thi sauter,
> And bidde for hem that ȝiueth the bred; for there ar bokes ynowe
> To telle men what Dowel is, Dobet, and Dobest bothe,
> And prechoures to preue what it is of many a peyre freres.'
> xii 16-19

The challenge is a double one. A man who lives, as William does, on other men's charity has no business to be writing poetry; and anyway such poetry is of dubious value. The latter point, suggested by Imaginative's use of the word *meddle*, is driven home by his reference to preaching friars. A friar will 'prove' what virtue is, but he will not put his knowledge to the proof of action. As Will himself says of the gluttonous friar in passus xiii, using *preue* in its other sense:

> That he precheth he preueth nouȝt.

The Dreamer has, in fact, already met a pair of friars, in the prologue to the vision which Imaginative concludes; but he learned little from their subtle exposition. Here Imaginative implies that his own poem may be equally useless. Will's reply is not convincing:

> I seigh wel he sayde me soth, and, somwhat me to excuse,
> Seide, 'Catoun conforted his sone that, clerke though he were,
> To solacen hym sum tyme, as I do whan I make;
> *Interpone tuis interdum gaudia curis, &c.*
> And of holy men I herde,' quod I, 'how thei otherwhile

Pleyden the parfiter to be in many places.
Ac if there were any wight that wolde me telle
What were Dowel and Dobet and Dobest atte laste,
Wolde I neuere do werke, but wende to holicherche,
And there bydde my bedes, but whan ich eet or slepe.'

xii 20-29[3]

The Dreamer scores little more than a debating point when he represents his huge poem as a simple 'gaudium', 'solace', or pastime; and his reference to the perfection of holy men creates an equivocal effect, here as in C vi 84 (and compare C vi 90). Nor is it easy to accept Will's claim that he will give up poetry altogether once he has found the final and definitive solution to the problem of the nature of the Three Lives. Imaginative said, authoritatively, that quite enough had already been written on that subject; and we suspect that Will would never be satisfied by any explanation. A simple, untroubled life of prayer, food and sleep seems, at the least, a long way off.

Passages such as this (and one might compare xi 81 ff) encourage one to suppose that Langland was in fact sensitive to the moral issues which his poem raised for him, as its maker. Was it legitimate for him to write such a poem? And was it necessary? Were there not already sufficient books on the Good Life? How could more words help, when what mattered were works and, above all, the secret will itself? Was he not perhaps brother under the skin to his chief enemies – the glib and hypocritical friars?

The effects of thoughts such as these can be traced, not only in the occasional passage where Langland raises them explicitly in the form of dialogue between Will and some personification representing a part of the poet's reason or 'wit', but also in the very progress of his poem – especially, I think, in the second and third visions, which between them comprise 8 of the 20 passus of the B-text.[4] These two visions, coming after the predominantly negative and satiric vision of Lady Mede and False, are concerned with developing the positive ideal of Truth – or, as it is called after the last part of passus vii, Dowel. The first is dramatic and pictorial in method: it presents the good life through the events and personages of the pilgrimage to Truth. The second is abstract and ratiocinative: it tells of the Dreamer's search for Dowel, and consists almost entirely of conversations with intellectual powers (Thought, Wit, Study, Scripture, Clergy and finally Imaginative).

The chief allegorical image of the good life in the vision of the pilgrimage to Truth is contained in passus vi, in the episode of Piers and his half-acre. The substitution of this episode for the expected pilgrimage is explained, I have already suggested, in the juxtaposition of Piers and the palmer. The latter represents a Pharisaic formalism which Langland goes out of his way to deprecate, by dropping the pilgrimage altogether from the allegorical action of the vision. We are left, then, with the new figure of Piers the Plowman, presiding over the ploughing, sowing, and reaping of the half-acre. Langland develops the image of the ploughing with great vigour and conviction in passus vi; and it seems to express adequately – more adequately, certainly, than the image of pilgrimage – his sense of what the good life really is. But in the next passus a fundamental difficulty makes itself felt. An allegorical action is, by definition, a matter of 'works'. The poet will show some people doing something – whether making a pilgrimage, ploughing, jousting or whatever – and say, in effect, 'that expresses what I mean by the good life'. But in real life such activities cannot possibly carry any moral guarantee, since you cannot ever be sure of a man's will from his works. So Langland (himself, I suspect, a somewhat literal-minded man) is faced with an intractable problem of poetic representation. A ploughman, however conscientious, may quite well, after all, be a damned soul (though less commonly, perhaps, than a palmer); so how can one rest content with ploughing as an image of the good life? How, indeed, could any image be found which would represent in an adequate and stable form the elusive inner reality which only Piers himself and Christ can perceive?

Considerations of this sort, I believe, lie behind what is the real crux of passus vii – the resolution of Piers, after tearing the pardon, to give up his plough and live a new kind of life:

'I shal cessen of my sowyng,' quod Pieres, 'and swynk nouȝt so harde,
Ne about my bely ioye so bisi be namore!
Of preyers and of penaunce my plow shal ben herafter,
And wepen whan I shulde slepe, though whete bred me faille.'

vii 117-120

I

Has Piers now learned something which he did not know when he first appeared to the pilgrims and put them to the plough? Yes and no both seem the wrong answer to such a question. A real change has occurred, not in Piers's attitude to his occupation, but in Langland's attitude to his image. It is as if the image has undergone, in little, something like the process which the Church is, in the *Dobest* section, represented as undergoing in its history since Christ – a gradual transition from the charismatic to the institutional, a mysterious loss of potency. As a result of this entropic process, the imagery of the half-acre, which at its first introduction as a contrast to the imagery of pilgrimage was full of all the right meanings, comes to seem in its turn just 'a way of putting it – not very satisfactory'. Langland projects this dissatisfaction dramatically in the person of his titular hero; and the startling result is that we see Piers the Plowman resolving to give up the very activity from which he takes his name.

It is not difficult to imagine why the C poet decided to cut out this episode of Piers's new resolution, together with his tearing of the pardon; yet he was surely wrong to do so. The episode marks the point after which we begin in both texts to feel that, however important he may continue to be, Piers's occupation is gone. It also helps to define the relation between the second and third visions, by suggesting that the imagery of ploughing and 'swink' which dominated the allegorical fiction of the second will be absent – as Piers himself is absent – from the third. Indeed, it heralds Langland's abandonment, for the time being, of the whole attempt to embody his conception of the good life in allegorical fiction. In the next vision, the fiction is a simple one of search, the Dreamer's quest for knowledge of Dowel; and that knowledge is achieved (so far as it is achieved) discursively, not dramatically, in the explanations of Thought, Wit and the rest. The poet tries whether 'words', or formulations, can do for him what 'works', allegorical actions, failed to do. Imaginative replaces Piers Plowman.

This third vision is generally held to be the driest and least pleasing part of Langland's poem. It does have faults; but it is really quite different from the flat didactic allegories with which it is sometimes compared. What chiefly distinguishes it is Langland's sense of the inadequacy and untrustworthiness of words, of neat formulations and improving sentiments. Instead of simply giving good advice, or proceeding in some orderly fashion towards a final definition of Dowel, the vision circles round and round something which is simple and familiar, yet also mysterious and easy to mistake.

At the beginning of passus viii, before Will falls asleep, he meets the pair of friars, Franciscans, who claim that Dowel lives with them, always has done and always will. This dubious claim suggests that the friars are Pharisees, like most of their kind in the poem; yet they support it with an entirely legitimate distinction between deadly and venial sin. This discrepancy between speaker and speech illustrates, of course, Langland's favourite moral point about words and works; but he does not make that specific point here. Rather he leaves the reader in a mood of general uneasiness and uncertainty about the status and value in the real world (for we are not yet in the dream) of any such talk about virtue. This uneasiness is strengthened by the parting words of Will to the friars:

'I haue no kynde knowyng', quod I, 'to conceyue alle ʒowre wordes,
Ac if I may lyue and loke, I shal go lerne bettere.'

viii 57-58

This 'kind knowing' is what Will is looking for in the third vision.[5] Its nature is illuminated by two passages in the *Visio*. At his first appearance, Piers says that he knows Truth 'as kyndely as clerke doth his bokes' (v 545). This suggests a direct, unratiocinative knowledge, different from book-knowledge, such as comes naturally to unlettered men. A similar meaning is suggested earlier, in the exchange between Will and Holy Church in passus i. Holy Church has been describing the life of Truth, and Will objects:

'Ʒet haue I no kynde knowing', quod I, 'ʒet mote ʒe kenne me better,
By what craft in my corps it comseth and where.'
'Thow doted daffe', quod she, 'dulle arne thi wittes;
To litel Latyn thow lernedest, lede, in thi ʒouthe;
  Heu michi, quod sterilem duxi vitam iuvenilem!
It is a kynde knowyng', quod he, 'that kenneth in thine herte
For to louye thi lorde leuer than thiselue;
No dedly synne to do, dey thouʒ thow sholdest:
This I trowe be treuthe. . . .'

i 136-143

So both Holy Church and Piers teach that man already has in his heart that direct or 'natural' knowledge of Truth for which he is searching. It is a large and simple thing, as God's real messages tend to be in *Piers Plowman*: Love your Lord and do no deadly sin. We are reminded of Truth's two-line pardon, and of the 'maundement' given by God to Moses on Sinai, with its 'two wordes' (*Dilige Deum & proximum tuum*) to which Will protests: 'Ben here alle thi lordes lawes?' (xvii 14).

If Truth and Dowel are essentially the same, as I believe, then these passages must raise doubts about Will's search for 'kind knowing' of Dowel in the third vision. His desire to 'savour' or 'conceive' the words of the friars, Thought, Wit and the rest is good in so far as it means that he is concerned, not with fine talk, but with the kind of direct knowledge which issues in action:

> Ac ʒet sauouriþ me nouʒt þi segging, so me God helpe;
> More kynde knowyng I coueyte to lere,
> How dowel, dobet & dobest don on þis erþe.
>
> A ix 102-104[6]

But what, then, is he looking for from his instructors? As Imaginative points out, there are already plenty of books and sermons to show what the good life is. And if it is not *that* he wants, then what is it? The truth is, if we are to believe Holy Church, that he is searching for a natural knowledge which he already possesses. This knowledge is perfectly simple; and the only difficulty for Will – or the will – is to come to terms and live with it. Yet this is a great difficulty, since human beings fix their experience and their knowledge in words; and words, like images and institutions, are subject to that process of atrophy by which easy and specious substitutes for the real thing form and lodge in the mind. So the problem for Langland, both as man and as poet, is much the same in the third vision as it was in the second. It is the problem of finding an adequate and stable representation for something which he already knows but cannot fix.

Much later, after Will has awakened from his dream of Hawkin at the end of the *Dowel* section, he says:

> Ac after my wakyng it was wonder longe
> Ar I couth kyndely knowe what was Dowel.
>
> XV 1-2

This remark confirms the reader, belatedly, in his feeling that such 'kind knowing' was not achieved in the third dream. The various descriptions and definitions of Dowel thrown out by the instructors there represent, it would seem, no steady progress towards the truth; and the dream culminates in Imaginative's restatement of a simple position which had already been reached five passus earlier, at the end of the *Visio*. He says that we may trust – though we cannot be sure – that God, being himself 'true', will reward truth in his creatures with a great meed in heaven. And that is just where we came in. Langland attempts to express his sense of Truth or Dowel by refraction, as it were, in a multitude of metaphors and formulations in the third vision; but he does not entrust it to any one of them, any more than he entrusted it to the allegorical images of the previous vision. They too remain 'a way of putting it – not very satisfactory'.

Langland's sense of the instability and uncertainty of works and of words, considered as external correlatives of the hidden will, intensifies in the second and third visions to the point of exasperation (and we may recall here that Langland seems to have abandoned the A-version of his poem altogether before completing the third vision). Yet these two visions are both, and especially the former, intensely Langlandian inventions; and they lie near the heart of *Piers Plowman*. Within the remaining visions, considered individually, the preoccupations with which we have here been concerned appear less important: they yield moral and satirical points, but hardly structural principles. But if we stand further back from the poem and contemplate it as a whole, we may see – or think we see – the structural peculiarities of the second and third visions matched in the overall relations of its parts. We see a core of three characters, Will, Conscience and Piers, all of whom at different times experience moments of intense impatience or dissatisfaction, whose origins are somewhat mysterious and not necessarily, except in the case of Piers, altogether reputable. These experiences set them off on quests along new paths. Like Piers at the end of the *Visio*, Conscience makes a fresh start, at the end of the Dinner Scene, and again at the very end of the poem, when he sets off in search of Piers. As for Will, it is his dissatisfaction with his successive visions which drives the poem along. The result is a structure more like that of Eliot's *Four Quartets* than Dante's *Divine Comedy*: not a linear sequence of ideas and images (though that is what the headings 'Dowel', 'Dobet' and 'Dobest' may well suggest), but rather a series of attempts, running in circles and epicycles, to embody adequately in ideas and images a cluster of perceptions about the secret inner world which Will represents.

Langland can be boring, clumsy and repetitive; but his imagination and intelligence are generally on the side of the 'real thing', the inner world, in its continual struggle, both in individuals and institutions, against counterfeits. He knows the difference between a lushburgh and a sterling; and that is one of the things that has kept his poem alive.

Conscience: The Frustration of Allegory

PRISCILLA JENKINS

Although *Piers Plowman* contains literal as well as allegorical incidents and characters, recent criticism of the poem has been particularly concerned with the nature of the allegory and the possible methods of interpreting it. It has therefore tended to overlook the literal elements in the poem or even, as in R. W. Frank's injunction to read the allegory literally,[1] to blur the distinction between the two modes. I suggest that the interplay between the modes forms the structural basis of the poem and that the contrast between the ranges of experience they can express is central to its meaning. Whether the allegory of *Piers Plowman* is single or multiple in significance, the mode itself suggests idealization and therefore simplification. It proposes a world of clear-cut moral distinctions; it deals in perfection of good or of evil. By contrast, the literal mode in *Piers Plowman* presents a world of compromise, confusion and frequent indifference to moral issues. The coexistence yet incompatibility of the two modes is a major theme in the poem, and is effectively established in the Prologue and first passus.

The B-text opens with all the conventions of the dream vision: the May morning, the rural setting, the river and the narrator falling asleep. In other poems which use a similar framework, such as *Le Roman de la Rose*, *The Book of the Duchess*, *Pearl* and *The Golden Targe*, the narrator begins to dream of a beautiful and idealized landscape and we expect the landscape to be peopled with allegorical figures or the dream to yield spiritual insight. But if the opening lines of *Piers Plowman* arouse this expectation it is derided by the rest of the Prologue. The narrator is at first baffled by the world of his dream:

> Thanne gan I to meten a merueilouse sweuene,
> That I was in a wildernesse, wist I neuer where.
>
> Prol. 11-12[2]

but it turns out to be the real everyday world in all its variety, and the Prologue ends, as if to assert its verisimilitude, with the ordinary street cries of London. Most of the inhabitants are heedless of their uncertain position between the tower and the dungeon and act with regard only to the laws of this world:

> A faire felde ful of folke fonde I there bytwene,
> Of alle maner of men, the mene and the riche,
> Worchyng and wandryng as the worlde asketh.
>
> Prol. 17-19

The limitations of this position are sometimes hinted at –

> And somme chosen chaffare, they cheuen the bettere,
> As it semeth to owre syȝt that suche men thryueth –
>
> Prol. 31-32

but during the Prologue the only context provided for disapproval of most of the characters is brief mention of Christ, the apostles, the Last Judgment and the Church.

A fuller and clearer context is established in passus i by the allegorical figure of Holy Church, whose first speech points out that the values of most of the literal characters are inadequate:

> 'The moste partie of this poeple that passeth on this erthe,
> Haue thei worschip in this worlde, thei wilne no better;
> Of other heuene than here holde thei no tale.'
>
> i 7-9

The Dreamer himself, however, does not recognize her, and in answer to his question she tells him who she is, explains the significance of the tower and the dungeon and gives him an account of some of the main Christian doctrines and obligations. She is impatient with him for his failure to recognize her and for his profession of ignorance. From her point of view this information is self-evident, available to anyone through 'kynde knowyng'. For

Holy Church, the problem which is to be dramatically presented in the episode of Meed, of how to place economic transactions in a moral perspective, is solved by a simple appeal to Scripture (i 43-53). The word 'truth', reiterated throughout her speeches, is invested with final authority at the end of the passus when she suggests that she is leaving the Dreamer with a framework which will provide adequate moral guidance for him:

> Forthi I sey as I seide ere by the textis,
> Whan alle tresores ben ytryed treuthe is the beste.
> Now haue I tolde the what treuthe is, that no tresore is bettere,
> I may no lenger lenge the with, now loke the owre lorde!
>
> i 204-207

The Prologue and first passus present us with a sharp contrast between literal and allegorical statements, almost between a practical and an idealistic way of looking at the world. At this point the reader is inclined to endorse the allegorical mode as presenting more of truth than the literal mode and the allegorical character of Holy Church as possessing the finest perception and the most informed judgment. Initially, we might say that the function of the allegorical mode is to correct the literal. But in the course of the poem allegorical characters come to be seen as variously inadequate, and the collision of the allegorical and the literal becomes more complex and disturbing. I can present this interpretation most clearly by focusing not on the ideal figure of Piers but on the episodes involving Conscience, the personification of the faculty which distinguishes between what is and what ought to be, between the actual and the ideal, or, frequently in this poem, between the claims of the literal and the allegorical.

The possibility that there might be limitations and falsifications in the allegorical, idealized mode of vision becomes clear in the episode of Meed. Despite Holy Church's implication that she has left the Dreamer with all the answers, he requests to be taught how to recognize the false. He is at once shown Meed and the controversy about her marriage. Various evil characters are interested in marrying Meed to Falsehood; the King would prefer her to marry Conscience who refuses to accept her unless commanded by Reason. Peace brings a plea against Wrong and Meed reveals her nature by attempting to buy Wrong off. Reason condemns Meed and 'alle riȝtful' agree with him. Most of the court call her a whore and there is no more talk of a marriage between her and Conscience. The King asks Reason to stay with him and Reason agrees, provided that Conscience will also be present. This story may seem rather inconclusive, particularly in its hasty shelving of the possibility of marriage between Meed and Conscience, and as an allegory it provides no satisfaction to the moralist other than the recognition of Meed's evil nature. It would be easy to sketch out an alternative fable in which Meed should represent Reward rather than Bribery (or, in Langland's terms, include in her nature 'measurable hire'[3]): she would then be morally neutral rather than permanently evil and could be reformed by being married to Conscience rather than to Falsehood. Such a story might seem at first to provide a more satisfying narrative and a more interesting moral. If, however, we regard Langland's story as deliberately frustrating the desire for allegorical tidiness, it appears more subtle and more profound. The quarrel between Wrong and Peace affords not only evidence against Meed but also proof of Langland's awareness of formal and moral problems inherent in allegorical writing. Since the nature of Peace is peaceful, peace-loving, peace-making *and nothing else*, his willing acceptance of the bribe and his readiness to forgive are inevitable. His response is perfect in one sense but foolish in another. The King points out that if Wrong is set free he will commit other crimes, and Reason refuses to have pity on Wrong until everyone in the world behaves perfectly and Meed has lost her power. In an ideal world, therefore, the ideal response of Peace would be appropriate; in the world as it is recognized to be by the King and by Reason it is a good response which will lead to further harm. Peace needs to be restrained almost as much as Wrong does. That Langland refuses to accommodate his realistic assessment of human behaviour in the simple moral scheme encouraged by the allegorical mode is further shown in the abandoning of the plan to marry Meed to Conscience. Such a union is no more than theoretically convenient: it could take place only in the ideal world sketched out by Reason in which he could have pity on Wrong. Since man is sinful his economic behaviour is corrupt; if Langland had married Meed to

Conscience he would have denied this fact. The understandable desire of the King that they should be reconciled – '3e shal sau3tne for sothe and serue me bothe' (iv 2) – has to be frustrated by Conscience.

If Langland is suspicious of the idealizing imagination as manifested in allegory, he is also deeply sympathetic towards it. Throughout the poem he pours scorn on literalism of belief. In passus i it is condemned several times by Holy Church:

> And that is the professioun appertly that appendeth for kny3tes,
> And nou3t to fasten a Fryday in fyue score wynter;
> But holden with him & with hir that wolden al treuthe,
> And neuer leue hem for loue ne for lacchyng of syluer.
>
> i 98-101

> Forthi chastite withoute charite worth cheyned in helle;
> It is as lewed as a laumpe that no li3te is inne.
> Many chapeleynes arne chaste ac charite is awey;
> Aren no men auarousere than hij whan thei ben auaunced,
> Vnkynde to her kyn and to alle cristene,
> Chewen here charite and chiden after more.
> Such chastite withouten charite worth cheyned in helle!
>
> i 186-192

Langland's attack on literalism is made most dramatically in the scene of the tearing of the pardon. I agree with R. W. Frank that Piers's gesture here is ambivalent, a mark simultaneously of acceptance and rejection.[4] Piers is accepting the pardon but rejecting the literalism of the priest who can only see that it is not a letter of indulgence and is, therefore, from his point of view, invalid. The priest, the Dreamer and, I think, the reader are surprised when the pardon is produced. After about a hundred lines of detailed paraphrase of its message, the brevity of the actual document must be meant to shock:

> 'Pieres', quod a prest tho, 'thi pardoun most I rede,
> For I wil construe eche clause and kenne it the on engliche'.
> And Pieres at his preyere the pardoun vnfoldeth,
> And I bihynde hem bothe bihelde al the bulle.
> Al in two lynes it lay and nou3t a leef more,
> And was writen ri3t thus in witnesse of treuthe:

> *Et qui bona egerunt, ibunt in vitam eternam;*
> *Qui vero mala, in ignem eternum.*
>
> vii 106-111

The Dreamer's implied amazement at the form of the pardon is exactly paralleled in passus xvii when Hope tells him of the covenant he made with God and of receiving the commandments:

> Thanne plokked he forth a patent, a pece of an harde roche,
> Wheron were writen two wordes . . .
>
> xvii 10-11

On these occasions the Dreamer seems to feel for a moment that 'two lines' and 'a piece of hard rock' cannot contain the vast meanings which are assigned to the pardon and the patent by Piers and Hope; initially, that is, he has difficulty in accepting the validity of a symbol.

There is another feature of contemporary religious life which Langland attacks at the literal level but approved in a symbolic sense, the pilgrimage. In the Prologue he condemns the actual instances of pilgrims and palmers in the field full of folk:

> Pilgrymes and palmers pli3ted hem togidere
> To seke seynt Iames and seyntes in Rome.
> Thei went forth in here wey with many wise tales,
> And hadden leue to lye al here lyf after.
> I seigh somme that seiden thei had ysou3t seyntes;
> To eche a tale that thei tolde here tonge was tempred to lye
> More than to sey soth, it semed bi here speche.
>
> Prol. 46-52

and the pilgrim in passus v, covered with souvenirs of his journeys, has never heard of Saint Truth. Immediately after the meeting with this pilgrim Piers is introduced for the first time and recommends to the seekers an *allegorical* pilgrimage. This speech with its somewhat automatic allegorization of Christian precepts as stages in the journey ('And so boweth forth bi a broke, Beth – buxum – of – speche,/Tyl 3e fynden a forth, 3owre – fadres – honoureth . . . That crofte hat Coueyte – nou3te – mennes – catel – ne – her – wyues –/Ne – none – of – her – seruauntes – that – noyen – hem – my3te.', v 575-576, 582-583) is a passage where Langland's method could be criticized as being mechanical and lacking in vividness. I would reply that a more detailed and even in one sense more interesting allegory might well have defeated the purpose here: the pilgrimage has to be recognized simply as allegorical and therefore inward. The method declares the meaning bluntly and uncompromisingly. Literal characters, in their preference for outward and visible signs, are prone to translate spiritual commands into material terms. From time to time it is suggested that the wanderings of the Dreamer constitute a too physical search for Dowel who should be found within himself:

> 'Dowel and Dobet and Dobest the thridde,' quod he,
> 'Aren three faire vertues and beth nauȝte fer to fynde.'
>
> viii 78-79

> 'Sire Dowel dwelleth,' quod Witte, 'nouȝt a day hennes.'
>
> ix 1

The allegorical mode as used in Piers's advice to the pilgrims is designed effectively to prevent such misunderstanding.

The *Dowel* section of the poem is particularly concerned with intellectual enquiry, the relationship between theoretical understanding and moral development, and the possible Christian attitudes towards learning. During the first half of *Dowel* most of the characters whom the Dreamer meets are mental faculties or aspects of learning: Wit, Study, Clergy, Scripture, Imaginatif. In passus xiii the more specifically moral qualities are re-introduced, Patience and Conscience, together with a literal character, the doctor of divinity, and we find again the tension between the modes of vision appropriate to literal and to allegorical characters and another dilemma in which Conscience has to choose a lesser good because total goodness is for the moment unattainable. The scene is a dinner party at which the Dreamer, Conscience, Clergy and the doctor of divinity are joined by Patience who is wearing pilgrim's clothes. The doctor of divinity outrages the Dreamer who has heard him preach in favour of abstinence by eating and drinking too much. The Dreamer and the allegorical characters, on the other hand, are served with purely spiritual food:

Conscience ful curteisly tho comaunded Scripture
Bifor Pacience bred to brynge and me that was his macche.

He sette a soure lof tofor vs and seyde, '*agite penitenciam*,'
And sith he drough vs drynke, *diu-perseuerans*.
'As longe,' quod I, 'as I lyue and lycame may dure!'
'Here is propre seruice,' quod Pacience, 'ther fareth no prynce bettere.'

xiii 46-51

The Dreamer's expression of approval is in the C-text assigned to
another speaker ('quath he' replaces 'quod I') as if the poet
decided that only an allegorical character could be fully satisfied
with such food and drink. If so, the use of allegory here is meant to
seem almost comically idealistic, as in the next passus when
Patience attempts to comfort Haukyn:

'And I shal purueye the paste,' quod Pacyence, 'though no plow erie,
And floure to fede folke with, as best be for the soule,
Though neuere greyne growed, ne grape vppon vyne.
Alle that lyueth and loketh lyflode wolde I fynde,
And that ynough shal none faille of thinge that hem nedeth.
We shulde nouȝte be to busy abouten owre lyflode,
      Ne solliciti sitis, &c: volucres celi deus pascit, &c:
      pacientes vincunt, &c.'
Thanne laughed Haukyn a litel and liȝtly gan swerye,
'Who so leueth ȝow, by owre lorde, I leue nouȝte he be blissed!'
'No,' quod Pacyence paciently, and out of his poke hente
Vitailles of grete vertues for al manere bestes,
And seyde, 'lo! here lyflode ynough, if owre byleue be trewe!
For lente neuere was lyf but lyflode were shapen,
Wherof or wherfore or whereby to lybbe . . .
Lyue thorw lele byleue and loue, as god witnesseth;
      Quodcumque pecieritis a patre in nomine meo, &c: et alibi,
      Non in solo pane viuit homo, set in omni verbo, quod procedit de ore dei,'
But I loked what lyflod it was that Pacience so preysed,
And thanne was it a pece of the *pater-noster, fiat voluntas tua.*
'Haue, Haukyn!' quod Pacyence, 'and ete this whan the hungreth,
Or whan thow clomsest for colde or clyngest for drye.'

xiv 28-50

Here the purely allegorical nature of Patience seems to be stressed
in the phrase 'quod Pacyence paciently' and the gulf between him
and the other characters expressed in Haukyn's derision and the
Dreamer's surprise ('*But* I loked') when he sees what Patience is
really offering. Man does not live by bread alone, but that does not

make bread as dispensable as Patience implies. Similarly at the dinner party the allegorical characters are completely satisfied with their insubstantial meal whereas the Dreamer is naturally enough angered by comparing it with that of the doctor of divinity.

The dinner party concludes in a discussion, started by the Dreamer, of the nature of Dowel. Clergy says that he is unable to give a definition since Piers Plowman considers all sciences value-less compared with love, and Conscience turns to Patience:

> 'Pacience hath be in many place and perauntre cnoweth
> That no clerke ne can, as Cryst bereth witness:
>   *Pacientes vincunt, &c.*'
>
> xiii 133-134

Patience speaks of the obligation to love friend and enemy and the next speaker (presumably Conscience) is rapturously approving: such counsel, he says, could protect one from any physical adversity, and all people, including those in the highest positions of authority, must feel bound to obey it. At this point the doctor of divinity interrupts:

> 'It is but a Dido,' quod this doctour, 'a dysoures tale.
> Al the witt of this worlde and wiʒte mennes strengthe
> Can nouʒt confourmen a pees bytwene the pope and his enemys,
> Ne bitwene two Cristene kynges can no wiʒte pees make
> Profitable to ayther peple,' and put the table fro him,
> And toke Clergye and Conscience to conseille, as it were,
> That Pacience tho moste passe, for pilgrimes kunne wel lye.
>
> xiii 172-178

The doctor of divinity is the least sympathetic character in this scene, but if his speech is brutal it is also realistic. The literal mode is now correcting the allegorical. The doctor's first line points out that the speeches of the allegorical characters operate only at a fictional level: when we look at the actual condition of the world we are swiftly disillusioned. At the same time his blindness to spiritual realities is suggested in his dismissal of Patience as a mendacious pilgrim. Langland initially characterized pilgrims as liars in the Prologue (line 49) but an allegorical personage in pilgrim's clothes must be accepted: he is the ideal which actual pilgrims do not represent. Therefore the doctor of divinity, by failing to realize that Patience in pilgrim's clothes is in a different category from actual pilgrims, betrays himself as only literal-minded. He knows what the world is like, but he has no idea of what it ought to be.

Conscience now makes the decision to go on pilgrimage with Patience rather than learn with Clergy:

> Ac Conscience carped loude, and curteislich seide,
> 'Frendes, fareth wel', and faire spake to Clergye,
> 'For I will go with this gome, if god will ȝiue me grace,
> And be pilgryme with Pacience til I haue proued more.'
> 'What?' quod Clergye to Conscience, 'ar ȝe coueitouse nouthe
> After ȝeresȝgues or ȝiftes, or ȝernen to rede redeles?
> I shal brynge ȝow a bible, a boke of the olde lawe,
> And lere ȝow, if ȝow lyke, the leest poynte to knowe
> That Pacience the pilgryme perfitly knewe neuere.'
> 'Nay, bi Cryste,' quod Conscience . . .
> Thus curteislich Conscience congeyde fyrst the frere,
> And sithen softliche he seyde in Clergyes ere,
> 'Me were leuer, by owre lorde, and I lyue shulde,
> Haue pacience perfitlich than half thy pakke of bokes!'
> Clergye to Conscience no congeye wolde take,
> But seide ful sobreliche, 'thow shalt se the tyme
> Whan thow art wery forwalked wilne me to consaille.'
> 'That is soth,' seyde Conscience, 'so me god helpe!
> If Pacience be owre partyng felawe and pryue with vs bothe,
> There nys wo in this worlde that we ne shulde amende,
> And confourmen kynges to pees, and al kynnes londes,
> Sarasenes and Surre, and so forth alle the Iewes
> Turne into the trewe feithe and intil one byleue.'
> 'That is soth,' quod Clergye, 'I se what thow menest,
> I shal dwelle as I do, my deuore to shewen,
> And conformen fauntekynes and other folke ylered,
> Tyl Pacience haue preued the and parfite the maked.'
> Conscience tho with Pacience passed, pilgrymes as it were.
>
> xiii 179-215

For the moment, despite the vindication of learning given by Imaginatif to the Dreamer (xii 72-191), virtue and learning seem to be opposed. Each is presented as a perfection incompatible with the other. Clergy claims that Patience never 'perfitly knewe' the details of learning; Conscience retorts that he would rather 'haue pacience perfitlich than half thi pakke of bokes!' Conscience feels that he must at present choose between Clergy and Patience: union with both of them would be ideal but is not possible. Such a union could put right all the ills of the world, but, as in the story of Meed, the happy ending is proposed only at the level of prophecy. It could change the imperfect world that the doctor reminded them of, but it cannot do it yet. Conscience's choice here is analogous to his rejection of Meed, but the reasons for it are less obvious. He is not, after all, rejecting an evil character but a character with great potentiality for good. His decision is received 'ful sobreliche' by Clergy who says that he will return. He and Clergy begin replies to each other with the phrase 'that is soth', suggesting a good deal of mutual understanding and agreement. The withdrawal of Conscience is most intelligible if seen as a response to the relationship between the literal and allegorical characters of the doctor of divinity and Clergy. Clergy himself may be suspect if an actual cleric can be so blind to idealism. To exemplify Patience, even imperfectly, must be virtuous; to exemplify Clergy imperfectly need not be. When learning and virtue perfectly unite, this distinction will be invalid; at the moment both the truth and the cynicism of the doctor's speech show that this is not the case. To accept the present situation would be either cynically pragmatic or naïvely idealistic. Therefore Conscience chooses to go on pilgrimage, to suffer with Patience until he has been made fit to return to Clergy. Clergy finally endorses this decision: he must continue to perform the actions characteristic of his nature, but he agrees that the first steps towards perfection have to be taken with Patience rather than with himself.

Finally I shall consider the behaviour of Conscience during the last part of the poem, *Dobest*. These two passus are concerned with the story of mankind after the Resurrection and with the struggle of the Church against the forces of evil. After the apparently final triumph of Christ in *Dobet*, Langland is working back to the situation with which the poem opened, the field full of folk, but its worldliness is now more sinister because seen with greater understanding. The drift towards pessimism in the last part of the poem is mainly expressed through the decline in the position of Conscience. At the beginning of passus xix the importance of his rôle as man's distinguishing faculty is emphasized: in a long passage (xix 9-193) he explains the symbolic function of Piers Plowman and relates the stages of the ministry of Christ to the terms Dowel, Dobet and Dobest. He announces the gift of grace to the Church (xix 202-205) and is regarded by Grace as the supreme authority within man: '. . . crouneth Conscience kynge' (xix 251). Enormous reliance is placed on Conscience and, even in passus xx when Antichrist is assailing the church, we are told that he alone is indestructible: 'Kynde . . . shal come atte last,/And culle alle erthely creatures saue Conscience one.' (xx 149-150.)

But during these last two passus the position of Conscience becomes increasingly vulnerable. As the keeper of Unity, the Church, he faces not only direct attack but, more insidiously, the perversion of values until he, of all faculties, will not be able to distinguish between right and wrong:

> Thise two [Surquydous and Spille-love, sent by Pride]
>   come to Conscience and to Crystene peple,
> And tolde hem tydynges, 'that tyne thei shulde the sedes,
> That Pieres there hadde ysowen, the cardynal vertues;
> And Pieres berne worth broke, and thei that ben in Vnite
> Shulle come out, and Conscience and зowre two caples,
> Confessioun and Contricioun, and зowre carte the Byleue
> Shall be coloured so queyntly and keuered vnder owre sophistrie
> That Conscience shal nouзte knowe by contricioun
> Ne by confessioun who is Cristene or hethen,
> Ne no maner marchaunt that with moneye deleth,
> Where he wynne wyth riзte, with wrong, or with vsure.'
>
> xix 337-347

We see their prediction fulfilled immediately in the perversion of the cardinal virtues when the lord describes how his auditor, steward and clerks deal with his reeve's accounts:

> With *spiritus intellectus* they seke the reues rolles,
> And with *spiritus fortitudinis* fecche it I wole.
>
> xix 460-461

and the more problematic cases of the king who claims that he can take anything from his country 'of *spiritus iusticie*' (xix 471) and the poor man who, according to Need, is free to beg and steal 'as by techynge and by tellynge of *spiritus temperancie*' (xx 8).

In the presentation of this dilemma the 'lewd vicar' seems to play a similar rôle to that of the doctor of divinity. When Conscience exclaims to the brewer who will not deal according to Justice, the voice of a literal character interrupts:

> 'But Conscience the comune fede and cardynale vertues,
> Leue it wel thei ben loste, bothe lyf and soule.'
> 'Thanne is many man ylost', quod a lewed vycory,
> 'I am a curatour of holykirke, and come neure in my tyme
> Man to me that me couth telle of cardinale vertues,
> Or that acounted Conscience at a cokkes fether or an hennes!
> I knewe neure cardynal that he ne cam fro the pope,
> And we clerkes, whan they come, for her comunes payeth.'
>
> xix 405-412

The vicar thinks as concretely as the doctor of divinity who mis-judges Patience in his pilgrim's clothes: he cannot attach the word 'cardinal' to anything but actual people, but, and partly *for* this reason, his judgment of the cardinals is realistic. He ends his speech with an exact analysis of the perversion of intellect pre-sented in *Dobest*:

> For *spiritus prudencie* amonge the peple is gyle,
> And alle tho faire vertues as vyces thei semeth;
> Eche man sotileth a sleight synne forto hyde,
> And coloureth it for a kunnynge and a clene lyuynge.
>
> xix 452-455

The vicar may only see the actual, but he sees that more clearly than some of the allegorical characters do.

These themes – the inability of a good allegorical character to act with full command of the situation, particularly in the context of intellectual perversion and economic corruption, the failure of learning to aid Conscience in the present state of the world, and the necessity for Conscience to withdraw, suspending immediate hope of a perfect solution – are all brought together in the closing episode of the poem.

Unity is now not only assailed from without but also vulnerable

within, and Conscience cries for help from the perfect idea of the
clergy against the actual examples of the clergy within the church:

> Conscience cryed, 'helpe, Clergye, or ellis I falle
> Thorw inparfit prestes and prelates of holicherche.'
>
> xx 227-228

The friars come to help and although Need warns Conscience that
they are motivated by avarice, Conscience welcomes them on
condition that they live according to their rule, leave logic and
learn to love. Envy immediately sends the friars to school to learn
logic and law and prove that all things ought to be held in common.
The desperate optimism which is displayed and refuted in this
episode is to characterize the behaviour of Conscience until the
closing lines of the poem.

Conscience makes Peace the porter of Unity. Unity is assailed by
Hypocrisy who 'wounded wel wykkedly many a wise techer/That
with Conscience acorded and cardinale vertues'. Conscience calls
for an effective doctor for their sickness, Shrift, who behaves
appropriately:

> Shrifte shope sharpe salue and made men do penaunce
>
> xx 304

and is therefore unpopular with some of the occupants of Unity
who ask for a gentler doctor such as Friar Flatterer. Surprisingly,
yet, in terms of the allegorical pattern which Langland has established, inevitably, three of the virtues, Conscience, Contrition and
Peace, agree to admit him. Contrition advises Conscience to do so
'for here is many a man herte thorw Ypocrisie'. (xx 315.) Presumably he must feel that any kind of contrition is better than none,
and is therefore apt to mistake the form of penance for the reality.
Conscience replies that they have no need of the friar and should
prefer certain authorized clergy, such as the parish priest, but then
gives in:

> 'I may wel suffre,' seyde Conscience, 'syn ȝe desiren,
> That frere Flaterer be fette and phisike ȝow syke.'
>
> xx 320-321

If 'syn ȝe desiren' is spoken to the people within Unity in general,
it suggests that Conscience, like Contrition, has to approve their

expressed desire for penance, even if it takes too mild a form. If, as I suppose, the phrase is addressed to Contrition, its implications are more complex. Conscience, whose nature is to distinguish between virtuous and vicious action, cannot refuse the promptings of a good quality even if this quality should be, through the limitations of its own virtue, mistaken.

When the friar arrives at the gate and is questioned by Peace, we find that the behaviour of Peace is consistent with his forgiveness of Wrong in the *Visio*. His choice is similarly, although it is no longer totally, blind. He tells the friar to leave and recalls the evil behaviour of one of his order, but, like Conscience, he soon capitulates:

> Hende-speche het Pees opene the ȝates –
> 'Late in the frere and his felawe and make hem faire chere.
> He may se and here, so it may bifalle,
> That Lyf thorw his lore shal leue Coueityse,
> And be adradde of Deth, and withdrawe hym fram Pryde,
> And acorde with Conscience and kisse her either other.'
>
> xx 346-351

It is not made clear whose courteous speech is thus allegorized: if it is that of Peace, we are being shown that his nature must include courtesy even when it is inappropriate to the situation, and that he has to give the benefit of the doubt to the friar who may, despite his probable evil life, do good through his learning; the meaning is not very different if we assign the courteous speech to the friar, but Peace's reaction to it is then even more clearly parallel to his behaviour in the episode with Wrong. He has to react favourably to any friendly overture, no matter how deceptive it may be.

The friar's first patient is Contrition himself whose illness has been mentioned by Peace. At this point again I think that the allegorical mode demands attention in itself as well as simple translation into literal terms. Of course the literal sense of Contrition's illness is that most of the Christians within the Church are rarely or never contrite. But in this context to say that 'Contrition is sick' seems to demand scrutiny of virtue itself as well as condemnation of those who fail to achieve it. Whittaker commented upon Conscience's reception of the friar as a possible doctor for Contrition: 'There is an impropriety in this; it was not the part of Conscience to complain that the parish priest was too severe a confessor.'[5] Where Langland commits apparent allegorical improprieties, I think that the breakdown of pure allegory is purposeful: an attack is being made on the habit of thought it encourages. The illness of Contrition is, after all, almost as 'out of character' as the speech of Conscience which it provokes. If a virtue becomes impossible for anybody to practise effectively, the concept of the virtue itself must be weakened. The feeble state of Contrition explains the 'improper' reaction of Conscience. Conscience, no longer advised by Reason as he was in the *Visio*, is in the state of moral and intellectual confusion which is one of the themes of *Dobest*. The failure of a virtue is so shocking that the allegorical mode itself is temporarily endangered: Conscience begins to compromise and suggest half-measures as though he were a literal rather than an allegorical example of Conscience.

If in this passage Langland has been suggesting criticisms and attempting violations of the allegorical method, he goes on to achieve his most destructive effect in the next lines where he describes Contrition's reaction to the comfort of the friar:

> Tyl Contricioun hadde clene forʒeten to crye and to wepe,
> And wake for his wykked werkes, as he was wont to done.
> For confort of his confessour contricioun he lafte.

> xx 367-369

The irony of the last line quoted hammers home the reversal of values which Conscience is confronting. If Contrition can be thus denatured, Conscience can no longer rely on any of the traditional moral categories, and after a final unanswered cry for help he sets out again on a pilgrimage:

> Conscience cryde eft and bad clergye help hym,
> And also Contricioun forto kepe the ʒate.
> 'He lith and dremeth,' seyde Pees, 'and so do many other;
> The frere with his phisik this foke hath enchaunted,
> And plastred hem so esyly thei drede no synne.'
> 'Bi Cryste,' quod Conscience tho, 'I wil bicome a pilgryme,
> And walken as wyde as al the worlde lasteth,
> To seke Piers the Plowman that Pryde may destruye,
> And that freres hadde a fyndyng that for nede flateren

And contrepleteth me, Conscience; now kynde me auenge,
And sende me happe and hele til I haue Piers the Plowman!'
And sitthe he gradde after grace til I gan awake.

xx 373-384

Conscience has in earlier episodes in the poem been a partially isolated figure, obliged because of the imperfection of the world to make choices which seemed inconvenient or even perverse to other virtuous characters. But when he refused the king's suggestion that he should marry Meed he was supported by Reason and when he left Clergy he was accompanied by Patience. Now in the total corruption of the world as represented by the metamorphosis of Contrition he is totally alone. His cry to Clergy presumably expresses a need for intellectual and moral guidance but there is no reply to it. It echoes the earlier appeal – 'helpe Clergye, or ellis I falle/Thorw inparfit prestes' (xx 227-228) – to an idea of perfection which is breaking down. After the dinner Clergy predicted that Conscience would finally need his counsel and refused to say good-bye to him (xiii 202-204), but now he fails to appear. The gap between the ideal and the actual which Conscience perceived in the earlier episode has widened disastrously. Even the awareness of the narrator which has been developing throughout the poem seems to be shrugged off in Peace's 'He lith and dremeth and so do many other', as if the whole form of the poem were being attacked. After so many assumptions have been destroyed, the poem ends, as it began, with the search for Truth. But the Church is no longer a perfect mentor who can provide the truth. It is Unity whose name points to an ideal which its nature belies. Having first rejected in Meed an evil quality, then in Clergy a capacity which can be used for good or ill, Conscience finally withdraws from the guardian of virtues because in an imperfect world virtue may take less than perfect forms. Yet the allegorical mode, almost destroyed by the coexistence of the literal, is finally asserted in the recourse of Conscience to the symbol of the pilgrim.

This analysis assumes that Langland was self-conscious in his opposition of the allegorical and literal modes and seeks to demonstrate that he questioned the habits of thought inherent in allegory. It therefore depends on a very different view of allegory from that presented by C. S. Lewis. In *The Allegory of Love* Lewis quotes

Dante's remark that 'love has not, like a substance, an existence of its own, but is only an accident occurring in a substance' and states: 'Symbolism is a mode of thought, but allegory is a mode of expression. It belongs to the form of poetry more than to its content.'[6] My view that the limitations of Peace are exposed in the Meed episode could be criticized on the ground that Peace is not in fact a 'substance' but an 'accident occurring in a substance': in an actual personality Peace would operate in conjunction with other qualities such as Reason and be tempered by them. There are several possible replies to this objection. One could, for example, argue from the form of the poem that, since Peace is presented by Langland as a distinct character, the reader does not naturally place him in a synthesis which is unattempted by the author. Or one could make an appeal to 'real life' and observe that such qualities as peacefulness and patience, however virtuous, are not necessarily the most effective in dealing with morally complex situations. Neither of these arguments seems to me totally satisfactory: the first is too allegorical, the second too literal. It seems preferable in discussing this poem to assert that allegory is a mode of thought which Langland is investigating and defining through the juxtaposition of allegorical and literal. This reading suggests that the allegorical habit of thought is indispensable in formulating moral concepts, but that, since these concepts are modified by actual situations, allegorization itself comes under increasing suspicion. By the end of the poem the mode has been so strained that 'perfect' characters behave inconsistently. Yet the desire for the idealism and intellectual coherence of allegory cannot be abandoned. The final image of the pilgrim re-instates the allegorical, not as a statement of a scheme, but in terms of a quest for the unknown.

Piers and the Image of God in Man

BARBARA RAW

I

One of the advantages Langland derives from casting his poem in the form of a series of visions is that the action need not be confined to any one logical time-sequence. The world described in the poem is at one and the same time the whole span of human history, from the creation to the time of Antichrist, and the world of the fourteenth century, concerned with the practical problem of justice in society and the theological problem of the salvation of non-Christians. Piers the Plowman, after whom the poem is named, moves constantly from one time sequence to the other, living sometimes in the fourteenth century and sometimes in the world of Biblical history. The Dreamer, too, lives in more than one world. Much of the time it is the world of his own mind, but he also, through the medium of the liturgy, follows Piers into the world of the Bible.

Piers enters the poem three times. His first appearance comes towards the end of the *Visio*.[1] During the previous sections of the poem the Dreamer has questioned Holy Church about the true and the false, has observed the activities of Mede, and has seen Repentance preaching to the Seven Deadly Sins. The repentant people have set out on a pilgrimage to Truth, but can find no one to direct them, and it is at this point that Piers offers to help them. We learn from this passage that Piers has been the servant of Truth (that is, of God the Father) for fifty years. He was recommended to Truth by Conscience and Natural Knowledge (Kynde Witte), promised to serve him for ever, and is fully satisfied with the conditions of service. As the servant of Truth Piers engages in three main activities: he instructs the pilgrims about the road to Truth, he organizes the ploughing of the half-acre and he receives pardon for himself and his helpers. The highway to Truth consists of the old law – the ten commandments – together with the new law: 'Thou shalt love the Lord thy God with all thy heart, and with all thy soul and with all thy mind . . . and thy neighbour as thyself'.[2] This road leads to the court of Truth, an allegorical edifice built of mercy, faith, love and brotherly speech. The search for Truth is no private, personal matter. Truth is to be found within the church: the centre of the court is Christendom and entry to it is across the bridge of prayer, through gates hung on almsdeeds, past pillars made of penance and, specifically, the sacramental penance imposed by the priest.[3] In order to gain entry to the court man must be contrite, must make amends for his sins, and must practise the Christian virtues: abstinence, humility, charity, chastity, patience, peace and generosity. He will then see Truth enthroned in his heart. In this section Piers is operating in an allegorical world. At the beginning of passus vi, when he offers to accompany the pilgrims on the road to Truth provided that they will wait until he has finished his ploughing, he moves into the world of the fourteenth century.

In passus vi Langland, through Piers, describes fourteenth-century society as it should be. His ideal society is divided into the three categories which were traditional in the Middle Ages, knights, clergy and commons, and each class has a specific task. The common people are to occupy themselves in farming; the duty of the knight is to protect the church from wasters and to be merciful to his tenants; the clergy must work by praying. The only people who are excused from work are the blind and the lame. The guiding principle of this reformed society is the duty of work. It is both a social duty and a religious duty, for work was imposed on Adam as a punishment for his sin, and work therefore forms the means by which man can return to God. Langland justifies this teaching by an appeal to natural law:

> Kynde witt wolde that eche a wyght wrouȝte
> Or in dykynge or in deluynge or trauaillynge in preyeres,
> Contemplatyf lyf or actyf lyf Cryst wolde men wrouȝte.
>
> B vi 249-251

The ploughing undertaken by Piers and his companions is to be understood literally, as the physical work which is as necessary to the life of the truly Christian community as the prayer of contemplatives is.

The third activity of Piers is to receive pardon on behalf of himself, his heirs and his helpers. Truth tells the workers to stay at home and continue with their work rather than going on pilgrimage, for the search for Truth can be carried on in the normal tasks of life: it requires no pilgrimage to distant parts. The conditions on which the pardon is granted, like the details of the ploughing, are related to the duties of the various classes of society: kings and knights are to protect the church and rule righteously; bishops are to preach to the ignorant and reform the wicked; merchants – who are mentioned only in the margin of the pardon – are to use the profits of their trade for charitable ends; lawyers are to plead for the poor and innocent; labourers are to work hard, and beggars must give up their profession unless they are genuinely sick. In the *Visio* Langland is concerned with a society ruled largely by natural law. He portrays this society in fourteenth-century terms, and he includes the church of the fourteenth century in his picture. There is no emphasis, however, on the hierarchical structure of the church or on its sacramental system.

In the first vision of *Dobet* Langland turns his attention from the community to the individual. In this vision, Piers, who is served by *Liberum arbitrium*, has the task of cultivating the tree of charity and protecting it against the attacks of the world, the flesh and the Devil.[4] His work is concerned with fruitfulness, and this is a constant element in his character, but whereas in the *Visio* the ploughing of the half-acre symbolised the outward activities of society, the tree in the vision of *Dobet* is related to man's inner life. It grows in man's heart; it is supported by the Trinity; its fruit is charity. This virtue is defined both morally – as those who exemplify the three degrees of chastity: virgins, widows and married people – and historically, when it signifies the patriarchs and prophets. In this section of the poem Langland is making use of two distinctions. He contrasts the inner life of man with his responsibilities to society, which had been portrayed in the *Visio*, and he does this by juxtaposing two historical periods. The shift from the period of the Old Testament to that of the Gospels occurs when Piers, at the Dreamer's request, pulls down some of the fruit, which is then stolen by the Devil. Piers, to protect his fruit, catches hold of one of the props which support the tree and strikes out with it against the Devil, and this action causes the incarnation.

In his third appearance Piers is involved once more in the farming activities which symbolize fruitfulness, and in the instruction and supervision which are appropriate to his position of authority.[5] He receives from Christ the power to absolve men from their sins. Like the apostles he receives the Holy Spirit. He becomes God's procurator and reeve, working together with grace. He ploughs, sows, harrows, builds a barn in which to house his corn, and carries home his sheaves. Once more Langland describes the establishment of a just society under the guidance of Piers, but this time it is the society of the church. Piers's responsibility to the community of the half-acre and to the people who will enter the barn of Unity is basically the same: he has to supervise the work and to ensure that all are fed. In the *Visio* he satisfies his workmen with material bread; in *Dobest* it is the spiritual and sacramental bread of the eucharist which he provides. In the *Visio* he summoned Hunger to coerce the idle. In *Dobest* he has other, more spiritual, sanctions; he receives power to absolve those who are contrite and willing to amend, and pardons those who have paid their debts; his horses are contrition and confession, and he is accompanied by priesthood, the normal administrator of the sacrament of penance.[6] In the two ploughing scenes Piers represents authority operating in secular society and in the church. Secular society, as Langland has shown in the *Visio*, has some hope of being reformed; the church, however, is so corrupt as to be unable to resist the destructive effects of pride. Here, once again, Langland links together a judgment on the society of his time and a statement about the nature of history. He compares the church with secular society, to the detriment of the former, and at the same time he distinguishes the just society of the Old Testament, symbolized by the ploughing of the half-acre, from the community of Christendom, established in the ploughing scenes of *Dobest*. The second society, despite its initial advantages, is destined to fail: not simply because the church is corrupt but because, given a Biblical view of history, the structures of this world must be shattered before perfection can be attained.

Piers's presence in the poem and influence on it are not confined to these three passages. During the two long visions of *Dowel*, which are devoted to an analysis of the Dreamer's mental struggles, Piers is mentioned only once, but it is at a crucial point for the Dreamer. Will is dining at Conscience's house and has asked the gluttonous doctor to define Dowel, Dobet and Dobest for him. Clergy is then invited to give his definition of the three lives, but he declines, saying:

> . . . one Pieres the Ploughman hath inpugned vs alle,
> And sette alle sciences at a soppe, saue loue one,
> And no tixte ne taketh to meyntene his cause
> But *dilige deum* and *domine, quis habitabit, etc.*
> And seith that Dowel and Dobet aren two infinites,
> Whiche infinites, with a feith, fynden oute Dobest
> Which shal saue mannes soule; thus seith Piers the Ploughman.

> B xiii 123-129

This definition marks a turning point in Will's progress, the change from the search for knowledge to the search for charity. It is true that he does not really assimilate the idea until Anima rebukes him for his pride,[7] but he has already come a long way since he set out on his search, or indeed since he lost himself in the land of longing; he has been taught by nature, and reminded by recollection of his approaching age. He is now ready to put into practice what he has learned, and he does this when he goes on pilgrimage with Patience and Conscience. In his definition of the three lives Piers returns to the Dreamer's preoccupation, voiced to Holy Church at the beginning of the poem: how may I save my soul?[8] To the pilgrims in the *Visio* Piers talked of natural justice, to be realized in society; to the Dreamer he speaks of inner qualities, the three theological virtues mentioned earlier by Imaginatyf, or recollection.[9] Dowel and Dobet seeking Dobest are the same as faith and hope searching for charity, or Abraham and Moses pursuing the Samaritan. The text on which Piers relies, and which is quoted again and again throughout the poem, is that carried by Moses: *Dilige Deum.*[10] It is a text which the Dreamer will not finally take to heart until he is faced by death.

In the scene at Conscience's house Langland reveals the intimate and necessary connexion between Will and Piers. The character Will represents both an individual man seeking salvation and the general human faculty of willing. Love is the object of his search, and love, we are told, is a matter of the will. Ailred of Rievaulx, in fact, identifies love with will.[11] But a man's will is something which is hidden, something of which only he is conscious, and this is why Piers is important to Will. Anima tells Will that he will never see charity without the help of Piers,[12] for only Piers can see into man's heart, and when Will asks where charity grows, it is to Piers that he is directed, and it is Piers who explains the tree of charity to him. Piers's connexion with Will is that of a guide: he is the one person who can understand the human will. But Piers is also connected with Christ. When Anima tells the Dreamer that only Piers can see into men's hearts, he seems to identify Piers completely with Christ:

Petrus, id est Christus.

B xv 206

This relationship between Piers and Christ is worked out in the jousting scenes, where Jesus fights in Piers's armour,[13] and it is because of this relationship that the renewed search with which the poem ends is a search for Piers.

The picture of Piers given in the C-text is similar to that outlined above, though there are one or two changes which should be mentioned. In the account of the great dinner at Conscience's house Piers is linked much more closely with Patience than he is in the B-text.[14] The speech on patience overcoming all things is attributed to Piers instead of to Patience, and Patience is said to look like Piers.[15] The definition of Dowel and Dobet as the two infinites who seek out Dobest is omitted, and Piers uses Patience's definition of the triad instead: learn, teach, and love God and your enemies. The other changes involve the relationship between Piers and Will. In the C-text Will is told by *Liberum arbitrium* (another name for Anima) that Piers is the best judge of charity, for God can see men's thoughts; the phrase, *Petrus, id est Christus* is omitted, and the poet concedes that one can sometimes discern charity in men's deeds.[16] The link between Will and Piers is lost here – Piers no longer sees the will – and this separation is found, too, in the fruit-farming scene where the tree is cultivated by *Liberum arbitrium*, who also explains it to Will.

Some characteristics are common to Piers in all his appearances. He is always shown in a position of authority, whether he is defining Dowel, directing the pilgrims to Truth, explaining charity to the Dreamer, or organizing the church. He exercises his authority in the two fields of secular society and the church, and ensures that men work in one of two ways, by labouring or by praying. His authority manifests itself through service: like the pope, he is *servus servorum Dei*. Piers's two functions – authority and service – are expressed by a series of metaphors connected with farming. The terms are traditional ones: the metaphor of ploughing, which is used of Piers in the *Visio* and the first vision of *Dobest*, is frequently applied to the functions of the bishop, in particular his task of preaching. The gardening metaphor is rather rarer, though it was used by Anselm and appears in the *Revelations of Divine Love* of Julian of Norwich, in the vision of the servant standing before his lord:[17]

> There was a treasure in the earth, which the Lord loved. I marvelled and thought what it might be. And I was answered in my understanding: 'It is a food which is lovesome and pleasant to the Lord.' For I saw the Lord sit, as a man, and I saw neither food nor drink wherewith to serve him. This was one marvel. Another marvel was that this worthy Lord had no servant but one, and him he sent out. I beheld, thinking what manner of labour it might be that the servant would do. And then I understood that he would do the greatest labour and the hardest travail that there is: he would be a gardener, delving and dyking and sweating, and turning the earth up and down: he would seek the depths, and water the plants in season; and in this he would continue his travail, and make sweet floods to run, and noble plenteous fruit to spring forth. This fruit he would bring before the Lord, and serve him therewith to his liking; he would never return until he had made this food all ready, as he knew it would please his Lord; then he would take this food, with the drink, and bear it full worshipfully before the Lord.

Julian explains the meaning of this parable: the servant is both Christ and Adam; the Lord is God the Father; the preparation of the fruit is the life and passion of Christ. This passage differs in detail from Langland's, but the general idea is the same – of a fruit which will not be ripe until the time comes for the redemption, and of a gardener who combines the qualities of man and God in his service of God the Father.

II

The meaning of Piers must be considered in relationship to the meaning of the poem which is named after him. The theme of the poem is defined by Holy Church when she is questioned by the Dreamer at the beginning of the poem. The Dreamer asks her:

> 'Teche me to no tresore but telle me this ilke,
> How I may saue my soule, that seynt art yholden?'
>
> B i 83-84

And Holy Church replies:

> 'Whoso is trewe of his tonge and telleth none other,
> And doth the werkis therwith and wilneth no man ille,
> He is a god bi the gospel, agrounde and aloft,
> And ylike to owre lorde, bi seynte Lukes wordes.'
>
> B i 88-91

Her answer is a startling one. Truth and charity, she says, will not only save man's soul but will make him 'a god'. This doctrine, that man can become like God, is of the greatest importance for the understanding of the poem. Man's perfection consists in his likeness to God. The more closely he resembles God, the more faithful he is to his own nature, for he was created in the image and likeness of God (*Genesis* i, 26). Medieval writers, following St Augustine, found this resemblance to God in the three faculties of man's soul, the memory, the understanding and the will, and they argued that this trinity of powers in man formed an image of the three persons within the one divine nature. This imprint of the divine nature was something permanent and inalienable. It could be obscured by sin but never completely destroyed, and it is because man bears this image of God within him that he is able to attain to knowledge of God through the use of his reason.[18]

It is important to remember that man is the image of God because he resembles him, not because he is equal to him. He is not a perfect image, but an inferior copy, imprinted on an alien nature as a king's image is imprinted on a coin:

> Et quia similitudo perfecta Dei non potest esse nisi in identitate naturae, imago Dei est in Filio suo primogenito sicut imago regis in filio sibi connaturali; in homine autem sicut in aliena natura, sicut imago regis in nummo argenteo.

> And because there can only be a perfect image of God where there is identity of nature, God's image is in his first-born Son as a king's image is in his son, who shares his nature; whereas it is in man as in an alien nature, like the king's image on a silver coin.[19]

The sin of Adam and Eve lay in their failure to realize this fact. Tempted by the serpent, they gave way to the desire to be equal to God, something which was quite impossible to created being. Ailred of Rievaulx defines Adam's sin not in terms of disobedience, but as an act of theft:

> [Adam] non intellexit quia qui fornicantur a Deo per superbiam, devolvuntur in insipientiam: et qui per rapinam Dei usurpat similitudinem, merito jumentorum induit similitudinem. . . . Sicque justissime actum est, ut qui contra Deum Dei appetebat similitudinem: quo voluit fieri curiositate similior, cupiditate fieret et dissimilior. Corrupta est itaque in homine Dei imago, non abolita penitus. Proinde habet memoriam, sed obnoxiam oblivioni; scientiam quoque, sed subditam errori, nihilominus et amorem, sed pronum cupiditati.

> [Adam] did not understand that those who are disloyal to God through pride, sink into folly, and whoever tries to acquire God's image by theft gets his deserts: he takes on the image of the beasts. . . . And so it is most just that the more a man tries to become like God, seeking a knowledge which is against God's will, the more unlike him he becomes through that cupidity. And so the image of God in man is damaged, though not completely destroyed. Thus man retains memory, exposed to forgetfulness; knowledge, but subject to error, and love, but prone to cupidity.[20]

By using the words *per rapinam* to describe Adam's sin, Ailred contrasts Adam's act of pride and self-assertion with Christ's emptying of himself when he became man:

> Qui cum in forma Dei esset, non rapinam arbitratus est esse se aequalem Deo, sed semetipsum exinanivit, formam servi accipiens, in similitudinem hominum factus. *Phil.* ii, 6-7

L

Who, being in the form of God, thought it not robbery to be equal
with God: But made himself of no reputation, and took upon him the
form of a servant, and was made in the likeness of men.

It was this act of self-abasement which made possible the restoration of God's image in man. Just as man had been made in the
likeness of God (*ad imaginem et similitudinem Dei*) so Christ would
be made into the likeness of man (*in similitudinem hominum*), and he
for whom it was no theft to claim equality with God would restore
the divine image, damaged by man's attempted theft.

Sacred history reveals the development of God's plan for the
world; the church made its effects available to man. If man was to
be united with Christ, he had to form part of Christ's body, the
church. When the chalice is prepared at Mass a drop of water is
added to the wine, to symbolize the union of the divine and human
natures in Christ, and the renewal of the whole of human
nature in Christ. The prayer said over the chalice makes this
symbolism explicit:

> Deus, qui humanae substantiae dignitatem mirabiliter condidisti, et
> mirabilius reformasti: da nobis per huius aquae et vini mysterium,
> eius divinitatis esse consortes, qui humanitatis nostrae fieri dignatus
> est particeps, Jesus Christus, Filius tuus, Dominus noster.

> O God who in a wonderful way created and ennobled human
> nature, and still more wonderfully renewed it, grant that by the
> mystery of this water and wine we may be made sharers in his
> divinity, who deigned to become a sharer in our humanity, Jesus
> Christ, your Son, our Lord.

This prayer must lie behind St Bernard's comparison between
contemplation and the mixing of water with wine:

> Quomodo stilla aquae modica, multo infusa vino, deficere a se tota
> videtur, dum et saporem vini induit, et colorem . . . sic omnem tunc
> in sanctis humanam affectionem quodam ineffabili modo necesse erit
> a semetipsa liquescere, atque in Dei penitus transfundi voluntatem.

> Just as a little drop of water, mixed with a lot of wine seems to lose
> its identity entirely, while it takes on the taste and colour of wine . . .
> so it will inevitably happen that in the saints every human affection
> will then, in some ineffable way, melt away from self and be poured
> out completely into the will of God.[21]

St Augustine sees the reception of communion as a means of establishing this union between Christ and humanity. Commenting on the words used in administering communion, 'Corpus Christi', he interprets them not simply as an assertion of faith in the presence of Christ in the host, but as a claim by the communicant that he belongs to the mystical body of Christ:

> Audis enim, Corpus Christi; et respondes, Amen. Esto membrum corporis Christi, ut verum sit Amen.
>
> For you hear the words, The Body of Christ; and you answer, Amen. Be a member of the body of Christ, so that your Amen may be true.[22]

By receiving the body of Christ in communion, man, a member of the mystical body of Christ, becomes what he receives. He becomes the body of Christ:

> Si bene accepistis, vos estis quod accepistis.
>
> If you have received [Christ] well, you will be what you have received.[23]

St Augustine expressed this idea at greater length in his *Confessions*:

> Et inveni longe me esse a te in regione dissimilitudinis, tanquam audirem vocem tuam de excelso: Cibus sum grandium; cresce, et manducabis me. Nec tu me in te mutabis, sicut cibum carnis tuae; sed tu mutaberis in me.
>
> And I found myself far from you in the land of unlikeness, and I seemed to hear your voice from on high: I am the food of the full-grown; grow and you will feed on me. You will not change my substance into yours, as you do with food for the body, but you will be changed into me.[24]

The restoration of the divine image in man is a gradual process. Historically, it will be complete only at the end of the world; for the individual man it will not be attained until his vision of God is made perfect. Until that time he possesses the image only in faith and hope.[25] And this restoration of the image takes place in three stages, both historically and individually:

> Unde imago Dei tripliciter potest considerari in homine; uno quidem modo secundum quod homo habet aptitudinem naturalem ad intelli-

gendum et amandum Deum, et haec aptitudo consistit in ipsa natura mentis, quae est communis omnibus hominibus. Alio modo, secundum quod homo actu vel habitu Deum cognoscit et amat, sed tamen imperfecte; et haec est imago per conformitatem gratiae. Tertio modo, secundum quod homo Deum actu cognoscit et amat perfecte; et sic attenditur imago secundum similitudinem gloriae. Unde super illud *Ps.*, *Signatum est super nos lumen vultus tui, Domine, Glossa* distinguit triplicem imaginem, scilicet *creationis, recreationis, et similitudinis.* Prima ergo imago invenitur in omnibus hominibus, secunda in justis tantum, tertia vero solum in beatis.

Thus God's image can be considered in man at three stages: the first stage is man's natural aptitude for understanding and loving God, an aptitude which consists in the very nature of the mind, which is common to all men. The next stage is where a man is actually or dispositively knowing and loving God, but still imperfectly; and here we have the image by conformity of grace. The third stage is where a man is actually knowing and loving God perfectly; and this is the image by likeness of glory. Thus on the text of the *Psalm, The light of thy countenance O Lord is sealed upon us,* the *Gloss* distinguishes a threefold image, namely the image of *creation, of recreation, and of likeness.* The first stage of image then is found in all men, the second only in the just, and the third only in the blessed.[26]

The restoration of the divine image in history and in the individual soul is the unifying theme of *Piers Plowman.* It governs the structure of the poem, the character of Piers and the development of Will.

The poem falls into four sections, each consisting of two visions. This eight-fold division of the poem is overlaid by a triple division, that of the *Dowel, Dobet, Dobest* triad, which corresponds to the three persons of the Trinity and to three periods of time. The *Visio* corresponds to the Old Testament period, and is concerned with the search for Truth, identified by Holy Church as the Creator, God the Father. The two visions of *Dobet* correspond to the Gospels: they describe the search for charity, a search which is dramatized in the Samaritan episode, where Abraham and Moses represent both the just men of the Old Testament awaiting the Messiah, and the theological virtues of faith and hope searching for charity.[27] The two visions of *Dobest* are concerned with the church, from its foundation to the end of the world: it is the task of the Holy Spirit to watch over and guide the church. As the search for Truth is associated with the *Visio* and the search for Charity with *Dobet*, so *Dobest* is associated with the search for Unity.

The restoration of the image in mankind as a whole comes about in three stages. In the Old Testament period the image is that of creation: man's natural aptitude for knowing and loving God. This stage is seen in the picture of the just society at the end of the *Visio* and in the first appearance of Piers. The second stage of restoration – that of re-creation – is brought about by Christ. It is shown in *Dobet*, in the dramatization of Christ's life and in the growing similarity of Piers and Christ. The third stage is the image of likeness, to be attained only in heaven. Langland does not show this stage, for his poem ends before the last judgment, but he indicates that Piers has achieved it when he says:

> And wel worth Piers the Plowman that pursueth god in doynge,
> *Qui pluit super iustos et iniustos* at ones.
>
> B xix 428-429

It is because Piers has this image 'by likeness of glory' that he is no longer to be found in this world.

The restoration of the image in the individual soul also comes about in three stages, each of which is related to one of the persons of the Trinity.[28] First man has to conform his will to God's, using his natural faculties, the gift of God the Father. Will goes through this stage in *Dowel*, when he debates with himself and with the external sources of authority, Clergy and Scripture. Next he must accept the gift of God the Son, the redemption and the grace which springs from it. Will does this in *Dobet*, when he watches the events of the passion. Finally, he must accept the gift of the Spirit, the love which unites the Father and the Son, and learn to love. Will never achieves this stage, for it is possible only in the next world.

These relationships, of course, are not expounded in detail in the poem. Langland takes a good deal for granted, and among the things he assumes in his audience is a familiarity with basic religious concepts. The doctrines of deification and of the restoration of the image were well known, even in the vernacular: they pervade the writings of Eckhart – in both German and Latin – and, in fourteenth-century England, they provide a major theme for Walter Hilton:

> By the grace of God I will tell you, then, how the soul is to be re-formed in the likeness of Him who first created it, and that is indeed the whole purpose of my writing.[29]

There would have been no need for Langland to explain this idea at length, though he makes a number of fairly specific references to it.

Langland uses three metaphors to express the concept of man as the image of God. The first, which is found in both the B- and C-texts, is the common medieval image of the coin:

As in Lussheborwes is a lyther alay and ȝet loketh he lyke a sterlynge,
The merke of that mone is good ac the metal is fieble;
And so it fareth by some folke now thei han a faire speche,
Croune and Crystendome, the kynges merke of heuene,
Ac the metal, that is mannes soule, with synne is foule alayed.

B xv 342-346

In these lines Langland compares man's soul to the counterfeit coins being imported from Luxemburg. To all appearances they are correctly stamped and of sterling silver, but in reality the metal is a light alloy. In the C-text the passage is expanded to show God, the owner of the mint, rejecting the false coin even though it bears his stamp:

> Men may lykne letterid men to a Lussheborgh, other werse,
> And to a badde peny with a good preynte.
> For of muche moneye the metal is ryght naught,
> Ȝut is the prente pure trewe and parfitliche graue.
> And so it fareth by false Cristine: here follouht is trewe,
> Cristendome of holykirke, the kynges marke of heuene;
> Ac the metal, that is mannes saule, of meny of these techeres
> Is alayed with lecherie and other lustes of synne,
> That god coueiteth nat the coygne that Crist hymself prentede;
> And for synne of the soule forsaketh hus owne coygne.

C xviii 72-81

The metaphor of the coin appears first in the writings of St Augustine, in the sermon *De decem Chordis*, then in Bede and Anselm, and later in the writings of St Thomas, who borrowed the image from Augustine.[30] In the *Proslogion* Anselm compares his own soul to a coin which is grimy from long use, and worn down by the friction of men's hands:

> Quia creasti in me hanc imaginem tuam, ut tui memor te cogitem, te amem. Sed sic est abolita attritione vitiorum, sic est offuscata fumo peccatorum, ut non possit facere ad quod facta est, nisi tu renoves et reformes eam.

> For you have created in me that image of yourself, in order that, remembering you I should think of you and love you. But that image is so worn away by the friction of vices, so blackened by the smoke of sins, that it cannot do that for which it was created unless you renew and re-form it.

Bede introduces the coin image in his commentary on the tribute coin. He represents man as a coin, stamped with God's image, which will pass through God's hands again at the judgment, when God, its maker, will ask: Whose image and superscription is this?

> Quemadmodum Caesar a nobis exigit impressionem imaginis suae, sic et Deus, ut quemadmodum illi redditur nummus, sic Deo reddatur anima lumine vultus eius illustrata atque signata.

> Just as Caesar demands from us the imprint of his image, so too will God: just as the coin is surrendered to the one, so God must receive back the soul adorned and sealed with the light of his countenance.[31]

In Bede, the image is that which was imprinted on man at his creation; in Langland, the stamp is that of baptism, but both writers are using the comparison with reference to the return of the coin to its maker.

The other two metaphors are found only in the C-text. The first is drawn from grammar. God is the antecedent and man is in correct relationship if he agrees with God in nature (*verbum caro factum est*), case (*credere in ecclesia*) and number (absolution of sins).[32]

> Ac adiectif and substantif ys as ich er tolde,
> That ys, vnite, acordaunce in case, gendre, and numbre;
> And ys to mene in oure mouth more ne mynne,
> Bote that alle manere men, wommen, and children,
> Sholde conformye to on kynde, on holy kirke to byleyue,

And coueite the case when thei couthe vnderstonde,
To sike for hure synnes and suffre harde penaunce,
For that ilke lordes loue that for our loue deyde,
And coueited oure kynde and be cald in oure name,
    Deus homo,
And nymen hym into oure numbre now and euere more;
    Qui in caritate manet in deo manet, et deus in eo.
Thus is man and mankynde in manere of a substantif,
As *hic et hec homo*, askyng an adiectif
Of thre trewe termysons, *trinitas unus deus*;
    Nominativo, pater et filius et spiritus sanctus.

C iv 397-409

In this passage Langland considers Christ in two ways: first he is the antecedent, with whom man must be in grammatical agreement (case and number); but (paradoxically) Christ decided to be in agreement with man and to accept man's case and number, and so Christ became the noun *homo*, which required an adjective, and the adjective, which is *deus* (i.e. *deus homo*), is triple since it implies the Trinity. The idea here is similar to that used by St Paul in the passage from the *Epistle to the Philippians*.[33]

The third metaphor is that of the tree, *imago dei*, which grows in man's heart:

Then louh *Liberum Arbitrium*, and ladde me forth with tales,
Til we comen into a contree, *Cor-hominis* hit hyhte,
Herber of alle pryuytees and of holynesse.
Euene in the myddes, an ympe, as hit were,
That hihte *Ymago-dei*, graciousliche hit growede.
Thenne gan ich asken what hit hyhte, and he me sone tolde –
'The tree hihte Trewe-loue', quath he, 'the trinite hit sette;

   . . . .

And therof cometh a good frut, the which men callen Werkes
Of holynesse, of hendynesse, of help-hym-that-neodeth,
The whiche is callid *Caritas*, Cristes owen fode.'

C xix 3-9, 12-14[34]

In this passage we have one of Langland's clearest statements about the nature of the image of God in man. The tree has been planted in man's heart by the Trinity, and in this it resembles the stamp impressed by the Trinity on the metal of man's soul in the coin image. But the metaphor of the tree differs from the coin image in one very important respect. A coin, once it has been minted, deteriorates with use. It can, of course, be recalled and reminted, but this possibility did not enter into the medieval use of this image: it was an image of man's imperfection, and therefore appropriate to an Old Testament view of man. The tree, on the other hand, is productive. Whereas the coin could only wait passively in the hope that God would clean it up, the tree, planted by God and cultivated by man, can develop and bear fruit. The fruit of the tree is charity, because it is through charity that the image is reformed in man:

Quomodo autem fiet ista renovatio, nisi novo charitatis praecepto, de quo ait Salvator: *Mandatum novum do vobis?* (*John* xiii, 34) Proinde hanc charitatem si mens perfecte induerit, profecto duo illa, quae aeque corrupta diximus, memoriam scilicet et scientiam, ipsa reformabit.

And how will this renewal come about, if not through the new commandment of charity, of which our Saviour said: *I am giving you a new commandment?* For if our mind is perfectly clothed in this charity, it will immediately re-form those two things which we have described as corrupt, that is the memory and the understanding.[35]

The passage on the tree, *imago dei* (or in the B-text, charity), forms the culmination of a long series of passages in which Langland makes use of the idea of the reformation of the image. When God created the world, says Langland, he distinguished man from the rest of creation by making him like himself in body and in mind:

'Kynde is a creator,' quath Wit, 'of alle kyne thynges,
Fader and formour of al that forth groweth,
The whiche is god grettest that gynninge hadde neuere,
Lord of lyf and of lyght, of lysse and of payne.
Angeles and alle thyng aren at hus wil;
Man is hym most lyk, of membres and of face,
And semblable in soule to god, bote yf synne hit make.'
                              C xi 151-157. cf. B ix 33

Man lost this resemblance to God when Adam and Eve aspired to know more than was fitting for them:

'It were aȝeynes kynde,' quod he, 'and alkynnes resoun,
That any creature shulde kunne al, excepte Cryst one.

. . . .

Coueytise to kunne and to knowe science
Pulte out of paradys Adam and Eue;
  Sciencie appetitus hominem inmortalitatis gloria spoliauit.'
                                      B xv 52-53, 61-62

It was not simple disobedience which caused their expulsion from
Paradise, but curiosity: they wished to be 'as gods, knowing good
and evil' (*Genesis* iii, 5). This point is made even more clearly in
the C-text, in Satan's address to Lucifer after the death of Christ:

'For thow gete hem with gyle and hus gardyn breke,
Ageyn hus loue and hus leue on hus londe ȝeodest,
Nat in forme of a feonde, bote in forme of an addre,
And entisedest Eue to ete by heore on,
     Ve soli!
And by-hihtest heore and hym after to knowe,
As two godes, with god, bothe good and ille.'
                                      C xxi 315-320[36]

Man's likeness to God is to be restored, not by reason but by
grace:

Whan the heye kynge of heuene sent his sone to erthe,
Many miracles he wrouȝte man for to turne;
In ensaumple that men schulde se that by sadde resoun
Men miȝt nouȝt be saued, but thoruȝ mercy and grace,
And thoruȝ penaunce and passion and parfit bylef.
                                      B xv 539-543

Natural knowledge, it is true, can lead man towards God – a point
which Holy Church tries without much success to impress on the
Dreamer at the beginning of the poem – but ultimately it cannot
save him:

Ac Kynde Witte cometh of alkynnes siȝtes,
Of bryddes and of bestes, of tastes of treuthe, and of deceytes.
    Lyueres toforn vs vseden to marke
The selkouthes that thei seighen her sones for to teche,
And helden it an heighe science her wittes to knowe.
Ac thorugh her science sothely was neuere no soule ysaued,
Ne brouȝte by her bokes to blisse ne to ioye;

For alle her kynde knowynges come but of dyuerse sightes.
   Patriarkes and prophetes repreued her science,
And seiden her wordes ne her wisdomes was but a folye;
As to the clergye of Cryst counted it but a trufle;
   Sapiencia huius mundi stulticia est apud deum.
For the heihe holigoste heuene shal tocleue,
And loue shal lepe out after into this lowe erthe,
And clennesse shal cacchen it and clerkes shullen it fynde.

B xii 130-143

It is the entry of God into his creation which will bring about
salvation. When Repentance calls on God to have mercy on the
contrite people, after the confession of the seven deadly sins, he
recalls this new creation which resulted from Christ's incarnation:

'Now god,' quod he, 'that of thi goodnesse gonne the worlde make,
And of nauȝte madest auȝte, and man moste liche to thiselue,
And sithen suffredest for to synne, a sikenesse to vs alle,
And al for the best, as I beleue, what euere the boke telleth,
   O felix culpa! o necessarium peccatum Ade! etc.
For thourgh that synne thi sone sent was to this erthe,
And bicam man of a mayde, mankynde to saue,
And madest thiself with thi sone and vs synful yliche,
   Faciamus hominem ad ymaginem et similitudinem nostram;
   Et alibi: qui manet in caritate, in deo manet, et deus in eo;

   . . . .

   Verbum caro factum est, et habitauit in nobis.
And bi so moche, me semeth, the sikerere we mowe
Bydde and biseche, if it be thi wille,
That art owre fader and owre brother, be merciable to vs'.

B v 488-494, 509-511

This statement of the brotherhood of God and man is clarified by
the Latin quotations, of which the first is the standard text on the
source of the divine image in man, while the second provides the
basis of the teaching that man is assimilated to God through
charity.

The emphasis on charity in this passage is important. The
search for charity is one of the major themes in *Piers Plowman*,
and is closely linked to the theme of the restoration of the image.
It will be remembered that Augustine said that the human soul

resembled the Trinity through its three faculties of memory, understanding and will. For many writers the way in which man could grow more like God lay in conforming his will to God's will. William of St Thierry, for instance, says:

> Velle autem quod Deus vult, hoc est jam similem Deo esse: non posse velle nisi quod Deus vult, hoc est jam esse quod Deus est, cui velle et esse, id ipsum est.

> For to desire what God desires, this is already to be like God; not to be able to desire anything but what God desires, this is already to be what God is, to whom to will and to be are the same thing.

This conformity of the will leads eventually to love:

> Et hoc non tantum ex judicio rationis, sed etiam ex affectu mentis: ut jam voluntas plus quam voluntas sit, ut amor sit, ut dilectio sit, ut sit charitas, sit unitas spiritus.

> And this not simply from a decision of the reason but from an impulse of the affections, so that already will may be more than will, so that it may love God, may delight in him, may live with him in charity and unity of spirit.[37]

The identification of will and love goes back to St Augustine, who used two different triads in his description of the soul, both of which were transmitted to medieval students through the *Sentences* of Peter Lombard.[38] The better-known was that of memory, understanding and will. In this triad the word memory refers to the soul's knowledge of itself. In the second triad, which consists of memory, understanding and love, the word memory refers to a memory of God. Ailred of Rievaulx, following Augustine, identifies will with love:

> Adhaesio plane ista non carnis, sed mentis est, in qua tria quaedam naturarum auctor inseruit, quibus divinae aeternitatis compos efficitur, particeps sapientiae, dulcedinis degustator. Tria haec memoriam dico, scientiam, amorem, sive voluntatem.

> Clearly, this clinging to God is not a matter of the flesh but of the mind, in which the creator has planted three powers, by which man is made capable of possessing God's eternity, of sharing his wisdom, and tasting his sweetness. These three I call memory, understanding, and love or will.[39]

III

All these passages testify to Langland's familiarity with the concept of the restoration of the image, but his use of the idea can be seen most clearly in the development of the two main characters in the poem: Piers and Will. Through the figure of Piers, Langland shows the restoration of the image in mankind as a whole. In the *Visio*, when he directs the pilgrims to Truth, supervises the ploughing of the half-acre, and receives pardon for himself and his heirs, Piers resembles the patriarchs and prophets. He is the just man living under Old Testament law. The directions which he gives to the pilgrims are drawn from the Mosaic law. The God he seeks – and whom he has served for fifty years – is Truth, and we know from Holy Church's explanation of the tower and the dungeon that Truth is the Creator, that is, God the Father, the God of the Old Testament. The way to salvation is through hard work, a conception which implies both the dignity of labour, and the necessity of it as a form of penance, consequent on Adam's sin:

> Go to Genesis the gyaunt, the engendroure of vs alle;
> '*In sudore* and swynke thow shalt thi mete tilye,
> And laboure for thi lyflode'; and so owre lorde hy₃te.
>> B vi 234-236

> The sauter seyth in the psalme of *beati omnes*,
> The freke that fedeth hymself with his feythful laboure,
> He is blessed by the boke in body and in soule:
>> *Labores manuum tuarum, etc.*
>>> B vi 252-254

The pardon, which consists of a quotation from the Athanasian creed, offers remission of both punishment and guilt to those who live justly: it depends on conditions which could be fulfilled before the redemption of man by Christ, not on the ministrations of the church. Even the implication in the pardon that faith is necessary as well as works (a constant theme in the poem) has an Old Testament ring about it, for it was the faith of the patriarchs and prophets which, together with their just lives, earned them a place in limbo, and the possibility of being snatched from there by Christ at the harrowing of hell. The part played by faith is explained at some length in the *Epistle to the Hebrews*: 'Now faith is the substance of things hoped for, the evidence of things not seen. For by it the elders obtained a good report.' (xi, 1-2). St Paul lists the patriarchs, instancing their acts of faith, and then continues:

> These all died in faith, not having received the promises, but having seen them afar off, and were persuaded of them, and embraced them, and confessed that they were strangers and pilgrims on the earth. For they that say such things declare plainly that they seek a country. And truly, if they had been mindful of that country from whence they came out, they might have had opportunity to have returned. But now they desire a better country, that is, an heavenly: wherefore God is not ashamed to be called their God: for he hath prepared for them a city.   xi, 13-16

Piers, like the patriarchs, is seeking a better country, through faith and a just life. Like them, he has some vision of redemption, for he mentions Mercy and her son, who are clearly to be identified with Mary and Jesus, and he realizes already that the brotherhood of man is based on the redemption.[40] But essentially his knowledge is a natural knowledge. He is in the position of the first group of men described by St Thomas, those who have a natural aptitude for understanding and loving God. He was taught to find Truth by Conscience and Kynde Witte, and this is in accordance with the *Visio* as a whole, where the emphasis is on natural knowledge. In this Old Testament context the pardon represents God's promise to the patriarchs and prophets that a just life will save them. It is sent to Piers and his heirs, just as God's promise was given to Abraham and his descendants.[41] It is a valid pardon. Ultimately, however, it is not enough, and this is why Piers tears it. He recognizes that the pardon, though valid and good, coming from God, must be abandoned, not because God is false and the pardon a cheat, but because the Old Testament dispensation must give way to the New. The promise made to Abraham was fulfilled in Christ; the pardon sent to Piers will take effect in the vision of *Dobest*, when the people pay their debts and receive absolution.[42]

Piers does not figure in the section on *Dowel*, at least in the B-text, though he is mentioned as the author of a definition of the Dowel, Dobet, Dobest triad, and in the C-text he appears and urges the duties of love and patience, and then vanishes again.

The chief emphasis in *Dowel* is on the Dreamer's individual re-
living of human history, and on his enquiries about Dowel: it will
be discussed in the section on the Dreamer's progress. The place
of Piers in *Dowel* is simply to foresee the coming redemption, and
he does this by his definition of the three lives as two infinites
seeking out Dobest.

In the vision of *Dobet* Piers is seen cultivating the tree of charity,
with the help of *Liberum Arbitrium*. He defends the tree against
the attacks of the world, the flesh and the Devil, using the three
props with which it is supported, that is, the power of the Father,
the wisdom of the Father (or the passion and power of Jesus), and
the Holy Spirit. When Piers describes the fruit of the tree to Will
he does so in two ways. The fruit represents the three grades of
perfection within the Church, marriage, virginity and widowhood,
but at the same time it is the patriarchs and prophets:

> For euere as thei dropped adown the deuel was redy,
> And gadred hem alle togideres, bothe grete and smale,
> Adam and Abraham and Ysay the prophete,
> Sampson and Samuel and seynt Iohan the baptiste;
> Bar hem forth boldely – no body hym letted –
> And made of holy men his horde in *lymbo inferni*,
> There is derkenesse and drede and the deuel maister.
> And Pieres for pure tene that o pile he lauȝte,
> And hitte after hym, happe how it myȝte,
> *Filius*, bi the Fader wille and frenesse of *Spiritus Sancti*,
> To go robbe that raggeman and reue the fruit fro hym.
>
> B xvi 79-89

In this scene Piers is still in the pre-incarnation era. He cultivates
charity, using free-will, and so prepares for the incarnation. His
fruit, which has to be recovered by Christ,[43] is the patriarchs and
prophets, the just men of the Old Testament. Historically the
incarnation marks the moment when the divine image was restored
in mankind. One would expect, therefore, that there would be
some major change in Piers when he strikes out with the second
prop and causes the incarnation. And so there is. From this point
onwards Piers becomes increasingly like Christ, and this assimila-
tion is symbolized in the poem by an increasing physical likeness
between the two. But it must be remembered that the restoration

of the image depends on two things: if man is to become god, God must first become man. At the beginning of section xviii the Dreamer sees a knight come riding into Jerusalem to the jousts. This figure, barefoot and riding on an ass, without either spurs or spear, resembles both Piers and the Samaritan: he resembles the Samaritan because, in the double allegory of that incident, the Samaritan represents both charity, pursued by faith and hope, and Christ, foreseen by Abraham and Moses. He resembles Piers because, as Faith explains to the Dreamer:

> 'This Iesus of his gentrice wole Iuste in Piers armes,
> In his helme and in his haberioun, *humana natura*.'
>
> B xviii 22-23

When, after the resurrection, the Dreamer falls asleep at the Easter mass, he dreams

> That Pieres the Plowman was paynted al blody,
> And come in with a crosse bifor the comune peple,
> And riȝt lyke in alle lymes to owre lorde Iesu;
> And thanne called I Conscience to kenne me the sothe.
> 'Is this Iesus the Iuster?', quod I, 'that Iuwes did to deth?
> Or is it Pieres the Plowman! who paynted hym so rede?'
>
> B xix 6-11

Conscience replies that the figure is Christ, conqueror of Christendom, dressed in Piers's arms.

We tend to see only Piers's resemblance to Christ. Langland reminds us that if the Dreamer cannot distinguish between Piers and Christ it is because Christ has become like Piers. The essence of the incarnation is that God became outwardly indistinguishable from man. Medieval writers made much of this stratagem by which God succeeded in outwitting the Devil. Langland does mention this aspect of the incarnation, but for him the importance of Christ's assumption of humanity lay not in the part it played in the long struggle between God and the Devil, but in its regenerative effect on mankind. In Christ the perfect image of God (his son) was united with the imperfect image (man), and it was in virtue of this that the imperfect image became capable of being restored to its first state.[44] At the Easter mass the Dreamer cannot distinguish between Piers and Christ, for the perfect and imperfect images have come together, but earlier the two are separate, not only when Christ enters Jerusalem, looking something like Piers, but still distinguishable from him, but earlier still, in the encounter with Anima, when the Dreamer asks about charity:

'By Cryst, I wolde that I knewe hym', quod I, 'no creature leuere!'
'Withouten helpe of Piers Plowman,' quod he, 'his persone seestow
neuere.'
'Where clerkes knowen hym,' quod I, 'that kepen holykirke?'
    'Clerkes haue no knowyng,' quod he, 'but by werkes and bi wordes.
Ac Piers the Plowman parceyueth more depper
What is the wille and wherfore that many wyʒte suffreth,
        Et vidit deus cogitaciones eorum.

                    . . . .

Therefore by coloure ne by clergye knowe shaltow hym neuere,
Noyther thorw wordes ne werkes, but thorw wille one.
And that knoweth no clerke ne creature in erthe,
But Piers the Plowman, *Petrus, id est, Christus.*'
                                        B xv 189-194, 203-206

At first, one might think that in this passage Piers is completely identified with Christ. But we know that Piers is distinct from Christ: it is his fruit that Christ comes to recover; it is his arms which Christ borrows; he teaches Christ medicine to protect his life. Moreover, in the C-text the words *Petrus, id est, Christus* are omitted, presumably because they did not represent Langland's conception clearly enough. The Latin, of course, involves a play on words: *Petrus*, Simon Peter, is the rock, *petra*, and the rock (according to St Paul) was Christ. Bede uses this very play on words.[45] But there is more to it than that. Piers, the image of God, can only be restored by becoming like the true image, by becoming a god that is. He becomes a god, to use St Thomas's distinction, by similitude, not by equality. It is, therefore, quite proper to say that Piers is Christ, but only in this sense of similitude.[46] The idea of the image explains, too, why Piers can see the will, or charity. This is not simply an assumption of divine qualities on his part, an imitation of God who searches the heart. It is because man looks into his own heart, and, through the memory and understanding, turns his will to God, that he recognizes the divine image in himself; he then becomes able to love God. It is because Piers has attempted through the Old Testament to hold on to the image of God within him, using his natural powers, that he and Christ can become one and the image can be truly restored by grace.

In the final two visions, those of *Dobest*, Piers has become a restored image, and receives from Christ the powers given historically to St Peter, the powers of binding and loosing. He founds the church, is praised because, like God, he feeds both the just and the unjust – that is, he has become completely like God – and then disappears. The poem ends with a renewed search for him. St Thomas in his discussion of the reform of the image, refers to the threefold impress of the image on man, the image of creation, of re-creation, and of likeness:

> The first stage is man's natural aptitude for understanding and loving God, an aptitude which consists in the very nature of the mind, which is common to all men. The next stage is where a man is actually or dispositively knowing and loving God, but still imperfectly; and here we have the image by conformity of grace. The third stage is where a man is actually knowing and loving God perfectly; and this is the image of likeness of glory.[47]

In the *Visio* Piers was in the position of the first group, using his natural faculties, as did the just in the Old Testament. In the visions of *Dobet* Piers is in the position of the second group, an image by the grace of Christ. Strictly speaking the third image is possible only in heaven, and should not therefore be possible to Piers while he is working in this world. St Augustine, for instance, points out that the image of God will only be made perfect in man when the vision of God is perfect; in this world we possess the image only in faith and hope, not in fact.[48] Yet Piers, it seems, has this image by likeness of glory, and this is why he cannot be found in this world. Piers is the embodiment of the image through history, and it is right that he should embody the final stage, in glory.

IV

Whereas Piers represents the imprint of the divine image on humanity as a whole, Will stands for the particular, individual man. Piers becomes a restored image through the whole of human history, and then demonstrates the application of this new ideal to fourteenth-century society; Will, being real, not imaginary or ideal, never becomes a fully-restored image, but follows Piers in the hope of becoming like him in the next world, and he does this in two ways, within the whole of his life and within the liturgy of one year.

The Dreamer is a complex character. In some respects he represents the poet. As is customary in fourteenth-century writing, the Dreamer carries the same name as the poet, and one presumes that he shares with him some details of character. The precise relationship between the ideas expressed by the Dreamer and those of the poet, however, is left ambiguous, and one should be cautious about foisting all Will's opinions on to his creator. Langland's Dreamer is both a fictive character who can introduce new topics by asking foolish questions, and an abstraction, the human faculty of willing, in constant conflict with wit or understanding: something to be overcome, suppressed, brought into line, and, in the end, converted into love.[49]

As an individual man, the Dreamer is given a personality and a life-history. The details of the Dreamer's life, which are found mainly in the C-text, may reflect the actual circumstances of Langland's life. The plea by the Dreamer to Reason and Conscience to allow him to continue his begging sounds like a cry from the heart. But even so, the passage, inserted between the vision of Mede and the repentance of the seven deadly sins, has a general significance.

The Dreamer at this stage in the poem is healthy and capable of physical work, but he prefers to drink and sleep:

> For as ich cam by Conscience with Reson ich mette,
> In a hote heruest whenne ich hadde myn hele,
> And lymes to labore with, and louede wel fare,
> And no dede to do bote drynke and to slepe.
>
> C vi 6-9

Reason asks the Dreamer whether he knows any craft which is of use to the community or which would help find food for the bed-ridden. The Dreamer retorts that he is too weak to work and too tall to stoop or to endure as a labourer. Reason then enquires whether he has any other means of livelihood such as lands or wealthy relations who will find food for him, or whether he is simply idle, a spender, a waster of time, begging his food at other men's hatches. The Dreamer claims that he should practise the craft he has learned, that is to labour with the *pater noster*, *placebo* and *dirige*, the psalter and the penitential psalms: he is a clerk and should not be forced to churlish work. The tonsured should serve Christ while those who are 'uncrowned' should cart and labour, because only the free, the legitimate and the well-born should be tonsured: it is fitting for bondmen, bastards and beggars to labour and serve lords. The Dreamer then bursts out into a great tirade against society, in which money has become the key to preferment, and ends with a plea to Reason not to criticize him: he knows in his conscience what Christ wishes him to do.[50] And the answer? the prayers of a perfect man and discreet penance are the labour which pleases God best, for man is not to live by bread alone. This passage plays its part in the long debate in the *Visio* on the necessity of work, whether active or contemplative, and brings the Dreamer into a closer relationship with the field full of folk than is found in the B-text, where he is largely an observer. In the same way, the references to a wife and daughter carry a meaning beyond the purely autobiographical.[51] Kit, the name of Will's wife, is a generic name rather than an individual one, as can be seen from the passage on Actif in the C-text:

> Thenne was ther on heihte Actif, an hosebounde he semed;
> 'Ich haue ywedded a wyf,' quath he, 'wel wantowen of maners;
> Were ich seuenyght fro hure syghte, synnen hue wolde,
> And loure on me and lyghtliche chide and seye ich loue anothere.
> For-thy, Peers plouhman, ich praye the telle hit Treuthe,
> Ich may nat come for a Kytte, so hue cleueth on me;
> > *Uxorem duxi et ideo non possum uenire.*'
> > > > > C viii 299-304

Will, the married man, is in the position of Actif, who is too bound up in the cares of this world to go on pilgrimage to Truth, or in the position of Haukin, who again is encumbered with a wife and so cannot escape sin:

> 'I haue but one hool hatere,' quod Haukyn, 'I am the lasse to blame
> Though it be soiled and selde clene; I slepe there-inne on niȝtes;

And also I haue an houswyf, hewen and children –
> *Uxorem duxy et ideo non possum venire* –
That wolen bymolen it many tyme, maugre my chekes!'

B xiv 1-4

These passages help to define the Dreamer at the beginning of
the poem as someone who is very much bound up with the world.
Will lives in and on the world. He is detached from it neither
physically, by celibacy, nor spiritually; before he can follow Piers
he must learn detachment.

At the beginning of the poem Will appears to be a rather arrogant young man. He wants above all things to know: to know both
good and evil:

> Yet I courbed on my knees and cryed hir of grace,
> And seide, 'mercy, madame, for Marie loue of heuene,
> That bar that blisful barne that bou3te vs on the rode,
> Kenne me bi somme crafte to knowe the Fals.'

B ii 1-4

He wants to be saved, but he is still capable of being enraptured by
Mede:

> Hire arraye me rauysshed, such ricchesse saw I neuere;
> I had wondre what she was and whas wyf she were.

B ii 17-18

It is hardly surprising that Will should later succumb to the
blandishments of Fortune and her attendants, concupiscence of
the flesh, covetousness of the eyes and pride of perfect living.[52]
Will spends more than forty years in the company of these young
women, and is recalled from his sojourn in the land of longing only
by age and poverty: he discovers the bitter truth that the friars are
no longer interested in him unless he will bequeath them his goods.
Finally, he hears Scripture preaching on the text, 'Many are called
but few are chosen' and, in his terror at the possibility that he is not
among the chosen, comforts himself with the thought that a man
who has once been baptized cannot renounce his belief, any more
than a churl can sell his possessions without permission from his
lord:

> For may no cherle chartre make ne his catel selle
> Withouten leue of his lorde; no lawe wil it graunte.

Ac he may renne in arrerage and rowme so fro home,
And as a reneyed caityf recchelesly gon aboute;
Ac Resoun shal rekne with hym, and rebuken hym at the laste,
And Conscience acounte with hym and casten hym in arrerage,
And putten hym after in a prisone, in purgatorie to brenne,
For his arrerages rewarden hym there to the day of dome,
But if Contricioun wol come and crye, bi his lyue,
Mercy for his mysdedes, with mouth or with herte.

                                        B xi 122-131

This is the turning point for Will. In the great vision shown to him by Kynde, he observes how the whole of nature is in harmony except man.[53] Reflection, symbolized by his encounter with Imaginatyf, or recollection, convinces him that he should return to God while he still has the opportunity:

I haue folwed the in feithe this fyue and fourty wyntre,
And many tymes haue moeued the to thinke on thine ende.
And how fele fernʒeres are faren and so fewe to come,
And of thi wylde wantounesse tho thow ʒonge were,
To amende it in thi myddel age, lest miʒte the faylled
In thyne olde elde that yuel can suffre
Pouerte or penaunce or preyeres bidde;
    Si non in prima vigilia, nec in secunda, etc.
Amende the while thow myʒte, thow hast ben warned ofte.

                                        B xii 3-10

The considerations put before Will by Imaginatyf lead to a complete change in his outlook. In the first vision of *Dowel* Will had questioned one character after another: first, the faculties of his mind, Thought, Wit and Study, then the sources of spiritual authority, Clergy and his wife, Scripture. In the second vision of *Dowel*, after his meeting with Imaginatyf, he finds himself in the company of Patience and Conscience. The conversations which he holds with these characters symbolize Will's psychological development. The will can be directed to either good or bad ends, and the decisions it makes between these ends are matters of conscience. But before the will can make any decisions it needs to be properly informed about the choice before it; this task is performed by memory and understanding. In the first vision of *Dowel* Will's knowledge was corrupted by error and his capacity for love was

restricted by his desire for the goods of this world.[54] He attempts
to inform himself, fails through pride, and is brought back by
Reason and Imaginatyf, that is, the memory and the understanding.
He is now in a position to make a practical decision, and this is
symbolized by his meeting with Conscience. In the second vision
of *Dowel* the Dreamer learns to direct his will according to the precepts of Patience and Conscience, and by the end of this vision he
is ready to follow Piers. These two visions dramatize the working
of the human will, and show how it can be directed to its proper
end, and transformed into love. In one sense, then, Will has
regained the lost image of God when, in his meeting with Anima,
he asks about Charity:

'What is Charite?' quod I tho . . .
'Where shulde men fynde such a frende with so fre an herte?'

B xv 145, 147

In another sense, the reform of the image has only just begun.
According to Ailred, the divine image is renewed in man in three
ways:

Reparatur tandem memoria per sacrae Scripturae documentum,
intellectus per fidei sacramentum, amor per charitatis quotidianum
incrementum.

The memory is restored by the teaching of Holy Scripture, the
understanding by the sacrament of faith, and love by the daily increase
of charity.[55]

Will's memory is reformed in his enquiring youth, when he
questions his own mind, together with Clergy and Scripture; this
process culminates in the meeting with Imaginatyf and is complete
by the end of the second vision of *Dowel*.

In *Dobet* Will enters the second stage, the reform of the understanding through the mysteries of faith. Whereas in *Dowel* the
emphasis was on debate, in *Dobet* it is contemplation that matters.
The Dreamer, who has already been reminded by Anima that man
will be saved by mercy and grace, not by reason, becomes an
observer once more.[56] He still asks questions, but his main task
is to watch, and to try to understand two major mysteries of the
faith. The first mystery is that of the incarnation, presented to the
Dreamer in the context of the theft of Piers's fruit, the patriarchs

and prophets. The second mystery is that of the Trinity, explained to the Dreamer by Abraham, in the account of his meeting with the three angels at Mambre, and by the Samaritan's two metaphors of the hand and the taper.[57] At the same time the Dreamer watches the historical events associated with these mysteries, in particular, the life of Christ, his death and resurrection.

In *Dobest* Will enters the third stage, in which the will, now transformed into love, is to be reformed. But in this section the parallel breaks down, because the image cannot be restored in this world. Will cannot become like Piers until after his death, and this is why, when Conscience calls on Kynde for help against Antichrist, Kynde comes in the company of Old Age and Death. It is the approach of death which, at long last, enables the Dreamer to learn what he has been told by one character after another throughout the poem:

> 'Conseille me, Kynde,' quod I, 'what crafte is best to lerne?'
> 'Lerne to loue,' quod Kynde, 'and leue of alle othre.'
>
> B xx 206-207

In these passages Langland shows the reform of the image in the individual man. Will's life, however, is not simply the history of one man: it recapitulates the history of the human race. In his youth he is like Adam and Eve: he wishes to be like God, knowing good and evil, and, in the end, he is rebuked for this desire by Anima:

> '3e, syre,' I seyde, 'by so no man were greued,
> Alle the sciences vnder sonne and alle the sotyle craftes
> I wolde I knew and couth kyndely in myne herte!'
>   'Thanne artow inparfit,' quod he, 'and one of Prydes kny3tes;
> For such a luste and lykynge Lucifer fel fram heuene:
>   *Ponam pedem meum in aquilone, et similis ero altissimo.*
>
>   . . . .
>
> Coueytise to kunne and to knowe science
> Pulte out of paradys Adam and Eue;
>   *Sciencie appetitus hominem inmortalitatis gloria spoliauit.*'
>
> B xv 47-51, 61-62

Will, by his insatiable desire for knowledge, is aspiring to the wrong kind of godlikeness, and, like Adam and Eve, he will lose his resemblance to God. He regains this resemblance, with the help of the Trinity, by following Piers through history.

In the first vision of *Dowel*, Will is in the position of the men of the Old Testament: he has to use his rational soul, the gift of God the Father, to answer his questions. Reason alone will not save him, since ultimately salvation depends on God not man, but he might make slightly more progress were he to follow the example of the patriarchs, or of Piers in his first appearance. Will, however, lacks humility, the prerequisite for learning. His favourite retort seems to be 'contra'. It is because of this arrogant self-reliance that Will cannot follow Piers directly. Whereas Piers is represented as a man of faith, Will puts his trust in reason. Where Piers makes use of natural knowledge in his pursuit of Truth, Will denies that he possesses the natural knowledge which would allow him to understand the directions of Holy Church.[58] Piers is always, even in his Old Testament period, possessed of the divine image; Will, though he has been baptized, and therefore possesses the imprint of God through baptism as well as nature, wanders into the land of unlikeness. Ailred says:

> Puto autem, quia si subtilius indagemus, quidquid nobis laboris oboritur, vel a carnis concupiscentia, vel a concupiscentia oculorum, vel superbia vitae . . . cognoscemus.

> I believe that if we consider the matter carefully we will see that all our troubles arise either from the lust of the flesh, or the desire of the eyes or the pride of life.[59]

Lust, curiosity, and vanity, all have to be curbed. Piers never suffers from this three-fold concupiscence or love of this world, but Will does, as the human will is prone to do until it becomes one with the divine will or charity, and so, unlike Piers, he is led by concupiscence into the land of unlikeness, the country where man loses even his own identity because he has lost his resemblance to God.

When eventually Will comes to his senses he finds himself still in the Old Testament period, but it is an Old Testament transformed by faith and hope. He watches while Piers, angry at the theft of his fruit, strikes out with the second prop from the tree and precipitates the incarnation. He meets Abraham and Moses, both of whom are pursuing the Samaritan, who is Christ. He is present at the death of Christ and at the harrowing of hell; he sees the founding of the church and the descent of the Holy Spirit on Piers; and finally, he is there when Antichrist attacks the church. Will's old age and approaching death are linked with the end of the world, and, by inference, just as the image will be made perfect in Will after his death, so the image will be made perfect in society after the destruction of the world.

The way in which Will succeeds in being present throughout history is by participating in the liturgy. The liturgical cycle not only commemorates the main events of Christ's life at the feasts of Christmas, Epiphany and Easter; it recalls the whole history of mankind. Just as in Advent, the beginning of the official liturgical year, the church reminds men of the prophecies of the incarnation, so during Lent, the time of renewal which leads up to Easter, she recalls those events in the Old Testament which looked forward to the redemption. The Breviary lessons for Septuagesima tell the story of the fall of man.[60] Will meets Abraham on Mid-Lent Sunday because on that day the account of Abraham's two sons and of the promise given by God to Abraham is read at Mass.[61] He meets Moses soon afterwards because the story of Moses occupies the Breviary lessons during the whole week beginning with Mid-Lent Sunday.[62] The feast of Palm Sunday coincides with the arrival of Jesus to joust in Jerusalem.[63] When Will wakes after watching the crucifixion, the harrowing of hell and the debate between the four daughters of God, he finds that it is Easter Sunday.[64] The Holy Spirit descends on Piers and his companions when Will has reached Pentecost in the liturgical year.[65]

V

In the two characters of Piers and Will Langland presents an account of the restoration of the divine image through history, and in the life of the individual, who enters into history through the liturgy, and whose psychological development forms a parallel to the development of mankind. He also links this historical view with a consideration of the restoration of the image in fourteenth-century society. In the *Visio*, Langland is concerned not simply with the duty of obeying the Mosaic law but with the right structuring of the society of his day. The duties he enunciates, those of work (either active or contemplative), of prayer, penance and almsgiving, and the patient endurance of poverty, are relevant to fourteenth-century society. Historically speaking, hard work was the punishment imposed on Adam as a result of the fall, and the way by which men living before the redemption could achieve some form of justice. But within the society with which Langland was concerned, hard work was the basis of the ordered life of the community. Prayer, penance and almsgiving, again, are elements in the just life of the Old Testament, but they are also the way in which the society of any one age makes the spiritual development of mankind its own.[66] To submit to poverty may be a Biblical virtue; for many people in the fourteenth century it was also a matter of making a virtue of necessity. Some details in the *Visio* apply solely to the church of the fourteenth century: there are references to the duties of bishops, penance refers to sacramental penance and prayer is prayer to the saints.[67] This section therefore is about the establishment of a just society in the world of the fourteenth century, using the Old Testament principles as a basis.

In *Dobet*, as befits a section concerned with grace rather than law, the emphasis is on the sacramental system. This is brought out particularly in the Samaritan passage. Historically this represents the patriarchs and prophets seeking Christ in faith and hope. But faith and hope (or Abraham and Moses) cannot help the wounded man:

> 'Haue hem excused,' quod he, 'her help may litel auaille;
> May no medcyn on molde the man to hele brynge,
> Neither Feith ne fyn Hope, so festred ben his woundis,
> Without the blode of a barn borne of a mayde.
> And be he bathed in that blode, baptised, as it were,
> And thanne plastred with penaunce and passioun of that babi,
> He shulde stonde and steppe; ac stalworth worth he neure,
> Tyl he haue eten al the barn and his blode ydronke.'
>
> B xvii 90-97

It is only the sacraments of baptism, penance and the eucharist which can heal men, sacraments which make present to him the passion of Christ.

Piers's connexion with the sacramental life of the church becomes explicit in the final sections of the poem, on Dobest. After the Holy Spirit has descended on Piers and his companions, Grace tells Piers and Conscience to summon the commons so that he can bestow grace on all men, a treasure which will sustain them till the end of their lives, and a weapon against Antichrist. The graces which he gives, like those enumerated by St Paul, are directed to the common good (1 *Cor.* xii, 7; Vulgate, *ad utilitatem*). They include occupations which are related not simply to the church but to society as a whole: there are not only preachers, priests and contemplatives, but lawyers, merchants, labourers of various kinds, mathematicians, painters, astronomers, philosophers, and justices.[68] If Conscience is to be the king of this realm, Craft is still the steward. This society is not an allegory of the contemplative life but a real society in which physical work plays its part just as much as contemplation does. The ploughing, on the other hand, has an allegorical meaning: it is concerned with the structure of the church, and the sacraments; moreover within the barn people grow holy through prayer, penance and pilgrimage, and are fed by the eucharist.[69] The food, and the conditions of obtaining it (*redde quod debes*), are spiritual, sacramental matters. This is the first difference between the society of *Dobest* and that of the *Visio*: grace plays a much larger part in the society of *Dobest*. One might expect that this society, helped by the sacraments, would be superior to the naturalistic, secular society of the *Visio* but this is not so. In the *Visio* we see a just and ordered society working under the direction of Piers, the image of God in man. Piers has trouble, it is true, in establishing this society: some help the ploughing by drinking and singing; others flatly refuse to work and threaten when they are rebuked. But in the end, the society is established; there is a due order; everyone contributes to the common good; all who have worked are rewarded. The society of *Dobest* is different. Based on Christian principles rather than on the Old Testament precepts, making use of the gifts of the Son and the Holy Spirit – grace and the sacraments – as well as the gift of the Father – the rational soul – it still cannot stand up to the attacks of Antichrist. These attacks are not simply those of superhuman powers; human weakness and sin are involved. The society of the *Visio* works. Piers achieves something, even though, eventually, he abandons this life for something better; but in *Dobest* Piers's work is apparently overthrown. Whereas in the *Visio* the natural forces such as hunger are working on Piers's side to support justice in society, in *Dobest* natural forces such as age, death and sickness, work against society, almost as though they were in league with the friars and the other agents of hypocrisy. It is a sad picture: in the *Visio* the seven deadly sins repented and turned to Truth, but in *Dobest* sin – a more diffuse, unpersonified sin this time – attacks the barn of unity so relentlessly that it can barely survive.

In these passages Langland draws together the different strands of his poem and shows how the society in which he lived resembles both the old age of man and the old age of the world. In the *Visio* the Dreamer observed those men who receive their reward in this world, who are obsessed with the goods of this world, and who are governed by cupidity. He also saw a picture of an ideal and regenerate society. Through his inner debates and struggles, which are described in the visions of *Dowel*, the Dreamer comes to see that in this world everything possesses order and harmony except man – the one rational being. By the end of the poem he is far less naïve and hopeful than he was in youth, and this change in his outlook is reflected in what he sees. He realizes that an ideal society is not possible in this world because such a society can only be realized under the guidance of the divine image, something which is possessed in this world only in hope. Will must die before he can meet Piers again, and Antichrist must destroy the world, because it is only through this final abandonment of this world that the divine image, symbolized by Piers, can be found.

The Rôle of the Dreamer in
Piers Plowman

DAVID MILLS

In 1953, in his edition of *Pearl*, E. V. Gordon referred to a 'difficult and important question for general literary history: whether the purely fictitious "I" had yet appeared in the fourteenth century, a first person feigned as narrator who had no existence outside the imagination of the real author'. He then offered the answer 'Probably not; at least not in the kind of literature that we are here dealing with: visions related by a dreamer'.[1] The idea that the narrator of a vision-poem is the representative of the poet himself has a particular attraction for critics of *Piers Plowman*,[2] partly because the poem is unique in its structure and effect, but more particularly because there are various 'biographical' references in the poem which can be assembled to provide a hypothetical biography of William Langland.[3] Moreover, if the poet is to be identified with the Dreamer, the poem can be regarded as the work of a man 'thinking aloud', wrestling with each problem in turn and becoming unduly concerned with detail to the detriment of the overall structure of the poem. *Piers Plowman* would then become valuable as evidence of the mind of its author and would reflect the concerns and problems of an articulate man in fourteenth-century England.

This approach to *Piers* has its attractions, and its supporters, but many critics would maintain that the Dreamer cannot be wholly identified with the poet and that the biographical element is of less importance than the fictional element in his presentation. D. C. Fowler, influenced perhaps by his belief in multiple authorship,

has objected very strongly to the emphasis given by the biographical approach:

> I will merely state my belief that the biography of William Langland,
> constructed from the literary character of the Dreamer, has perhaps
> done more to prevent an accurate reading of *Piers the Plowman* than
> any other single thing in the stormy history of criticism of the poem.[4]

By this modified approach, the Dreamer is a naturalistically conceived creation of the poet's imagination whose character provides
the key to the meaning of the visions. The poem is a revelation of
the Dreamer's mind and progress, and the confusions and contradictions of the poem are evidence, not of Langland's own confused
mind, but of his awareness of the confusions in the minds of others
which he has incorporated into the structure of his poem. As
J. Lawlor has said:

> The Dreamer, however he may stand in relation to the author, is that
> one man whose experience we follow. Thus, the mere sequence of
> thought is not the whole truth; the Dreamer's failures and false
> conclusions ... are no less important than his true inferences and
> unshakeable assertions.[5]

Other critics, however, have questioned the underlying assumption that the Dreamer is naturalistically conceived. Supporters of
the 'pan-allegorical' school of criticism would argue that a concept of
'character' is not relevant to medieval literature since such literature
was not primarily an imitation of reality. D. W. Robertson states
that 'human behavior was thought of in terms of abstractions
which retained their individuality without reference to the psychological condition of the subject'.[6] Applied to *Piers*, this means that
the Dreamer must be seen as an element in the allegorical framework:

> Will is merely a device by means of which the poet may set off the
> actual against the ideal in the poem and so develop his major theme.[7]

As propounded by Robertson and Huppé, this interpretation of the
Dreamer's rôle is dependent upon their theory of the poem's
central didactic purpose, but it should be noted that it is possible
to regard a literary figure as a structural device, and not primarily
a naturalistic creation, without subscribing to the allegorical

approach to literature. Character can be seen as part of a rhetorical structure, as G. T. Shepherd regards it in Chaucer's *Troilus and Criseyde*:

> The plot is central. But the story, as Chaucer tells it in its wholeness and fullness, generates the characters it needs. If we insist on assessing the individuality and psychology of these characters we do it from outside the poem. They needed not to be psychologically coherent as long as their presentation sustains and gives substance to the *narratio*.[8]

Here the Dreamer would be a rhetorical device, generated by the argument of the poem, and need not manifest naturalistic behaviour or show any plausibly motivated development.

It should be evident that a study of the rôle of the Dreamer in *Piers* is not merely the study of a particular aspect of a particular poem. A. C. Spearing has said that 'despite the great quantity of scholarly work that has been done on it [*Piers*], it appears that we are still at the stage of having to make up our minds what *kind* of poem it is'.[9] Indeed, we must do even more. We must decide what we mean by *poetry* and whether *Piers* can justly be considered as a poem at all. Often it seems to be regarded as something requiring explanation rather than response, a philosophical argument made more obscure by being written in the form of a verse allegory, with certain passages being singled out for their poetic value. Perversely, its alleged poetic deficiencies are cited in justification of its extra-poetic interest. M. W. Bloomfield claims that –

> Langland fails, in part, to satisfy these claims [the contending tensions of his age] completely and in perfect artistic form because his aim is to show the spiritual confusion of his own times. Spiritual confusion demands to some extent artistic confusion.[10]

It is hard to believe that an impression of the spiritual confusion in the world can be effectively conveyed by a poem that is at all confused in its own structure. Rather, poetic confusion produces impatience and boredom, and it matters little whether we attribute that confusion to a confused poet or a confused Dreamer. *Piers* may be explained and even excused by this means, but it cannot be justified.

In *Piers Plowman*, I would claim, it is not possible to distinguish 'thought' from 'expression'. The work is a complete unity in which the poet explores the relationship between the finite and the infinite on a number of inter-related levels, and the Dreamer's rôle is to represent the finite on all these levels in contrast to Piers Plowman who represents the infinite. The resulting poem is complex and difficult, but it is nevertheless a poem, self-contained, whose structure is its meaning, and, like any work which has structural and thematic unity, it demands an emotional as well as an intellectual response from its readers. It is a poem with many aspects but, for the sake of convenience, it may be considered to have four levels – contemporary reality, dream-experience, narrative and total structure.

The contemporary world, with its social complexities and philosophies of life, is the starting point and 'raw material' of the poem. It is true that this reality is mostly presented through the vision-form, but the basic problems of the medieval world are not in doubt. Man has two inter-related obligations – to his fellow men in society and to God. Society presents an order which essentially is a moral order but which is overtly enforced by human law under the king. It also has an economic basis, again to be interpreted in terms of moral obligation, but overtly controlled by manufacture and trade and measured in terms of wealth. God is represented in society by His Church which is the means whereby Man is directed to God. From the Church Man learns his moral obligations which are consonant with the principles of social order, though wider reaching and of greater importance, and within the Church he can attain grace. Yet the reality to which *Piers Plowman* returns constantly is one in which human law and social order are overthrown by an excessive concern with material goods and in which moral obligations are ignored by laity and clergy alike in their desire for gain. In reality the unity envisaged in theocentric theory has been destroyed in every aspect.

The rôle of the Dreamer at this level is to represent contemporary man, almost the only 'real' person in the poem, and the opening lines of the poem go some way towards establishing this rôle:

> In a somer seson, whan soft was the sonne,
> I shope me in shroudes, as I a shepe were;
> In habite as an heremite, vnholy of works,

N

> Went wyde in this world wondres to here.
> Ac on a May mo: nynge on Maluerne hulles
> Me byfel a ferly, of fairy me thouȝte.
>   B Prol. 1-6

Burrow notes:

> For Langland, the dream is a structural device; and he does not
> exploit its decorative possibilities in the manner of *Wynnere &
> Wastoure, The Parlement of the Thre Ages,* or *Pearl.*[11]

The result, however, is to divorce the preamble from a set literary
convention; in this context the *May mornynge* is not only out of its
conventionally decorative context but is allied to the precise
Maluerne hulles and both suggest a definite time and place. They
are the first of a number of precise and unexpected statements
which relate the Dreamer to a background of space and time; e.g.:

> . . . er I hadde faren a fourlonge, feyntise me hente.
>   B v 5

> Tyl it bifel on a Fryday two freres I mette.
>   B viii 8

> . . . lened me to a lenten, and longe tyme I slepte.
>   B xviii 5

> In myddes of the masse, tho men ȝede to offrynge,
> I fel eftsones aslepe.
>   B xix 4-5

> And it neighed nyeghe the none, and with Nede I mette.
>   B xx 4

The Dreamer is set against a precise background, never realized
by detailed description but created by a few brief references. The
'biographical' references to him living with his wife Kit in a cottage
on Cornhill (C vi 1-5) and to *Kitte my wyf and Kalote my douȝter*
(B xviii 426) similarly serve to establish him in a precise context,
and with the same conciseness. Moreover, the Dreamer is presented
in the temporal context of his own life, as described by Imaginative:

> . . . of thi wylde wantounesse tho thow ȝonge were,
> To amende it in thi myddel age, lest miȝte the faylled
> In thyne olde elde.
>   B xii 6-8

and represented in his visions by the assaults of Elde upon him (B xi 26-32; xx 182-197). These precise references, both circumstantial and 'biographical', and the lack of accompanying conventional poetic descriptions help to establish the Dreamer as 'real' and enable him to fulfil the function of dreamer noted by Gordon:

> Tales of the past required their grave authorities, and tales of new things at least an eyewitness, the author. This was one of the reasons for the popularity of visions: they allowed marvels to be placed within the real world, linking them with a person, a place, a time, while providing them with an explanation in the phantasies of sleep, and a defence against critics in the notorious deception of dreams.[12]

Yet, if the Dreamer belongs to the real world, it is clear that he stands outside society. What is less clear is the significance of his rôle as outsider, for even in the opening description he is an ambiguous figure. The physical comparison, *as I a shepe were*, is a grotesque and suggests the uneasy awareness of the absurdity of his position, considered objectively, which the Dreamer shows elsewhere – for example, in his pose of social rebel (B xv 1-15) – and which is also reflected in the rebukes which he receives – for example, from Dame Study (B x 1-134). But although the Dreamer may often seem comic, there is a serious overtone in his absurdity. Here *shepe* suggests a number of wider meanings:

OED 2a in allusions to

    (a) the sheep's timidity, defencelessness, inoffensiveness, tendency to stray and get lost.

    (b) the fabled assumption by a wolf (or other beast of prey) of the skin of a slaughtered sheep.

    (c) the division into 'sheep' and 'goats' at the Last Judgement.

OED 4. In biblical and religious language (as collective plural) to persons, in expressed or implied correlation with *shepherd*.[13]

The obvious sense here, stressed by Robertson and Huppé,[14] is the 'wolf in sheep's clothing' which is suggested by the reference to dress and the outward similarity to a hermit. Yet at the same time the idea of a 'straying and lost sheep' is present in the reference to wandering, and perhaps against it stands the idea that the Dreamer wishes to be a 'sheep' as opposed to a 'goat', one who is among God's chosen and will be saved, and both these senses become stronger as the poem progresses. Moreover, this ambiguity is continued in the next line by the play on *habite* which strengthens the link between outer appearance and inner nature. *Vnholy of workes*, as many critics have pointed out,[15] implies that the Dreamer is a wastrel masquerading as a hermit, like the false hermits in the Field (B Prol. 53-57). Yet the phrase could also imply the contrast of the contemplative and the active life which is an important concept in the poem. On the one hand, the Dreamer's withdrawal from the world may mean that he does no evil but also does no good works, is guilty of sins of omission.[16] On the other hand, it suggests his desire to fulfil the rôle of a true hermit, standing apart from the world and relying upon prayer and contemplation; the Dreamer aspires to a special faith, and perhaps a special grace and knowledge.

This initial ambiguity is never resolved and leaves some doubt about the value of what the Dreamer says; his physical isolation from his fellow-men, reinforced by the absence of any definite indication of his social status, has a counterpart in his critical attitude towards the contemporary world. Is he shirking his social responsibilities, living upon society, like a false hermit or beggar? Is he preaching false doctrine, like an evil preacher? Is he talking idle nonsense, like an entertainer or minstrel?[17] The ambiguity may be 'a defence against critics', but it contributes to the general sense of uncertainty that *Piers* leaves. The Dreamer is seeking not only the answers to the problems around him, but also the answers to his own identity and value, and his request to Holy Church, *Kenne me bi somme crafte to knowe the Fals* (B ii 4), has personal as well as social reference. Is he a sinner, a guide to salvation, or both?

In another way the Dreamer's 'real' situation can be related to his visionary situation, for he is like a pilgrim – like all pilgrims – in search of Truth. Yet, as he recognizes, there are true and false pilgrims, and pilgrimages may be undertaken for idle pleasure as well as for true devotion. Certainly it is in this spirit of idleness that the Dreamer begins, for his journey seems motivated by nothing more than the fine weather and consists in pointless wanderings (*went wyde*). His avowed intent, *wondres to here*, suggests an idle curiosity and a concern with hearsay rather than deeds.[18] This sense of aimlessness seems to appear whenever the Dreamer awakes; e.g.:

> Thus yrobed in russet I romed aboute
> Al a somer sesoun for to seke Dowel.
>
> B viii 1-2
>
> And I awaked therewith, witles nerehande,
> And as a freke that fre were, forth gan I walke
> In manere of a mendynaunt many a ӡere after.
>
> B xiii 1-3
>
> Wolleward and wete-shoed went I forth after,
> As a reccheles renke that of no wo reccheth,
> And ӡede forth lyke a lorel al my lyf-tyme.
>
> B xviii 1-3

and at the very end, before his final vision, he is still in doubt and perplexity:

> Thanne as I went by the way, whan I was thus awaked,
> Heuy-chered I ӡede and elynge in herte;
> I ne wiste where to ete ne at what place.
>
> B xx 1-3

The physical picture may well be an image of search, but it is also an image of aimlessness and one which becomes associated increasingly with despair. It may also be seen as an image of the Dreamer's own lack of steadfastness, of his own instability, which makes him incapable of progression. Yet it could be suggested that the abandonment of the idle gaiety of the opening is a sign of progression which is a counterpart to the Dreamer's spiritual growth in the visions.[19] The parallels and contrasts of the physical journeys are evident, but the values to be set upon them are far from clear.

Yet these difficulties are small compared with those which the reader encounters in evaluating the dream-experience. Here the initial problem is to determine what kind of dream-experience this may be. This is not the place to attempt a detailed discussion of medieval dream-theory,[20] but basically the problem is to decide if the dream has its origins in the Dreamer's own confused mind or if it is a prophetic dream impressed upon his mind by a celestial intelligence. If the dream is from the Dreamer's mind alone, it is unlikely to have any wider value and the Dreamer's rôle is to create his own dream. If it comes from outside him, however, his rôle is that of prophet, to receive a divine revelation and communicate it to his fellow-men. Even so, the two types are not totally distinct, and it is possible that the dream is part revelation, part personal creation, so that the problem of distinguishing between the various elements also arises.[21]

These difficulties are clearly inseparable from those involved in the Dreamer's relation to society. Indeed, at the start of his dream, his position is comparable with his situation at the start of the poem:

> Thanne gan I to meten a merueilouse sweuene,
> That I was in a wildernesse, wist I neuer where.
> B Prol. 11-12

The reference to the *wildernesse* takes up the earlier picture of the Dreamer as a hermit. He is outside the structure of his dream – tower, field and dungeon – and merely observes. At the same time the wilderness may suggest his inner aridity. Yet it also evokes the image of a desert-father, a prophet. The lack of purpose is taken up in *wist I neuer where*, but at the same time this contrasts with the firm reference to the Malvern Hills where the Dreamer falls asleep, suggesting both uncertainty and a liberation from earthly restriction.

If indeed there is a parallel between the Dreamer's relation to society and the Dreamer's relation to his vision, there is also an evident distinction between the vision and society. The dream is a form of escape, a kind of pleasant entertainment evoked by the pleasant natural scene. An image-pattern develops – '*wondres* to here', 'me byfel a *ferly*', 'it sweyued so *merye*', 'a *merueilouse* sweuene'. Initially the dream is a pleasant experience, but nothing more. Yet the value of the experience is still not clear. On the one hand, the Dreamer seems to suggest that the experience is an escape from doubt to certainty:

> . . . folke helden me a fole, and in that folye I raued,
> Tyl Resoun hadde reuthe on me and rokked me aslepe.
> B xv 10-11

Here the dream is inspired by Reason as a means of leading the

Dreamer from the folly induced by his misunderstanding of the previous vision. On other occasions the Dreamer sees his experience as a total renunciation of a hopeless world:

> ... I wex wery of the worlde and wylned eft to slepe.
>
> B xviii 4

On other occasions, however, it is not clear if the dream represents a movement into a more meaningful experience or an escape from a personal duty:

> And so I babeled on my bedes thei brouʒte me aslepe.
>
> B v 8

> In myddes of the masse, tho men ʒede to offrynge,
> I fel eftsones aslepe ...
>
> B xix 4-5

Does religious observance inspire a divine revelation, or is the dream a rejection of a meaningless ritual? Does the Dreamer fall asleep in church through boredom, or conveniently because he must make his offering, or in revolt against the worldly church, or because the worldly offering leads him naturally to think of God's offering for Man, the subject of his vision?

Perhaps most important of all, however, is whether the dream-experience can answer the Dreamer's questions. What the Dreamer seeks in the *Vitae* section is to know Dowel, Dobet and Dobest, but paradoxically this knowledge involves 'doing'. By his position outside society the Dreamer has cut himself off from the possibility of acting effectively, but by his further withdrawal from reality into a dream-experience he has cut himself off from the possibility of knowing what doing well may be. Perhaps the clearest statement of this dilemma is to be found in the C-text where the speaker is the Dreamer:

> ... And sayde anon to myself: 'slepynge, ich hadde grace
> To wite what Dowel ys, ac wakynge neuere!'
>
> C xiv 218-219[22]

It is difficult to see how the Dreamer can know Dowel when he is asleep and not when awake, although it is easy to translate this opposition into a contrast of the will and the deed such as St Paul makes.[23] But such a contrast is made impossible by the Dreamer's continuation:

> And thenne was ther a wiȝt – what he was ich nuste –
> 'What ys Dowel?', quath that wiȝt. 'ywis, syre,' ich seyde,
> 'To see muche and suffren al, certes, syre, ys Dowel.'
>
> C xiv 220-222

The idea of activity is transformed into one of passivity – to do well is to do nothing but observe uncritically; it is a reinforcement of the Dreamer's withdrawal since, although the Dreamer would have 'done well' to have listened to Reason, he has made an absurd generalization from a particular case. His act of dreaming is used as a substitute for experience as well as an extension of experience and his medium of revelation is also a means of withdrawal.

Hence the Dreamer remains as uncertain of the value of his dream as he is about his own rôle in the world. It is, he says, a dream *of fairy me thouȝte* (B Prol. 6); *MED* defines *fairy* as 'supernatural contrivance: enchantment, magic, illusion: also, something supernatural or illusory, a phantom'. It is to be associated with the sequence of 'marvel' terms in the opening lines of the poem, but it also suggests an illusion as opposed to a reality, and a fantasy as opposed to a revelation. Yet later, at the end of the *Visio*, he wonders:

> Ac I haue no sauoure in songewarie, for I se it ofte faille.
>
> B vii 148

and then proceeds to give an account of dream-theory which stresses above all the prophetic dreams of the Bible. Later still, as has been noted, a dream is inspired by Reason. Yet, significantly, when the Dreamer comes to interpret his vision after his discussion on dreams, he concludes only that written pardons are unsafe, and then embarks upon a quest for Dowel which leads him to despair and to a statement of predestination with which the A-text ends. The Dreamer's difficulty is to find the prophetic element in his vision, and he remains constantly unable to do so. The dream may be prophetic but the Dreamer is not.

To appreciate this problem, we must examine in more detail the distinction between dream-experience and reality. The advantage of the dream-vision is that it allows an escape from reality, which in this poem means particularly from space and time. *Piers Plowman* is often compared with the mystery cycles[24] both in contemporary reference and in the selection of Biblical episodes. V. A. Kolve has sought to reconcile this reference and selection with medieval theories of time and place.[25] On the one hand:

> The Corpus Christi drama . . . establishes by costumes, settings and verbal reference a time and place that are roughly contemporary, and more or less English.[26]

On the other hand:

> For several hours of mimetic performance, the audience is invited to contemplate [God's plan for man's redemption] in its temporal sequence, as a thing outside them, as a rhythm that passes by the audience's moment in time in order to talk about times more significant to the history of the race.[27]

Within the dream there is neither time nor place. Man's Fall, Christ's Crucifixion and the Harrowing of Hell, among other events, are all 'now', as is the coming of Antichrist. The Field Full of Folk, and Piers's half-acre, and the garden of Man's heart, among other places, are all 'here'. This fusion, which is inseparable from the allegorical method of the poem, contrasts with the concern with time and place which is associated with the Dreamer and his outlook. It has the effect, furthermore, of denying the unique importance of the present and hence of the Dreamer who is part of the present. The Dreamer's quest for identity must therefore take place in a framework which denies his criteria for that identity, denies that he is any different from any other man.

The Dreamer has a dual rôle, as Dreamer and as a figure in his own dream, but his function within his own dream is to assert the primacy of the present and of the individual against the denial which the dream-experience proposes of any such primacy. It is this assertion which destroys the unity of the vision but which also makes the vision uniquely the Dreamer's. It corresponds to the distinction between the prophetic and personal elements within the dream and between the analogical correspondences and 'real' elements of the vision, for the Dreamer becomes the means of asserting a sinful and worldly reality against the advice and claims of the figures in the *Vitae*. For this reason, the dream must always return to reality, both because the Dreamer must awake, and also because within the dream there is always the assertion of a reality which contradicts the ideal. But the great achievement of Langland is to set against the figure of the Dreamer that of Piers who epitomizes the fusion of time and space. Piers is timeless and universal as the Dreamer is not. But Piers is also a part of the social world which the Dreamer rejects, for Piers has a definite social function – he is always Piers *the Plowman*. As such – surprisingly, perhaps – he exemplifies action and involvement against the Dreamer's thought and withdrawal.

It seems assumed that when the Dreamer asks questions, he asks the right questions. Yet, given his attitude to society and the concepts of time and place which he represents, it would be strange if his questions were always valid. His remarks to Holy Church are a case in point. He has noted, it might seem, the concern of those in the Field with money, and he asks a most pertinent question:

> Ac the moneye of this molde that men so faste holdeth,
> Telle me to whom, Madame, that tresore appendeth?
>
> B i 44-45

Yet this is a strange, childlike question which presupposes that *someone* must own the treasure, and Holy Church's answer, *Reddite Cesari*, never faces this presupposition; it is merely a statement on the use of wealth. It is significant that the Dreamer supposes that his question can have an absolute answer, for he continues, having discovered Holy Church's identity, to question in a way which indicates that he has not understood her answer:

> Teche me to no tresore, but telle me this ilke,
> How I may saue my soule, that seynt art yholden?
>
> B i 83-84

Holy Church has already made it clear that worldly wealth has a place in man's existence but must be governed by moral law. The Dreamer's new question is doubly childlike; it presupposes an opposition of worldly goods and salvation which is only partially true and it suggests that Holy Church can tell him how to save his soul. In fact, neither presupposition is correct. Holy Church patiently tries again:

> 'Whan alle tresores aren tried,' quod she, 'trewthe is the best.'
>
> B i 85

where the 'treasure' image is an assertion of a comparative scale of values against the Dreamer's totally exclusive categories – the things of this world cannot be totally rejected but must be correctly valued. And as a counsel of salvation, it is unintelligible to the Dreamer:

> . . . ȝet mote ȝe kenne me better,
> By what craft in my corps it [Truth] comseth and where.
>
> B i 136-137

Small wonder that Holy Church, like an exasperated mother, loses control – *Thow doted daffe* (i 138) – and, after another attempt, concludes hastily 'I've had enough; I'm going!' (i 206-207) and to the Dreamer's howl of 'But *please!*' she replies hastily 'Look for yourself!' The Dreamer expects that there will be an absolute explanation and denies that he has any 'natural understanding' (*kynde witte*) to apply precepts to individual situations. He is therefore limited to a sequential vision, a system of logical and definable causes and effects, in which each answer is final.

Thus when he sees his visions, they correspond ostensibly to his questions and to Holy Church's answers. The trial of Meed follows the pattern of Holy Church's advice on worldly goods, while the pilgrimage to Truth is the answer to the Dreamer's demand for salvation. Yet the correspondence is only apparent, for the illogical division which the Dreamer made between wealth and salvation is made clear when the vision breaks down. In the trial of Meed, although the king, guided by Conscience and Reason, can limit the interference of Meed in the order of society under law and can help to enforce a *mesurable hire*, no one owns Meed – she owns them and she is more enduring than they are. At the end of the trial, Meed is still present and still has her supporters. And in the pilgrimage to Truth, the necessity to earn one's living in society becomes an important element in the pilgrimage and is a feature of the pardon. Although the individual may repent, the Sins, like Meed, are allegorical figures, enduring and incapable of change, and contrition and repentance are useless without obedience and love. Finally, the pardon episode is an example to the Dreamer that no simple definitive answer, of the kind which he expected from Holy Church, will suffice unless interpreted with 'natural understanding'. The priest is logically correct – good deeds are not enough; but from all that has gone before in the poem we know this. The text has to be set in its context – of the poem, or, as Robertson and Huppé point out,[28] in its original context of the Athanasian Creed. The priest could certainly have done the latter, and every reader can do the former, but the priest treats the pardon in the isolating, definitive manner which we come to recognize as characteristic of the Dreamer himself.[29]

The Dreamer, however, bound by his own experience in time and space, cannot escape from his sequential vision. From time to time he interposes, as Dreamer, his comments on the action showing that he is still no nearer an understanding of the true meaning of his vision. Thus, the incident of the shriving of Meed draws the trivial comment that the rich should not endow stained-glass windows (iii 64-99),[30] while his conclusion on the pardon-scene, that one should trust Dowel and not a paper pardon, is certainly true but misses the personal lesson to be learned from the priest's literalism.[31]

The pardon-scene, however, marks a turning-point in the poem, since the quest for Dowel, Dobet and Dobest follows. If the questions with which the Dreamer directed the *Visio* were based on false assumptions, the suppositions underlying the *Vitae* are more obviously false. The Dreamer's quest originates, significantly, in the priest's comment on the pardon:

> 'Peter!' quod the prest tho, 'I can no pardoun fynde,
> But Dowel, and haue wel and god shal haue thi sowle,
> And do yuel, and haue yuel, hope thow non other
> But after thi ded-day the deuel shal haue thi sowle!'
>
> B vii 112-115

Dowel is very clearly a 'verb-adverb' construction suggesting a finite action, but the Dreamer, oddly, treats it as if it were a noun,

> Thus yrobed in russet I romed aboute
> Al a somer sesoun for to seke Dowel.
>
> B viii 1-2

that is, as if it were a definite thing which could be sought out and found – like the person who owns all the treasure in the world. Then, to heap confusion upon confusion, Thought supplies a comparative and superlative:

> 'Dowel and Dobet and Dobest the thridde,' quod he,
> 'Aren three faire vertues and beth nauȝte fer to fynde.'
>
> B viii 78-79

Dowel is a syntactical impossibility, a verbal phrase indicative of action frozen into a noun which implies an objective existence, an entity or state. One cannot seek Dowel, one can only *do* well, so that the Dreamer's lack of involvement has now been turned to the pursuit of the non-existent. Thought's comment erects a comparative and superlative upon a positive that has no objective existence. Every adviser that the Dreamer encounters can define Dowel for him only by limiting its reference to something which does exist, and hence provides only a partial definition. The Dreamer is looking for the impossible in his attempts to impose an order upon and direct the course of his own vision.

Yet the advice of Thought raises another problem, for surely Thought is advising the Dreamer correctly. Again, it is usually assumed that the abstractions in the poem have an objective existence,[32] and this seems true of the abstractions of the *Visio*. Yet in the *Vita*-section, where the Dreamer is taking a more obviously active rôle, the division between the subjective and objective aspects of the figures is often difficult to maintain. Thought is a good example:

> A moche man, as me thouȝte, and lyke to myselue
> Come and called me by my kynde name.
>
> B viii 70-71

The reference could be ironic – Thought is a great man in every sense of the term and hence an ideal for the Dreamer, and more-over the Dreamer, with his hasty judgments, is surely the anti-thesis of Thought. Yet Thought, logically, can be only the collective Thought of mankind in which the Dreamer's own thoughts have a share, or mankind's faculty of thinking, which is capable only of personal manifestation. The reference *lyke to myselue* suggests a peculiarly close connexion between this figure and the

Dreamer; it may, of course, be merely that Thought, like the Dreamer, is speculative and without preconceptions of intuition or faith, but if so Thought's advice is not necessarily valid. It would be simpler to assume, however, that Thought here is a personal faculty and that the Dreamer, on the basis of his initial syntactical misunderstanding, creates a false triad in his own mind which he then attempts to establish as an objective reality. The Dreamer's dispute with Thought (B viii 112-113) is thus an internal dialogue. This hypothesis would explain why Thought addresses the Dreamer by his *kynde name* and also why he tells the Dreamer in answer to his request to know his name:

> 'That thow wost wel,' quod he, 'and no wyȝte bettere.'
>
> B viii 73

Why should the Dreamer know him better than any other unless he is peculiarly the Dreamer's thought?

One cannot press the personal reference quite so far for the other abstractions, but it is possible that they are subjective as well as objective, so that the Dreamer continues his dialogue with himself. Logically, his own Thought, Wit, Study, Clergy, Conscience have a share in a collective Thought, Wit, Study, Clergy, Conscience, much as the sins of individuals have a share in the collective allegorical Deadly Sins of the *Visio*. And structurally these abstractions are part of the Dreamer's own dream which, as has been noted, may be objective and prophetic or subjective and fantastic, or most probably both. By avoiding any clear-cut division between the Dreamer's faculties and the objective faculties which must provide him with new knowledge, Langland has created a situation in which the reader must question the arguments advanced by the abstractions at every point.

Structurally, the concept of Dowel, Dobet and Dobest sets up an impression of progress towards an absolute goal which contrasts with the impression of balance created by the Dreamer's questions to Holy Church which are developed in the two episodes of the *Visio*. Ostensibly the Dreamer's rôle changes from that of observer to that of protagonist, since he is now a figure actively engaged in his own dreams. But just as Dowel, Dobet and Dobest develop from the pardon scene, so also does the idea of conflict and dispute, with the Dreamer taking over the priest's rôle and rigorously questioning the meaning of all that he encounters. Since the priest could not see the truth in the pardon sent by Truth, it is unlikely that the logical Dreamer can see the truth in his revelation. And since the Dreamer has begun by postulating a triad which has no objective existence, he cannot receive a satisfactory definition of it and hence progression becomes impossible, for he is asking the impossible. At the end of the poem he is still being given the same answers that Holy Church gave him – learn to love and do not set great store by worldly needs (B xx 206-210) – and from what we have seen of the Dreamer we can feel no confidence that he is capable of understanding these injunctions, particularly when his guide is not a perfect Holy Church but a disunited earthly church.

This is not to say that there is no concept of progression in *Piers*, but it is a 'progression' only in a limited sense. In the *Visio* there is an implied causative relationship between the trial of Meed and the pilgrimage to Truth; but with the breakdown of the pilgrimage it becomes clear that this is not a progression but a cycle, a sequence of aspiration and failure. In the *Vita*-section this concept of progression is more complex since it includes a historical perspective. The Fall of Man, the Harrowing of Hell, the Coming of Antichrist; Abraham, Spes (Moses) and the Good Samaritan exemplify a chronological progression, and the Dreamer's own position in a historical sequence, established by references to him in the real world, is assimilated to this pattern. Firstly, the introduction of his internal dialogues into the framework points a connexion between his situation and the historical pattern, and secondly, at the end of the dreams, the Dreamer is stricken by Elde and driven in fear to Unity (B xx 188-205); the coming of Antichrist preludes both the ordained end of the world and the physical end of the Dreamer. On the one hand, progression is progressive decline, but on the other hand it is increasing awareness of one's need; as Kolve says:

> For the most part, the Middle Ages was chiefly conscious of degeneration, of the times growing ever worse and worse. Only one medieval conception of present time had an affirmative tone, and its beginning is staged by the central story of the Corpus Christi cycle: whatever else 'now' might be, it was historically the time of mercy.[33]

Yet this sequential concept of progress is secondary, for the sequence can only figure a unity. Thus Father, Son and Holy Ghost; Faith, Hope and Charity correspond to the historical triads above but represent a progression in degree, within a single unity, and are active, ever-present forces and principles. And Piers Plowman himself stands as an active, present force, the present manifestation of social man, spiritual man, Christ and St Peter. This rôle is something which the Dreamer cannot understand and he applies to Piers the same finite vision that he applied in his questions to Holy Church:

> 'Is Piers in this place?' quod I.
> B xviii 21

> 'Is this Iesus the Iuster?' quod I, 'that Iuwes did to deth?
> Or it is Pieres the plowman; who paynted hym so rede?'
> B xix 10-11

Piers for him must exist in one place and as one person (Iesus . . . *or* . . . Pieres) and this limited vision is the main barrier to the Dreamer's understanding. Basically, Dowel, Dobet and Dobest is a triad of unity, like the Trinity, not a triad of progression, like the historical groups. This is made quite clear by Clergy:

> For one Pieres the Ploughman hath inpugned vs alle,
> And sette alle sciences at a soppe, saue loue one . . .
> And seith that Dowel and Dobet aren two infinites,
> Whiche infinites, with a feith, fynden oute Dobest
> Which shal saue mannes soule; thus seith Piers the Ploughman.
> B xiii 123-124, 127-129

The Dreamer's false premises, like his earlier misguided questions, form the starting point for the exploration of a profound truth. Syntactically he has sought to define action as state, verb as noun, and has carried this further by establishing a progressive sequence of states which can be regarded only as a progressive intensity of action. The definitions which he receives are given in finite terms but the terms are infinites – syntactically incomplete and hence logically lasting for ever. The infinite can be approached and known only through the finite, and in one sense this is the progression of the *Vita*, but finite examples, existing in time and space, are inadequate manifestations since they are complete and cyclical. They represent the verbal aspect of the Dreamer's categories which must be reconceived in terms of the infinite noun-categories to which the Trinity and Faith, Hope and Charity belong. The recognition that states are subject to change is the basis of the poem's pessimism – the real world of change and corruption breaks in upon the 'ideal state' of the dream-experience with its unchanging allegorical figures, while the Dreamer hovers uncertainly between the two, demanding that a verb should be a noun and objecting because it cannot be. Meanwhile, Piers Plowman stands as the assertion of the nominal, himself an infinite in whom all triads meet and who unites time and space and defies change.

The Dreamer and Piers are in complementary rôles, but without the Dreamer there could be no poem, for one cannot dramatize a state. The conflicts of the *Vita* are foreshadowed in the *Visio* in a much simpler form. What the Dreamer sees is a physical picture, with the Tower of Truth, the Field of Folk and the Dungeon of Care, and when a pilgrimage to Truth is suggested one assumes that it will present the inhabitants of the Field ascending the hill to the Tower – a physical journey figuring a spiritual journey, with the duration of the journey being equivalent to the life of man. Piers, however, effects a characteristic fusion by destroying the Dreamer's physical picture. The people are to stay where they are and find Truth in their hearts and, as Burrow has pointed out,[34] a brief labour in the field becomes a substitute or an equivalent for the pilgrimage and an image of a lifetime's labour in the world. Yet the pilgrims cling to the physical image – they complain about the distance (vi 1-2), refuse to work in the field; and finally Truth's pardon is declared false on logical grounds by the priest. The intersection of the finite image of physical pilgrimage by the 'infinite' spiritual pilgrimage has its counterpart in the breakdown of the action. The point of the pilgrimage account is the sheer inadequacy of the image to sustain the meaning. The pilgrims are not first to 'honour their fathers' and next to 'swear not in vain' but are to do all these things simultaneously, and the spatial and temporal concepts of pilgrimage obscure the essential unity of Piers's message.

Piers's problem in directing the pilgrims is that of the Dreamer in his rôle of narrator, for although the dream-experience admits the infinite, any verbal expression, whether sentence or poem, is finite and limited. Just as dream-experience cuts the Dreamer off from reality, so the necessity of poetic expression prevents him from understanding or communicating the meaning of his dream. In contrast to the normal practice of a dream-poem, *Piers* presents a dream-experience in opposition to its verbal manifestation and demonstrates that an 'idea is translatable into words and fictions, but these may not faithfully represent the original.'[35] As narrator, the Dreamer sets a verbal barrier between the reader and his experience, and the poem becomes an expression of the limitations of poetry.

When Holy Church attempts to explain love to the Dreamer, she is compelled to use images, but shifts reference so frequently that the image breaks down:

> For trewthe telleth that loue is triacle of heuene;
> . . . And also the plente of pees, moste precious of vertues.
> For heuene myȝte nouȝte holden it, it was so heuy of hymself,
> Tyl it hadde of the erthe yeten his fylle.
> And whan it haued of this folde flesshe and blode taken,
> Was neuere leef vpon lynde liȝter therafter,
> And portatyf and persant as the poynt of a nedle,
> That myȝte non armure it lette ne none heiȝ walles.
> Forthi is loue leder of the lordes folk of heuene . . .
>
> B i 146, 150-157[36]

In the first line *triacle*, 'sovereign remedy', suggests a medicinal image, and *of* stands in a double sense – love is the remedy *from* heaven but is also the remedy which heaven exemplifies. The image then shifts to a botanical reference with a backward look to the opening medico-moral reference in *precious* and *vertues*. *For*, at the start of the next line, conceals a lack of logical connexion; if love was at first both 'of' and 'from' heaven, the two ideas are now separated, for heaven cannot contain love. Logically, the 'remedy' and 'peace' cannot exist while Man is separated from God, and hence God is *heuy*, 'sorrowful' as well as 'weighed down with love'. The plant of love has grown too big for its heavenly container – the image is becoming grotesque – and we are about to move from the idea of state to the idea of historical action, from objective love to its human manifestation. Yet the transition is too much for the image. The 'plant' now 'eats its fill', in apparent contradiction of the idea that it was already too heavy for heaven, and the eating image raises incongruous associations which can be eliminated only by rejecting the plant-image altogether (*flesshe and blode*); yet the tension still persists since the phrasal parallels suggest that *yeten his fylle of the erthe* is re-expressed in *taken flesshe and blode of this folde*. The whole problem is summarized in the reference to the earlier plant-image (*leef vpon lynde*) which has been proved inadequate, and to the paradox of the weight/eating image (*lyȝter*) which has also been shown to have limited application. Now a new idea, *persant*, is introduced and a new pattern develops. Firstly, the shape and size of the leaf is compared with *the poynt of a nedle*, then this visual image is abandoned for the more aggressive idea of a lance (*non armure it lette*), and then the idea of a 'point' is abandoned for the image of the battering-ram (*none heiȝ walles*), a progressive evocation of force. Finally, the depersonalized images are abandoned as love is personified as *leder*, continuing the idea of military conquest. The development is one of association – salve, plant, weight, food, flesh; leaf, needle, lance, ram, leader. The totality of love as a state and a force can be conveyed only through a succession of partially adequate images, and the two basic ideas of growth and conquest, vegetation and human endeavour, are both complementary and contradictory; the inadequacy of a single finite image to convey the infinite is the point of the passage. This is not the kind of language which the definitive Dreamer can understand, and it is not surprising that he tells Holy Church that she must do better, or that Holy Church points out to him that there are some things that cannot be, and should not have to be, explained.

On a larger scale, the same inadequacy of imagery can be seen in the description of the Tree of Charity which, even in its poetically superior form in the C-text,[37] utilizes an inadequate image. The account opens with the Tree attacked by the three wicked winds of the World, Flesh and Devil and protected by the props of the Trinity, but even this simple image is not fully sustained. Firstly, the image of the prop gives way to an image of violence:

> The Worlde is a wykked wynde to hem that wolde treuthe;
> Covetyse cometh of that wynde, and *Caritas* hit abiteth,
> And for-freteth that frut with manye fayre syghtes;
> And with the ferste plaunke ich palle hym doune,
>   *Potencia-dei-patris.*

C xix 31-34

The increasing violence of the verbs – *wolde, cometh, abiteth, for-freteth, palle* – gives the passage a rhetorical climax which obscures the fact that *palle* is an abandonment of the 'prop'-image – 'Langland's 'active' imagination immediately transforms props into weapons'.[38] Yet the *hym* against which the weapon is used is the world, and the world is a wind! Secondly, the image is again threatened in:

> Thenne fondeth the Feende my frut to destruye,
> And leith a laddere therto, of lesynges be the ronges.

43-44

though the rhetoric of the passage, its verse-movement and cumulative effects leading to simple, forceful assertions (*certes hit sholde nat stonde, and thus gat ich the mastrye*) conceals the abandonment of the 'wind'-image. The idea of the devil as a thief stealing apples and being beaten like a naughty boy would be comic if the passage was not the climax of a serious theme and did not carry the reader over its incongruities by the speed and skill of its rhetorical structure.[39]

The next section of the description is simpler and far closer to expository sermon-allegory in which the image is stated and then directly interpreted. The fruit of the tree is the three degrees of Virginity, Widowhood and Matrimony, represented by maidens and monks, widows and married men. The image is consistent in itself (although the visual suggestion of people hanging from a fruit-tree would, with consideration, seem odd), but it does shift the emphasis firstly from the concept to humanity, and secondly from state to historical events:

> Adam was as tree and we aren as hus apples.

68

Adam is not 'charity' and his association with 'tree' evokes the historical tree of the Fall;[40] Adam fell to the three temptations that the props of the first image ward off. Yet the passage is successful.

It is only in the third part of the account that the latent problems of the earlier images are brought to the fore. The basic contradiction occurs when the Dreamer asks that the tree be shaken by *som leef* and Elde, the enemy of life, appears. The notion of change and decay, of the passage of time, is introduced into what has been primarily a pictorial allegory. *Falle* (107) suggests the physical descent, but also the historical Fall and the idea of decline. Suddenly, by putting together the elements of the first and second sections, the Dreamer breaks the tree-image down:

> He waggede Wedewehode, and hit wepte after;
> He meuede Matrimonye, hit made a foule noyse.
> For euere as Elde hadde eny doun, the deuel was wel redy,
> And gederide hem alle togederis, bothe grete and smale,
> Adam and Abraham and Ysaye the prophete,
> Sampson and Samuel and seynt Iohan the baptist,
> And bar hem forth baldely – no body tho hym lette –
> And made of holy men hus horde in *limbo inferni*,
> Ther is derknesse and drede and the deuel maister.
>
> 109-117

The opening lines fuse the physical image (*waggede, meuede*) from the first section and the human image (*Wedewehode, Matrimonye*) from the second, but develop the image in the direction of sorrowing humanity (*wepte, made a foule noyse*) so that the original effect is left behind. *Grete and smale* refers to status, not size, and actual examples replace the fruit-image of the second section. Again a cumulative sequence is broken by the short, telling phrase, but here the phrases convey defeat and intensify the desolation contained in *wepte – no body tho hym lette, and the deuel maister*. Echoes of the earlier image reinforce its inadequacy – *waggede the rote* giving way to *waggede Wedewehode, his horde* offset by the terror of *derknesse and drede*. Now the image of misdirected violence, latent in the first passage, emerges:

> . . . hitte after the fende, happe hou hit myghte.
>
> 120

The three 'props' are now active agents and the image of the apple-thief stands as an irrelevant triviality against the sense of desolation and the seriousness of the ensuing action:

> *Filius*, by the faders wil, flegh with *Spiritus Sanctus*,
> To ransake that rageman and reue hym hus apples,
> That fyrst man deceyuede thorgh frut and false byheste.
>
> 121–123

That last line provides the moral and historical perspective and destroys the image of unchanging state that the Tree of Charity introduced. We pass through a further grotesque – a knight jousting with a thief for a hoard of apples – to the account of Christ.

This passage, on a larger scale, exemplifies the same inadequacies as Holy Church's account of love. The image is incapable of sustaining the two ideas of state and change simultaneously and hence breaks down. This breakdown is emphasized by the reference back to the starting point, so that the reader is made doubly aware that the image is inadequate, so that the breakdown is functional. But, above all, this breakdown of expression at narrative level corresponds to the breakdown of the dream-state by the Dreamer's logical interventions, and to the breakdown of an ideal reality by the forces of worldliness.

It is not surprising that the Dreamer's first question, *what is this to mene?*, is the most important, for it concerns not only the 'meaning' of life but also the 'meaning' of words. The Dreamer's problem in defining Dowel, Dobet and Dobest is essentially verbal, although verbal definition is impossible. In the same way, a number of terms are employed which cannot be verbally defined. *Truth* is used to refer to the owner of the tower on the hill, not *God*, for Truth is not only synonymous with God but also an active principle (contrast *False*) and its manifestation (contrast *Falsehood*). At the end of the poem Piers builds *Unity*, not *Holy Church*, for Unity is the harmony of God and Man, of man and man, and of man within himself; it is the manifestation of love, and hence wider than Holy Church. Yet because experience is fragmented, we can never understand these terms fully. The poem ends thematically where it should end – in Unity; but the real world intrudes, for there is disunity within the earthly unity. How then can the

Dreamer come to Unity? How can he know Truth when all he sees is False? How can he know Charity when all that he can see is false charity and covetousness (xv 147-159)? He is faced with the problem of talking about an ideal infinite with the outlook, and language, of a corrupt finite. If language is inadequate to convey meaning, and experience is too limited and corrupt to give understanding, how can he attain salvation?

If we regard the Dreamer as the representative of reality, of logical reason, of definitive language, it is clear that his account of his visions is going to be weighted heavily in the direction of the very world which he is trying to reject. Thus, when we read the account of the Field of Folk, we are aware that it is an uneven account, and for two reasons. Firstly, there are far more evil-doers than virtuous men. This may be attributable to the actual state of society or to the selective nature of the Dreamer's vision which may or may not come from him; but it may be the result of the Dreamer, as narrator, selecting the evil element in society. This latter view is strengthened by the second reason, that the treatment of the figures endows the evil-doers with the greater poetic vitality. It is the friars, the beggars, the pardoner who remain in the mind. Even when he refers to the virtuous, it is the image of the bad which remains:

> Some putten hem to the plow, pleyed ful selde,
> In settyng and in sowyng swonken ful harde,
> And wonnen that wastours with glotonye destruyeth.
>> Prol. 20-22

It is not merely the detail that strikes us, it is also the expression – the climactic movement, emphasized by the phrasal parallel of the b-lines, rising to *wonnen* and falling away in an irregular line with weak caesura and irregular alliterations; the parallelism of the half-lines is broken and *destruyeth* has a strong physical sense. And when he comes to real evil-doers, the friars, he gives an extended account which exploits the opposition of worldly and spiritual values in terms such as *profit, good, money and marchandise,* culminating in the unforgettable

> For sith charite hath be chapman and chief to shryue lordes.
>> Prol. 64

with its reversal of values fused in the physical image, with its absurd notion of the pedlar-confessor and the ideas of brotherly love and material gain contained in *charite*. Reality may be dominated by evil, but in presenting reality the Dreamer (who is not here dreaming words!) makes the sin memorable. He certainly could draw upon a sermon-tradition of denunciation which provided satiric models, but this kind of poetic vitality demands some compensating element. The appropriateness of the physical references, in detail and language, contrasts with the inadequacy of the imagery found in much of the exposition, where words convey an abstract fusion and there is a breakdown and loss of precision.

This lack of poetic balance is a continuing problem in *Piers Plowman* and affects the reader's response. Meed contrasts with Holy Church in appearance and characteristics, but Meed is far more vital than Holy Church and emerges as a much stronger figure. As a vice she is necessarily dynamic, and as that particular vice she is concretely manifested in an interesting variety of forms and is capable of dramatic action. Having real manifestations, she serves as a vehicle for lively social satire, aided by the fact that she is an allegorical figure with no moral faculty and hence is completely unable to evaluate her actions. This gay immoral consistency is attractive and Meed is the one figure at the trial who holds our attention and captures our imagination. Yet Meed, as an allegorical figure, cannot question or change herself, but can only manifest herself and attempt to justify her existence. Even at the end of the trial, Meed has not been changed into something capable of reconciliation with Conscience, nor has she ceased to exist. She has only been denied control of one king for a moment, and her continuing existence is a justification both for her prominence in the real world and for her vitality in the scene which the Dreamer narrates. The visions of the ideal state put forward by Conscience and Reason lie in a future in which Meed does not exist and have no reference to the corrupt present, nor does the poem hold out any hope of the realization of the ideal by investing it with immediacy or conviction.

This lack of poetic balance is continued in the confessions of the Deadly Sins. Many critics, following the 'thought' of the poem, would argue that the confessions of the sins represent the collective confessions of the people; thus Dunning says:

> The Confessions are real confessions . . . they are the Sacrament of Penance and not mere self-declarations or public displays of their characters by the Sins. . . . The Confessions are made on behalf of, and stand for, the confessions of the folk.[41]

But the dominant impression left by these confessions is not of repentance but of sin, and the vitality both of the manifestations of the sins and of the language in which they are described and describe themselves weights the poetic emphasis towards sin rather than repentance. As has been noted, part of the problem is the nature of allegory, for a sin is incapable of passing moral judgment upon itself; it may be sorry that it is a sin, but it cannot become a virtue, and indeed no absolution is pronounced upon the sins, and sinners appear among the crowd of pilgrims to Truth, unable to understand the nature of the 'journey' and finally disrupting the ploughing of the half-acre.[42] But the other part of the problem is the vigour with which the sins are realized. Had all the sins been portrayed with the brevity of Superbia and Luxuria, the idea of repentance would have been realized, but other portraits are longer, with more varied manifestations. And the language has strong imaginative vitality, e.g.:

> 'I am Wrath,' quod he, 'I was sum tyme a frere,
> And the couentes gardyner for to graffe ympes;
> On limitoures and listres lesynges I ymped,
> Tyl thei bere leues of low speche, lordes to plese,
> And sithen thei blosmed obrode in boure to here shriftes.'
>
> B v 136-140

There is no penitent note here. The idea of grafting sprigs of lies is comically appropriate and is worked out skilfully, with none of the complexities of the expository images such as the plant of love. When sin is so vividly realized, the idea of penitence recedes, much as it does in the worst morality plays where the comic vice steals the scene. When a figure like Inuidia says:

> 'I am sori,' quod that segge, 'I am but selde other,
> And that maketh me thus megre, for I ne may me venge.'
>
> B v 127-128

we can see little hope of reformation. The breakdown of order in Piers's half-acre is a logical continuation of such sin-centred poetry which is explicable as an illustration of the Dreamer's own outlook.

In contrast to this vitality, Piers's own account of the journey to Truth is very poor poetry. Much can be said in favour of the simplicity and clarity of this 'signpost allegory'[43] and there is no doubt that it occupies a key position in the development of the poem, but there is something in Ker's comment that:

> It is tedious to be told of a brook named 'Be buxom of speech', and a croft called 'Covet not men's cattle nor their wives', when nothing is made of the brook or the croft by way of scenery.[44]

It is still more tedious when compared with the racy, vital treatment of sin which has preceded this account. In fact, the inadequacy of the poetic method here parallels the inadequacy of the whole pilgrimage image which has been discussed above – it is comparatively simple to convey the idea of a sinful rebellion but extremely difficult to convey the concept of obedience. At a poetic level this unevenness is a further manifestation of the opposition between the dynamic and finite and the static and infinite. The Dreamer's account of the confessions of the sins presents a much more attractive and intelligible realization of sin than his report of Piers's address on the journey to Truth does for virtue.

At this point it is impossible to decide if the emphasis upon sin is intended to reflect a bias in reality, or in the dream, or in the Dreamer's account of the dream, but it is true to say that the Dreamer emerges as the representative of all the disruptive forces which he deplores. In a key passage, the dialogue with Anima, we find:

> '3e, syre,' I seyde, 'by so no man were greued,
> Alle the sciences vnder sonne and alle the sotyle craftes
> I wolde I knewe and couth kyndely in myne herte!'
> 'Thanne artow inparfit,' quod he, 'and one of Prydes kny3tes;
> For such a luste and lykynge Lucifer fel fram heuene.'
>
> B xv 47-51

It is a culmination of the warnings given to the Dreamer by Study, Reason and Imaginative against seeking illegitimate knowledge and it provides the key to the Dreamer's widest rôle. He does not seek in a spirit of humility but in a spirit of speculative curiosity, and the basic failure of his questionings is the strong personal element – 'How may *I* save *my* soul?' His quest for knowledge becomes side-tracked by irrelevancies. In passus xi he sees himself following Fortune through Lust of the Flesh and of the Eyes, but as old age approaches he demands burial in his parish church and is deserted by the friar-confessor; the thought of death should inspire remorse, but instead the Dreamer is sidetracked from self-knowledge into an attack upon the covetous friars. In passus xix he asks Conscience whether the figure he sees is Jesus or Piers, but instead of pursuing this key question, he is sidetracked into asking why Conscience calls Jesus 'Christ'. Even in passus xx, when beset by Elde once more, the Dreamer's cry is not for grace but for vengeance – 'Awreke me' (202). The Dreamer's inability to understand the nature of his own need makes him unable to distinguish between necessary knowledge and idle speculation. It is ironic, then, that this figure who, as Dreamer, has persistently diverted and misdirected his own vision, and, as Narrator, has distorted his account by giving a misleading poetic emphasis to certain aspects of his sub-ject, should now attempt to enter Unity, only to find that it no longer exists. The lack of unity in vision and poem are reflections of the Dreamer's own doubts about his identity, his rôle in society and his relationship to God – in fact, his own lack of unity. The sophistry and scepticism which he has expressed during the poem reflect the destruction of his means to salvation in his moment of greatest need.

Yet, if order and unity cannot be taught, they can be mani-fested, and Piers's rôle in the poem is this manifestation. He is a man in society, a ploughman in the real world with social and religious obligations, but he is also a figure in a dream who re-appears at various times in various functions, and as such he becomes a figure in the Dreamer's allegorical poem. The analogical principle is a two-way principle – the man who conforms to the will of God manifests God in the world.[45] Hence Piers, a plough-man, is also like Everyman, like an earthly ruler, like Christ, and the Good Samaritan, and St Peter. As the symbol of an ultimate Unity he is the fitting founder of Unity on earth and the mirror of the ideal pope. In a time of disunity, it is this unifying principle and agent that Conscience finally seeks. Piers is, apart from the Dreamer, the only figure to belong to all levels including the real, and he asserts the unifying principle of reality and of the poem against the Dreamer who at all levels disrupts the concept of order.

It is important to recognize the unity which Piers represents, since this constitutes the positive element of the poem. The Dreamer, as narrator, is bound by the demands of his poem's structure. Just as his first appearance, as a wanderer, seems to serve no purpose except a withdrawal from society, so his wanderings through the poem and dream in search of Dowel, Dobet and Dobest serve no purpose, since a dream is remote from the world of experience and no verbal statement can convey the meaning of Dowel. Ironically, the Dreamer's concern with the value or otherwise of learning reflects not only upon the ability of books to teach him, but also upon the ability of his book to teach his readers. If Piers, who has the certainty of Truth, cannot convincingly exhort the pilgrims, how can the Dreamer, without such certainty, ever convey the meaning of his vision?

The answer lies in the final level, the total structure of the poem, for both the Dreamer and Piers are figures in Langland's poem. It might seem so far as if the Dreamer's rôle in the total structure is that which he has in his own dream, to contrast with Piers. But although the Dreamer does contrast with Piers, it is evident that, in an allegorical poem, he need not contrast and that, indeed, because Piers is part of the Dreamer's vision, it is possible that the Dreamer has a part of him. A starting point may be Anima's statement:

> Therefore by coloure ne by clergye knowe shaltow hym neuere,
> Noyther thorw wordes ne werkes, but thorw wille one.
> And that knoweth no clerke ne creature in erthe,
> But Piers the Plowman, *Petrus, id est, Christus.*
>
> B xv 203-206

Clearly Piers is not Christ in the sense that he acted Christ's historical rôle, but only in the sense that in striving to be Christ-like he manifests Christ in the contemporary world. But is Piers then any different from any other man? He knows Truth *kyndely* where no other man does, and he manifests Christ as *no creature in erthe* does, but Piers is then the realization of the potential in every man, differing only in degree from others. If Christ is the historical pattern, Piers is the contemporary reflection of that pattern and to be Piers-like is to be Christ-like.

It is hardly surprising, therefore, that in the picture of Haukin, the active man, we have echoes of the ploughing of the half-acre. Like Piers, Haukin works for all, is the universal provider of bread, and he recalls a time of famine which reminds us of the previous episode of Hunger. Yet, unlike Piers, Haukin is sinful; but unlike the allegorical sins, Haukin is human and can repent, so that in him there is progress towards the ideal of Piers. Yet Haukin also reminds us of the Dreamer. He is a minstrel, though one of no talents, and a wanderer. He represents the intervening state of humanity between the observing Dreamer and the involved Piers, and his repentance marks the progression that the Dreamer seems unable to make. His penitence has a dramatic force which the picture of the Dreamer's entry into Unity, backed by the dominant image of a sceptical Dreamer and the immediate motivation of fear of Elde, lacks. The fact that the Dreamer in his arguments reminds us of the priest of the *Visio* or the idle speculators condemned by Dame Study marks his isolation from the ideal of Piers. His analytical observations undermine the unity that Piers asserts and his presence in a disunited church is final evidence of its failings.

Piers knows and manifests Truth but cannot explain his knowledge, while the Dreamer expresses himself but does not know or manifest Truth. The division between the letter and spirit of the law is the key to the poem. If the Dreamer could attain Piers's knowledge, then he would manifest Truth, or, more simply, the Dreamer would be Piers. Yet finally, when the opportunity reaches the Dreamer, he is incapable of taking it and Conscience has to set off again in search of Piers. The picture of total disunity at the end of the poem is not unexpected, but Conscience, like all allegorical figures, is both collective and personal. It seeks the ideal leader, the successor of St Peter, but it seeks also the Piers-like quality in the individual, the promise of which Piers held out to the pilgrims in the *Visio* and which is available to the Dreamer himself.

But it is here that poetic structure takes over from philosophy.

Paradoxically, although Piers is a creation of the Dreamer, Will cannot make the act of will which Anima says is necessary to knowledge. He must remain outside as well as inside his own vision, so that, while the identity of the Dreamer's own persona and Piers within the vision is possible, the Dreamer-narrator cannot step into the vision which he sees and sever his contact with the real world in which he began. Any man can be Piers-like, and hence Christ-like, for a moment, but no man can be Piers-like for ever, since the concept of a timeless, universal figure is a pattern imposed by a dream upon a changing reality. This is the final complexity of the poem – that the Dreamer and Piers are two sides of one man, William Langland, so that the poem represents the tension between the earthbound poet, imprisoned by his environment and language, and all his irrational hopes and visions which can never be known either through experience or through words.

Action and Contemplation in *Piers Plowman*

T. P. DUNNING

Twelve years ago, both the general editor and the present writer discussed certain aspects of this subject.[1] Dr Hussey showed that neither the triad active, contemplative and 'mixed' (in the Hilton sense) lives, nor the triad purgative, illuminative and unitive states is completely satisfactory as a definition of Langland's Dowel, Dobet and Dobest. I was principally concerned with the relationship between the *Visio* and the *Vita* in B; but in a brief third section of my paper, I sought to show how Langland, as a poet, had made use of the traditional teaching on the stages and grades of the spiritual life. The purpose of the following essay is to examine Dowel, Dobet and Dobest more closely in the context of late fourteenth-century and early fifteenth-century writings on Christian perfection and in the light of more prolonged meditation on what Professor Lawlor so rightly calls the 'non-sequential nature of the *Vita de Dowel, Dobet and Dobest*'.[2] I shall presuppose the main thesis of my earlier paper, that the *Visio* is concerned with the *animalis homo* and with the first stage of his regeneration; the *Vita* with the spiritual life proper. The *Visio*, therefore, does not represent, in my view, the 'active' life discussed by Bromyard and the popular treatises on the Paternoster, Ten Commandments, and the Creed: although the active religious life of the good Christian does include works of charity to the neighbour, it is essentially a life of prayer and penance – of worship of God; and it is the life to which Piers is called by the Pardon, as he so clearly sees (B vii 116-129). The message of the Pardon, repeated in so many popular religious works of the fourteenth century, is: *Non in solo pane vivit homo*.[3] In this essay, I shall be concerned with a closer interpretation of B, passus viii-xx.

I

The terms 'Action' and 'Contemplation' were widely current in England in Langland's time, as, indeed, they had been throughout the Western Church for centuries; but it is important to note that the terms are used chiefly in treatises written for religious, that is, for those who have left the world and bound themselves by vow to a special way of life. Since Langland's scope is the world, surer guides to his thinking are, on the one hand, scientific theological writings which explore all aspects of the good Christian life; and, on the other, popular manuals and sermons addressed to all Christians, in whatever state of life. The close correspondences Owst has shown in thought and sometimes even in words between *Piers Plowman* and some of these manuals and sermons seem to me to indicate that Langland is not really in search of anything. The questions the Dreamer asks in *Dowel*, *Dobet* and *Dobest* are rhetorical, designed to lead in the poem to exposition and discussion and to stimulate attention and a change of heart in its readers. The poem is a conscious literary work in which the traditional teaching is presupposed all through, and in which various aspects of this teaching relevant to present conditions in England are singled out and manipulated with often superb artistry in order to bring home the need for reform and to make clear the way in which it might be achieved. The motivation of the poem is Langland's passionate concern with the reform of Christian society, with the realization of the ideal city on the hill of *Isaiah* ii and Conscience's speech at the end of passus iii, a concern he shares with Bishop Brinton and with other preachers of the time, as Owst's still 'neglected chapter' abundantly shows.[4] For this reason, Langland is not greatly interested in the contemplative life as a state or way of life. His one extended reference in the poem to this way of life in common is laudatory, but relatively brief, and in a context which indicates that it is not a main concern of his if properly lived (B x 291-303). Otherwise, the contemplative way of life is represented in the poem mainly by anchorites and hermits: these are constantly mentioned, always very briefly, and always in regard to their being worthy of material support only if they fulfil their profession of a life of prayer. Langland is interested in the higher stages of the spiritual life chiefly in so far as a high degree of holiness is needed in ecclesiastics who have the care of souls, if they are to fulfil their responsibilities; and this interest is *always* directed towards the Christian people in general whose reform largely depends on the prelates and priests and the religious who teach and preach:

> The heuedes of holicherche, and thei holy were,
> Cryst calleth hem salt for Crystene soules;
>   *Et si sal euanuerit, in quo salietur.*
> Ac fresshe flesshe other fisshe whan it salt failleth
> It is vnsauory, for soth, ysothe or ybake,
> So is mannes soule sothly, that seeth no good ensaumple
> Of hem of holycherche that the heigh weye shulde teche,
> And be gyde and go bifore, as a good baneoure,
> And hardy hem that bihynde ben, and ʒiue hem good euydence.
>
>   B xv 422-429

II

In both the scientific theological treatises and in the popular manuals, the terms 'contemplation' and 'contemplative', while usually clearly defined, are also often used to denote the means by which the mind is led to the contemplation of God: withdrawing from bodily activities, reading, reflection, and, above all, medita-tion.[5] That is, the terms often denote a series of practices or set of activities. And these are generally discussed as practices which *every* Christian should undertake. For, unless the writer is expressly referring to the religious *state*, he uses the terms 'active' and 'con-templative' to denote two forms of activity of the *one* person, two aspects of the spiritual life of every man. St Aelred of Rievaulx warns every Christian that the Lord 'did not determine that we should be intent about Mary's contemplation and overlook Martha's labour, but he commended both to us and allotted certain times for the work of each':

> But those who think that some should be Marthas and some should be Marys are making a mistake and do not understand aright. Both these

P

women live in one castle, in one house; both are pleasing and acceptable to the Lord, both beloved by the Lord . . . Let them tell us which of the holy Fathers reached perfection without both these actions. But because both these roles must be played by each one, at certain times we should do those things which are Martha's; at other times, those things which are Mary's, except in the case of necessity which knows no law. . . .[6]

This principle is the very basis of St Thomas Aquinas's treatise on Action and Contemplation, which is mainly a summary and systematization of the doctrine of St Gregory and St Bernard.[7] The traditional teaching is echoed in English manuals and sermons. All through the second *articulus* of *Vita* in the *Summa Prædicantium* the spiritual life of the Christian, considered under Action and Contemplation in the first *articulus*, is referred to as *hæc duplex vita*:

Ad hanc autem duplicem vitam habendam multum movere deberet omnes mortales vitae presentis miseria.   436 r

But the miseries of this present existence ought greatly to incline all men to enter upon this two-fold life.

The author of the *Speculum Vitæ*, after outlining the practices of the contemplative life, declares that it may not be without active life:

Contemplatif lif is holy studye aboute þe loue of God and þe blisse of heuen. leue in fulle charite. Sette þe herte al in God and byleue. This lif semeþ a lif of grete reste. but who so useþ it wel hym behoueþ to be besy principaly in þre þynges. In redynge. praier. and byþenkyng . . . But ȝit contemplatif lif may not be. but it be medlede with actif lif. for fro þese two lyues comen alle goode werkes.[8]

And Bishop Brinton in a sermon preached on the first Sunday of Lent 1376 to what appears to have been a general audience, exhorts his listeners to alternate in their lives active and contemplative exercises:

Tercio vt in nouitate vite ambulemus opus est quod vitam actiuam et contemplatiuam alteremus frequenter. Exemplum in natura [Example of the quail follows] . . . Sed oportet quod frequenter descendat in mare mundi propter necessaria vite corporalis. Requiritur vt postquam erexerit alam deuocionis se occupando in operibus vite contemplatiue, sicut est orare, vigilare, studere, predicare, legere, et docere ac meditari, postea descendat ad opera vite actiue, sicut est pascere famelicos, potare sicientes, vestire nudos, sepelire mortuos . . . (*op. cit.* p. 349)

Thirdly, in order that we walk in newness of life, it is necessary that we alternate the active and contemplative life often. An example from nature [Example of the quail follows] . . . But it is necessary that one frequently comes down into the sea of the world because of the demands of the bodily life. So it is necessary that, just as when one has lifted up the wing of devotion, occupying oneself in the works of the contemplative life – such as praying, watching, studying, preaching, reading, and teaching and meditation – so one afterwards must descend to the works of the active life: for example, feeding the hungry, giving drink to the thirsty, clothing the naked, burying the dead . . .

Uthred of Boldon, in *De perfectione vivendi*, written c. 1374-76, sees the perfection of life in the Church Militant as what he calls the 'quadruple life', for he distinguishes 'inferior' and 'superior' grades in both the active and the contemplative life:

'The life of the Church Militant is divided thus:

1. Contemplative life, (a) superior, concerned with divine things (superior reason), (b) inferior, concerned with *sciencia* (inferior reason); cf. the speculative life, according to the philosophers, concerned (a) with immaterial, (b) with material things;

2. Active life, (a) concerned with the utility of the soul, (b) concerned with the necessities of the body; cf. the practical life, concerned (a) with moral virtues, (b) with bodily governance.

'The quadruple life, exercised now in one way and now in another, is the perfect life, as exemplified in Christ, St. John the Baptist, and the Apostles.'[9]

Uthred goes on to say that everyone is bound to this life in so far as he can fulfil it.[10] Furthermore, all these writers – and the tradition of Western spirituality since Gregory the Great – either explicitly or implicitly agree with St Thomas Aquinas that the division of human activities into active and contemplative is sufficient and complete.[11] Walter Hilton's 'medled lif', therefore, introduces an unnecessary and misleading distinction. As Dr Hussey has shown,

Langland mentions only active and contemplative lives, and shows no sign of having read Hilton. All teachers, however, agree with Uthred of Boldon that the higher the ecclesiastical office in the Church Militant the greater the obligation of perfection for the holder. Here we come to that 'second part of the active life' which is discussed at some length in the *Meditationes Vitæ Christi* and by Bromyard in the *Summa Prædicantium*, s.v. *Vita, articulus primus*. Since the pastoral care is ideally *contemplata tradere*, the good pastor ought to be *in statu perfectionis acquisitæ*.[12] That is 'how the contemplative life precedes the second part of the active life, and how the contemplative part stands midway between the two sections of the active life.'[13] Bromyard does not at first distinguish the two kinds of active life, which might indicate that he is dealing with a well-known traditional doctrine. His argument is that *vita contemplativa est securior: sed activa fructuosior*; and he develops his point chiefly by means of a comparison between two soldiers, referring on the way to the standard types of the two lives, Lia and Rachel, Martha and Mary: the soldier who defends his country in the field against its enemies performs more useful service than one who attends his sovereign amid the pleasures of palace life. But when he comes to the example of Moses coming down from the mountain of contemplation to provide for the religious needs of his people, and to the decrees of various Popes who refused the requests of bishops asking to be released from their pastoral charge to devote themselves entirely to a life of contemplation, it will be seen that his teaching is completely in line with that of the *Meditationes*:

> In the first part of the active life, it behooves the soul to be purified, corrected, and strengthened by the practice of virtues. Then in the contemplative life it has to be informed, illuminated, instructed, and trained. After that it can confidently go forth to help others and work at their perfection.[14]

In Bromyard, as in the other writers mentioned above, 'contemplative life' denotes mainly 'the practices of the contemplative aspect of life', as Bishop Brinton and the author of the prose *Speculum Vitæ* make explicit.[15] 'For we are always living, as it were, this twofold life, active and contemplative, and we often do not know how we ought to live, which is a great danger and the cause of great loss.'[16] Contemplation, properly so-called, is the fruit of the supernatural gifts of understanding and wisdom, as, for example, *The Book of Virtues and Vices* teaches.[17] But prayer and meditation, as Friar Lorens makes clear, must be part of the 'active' spiritual life, as well as asceticism, the practice of the theological and the moral virtues, and the exercise of the five other gifts of the Holy Ghost, if a Christian is to achieve the 'riȝtful knowynge of God' and 'parfiȝt loue'. This full perfection of Christian life is possible to everyone, in every walk of life, as *The Book of Virtues and Vices* clearly implies and as Uthred is careful to note:

> Nec gradus aliquis nec status in Christianismo secularis, religiosus aut ecclesiasticus qualiscumque reddit aut efficit hominem sic perfectum esse, sed eius conversacio virtuosa, quamvis gradus et status huiusmodi multum iuvent . . .[18]

> Neither does any office or state in Christian society, secular, regular, or ecclesiastical, cause or bring it about that a man is thus perfect, but his virtuous manner of life, although office or state of this kind may help greatly.

Uthred seems aware, too, of the distinction made by St Thomas, that the 'regular' or religious life is called the state of perfection, not because its members are perfect, but because they solemnly bind themselves to strive for perfection,[19] for although he is himself a monk and is writing primarily for monks, he roundly declares:

> alicui homini utilis et perfecta est conversacio secularis, cui foret vita regularis inutilis et penitus inperfecta.

> For a particular man, the secular life may be profitable and perfect – one for whom the regular life would be unprofitable and wholly imperfect.

III

According to the traditional teaching, then, doing-well, doing-better, and doing-best, in so far as these terms relate to personal Christian perfection, have no essential relation to states or ways of life; and this is surely Langland's view. So, too, *The Book of Virtues and Vices*, which leads 'euery cristen man' from the Commandments to contemplation, distinguishes 'þre staates of Godes children in erþe' not with reference to walks of life, but with reference to the gifts of the Holy Ghost: 'þorwe tweie þinges is a man holy: for to flee euele and to do good'. The first gift achieves the first 'þinge'; the remainder of the gifts the other: 'For to flee þe euele and to hate it makeþ þe ʒifte of drede; þe oþere sixe makeþ vs to do wel.' One is here reminded of the conversion of the folk in the field by Reason's sermon in passus v and of the message of the Pardon in passus vii. With reference to the other six gifts, Friar Lorens considers the three 'staates' of God's children, 'þe whiche þe Holy Gost ledeþ and conduceþ in erþe, as seynt Poule seiþ':

> Þat on staat is of hem þat beþ in þis world and lyuen as God comaundeþ and as þei bileuen and heren of here prelates. Þat oþer staat is of parfiʒt men and wommen þat han al y-sette here hertes oute of þis world and þat seen God as moche as a man may in þis lif, and han here conuersacioun in heuene and þe bodies in erþe and here hertes wiþ God. Þe þridde ben in þe mene staate, and gouernen hemself wel and oþere and lyuen after þe comaundementes.[20]

While the bulk of Langland's people are in the first and third of these states, the poet does denote the true line of progress for every Christian. Will's adventures in *Dowel* denote the man who has set himself to live the Christian life in earnest and is following the advice of Bishop Brinton and is giving himself to the practices of the contemplative life: the reflection begun with Piers's speech in vii (117-129) is continued throughout viii, ix, x, xi, xii. Scripture underlines the character of these passus at the beginning of xi, stimulating Will to meditate on himself[21] and then on creatures: this is the beginning of good Christian living:

> And þis manere of consederacyone es called medytacyone, ffor by þis maner of knawynge of þi selfe and by þis maner of medytacyone sall þou come to þe knaweynge of Gode by haly contemplacyone. Wiet þou þat þare es thre manere of contemplacyone. The fyrste es in creaturs. The toþer es in haly scripture. The thirde es in Gode hymselfe in his nature.[22]

The chief problem which exercised Will in his meditation, the place of learning in the good life, is resolved by Ymagynatyf in xii. In xiii, Will's setting off with Patience denotes the practice of the moral virtues. Passus xiv, in my view the climax of the poem, indicates the limits Langland sets himself in delineating progress in perfection. With Haukyn, who represents the bulk of the folk in the field, we are at the opening stages of the life of Christian perfection; and we remain there. But these *are* definite stages, namely the sacrament of Penance and patient poverty; and they are definitely and firmly presented. No progress in holiness is possible except through and by means of these. The beginning of the good life is the cleansing of sins in the sacrament of Penance:

> Christus . . . opera per peccatum mortificata viuificat tribus modis: contricione, confessione, et satisfactione.

> (Christ . . . brings back to life works dead through sin in three ways: by contrition, confession and satisfaction.)

> Confession is þe firste begynnynge to all good lyvynge. And it shuld be done afore all oþur good werkes.[23]

The next step is patient poverty – to be poor in spirit, the gateway to all Christian perfection: after counselling the practices of both the active and contemplative life, the prose *Speculum Vitæ* continues:

> þe þridde stappe of this laddre is poornes of herte. for in the kingdome of heuenes may no man be crowned but he that wonne hit here with poornes. and with victorie of his thre enemyes. that is the worlde. the flesche. and the deuelle.

(and the writer goes on to show how these may be vanquished by 'wilfulle pouerte', 'stidfaste suffraunce of hert' and 'uerrei meekenes').[24] This is the ideal set before Haukyn, but he is clearly in that third 'staate' mentioned in *The Book of Virtues and Vices*. He:

> Swowed and sobbed and syked ful ofte
> That euere he hadde londe or lordship, lasse other more,
> Or maystrye ouer any man mo than of hymself.
> B xiv 326-328

In passus xv, Langland turns to those who in virtue of their

office – *status vel gradus* – in the Church Militant are obliged
to practise patient poverty and to advance in contempt of the
world's goods and in the love of God. The line of progress is
maintained:

> Secundo vt in nouitate vite ambulemus requiritur vt vitam sanctorum
> imitemur feruenter. (Brinton, p. 348.)

> Secondly, so that we may walk in newness of life, it is required that
> we must fervently imitate the lives of the saints.

In passus xv, the lives of the Saints are indeed held up for imitation
and the highest perfection of charity inculcated, but always with
reference to prelates, priests, and religious, whose sound teaching
and good example is needed by the people.

If the *Vita de Dobet* be examined soberly, it will be perceived
that it does not imply any real progress from the point reached at
the end of passus xiv. Langland indicates, it is true, the *line* of
progress, by recalling us, in a striking way, to meditation of the life
of Christ; and in placing before us the figure of Christ, the Way,
the Truth, and the Life. The preacher of Sermon 45 of MS Royal,
taking the same text as Brinton in his Sermon 76, *In nouitate vite
ambulemus* (*Romans* vi 4), distinguishes four ways 'the qwych leden
men to heven that hem holden': 1. Of Christ's holy commandments; 2 Righteousness in word and deed, 'in þat þou may';
3 'the way of sothfastnes . . . *in veritate ambulantes*' (3 *John*, 4); and
4. 'the best and hyest of all, for all thyse other been bot pathes of
this hye waye . . . For Cryste hym-selfe is this waye, bothe lyfe
and trewth: Iohannis xiiii, "Ego sum via, veritas, et vita." . . .
Paciens and mekenes, svetelofe and kyndenes, mercy and pyty,
pouerty and penaunce – þise brengyn men to Cryste, þat is the
hye waye.'[25] But this last is the way Patience taught Haukyn; and
we are at once recalled to Haukyn in the opening lines of passus xvi.
The main object of *Dobet* and *Dobest* is to establish the very founda-
tions of Christian life within the Christian Church. As Uthred of
Boldon points out, affirming the traditional doctrine, the way of
perfection in this world is the way of *reparacio graciosa* through
Christ. Perfection consists essentially in the exercise of the
theological virtues of Faith, Hope, and Charity. Man is wounded
and deprived of these by sin; but by the sacrament of Penance

they are restored, through the victory of Christ.[26] Bishop Brinton neatly expresses the same doctrine in a sermon on Confession:

> Nobis subiugatis diabolo per violenciam *Christus obtulit semetipsum* in ducem nostre liberacionis; igitur ei offeramus cor nostrum mundatum. [And our heart is cleansed] per contricionem et nudam confessionem.[27]
>
> When we were subject to the devil through violence, Christ offered Himself as leader of our liberation; therefore let us offer to Him our heart which has been cleansed . . . through contrition and complete confession.

It will be seen, however, that Langland's technique in *Dobet* is a 'descending' one, descending, that is, from the point reached in passus xiv: the long discussions of Faith (for the Christian, essentially faith in the Blessed Trinity), Hope, and Charity precede the dramatic account of Christ's victory, which has made these gifts available to us. This is, no doubt, the reason why the poet, in the dream within the dream, follows his account of the Devil's carrying off holy men to *lymbo inferni* with a summary of our salvation (xvi 79-89; 90-166), which looks ahead to the Harrowing of Hell at the end of passus xviii, and thus gives point to the discussions of Faith, Hope and Charity during the rest of xvi and throughout xvii. But even by the end of passus xviii we are only at the very threshold of Christian life. Nicholas Love's mirror for simple souls (and his exemplar, *Meditationes Vitæ Christi*) *begins* with the debate between the four sisters, Mercy, Peace, Truth and Justice, which is an image of the manner in which the Blessed Trinity brought about our Redemption. The means by which we make use, as it were, of Christ's victory have yet to be established: the Church and the Sacraments, the subject of passus xix. The 'lewed vycory's' speech at the end of xix brings the Church up to the present time; and the world presented in passus xx is once again the world of the Prologue, where Haukyn has taken his place with the folk in the field. But this world is viewed here in passus xx in the perspective of passus xvi-xix and in the light of passus xiv and xv. Christian society is the Church, the Barn of Unity; and not only do men enter this barn by way of Contrition and Confession (xx 212-215), but they need this sacrament of Penance to be healed of the wounds caused by the deadly sins and to remain fast in Unity: Contrition keeps the gate of the Barn (xx 374) for

> þis sacrament of confession bryngeþ grace vn-to mans soule – not only grace but all oþur good werkes wurchynge, veritas et vita[28]

So the people are dependent upon good priests, in particular upon good confessors, to help them withstand the attacks of the seven deadly sins, champions of Antichrist:[29]

> Conscience cryed, 'helpe Clergye, or ellis I falle
> Thorw inparfit prestes and prelates of holicherche'.
>
> xx 227-228

Finally, the people are led astray by friars (see especially xx 275-291), as Bishop Brinton, no less than Langland, roundly declares.[30]

'Confession is þe firste begynnynge to all good lyvynge'.[31] By the exercise of Faith, Hope and Charity, by meditation of the life of Christ, especially on his Passion, by union with Christ in poverty of spirit and in meekness, we do well and are on the way to doing better. By making use of the means of holiness, of union with Him, Christ has provided in the Church, we can even do best. But if those who are our guides and the dispensers of these means do not themselves strive to do best, the majority of Christians will find it difficult even to do well. This, it seems to me, is the highly original use Langland makes of traditional concepts, *incipientes*, *proficientes*, *perfecti*, on the one hand; and the concept of states, *gradus*, in the Church on the other. Langland is certainly not thinking about 'the contemplative state' as such anywhere in the poem: in passus xv and again in passus xx he is directly concerned with *gradus religiosus* and *gradus ecclesiasticus* in the Church Militant, and with the principle stated by all theologians, 'et quanto gradus superior, tanto perfeccior',[32] for

> ȝif presthod were parfit the peple sholde amende
> That contrarien Crystes lawe and Crystendome dispise.[33]
>
> xv 530-531

Langland is concerned in his poem with the Church Militant in the England of his time, the greater part of which consists of ordinary people living in the world. These are presented in the

Prologue, brought to a focal point, as it were, in the person of Haukyn at the centre of the poem, and again recalled in passus xx, not this time in the political framework of the Prologue, but in the full perspective of Christian society, the Church, built up throughout passus i-xix. And his end is contained in his beginning: at the very end, we see dramatically presented just how the friars' merchandise and money march together; and how, because Holy Church and they are not holding better together,

The moste myschief on molde is mountyng wel faste.
                                                    Prol. 63-67

The Langland Country

R. W. V. ELLIOTT

In a poem as subject to diverging critical interpretations as is *Piers Plowman* it is perhaps as well to seek some common ground. For the reader of both the poem itself and its critics this may be a help, for *Piers Plowman* is as complex a poem as it is a rewarding one, complex in structure, in thought and intention, and in the movements and settings of its numerous episodes.

Much has been written in attempts to illuminate and interpret the spiritual pilgrimage or quest which most critics acknowledge as the central theme of *Piers Plowman*. The following examples, drawn from an embarrassing opulence of critical comment over the past twenty years and here arranged simply in chronological order, may serve as illustrations. E. Talbot Donaldson distinguishes between the concern of the *Visio* with salvation and of the *Vita* with perfection;[1] Elizabeth Suddaby takes the line:

> 'Lerne to loue,' quod Kynde, 'and leue of alle othre,'
>
> B xx 207

to be the poet's 'final statement' and the most 'adequate summing-up of the theme of the poem and the spirit in which it is written.'[2] S. S. Hussey concludes that it is 'the practice of the good life leading to salvation which I believe it was the Dreamer's (and so the poet's) chief concern to find.'[3]

Elizabeth Zeeman (Salter) writes:

> The deepest theme of *Piers Plowman* might, then, be viewed as an exploration of the journey to God through Christ – the reaching of the "treasure of Truth" along the highroad of Love: a study of the way in which Christ, with his doctrine of love, enables the pilgrim to Truth and his goal, Truth, to become one.[4]

Morton W. Bloomfield sums up the thesis of this book, *Piers Plowman as a Fourteenth-century Apocalypse*, in these words:

> Briefly, the thesis of this book is that *Piers Plowman* is concerned with the subject of Christian perfection rather than with salvation. The former is the creation of the monastic tradition and is the older and more social Christian world view. This tradition was still alive in the fourteenth century and in England. It is oriented towards the King-dom of God and eschatology. It finds its natural expression in the apocalyptic frame of mind and in corresponding literary forms. *Piers Plowman* can be best understood as an apocalypse that reflects this older Christian tradition.[5]

John Lawlor regards 'the awakening to self-knowledge as the precondition of understanding the truths so long accepted' as constituting 'the imaginative authority of Langland's work',[6] while Edward Vasta expresses a similar view succinctly in the words: 'What never changes is the subject of the poem: growth in the spiritual life.'[7]

Most of these views do not exclude or contradict each other; their divergence is rather a matter of varying emphasis than of irreconcilable differences in approach or interpreting what Lang-land said. And fundamental to every interpretation of *Piers Plow-man* (the common ground, if we like) is an awareness that the poem describes a search, however circuitous, however incon-clusive it may be, directed in the first instance 'to Treuthes dwellyng-place' (B v 564) and in the last instance 'to seke Piers the Plowman' (B xx 380). The theme of the 'search' or 'quest', whether in spiritual terms or in terms of knight-errantry and romantic adventure, is a medieval commonplace. We owe to this theme the greatest achievements in medieval literature, like Dante's *Divina Commedia* or *Sir Gawain and the Green Knight*, as well as the tedium of episodic narratives in which an idealized hero ac-complishes whole series of unlikely feats of arms and *amour*. But the one thing that all of these have in common – including even the mystical writings making use of symbols of ladders or journeys or pilgrimages – is some endeavour to create what Charles Musca-tine has called 'the locus of the characters and actions and their spatial environments',[8] a setting, if we like, or what John Lawlor, speaking of *Piers Plowman*, aptly calls the 'terrain' of the poem.[9]

How much these settings can differ, even among poems as closely associated in place and time as those of the fourteenth-century alliterative revival in the West Midlands and North-West of England, can be seen by placing side by side *Sir Gawain and the Green Knight* and *Piers Plowman*. The former contains a number of remarkably particularized landscape descriptions in which the selection of unusual features and the use of rare topographical terms suggest an indebtedness to real English landscapes known to poet and audience alike;[10] while in *Piers Plowman*, on the other hand, 'often the background against which characters meet is quite unknown, and this gives an impression of vagueness and greyness to the poem',[11] hence the justice of Lawlor's 'highly individual terrain'.[12] It is the purpose of this essay to examine the 'terrain' of *Piers Plowman* – what for convenience I have called the 'Langland Country', – in some detail in the hope that such a study may help in some way towards a fuller appreciation of Langland's poem and of his art.

The medieval dream poem, *Pearl*, for example, or Chaucer's *Book of the Duchess*, generally distinguishes between two settings, that of the actual world in which the dreamer falls asleep and that of the dream experience. In *Pearl* there is a marked difference between the subdued calm of the poet's confined 'erber grene' and the brilliance and spaciousness of the dream world of 'downeȝ' and 'klyffeȝ' and 'holtewodeȝ bryȝt'. In the *Book of the Duchess* the poet uses his bedroom as a setting to link his waking experience with the start of his dream, but soon wanders forth 'to the feld', 'doun by a floury grene' into 'the woode' where the Black Knight was sitting. Often the 'real' setting is heavily indebted, as in *Wynnere and Wastoure* or *The Parlement of the Thre Ages*, to what has become known as the 'May-morning convention', – the painting of a convenient opening picture combining pretty landscape ingredients – a convention which owes something to medieval rhetorical precept, something to the model provided by the *Roman de la Rose*, and very little to observation of nature.[13] *Piers Plowman* opens in this manner in the A and B texts:

> Ac on a May mornynge on Maluerne hulles
> Me byfel a ferly of fairy me thouȝt;

I was wery forwandred and went me to reste
Vnder a brode banke bi a bornes side,
And as I lay and lened and loked in the wateres,
I slombred in a slepyng, it sweyued so merye.

B Prol. 5-10

In C it is also 'May morwenyng on Maluerne hulles', but the bank
by the stream with its sweetly rippling water becomes simply a
'launde', probably just some grassy plot. The 'real' setting among
the Malvern hills is not elaborated further, although the vision
that follows may well have owed some topographical details to a
scene which Langland knew,[14] and it provided the poet with a
striking image:

Thow my3test better mete the myste on Maluerne hulles,
Than gete a momme of here mouthe but money were shewed.

B Prol. 214-215

We are told, in B vii 141-142, that the Dreamer awakes, after the
episode of the Pardon,

Metelees and monelees on Maluerne hulles,
Musyng on this meteles; and my waye ich 3ede,

but the 'waye' is left unspecified, a vague 'roaming about'

Al a somer sesoun for to seke Dowel.

B viii 2

Apart from the Malvern hills, only London provides Langland
with another 'real' setting, in the opening lines of C vi, and again
the poet makes no effort to elaborate. Clearly, what interested him
in his own actual environment was not its physical but its social
and spiritual landscapes, and it is these which he imaginatively
transformed into the visionary terrain of *Piers Plowman*. It is not
that Langland was any less aware of actual places than of people
and of spiritual matters, but his awareness was not expressed in
geographical or topographical terms so much as in imaginative
ones. Westminster is a place where worshippers of Meed live
(B iii 12), a place of law and the abuse of law (C xi 239, B xx 282 ff);
Winchester fair offers scope for dishonest trading (B v 205);
Dunmow, for all its gastronomical overtones, has primarily a
matrimonial relevance (B ix 168); Abingdon was of interest because

of its abbot, apparently a man sufficiently 'redoubtable' for the allusion to be watered down in the C-text to the innocuous 'Engelonde';[15] the mention of Pamplona (B xvii 252), an allusion to the Hospital of St Mary Rounceval at Charing Cross, linked here with Rome, shows Langland's bitter reaction to the dispensation of fraudulent foreign pardons from the hospital.[16] And similarly with the whole atlas of places whose names figure in *Piers Plowman*, from Babylon and Bethlehem to Bruges and Buckinghamshire.

The 'Langland country' is a constantly, often rapidly changing terrain, and it both reflects and contributes to the at times direct, often tantalizingly circuitous argument of the poem. Setting follows setting, each supplanting the next 'according to a very loose and vague imaginative logic in the *Visio*, and no logic at all in the *Vita*'.[17] From the field full of folk we travel to the king's court; the pilgrims to St Truth 'blustreden forth as bestes ouer bankes and hilles' (B v 521), blindly, helter-skelter; the poet wanders onwards

> wide-where walkyng myne one,
> By a wilde wildernesse and bi a wode-syde.
> B viii 62-63

Sometimes (as in the lines just quoted) we are in the real world; sometimes we traverse a dream landscape which has topographical features that can be visualized, however indistinctly; and at other times again such topographical features become the vehicle of allegory as in Piers's description of the way to Truth

> 'bi a broke Beth-buxum-of-speche,
> Tyl ʒe fynden a forth ʒowre-fadres-honoureth,'

and so on past 'a crofte' and 'a berghe' to 'a courte', all named in similar manner (B v 575 ff.), 'baffling' enough for W. P. Ker to have complained that 'nothing is made of the brook or the croft by way of scenery; the pictorial words add nothing to the moral meaning'.[18] Ker's complaint is understandable, but he was wrong in his conclusion. The topographical words do create a sense of terrain, an awareness of obstacles, of roads forking, of movement, indeed of possible if not actual progress. The symbol of the 'high road' is a persistent one in *Piers Plowman* and it is supported by occasional references to topographical features, however unconnected these may be into any properly composed landscape. To us, no longer reared on *The Pilgrim's Progress*, such directions as Piers's or Study's (B x 157 ff) or Scripture's (A xii 51 ff) may seem heavy-handed, oppressively artificial, but they are as much part of Langland's imaginative topography as the field full of folk or the vision from the 'mountaigne that Mydelerd hyʒte' (B xi 315) or the place of the jousting at Jerusalem in B xviii. What Langland's 'pictorial words' as well as his shifting settings and devious journeyings add to the moral meaning of *Piers Plowman* is suggested by Muscatine:

> His use of place and location – along with the other traits I have mentioned – suggests that for him, despite his doctrinal orthodoxy, the structure of the moral world – to which most of his predecessors could give coherent spatial expression – had become a thing newly problematic.[19]

The high road to Truth, to salvation, to perfection, to social reform was not, for Langland, as it turned out, the seemingly simple route mapped out by Piers. To this fact the poem bears witness, and it does so not least by the 'serpent-like movement' which John Burrow has shown to be 'essential to the progress of Langland's poem'.[20] Langland, as the critics have reminded us, is 'learning', 'growing', 'exploring', 'awakening' as he moves across the terrain of his experience and the topographical words are used not to provide landscapes as in *Sir Gawain and the Green Knight* but landmarks. No matter how we regard the latter poem, whether as a serious investigation into the ethics of Christian chivalry or, as I prefer to do, as a festive entertainment, comic in the fullest sense of that word, we may agree that the icy north-western landscapes of Arthurian 'faerie' as much as the lawlessness of fourteenth-century Cheshire are part of the challenge and the testing of Sir Gawain. In *Piers Plowman* there is no such attempt to integrate landscapes into the texture of the poem, but there is the endeavour to let the Dreamer's journeying and the terrain which he traverses express some of the questioning, the confusion, the bewilderment, as well as the growing understanding of his quest.

The keyword in all this is *movement*, for even the longer passages of debate and dissertation are not free from an undercurrent of restlessness which every now and then erupts into an orgy of motion. Langland's Dreamer is a wanderer:[21] from the opening lines of the poem to the final resumption of the pilgrimage in its last few lines there is movement, sometimes leisurely, sometimes, as John F. Adams has said, the 'poetic effect is one of immediacy and urgency: time *is* running out'.[22] At some points of the journey there is a deep sense of frustration:

> 'This is a longe lessoun,' quod I, 'and litel am I the wyser;
> Where Dowel is, or Dobet derkelich ȝe shewen.'
>
> B x 372-373

at others a sense of renewing hope:

> 'Sire Dowel dwelleth,' quod Witte, 'nouȝt a day hennes.'
>
> B ix 1

But through it all the Dreamer is carried forward, eager to persevere though often 'wery for-walked' (B xiii 204), meeting on his journey that numerous and varied company of figures – Thought and Clergy and Anima and Conscience and the rest – who people 'the weye' of the 'Langland country'. Much of the movement is steady, however uncertain the direction, but at times Langland accelerates his tempo, as in the Samaritan episode in B xvii 47 ff where the verbs of motion gather into a veritable *presto*: 'ac he flegh on syde', 'Hope cam hippyng after, and thus on to:

> 'For I may nouȝt lette,' quod that leode, 'and lyarde he bistrydeth,
> And raped hym to-Iherusalem-ward the riȝte waye to ryde.
>   Faith folweth after faste and fonded to mete hym,
> And *Spes* spaklich hym spedde, spede if he myȝte,
> To ouertake hym and talke to hym ar thei to toun come.
> And whan I seyȝ this, I soiourned nouȝte but shope me to renne,
> And suwed that Samaritan that was so ful of pite . . .'
>
> B xvii 78-84

All the major characters in *Piers Plowman*, as Elizabeth Zeeman has reminded us, are involved in 'the activity of travel, whether material or spiritual':[23] in B iv 23 ff. Conscience 'kaireth forth faste'[24] with Reason and others following; the friars of B viii 8 ff:

> ben men on this molde that moste wyde walken,
> And knowen contrees, and courtes and many kynnes places,

Bothe prynces paleyses and pore mennes cotes,
And Do-wel and Do-yuel where thei dwelle bothe.

B viii 14-17

Ymagynatyf, in B xi 429, 'shope hym for to walken'; Conscience
and Patience 'passed, pilgrymes as it were' (B xiii 215),

And as thei went by the weye, of Dowel thei carped

B xiii 220

a touch of medieval verisimilitude, to be sure, for it was then possible to discourse *en route*, as the Canterbury Pilgrims also did,
before the internal combustion engine and the jet engine made
such civilized activity impossible. At B xviii 112 ff Mercy and
Truth, and later Righteousness and Peace, come, respectively
'walkynge,' 'softly walkynge,' 'rennynge,' and 'playinge'. Langland
knew how to use verbs; as Rosemary Woolf has astutely observed:

> Whilst the dominant tone of the *Pearl* and *Sir Gawain* is set by their
> recurrent adjectives, that of *Piers Plowman* is set by the verbs, which
> constantly suggest abrupt and vigorous action – action such as leaping,
> jumping or rushing.[25]

While this is less applicable to the Dreamer himself than to those
whom he meets 'in the weye', for the verbs used to describe his
journeying are mostly *gon*, *walke*, *wenden*, and *rome*, it is true that
all the verbs of motion in *Piers Plowman* contribute something
towards the feeling of persistent exploration which the poem is
undoubtedly intended to convey.

That we are by no means always sure whither the exploration
is directed or whither it is leading may also have been part of what
Langland intended; it is certainly one of the principal impressions
the poem makes on the reader. Such vagueness is in part the
vagueness of dreams, and one wonders how far Langland was
deliberately reaching beyond the familiar use of dream allegory
into some kind of dream psychology. 'He does not exploit its [the
dream's] decorative possibilities'[26] because, unlike the poets of
Pearl or *Wynnere and Wastoure*, he is not interested in the embel-
lishment which rich description or colourful pageantry provide in
these poems. But, unlike these poets also, he is able to convey
aspects of dream experience which are much more akin to Freud
than to Macrobius. Perhaps Fr. Dunning dismisses too readily the

brief discourse on dreams in A viii 131 ff as 'of no particular significance or interest',[27] for Langland's comments, however unoriginal, are at least pertinent to his search for certitude:

> Manye tyme þis metelis han mad me to stodie,
> And for peris loue þe plouȝman wel pensif in herte,
> For þat I saiȝ slepyng ȝif it so be miȝte.[28]
>
> A viii 131-133

It is one of those moments in the poem of 'tantalizing awareness – of having been several times on the brink of knowing' which John Lawlor characterizes as 'very faithful to dream-experience recaptured in the first moments of waking'.[29] But equally true of *Piers Plowman* is Langland's refusal to 'strictly observe a line of demarcation between sleeping and waking',[30] hence the peculiar character of the 'Langland country', the wide sweeps across whole continents of spiritual experience as well as the sudden intimacy of two figures earnestly discoursing along a fourteenth-century English highway. To the world of dream experience belong also those shifts in time, ('Al a somer sesoun', B viii 2; 'thre days we ȝeden', B viii 112; 'many a ȝere after', B xiii 3; etc.) which make the chronology of *Piers Plowman* as hard to establish as its topography.[31] In the dream world of *Piers Plowman* anything becomes possible, 'for the fertile imagination of the allegorist works much after the manner of dreams' – so that (to vary Stanley J. Kahrl's argument somewhat) events, scenes, figures 'follow one another more by free association than by organic unity'.[32] The method served Langland well, for it allowed him to be both vague and specific, to combine the abstract with the concrete, to counterpoise the actual and the spiritual. Those who take the poet to task for an ill-structured poem[33] overlook the poignant reflection which *Piers Plowman* provides of a perplexed soul seeking certitude. Those who censure the shifting time of the poem ignore the co-existence in any man's life of years and seconds. Those who feel lost in the uncertain terrain of the 'Langland country' must remember that poet and Dreamer were at home as much in the Malvern country and Cornhill as 'on a mountaigne that Mydelerd hyȝte' and 'in Piers berne the Plowman'.

If the argument of Langland's poem is often riddling, his diction is remarkable for its simplicity, remarkable not solely because he is often probing profound spiritual problems, but also because the alliterative tradition throve on ornamentation. That this is true of his topographical vocabulary we shall see in a moment; that it is true of his diction in general has frequently been commented upon[34] but is worth re-stating in this context. No doubt Burrow is right in suggesting that Langland was writing for an audience which included many people not familiar with the rich vocabulary of other alliterative poets,[35] and we may assume that it was also an audience of to no small extent unlettered, 'lewed' people, whose familiarity with the techniques and diction of contemporary sermons would have provided some equipment towards an understanding of Langland's thought.[36] It is Langland's great merit to endow abstractions with flesh and blood, as in his justly celebrated portrayal of the deadly sins in B v, and to dramatize ideas, as in the building of Unity and the assault of the forces of Antichrist in B xix and xx. His use of simple figures of speech, as R. E. Kaske has shown, is just one device 'of stating ideas that are in some way difficult to express, in terms that will make them at once intellectually understandable and poetically stimulating'.[37] His use of colloquial language, even slang, is another: 'doted daffe' (B i 138; cp. B xi 417, 424); 'blynde bosarde' (B x 266); 'lewed Iottes' (B x 460); and so forth. But above all else it is Langland's command of what Lawlor has called 'a kind of natural rhetoric'[38] that enables him to express vigorously and often memorably what many a lesser poet has sorely travailed to express:

> Thus thei dryuele at her deyse the deite to knowe,
> And gnawen god with the gorge whan her gutte is fulle.
>
> B x 56-57

> That preyeres han no power these pestilences to lette.
> For god is def now a dayes and deyneth nouht ous to huyre.
>
> C xii 60-61

> He shal haue a penaunce in his paunche and puffe at ech a worde.
>
> B xiii 87

Langland's gift 'to see the highest spiritual conceptions in terms of a rooted concreteness, a firm grasp of the particular',[39] enables him also to describe the terrain of his spiritual pilgrimage in words firmly rooted in English topography. It is not a large vocabulary and many words which add a distinctive colouring to poems like *Pearl, Sir Gawain and the Green Knight, The Wars of Alexander,* or the alliterative *Morte Arthure,* are conspicuously absent from *Piers Plowman.* Characteristically, the largest group of topographical words in *Piers Plowman* is that describing whole realms and regions, words like *reame, rewme* or *contreie* or *londe.* It is to such words that the poem owes something of its macrocosmic quality, that sense of expansiveness which embraces kingdoms and continents, and which is reminiscent of the cosmic imagery of *Antony and Cleopatra:* '*Piers Plowman* is planned, as the opening lines tell us, on a cosmic scale: its dream province spans Earth, Heaven and Hell'.[40] The words in this group are mostly common words: *contray, coste, erde, erthe, folde, grounde, kyth, londe, marche, molde, reame, shire.* Their use varies, as in other alliterative poems, from the specific to the often meaningless tag, and in some other poems, too, notably *The Wars of Alexander,* their frequent employment creates a similar spaciousness of terrain as in *Piers Plowman.* Many of these words, admittedly, are but the staple of alliterative formulae,[41] and Langland's use of them is often mechanical:

> The moste myschief *on molde* is mountyng wel faste.
> > B Prol. 67

> Riden and rappe down *in reumes aboute.*
> > B i 95

or in this line from Skeat's A-text, with its instructive variants in other manuscripts and in the other versions:

> Was neuer gome *vppon grounde* seththen god made heuene,
> > A xi 170

where Kane's A-text has 'vpon þis ground' (173), as also in Skeat B x 224, while another manuscript (Kane's M) substitutes *moolde* for *grounde.* Not that it makes much difference, although the use of the demonstrative pronoun always modifies a mere formula towards more specific meaning:

> For thei ben men *on this molde* that moste wyde walken.
> > B viii 14

The moste partie of this poeple that passeth *on this erthe.*

B i 7

The word *londe* is frequently associated with 'lord' or 'lordship' in *Piers Plowman*, an alliterative convenience which Langland is happy to make use of:

Til thow be a lorde and haue londe	B xi 22
In londe and in lordship	B xiv 262
The lordeship of londes.	B xv 517

That many of these words are semantically dispensable in their contexts is shown by the gain in the reviser's

Out of the west, as it were a wenche, as me thouhte

C xxi 118

as against the earlier 'Out of the west coste' (B xviii 113).

A few less common words should perhaps be added to this group: *greot* in the sense of 'the earth, ground' is not common in the alliterative poems, nor for that matter outside them,[42] and in *Piers Plowman* it occurs but twice in the C-text (xiv 23, 177); *sokene* 'a district, soke' occurs only once (as 'Rutland soke' in A ii 75 (Kane), and B ii 110, and as 'Banbury soke' in the corresponding C iii 111); I have not found it elsewhere in the alliterative poems, although it occurs in place-names, mainly in the South Midlands and in southern England.[43] The word *waste* 'waste land' occurs once only in B Prol. 163 in the formulaic 'bothe in wareine and in waste', and is not common in other alliterative poems. The *Gawain*-poet uses it forcefully to describe the region of the Green Chapel:

Þer wonez a wyȝe in þat waste, þe worst vpon erþe.[44]

On the other hand, the related *wildernesse* occurs more often and provides Langland with a word that conveys vigorously something of the perils of spiritual journeying:[45]

For went neuere wy in this worlde thorw that wildernesse,
That he ne was robbed or rifled, rode he there or ȝede.

B xvii 98-99

That Langland was not always so sensitive to the power of a word such as *wildernesse* is sadly apparent from the incongruous apposition of 'a wilde wildernesse' with the sweet song of birds in a woodland setting that recalls many a medieval Maytime daisy meadow:

> And thus I went wide-where walkyng myne one,
> By a wilde wildernesse and bi a wode-syde.
> Blisse of tho briddes abyde me made,
> And vnder a lynde vppon a launde lened I a stounde,
> To lythe the layes the louely foules made.
> Murthe of her mouthes made me there to slepe.
>
> B viii 62-67

Words denoting fields and moorland, forests and woodland, add further dimensions to the broad terrain of the 'Langland country', although they are more sparingly used than words like *londe* or *molde*, and in the main more specifically, as in B xi 342-344:

> And ʒet me merueilled more how many other briddes
> Hudden and hileden her egges ful derne
> *In mareys and mores* for men sholde hem nouʒt fynde.

the last line of which the C version (xiv 168) reinforces into a double formula without losing the contextual aptness:

> In mareis and in mores, in myres and in wateres.

The temptation to be sometimes merely formulaic, apparent in this example, is as irresistible with words of this group as of the first; so we find 'in frythes and in forestes' (C x 224); 'the floures in the fryth' (B xii 219); 'on laundes' (B xv 293, 299); 'wylde wormes in wodes' (B xi 320, xiv 112); and others. Yet Langland was not devoid of sensibility in the use of some of these topographical words. Perhaps he owed the word *croft*, in the sense of a small, usually enclosed, piece of agricultural land, to his own roots in the countryside of the West Midlands, for while the word is common in field names it is rare in fourteenth-century poetry. Piers uses it in his allegorical directions in B v 581 and in the appropriately rustic register of:

> And bi that, I hope to haue heruest in my croft.
>
> B vi 292

Uncommon also and equally well chosen is *wareine* 'warren', first recorded in *Piers Plowman* (B Prol. 163) according to the *New English Dictionary*, though increasingly common in later field names. Other words in this group beside those mentioned are the *shrobbis* of C i 2 (Skeat; Salter and Pearsall's text has *shroudes* as in A and B), *felde, hethe, leye,* and perhaps we should include *gardyn* and *herber.* That Langland altogether eschews the phrase *on bent,* so common in the alliterative poems, and more often than not a mere tag, should perhaps be accounted to his credit. That he did not know it is unthinkable, especially if, as is likely, he knew *Wynnere and Wastoure* where the word *bent* occurs four times. Even the *Gawain*-poet, whose topographical vocabulary is particularly interesting and who uses *bent* discerningly a number of times, is not above making a tag of it.

A third group of topographical words adds its share to the theme of the wayfaring and wandering of Langland's Dreamer, although only two of them, *gate* and *wey,* are used extensively. The other three words, *lane, path,* and *strete,* are as exceptional in *Piers Plowman* as elsewhere in fourteenth-century poetry. *Lane,* for example, I have found only in *The Pistill of Susan* and once in Chaucer (*Canon's Yeoman's Prologue* 658) in a line strongly reminiscent of alliterative verse in general and *Piers Plowman* in particular:

Lurkynge in hernes and in lanes blynde,

which recalls Langland's 'lorkynge thorw lanes' (B ii 216) as well as his 'hidden hem in hernes' (B xviii 402). For the constant reference to the Dreamer's (and the poet's own) road Langland prefers *gate* and *wey,* often the 'heiȝe gate' (as in B iv 42) or the 'heigh wey' (as in B xii 38). The theme of people going 'forth in here wey' (B Prol. 48) is a persistent one in *Piers Plowman,* and the poet's virtual restriction to the two most familiar words (which, incidentally, are the only two the poet of *Sir Gawain and the Green Knight* uses) may be a deliberate emphasising that the Dreamer's spiritual pilgrimage is indeed a quest common to all men along the familiar 'heigh waye to-heuene-ward' (B xiv 211).

If the 'road' words denote movement and progress, however circuitous, the small group of 'cave' words and the larger group of words denoting hills and valleys add little variety to the landscapes of *Piers Plowman.* The three words denoting caves are negligible to the meaning of the poem, although *spekes* appears to be unique to *Piers Plowman* in the phrase 'in spekes and in spelonkes'

(B xv 270). The latter word occurs also in *The Wars of Alexander* and in *Mandeville's Travels* and is twice used of the coffin in *St Erkenwald*. *Herne* derives from Old English *hyrne* 'corner' and effectively conveys the sense of a hiding place in the phrase quoted above and in the forceful movement of the line

> Alle fledden for fere and flowen into hernes.
>
> B ii 233

Compared with *Sir Gawain and the Green Knight* as well as with other alliterative poems, *Piers Plowman* is not rich in 'hill' words, – *berghe, bonk, doune, hulle, mount, mountaigne, toft*, – and of these only the last is of lexical interest. It derives from Old Norse *topt* and appears in late Old English as *toft* with the meaning 'homestead, site of a house' or 'a place where a messuage has stood', which is the meaning Dr Johnson, for example, records. In dialect, however, it developed the meaning of 'a hillock in flat country', which the *New English Dictionary* first records in *Piers Plowman* where the word occurs in B Prol. 14:

> I seigh a toure on a toft trielich ymaked,

and in B i 12:

> 'The toure vp the toft,' quod she, 'Treuthe is there-inne.'

Some of the A-text scribes, according to Kane's variants, appear to have been sufficiently unfamiliar with *toft* to have substituted other words. The C-text retains the second occurrence of *toft*, but for B Prol. 14 is has the rather feebler:

> And sawe a toure, as ich trowede, truthe was therynne.
>
> C i 15

It would be foolish to claim that the handful of 'hill' words in *Piers Plowman* achieves anything like the superb scenic effects which the *Gawain*-poet manages to create with vigorous words like *clyffe, cragge, felle, knarre, knot, scowte*. For such effects a much more consistent depicting of landscape is required as well as the pictorial and auditory qualities of the words themselves. Langland is content with a bare mention or two of 'Maluerne hulles', with the 'berghe Bere-no-false-witnesse' as a piece of moral topography, with the 'mountaigne that Mydelerd hyȝte', and a few other protuberances in his spiritual landscape. Perhaps the gentle slopes of the Malvern hills were inadequate to produce in Langland the sense of scenic grandeur evinced by the '*Gawain* country'; perhaps, and rather more probably, Langland saw the world, whether as the field full of folk or from the mountain of Earth or in the final passus of the poem, as 'the plain of earth, set between Heaven and Hell . . . seeing everything at a glance – a God's eye view',[46] in which a mountain is aptly called a *toft* – a hillock in flat country. Similarly, the wanderer's more earth-bound vision from the 'heigh wey' is flat, broken by journeying figures rather than by natural features.

And if hills are few in *Piers Plowman*, valleys are even fewer. Again the interest of the words here is lexical rather than artistic. Apart from the reference to the 'pas of Altoun' in B xiv 300, Langland uses the common words *dale* and *vale*, as well as the rarer *valay* and *bache*. Both these appear to have troubled the copyists. Where A vi 2 (in Kane's edition) has 'ouer [baches] & hilles', the variants record *valeis* (thus Skeat, and Knott and Fowler[47]), *dales* and *bankes*. The B-text in Skeat (v 521) has 'ouer bankes and hilles', a safe formula for which the alliterative poems provide numerous parallels. The C-text (viii 159) reverts to 'ouer baches and hulles'[48] which is probably what Langland wrote, for *bache* is a good west-midland word for a valley or stream and is found in place-names in Cheshire, Shropshire, and Herefordshire, the 'real' Langland country, if we like.

There is no watery obstacle in *Piers Plowman* such as confronts the Dreamer in *Pearl*, and although the *borne* at the opening of *Piers Plowman* 'sweyued so merye', holding out promise of 'plesaunces' to come, little topographical use is made of water in the poem. It plays a part in the spiritual landscape, to be sure, but it is a minor rôle, and the words Langland uses are all plain ones: *borne, broke, dich, flode, ryuer, see, welle*, and the word *water* itself. Langland's wanderer is no seafarer: the only river he knows well, as befits one living 'in Londone and on Londone bothe' (C vi 44), is the Thames, and the only expanse of water with which he is at all familiar is Noah's Flood.

This brief survey of Langland's topographical vocabulary will have confirmed two important points made earlier in this essay: the plainness of much of the poet's diction, and the essentially macrocosmic character of the terrain of *Piers Plowman*.

The simplicity of Langland's diction, as far as his topographical

words are concerned, is not only that of the common words on
which he mainly relies, but also, paradoxically, that of his uncommon words, for words like *bache* and *toft* and *wareine* are
country words, some of them more particularly west-midland
words. Despite his residence in London, Langland was a west-
midland man, and to the evidence examined by M. L. Samuels to
determine the linguistic provenance of the three texts of *Piers
Plowman*,[49] may well be added such modest pointers as the reappearance of *baches* in the C-text, which Samuels concludes to
have circulated in the poet's own native areas of the Malvern Hills.
But such words are few, and it is more sensible to argue that the
whole of Langland's topographical vocabulary must take its place
with the colloquialisms and the domestic imagery (as in B xvii
315 ff), the numerous proverbs and much else besides as constituting the characteristic idiom of the poem, as well as contributing
towards the poet's power of making the abstract palpable.[50]
Piers's allegorical signposts to Truth point along a spiritual highway, but the landmarks are firmly grounded in English topography:
a brook, and a ford, and a croft, and a hill, leading to a stronghold
such as must have been familiar to every medieval English way-
farer. Langland probably had no particular landscape in mind, it is
too much a set piece for that, but he knew the English countryside
and used its vocabulary to create the spiritual *reame* in which the
quest for Truth was to take place. Anything less firmly rooted in
the facts of topography might have smacked too much of 'faerie'
for so serious an enterprise. And, *mutatis mutandis*, these comments
may be applied to other sections of the poem, both *Visio* and *Vita*,
in which setting or terrain is at all elaborated.

The opening vision of the field full of folk immediately estab-
lishes the duality of the 'Langland country': its mingled, sometimes
confused, spiritual and, in contemporary terms, realistic features.
Within a few lines of his opening Langland can say, without
incongruity:

> Some putten hem to the plow . . .
> And some putten hem to pruyde . . .
> B Prol. 20, 23

a juxtaposition as warranted in the context of this vision as is the
sight of hermits going to 'Walsyngham' (B. Prol. 54) when we have

only just been taken into 'a wildernesse wist I neuer where' (B Prol. 12). No wonder that in a poem so eager to plunge *in medias res* the course should be a 'riddling' one, that we should lose all count of time, and that we should find ourselves at one moment in an English tavern and at another on Calvary. Langland's topographical vocabulary is a small ingredient in all this, but it adds its share: positively, by establishing a spacious flatness across which Langland's 'gates' and 'ways' criss-cross like a modern road map of England; negatively, by not mapping movement too clearly, by not suggesting either progress or stagnation unequivocally. Comparison with other poems is instructive here. In *Pearl* the Dreamer's progress also takes place in no man's land:

I ne wyste in þis worlde quere þat hit wace —[51]

but it is orderly progress, and the landscape, for all its symbolic opulence and mystical colouring, can be visualized step by step. In *Sir Gawain and the Green Knight* the hero leaves the world of Arthurian romance to cross into Wirral, a deliberate signpost, as I believe, to that other landscape in which 'an old caue, Or a creuisse of an olde cragge' is the central feature. And when the *Gawain*-poet wishes to indicate a different type of movement, as in the confused entanglement of the fox hunt or the wide sweeps across country, around hills and along valleys, as in the boar hunt, he uses significant topographical words and appropriate verbs to create the desired effect.

Langland's mode, as we have seen, is different, 'an alternate dawdling and darting movement'[52] against a changing background that allows 'realistic' fourteenth-century scenes to melt into biblical landscapes and into a spiritual terrain where ideas become figures and words are made flesh. And it all ends where it began, among 'folk' like the 'brewere' and the 'lewed vycory', a 'lorde' and a 'kynge', a 'mansed preste of the marche of Yrlonde' and the friars. The 'Langland country' is circular, like the world which it represents.

A study of the 'terrain' of *Piers Plowman* and its vocabulary can thus in some way contribute to our understanding of Langland's design and an appreciation of his art. Perhaps such a study does no more than confirm the perplexities of the Dreamer's search, but then these are a central fact in the poem. Perhaps it does no more than underline the poet's 'natural rhetoric', but then this is the mainstay of his art. In the study of a great poem, such as *Piers Plowman* is, no detail is so unimportant as to warrant neglect. And not only the poem, but the poet himself,[53] may become a little more familiar. The words drawn from the west-midland country-side are few in *Piers Plowman*, but they are genuine; the knowledge of actual places which the poem evinces is meagre, but the intimate scenes of the poem are sharply and authoritatively drawn; the actual distances which William Langland travelled in his life were probably short ones, even by medieval standards, but in his spiritual wayfaring the poet of *Piers Plowman* traversed the *reames* of all human experience.[54]

Charity in *Piers Plowman*

W. O. EVANS

However else *Piers Plowman* may be described, it is above all a work of personal exploration, an attempt by a man we call William Langland to examine his own life in its spiritual, intellectual and physical totality. And this man, strong and passionate, was honestly and completely committed to finding out how to live best in accordance with God's will, in his particular society; he was concerned with setting out the difficulties and contradictions of life and coming to terms with this complexity in all its fullness, and was prepared to examine in public the apparently irreconcilable answers about life and death offered to him by his own natural understanding, his learning and his religion. We can be certain, then, that because of the nature of the poem we can arrive at no clear-cut tidy definition or exposition of what Langland considered essential to a life dedicated to God's will – charity or love. The more a man ponders the meaning of life and how it should be lived, the more he is likely to see many sides to any particular problem; he is likely to be less certain of earlier exclusive enthusiasms, and more able to entertain apparently contradictory views even at one particular moment in time. After all, a conviction in a matter of faith may be held on fifty-one per cent belief and forty-nine per cent doubt, and Langland is prepared to expose all the complexity of his thought, belief and counter-belief. The reader is not helped, either, by the fact that in *Piers Plowman* the complexities and difficulties are not objectified, 'distanced' from the author, by being set in fables and controlled by the total form of the work as, for example, in Chaucer and Shakespeare. In spite of his use of allegorical figures, Langland does not objectify in this sense. The poem is referable, rather, to the art of the pulpit[1], specifically didactic and polemical, and the whole expresses a fierce personal wrangle within the poet. Such form as it has mirrors life most closely – wandering, searching, progressing and then apparently retrogressing – the life of a man continuously in search of living as God would wish him to live. Significantly, the poem has no formal end.

No definitively formed answers can be expected from such a work; or, rather, so many answers may be found, and they may be so contradictory, that none will be an adequate statement of Langland's position. The best we can do is abstract recurring and dominant attitudes and infer from these the onus and general drift of Langland's thoughts and beliefs. To do this is, of course, to lay oneself open to the charge that quotations have been selected and presented out of context to substantiate a predetermined view, that the poem is being used, indeed, as it was used in the fifteenth and sixteenth centuries and as the Bible has been used from time to time. In fact, few interpretive statements can be made about *Piers Plowman* which are not open to counter demonstration because the method of argument often used by Langland is the traditional one used, for example, by Peter Lombard in his *Sentences* and by other theological writers: the pitting of scriptural quotations expressing one view against other quotations expressing a seemingly contrary view and the seeking of a compromise answer which would reconcile the two. Although the method may be similar, the purpose is different, for Langland is not writing a theological textbook but a poem of personal exploration, so he will return to the same problem again and again, worrying it to find an answer to satisfy himself. Often he finds no final answer, but we can infer the direction in which his mind was moving. Needless to say, any such inference should be checked by the reader against his own reading of the text.

Another problem inherent in determining Langland's dominant attitude in any matter is this: how much weight or authority did the author intend to give to his various abstractions or personifications, whether of 'faculties' or 'accidents' of the individual soul or externals such as Scripture or Study? We cannot assume with certainty a hierarchy in Langland's mind, since often the theologians them-

selves were not in agreement: for instance, as to whether reason or
conscience was the superior faculty of the soul. Instead we have to
assess the tone of the verse to determine the weight of his conviction. And this is not easy to do, especially since contradictions
may be posed by a single character in the course of the same speech.
There is one instance where Riʒtwisnesse, usually reliable and
without modern connotations of self-righteousness, is proved
absolutely wrong by Pees.[2] Obviously, specific points of view can
easily be common ground to most of the abstractions or personifications, and with this possibility of overlapping comes an almost
inevitable carelessness at times in ascription of ideas to speakers.
This is why it is so important to remember that the author has
written *all* the parts and manipulates *all* the puppets. These
abstractions are projections of arbitrary, and not always very
satisfactory, distinctions in the author's mind, and one distinction
apparently rejected in one instance may well triumph in another.
And in this context we might remember that Langland even puts
the first genuine clue to a definition of Dowel into the mouth of a
representative of a class he hates consistently and unequivocally –
the friars: it is a friar who first tells the Dreamer that Dowel is
'Charite the champioun' (viii 46).[3]

What general impression of the author's character emerges
from the poem? A superficial reading might seem to render doubtful a claim that the poem's main message is that charity or loving-
kindness is the universal panacea, for Langland himself appears as
an extremely irascible man, with a very long list of fiercely
expressed dislikes and even hates. The clergy bear the brunt of his
anger, from members of the papal and bishops' courts to ordinary
parish priests, pardoners and especially friars. Next in his rogues'
gallery come all those connected with the law, followed by doctors,
grocers, minstrels, vulgar jesters and shoddy workmen of any kind.
Very few escape his abuse at one time or another, but Langland is
very clearly aware of his failings in this respect because he makes
various abstractions rebuke them in the Dreamer, who in this case
can safely be identified with the author. The Dreamer is upset and
disturbed when Scripture attacks him directly:

> Thanne Scripture scorned me and a skile tolde,
> And lakked me in Latyne and liʒte by me she sette,

And seyde, '*multi multa sciunt, et seipsos nesciunt*'.
Tho wepte I for wo and wratth of her speche,
And in a wynkyng wratth wex I aslepe.

xi 1-5

And, a little later, Reason advises the Dreamer to learn how to
control his tongue better, 'And ar thow lakke eny lyf, loke if thow
be to preyse!' (379), because no one is perfect; at this rebuke the
Dreamer is ashamed and begins to blush. Almost immediately
after, Ymagynatyf ('Creative reflection')[4] tells him that he might
be a philosopher if he could manage to keep quiet – *Philosophus
esses, si tacuisses* (406); Ymagynatyf even couples the poet's occupation with that of the hated friars, and the Dreamer humbly accepts
the criticism, together with a rebuke for mocking at logic, law and
learning generally, and particularly for despising priests. One of
the assets in the marriage charter of Falsenesse and Mede is that
they may 'iugge here euene cristene' (ii 94), which is what Langland seems to do a great deal of the time. Indeed, the poem is
studded with indications that Langland was very much aware of,
and concerned about, his own impatience and lack of charity in this
respect. One can see the implied self-rebuke, for instance, in the
different attitudes of the Dreamer and Patience at Conscience's
dinner: the Dreamer frets at the doctor's fine food and the way
he gulps it, while Patience expresses only gratitude for his own
meagre provision.

Sometimes Langland tries to justify his practice of denunciation.
In passus xi, for instance, complaining, within the framework of a
dream, about the venality of friars, the Dreamer concludes by saying how much he would like to tell this dream openly among the
people. Lewte (Loyalty or Good Faith) replies, why on earth
should you not? and quotes '*Non oderis fratres secrete in corde tuo,
set publice argue illos*' (xi 87). The Dreamer says that this could be
countered by '*Nolite iudicare quemquam*' (that ye be not judged).
On the other hand, says Lewte, there is little point in the (moral)
law if no one is to stand out against evil. The conclusion of this
discussion is that what is unknown to others should be left hidden,
but what is already known denounced:

Thinge that al the worlde wote, wherfore shuldestow spare
To reden it in retoryke to arate dedly synne?

Ac be neuere more the fyrste the defaute to blame;
Thouȝe thow se yuel, sey it nouȝte fyrste, be sorye it nere amended.
No thinge that is pryue publice thow it neuere,
Neyther for loue laude it nouȝt ne lakke it for enuye.

xi 97-102

Here is an example of Peter Lombard's method of arguing, not, however, for the requirements of a theological or moral manual, but for trying to resolve difficulties in the poet's own mind.

But Langland's apparent anti-charity, his irascibility, his quickness to condemn and rebuke are in any case not necessarily contrary to the concept of charity we shall see emerging from his work. As long as it is directed, like Chaucer's Parson's 'goode ire,' against evil and towards the correction of the individual, towards ultimate good and the greater glory of God, it is far more charitable than, for instance, the pleasant flattery of Haukyn which is directed towards his own self gain.

II

Langland is deeply convinced that love is the panacea for all troubles; he believes it can achieve anything. For instance, when the Dreamer, old and destitute, asks Kynde (Nature) what he can do with his life, Kynde tells him to leave every other occupation and learn to love. But how is the Dreamer to keep alive?

'And thow loue lelly,' quod he, 'lakke shal the neure
Mete ne worldly wede whil thi lyf lasteth.'

xx 209-210

This love is what the clergy should preach and practise, and when Langland complains about them, as he does so frequently, his bitterness springs from the feeling that because they themselves lack charity they are nullifying or making inoperative the great spiritual power they possess. His particular vision of the Golden Age is of a time when charity reigned supreme, when clerics rejoiced only in the Cross of Christ rather than in the cross on a gold piece. In those days there 'was plente and pees amonges pore and riche' (xv 500). Charity is superior to all other virtues: at the beginning of the *Visio* Holy Church instructs the Dreamer that 'chastite withoute charite worth cheyned in helle' (i 186) – not a frequently expressed sentiment in the Middle Ages; Scripture says that faith without charity is of no avail; and the Samaritan tells the Dreamer:

> Be vnkynde to thin euene-cristene, and al that thow canst bidden,
> Delen and do penaunce day and ny3te euere,
> And purchace al the pardoun of Pampiloun and Rome,
> And indulgences ynowe, and be *ingratus* to thi kynde,
> The holy goste hereth the nou3te ne helpe may the by resoun.

xvii 250-254

Trajan says that only love could have dragged him out of hell; no study or learning could have achieved it. 'The seuene artz [the subjects of the Trivium and Quadrivium] and alle' (xi 166) are useless unless informed by and directed towards love. And when Conscience asks Clergy (Learning) for his explanation of Dowel, Clergy dare not answer until he and his seven sons are of accord:

> For one Pieres the Ploughman hath inpugned vs alle,
> And sette alle sciences at a soppe, saue loue one,
> And no tixte ne taketh to meyntene his cause,
> But *dilige deum* and *domine, quis habitabit, etc.*

xiii 123-126

This, of course, derives from St Augustine's doctrine that the only legitimate end of study and art was 'to promote the reign of charity'. There are so many instances in the poem which insist on the uselessness of study and learning without charity that one is left with the impression that Langland really thought them inimical to charity and therefore a danger to the soul; he thinks them closely allied with pride and where there is pride there is no love.

All attempts within the poem to define Dowel, Dobet and Dobest, however disparate they may appear, have in common some element of charity, and inadequate as many of the definitions are they are surely genuine attempts at discovery; they imply degrees of excellence in loving God and man. To generalize further, Dowel is often associated with a kind of passiveness – loving God by keeping free from sin; Dobet extends to concern for other men, helping and being charitable to them; Dobest is usually associated with active militancy in trying to oppose evil and save other men's souls. The progression is one of degree of effort and concern applied to loving God and man. Possibly the most satisfactory, even though the vaguest, definition is that by Clergy, immediately following the passage quoted above saying that Piers the Ploughman has shrugged aside all concerns other than love:

And seith that Dowel and Dobet aren two infinites,
Whiche infinites, with a feith, fynden oute Dobest,
Which shal saue mannes soule; thus seith Piers the Ploughman.

xiii 127-129

In other words, Dowel and Dobet are stages on the road to Dobest and can only be achieved by trying to Dobest – love, of God and man, cannot be limited in degree; it must aim at completeness. One cannot say: I will love God so much, to the extent, perhaps, of Dobet; Dobet is achieved only by aiming at perfect love, Dobest.

The commandment to love is in two parts, love God and love man, but the emphasis in *Piers Plowman* is on realizing the former through the latter. It is true that Anima applauds the lives of saints and hermits who have shut themselves away from the world so as to worship God in solitude and thereby practise the first part of the dual commandment directly, but in Langland's work the emphasis is not on contemplation of God's goodness or any mystical coming together with Him in private devotion; it is realized through an imitation of Christ, an imitation of the dealings of God *as man* with other men. There is comparatively little concern for, or admonition to, the practice of formal religion in the poem – not that Langland implies that religious devotions are unnecessary or unimportant, but it is clear, I think, that he considers them of secondary importance compared with the practice of charity; in any case, however necessary they are for the Christian, they are of no avail unless informed with charity. At the very beginning of the poem, when the Dreamer sees the clergy moving towards the acquisition of wealth and soft lives, he is led to think of the Sacrament of Penance, 'How he (Christ) it left with loue' (Prol. 102) and how it is being abused and presumably invalidated by venality. A conflict in the Dreamer's mind between the relative merits of charity and faith with all its implications – knowledge of theological explanations of God, etc. – is made explicit towards the end of the poem in the Dreamer's encounter with Abraham (Faith) and Hope: Faith's recommendation for salvation is by way of belief in the theological teachings of the Church, whereas Hope has given a new law, saying nothing of these but:

> To byleue and louye in o lorde almy3ty,
> And sitthe ri3t as myself so louye alle peple.
>
> xvii 34-35

The Dreamer does not know which law to follow and when he puts his problem to the Samaritan he is told to follow both:

> 'After Abraham,' quod he, 'that heraud of armes,
> Sette faste thi faith and ferme bileue.
> And, as Hope hi3te the, I hote that thow louye
> Thyn euene-crystene euermore euene-forth with thiself.'
>
> xvii 131-134

Love is not a substitute for religious belief or practice, but the most essential element in both. Langland is concerned not to seem, and probably not to be, heretical – as he points out at the end of the *Visio*:

> And so I leue lelly (lordes forbode ellis!)
> That pardoun and penaunce and preyeres don saue
> Soules that haue synned seuene sithes dedly.
> Ac to trust to thise triennales, trewly me thinketh,
> Is nou3t so syker for the soule, certis, as is Dowel.
>
> vii 176-180

Probably the most remarkable feature of Langland's concept of the second part of the dual commandment, 'love man', is his continual stress on the main aspect of Christian charity which distinguished it from other ethical systems it was striving to replace. Hebrew law, the *pietas* of the Classical world, the allegiances of Germanic society, and many other systems and societies, had as their starting point concern and responsibility for those with whom the individual was most closely associated, either by blood or organization; and as the degree of association was less close, so was the obligation of concern and responsibility less in proportion. The obligation stopped where other ties stopped, and at that point hostility might automatically take over. One might think that such an attitude is natural and even necessary to survival in primitive societies, and possibly not only in primitive societies, but this was not the system preached by Christ and recorded in the

Gospels and St Paul. The New Law preached universal brotherhood, concern for *all* men, even those who considered themselves
enemies, aiming thus at the complete eradication of enmity.
Typified by Christ's admonition to leave father and mother and
follow Him, it cut across the tenets of any system concerned
exclusively with close ties, and across the idea of enmity for anyone. This is not to say that Christians behaved in the prescribed
manner. It was hardly to be expected in the early Church, a
minority fighting for survival, and is certainly not very evident in
medieval Europe with its Inquisitions, Crusades, its persecutions
of the Jews. We are familiar in Anglo-Saxon literature, for instance,
with the genuinely pious expression of the attitude of *us* the saved
Christians, and *them* the doomed enemies. Nevertheless the basic
Christian message is the brotherhood of *all* men, even though there
are still in the twentieth century very many presumably genuine
practising Christians throughout the world who obviously have no
idea of it. We return to *Piers Plowman* with all the more wonder at
a man writing in English in the fourteenth century with such a
strong grasp of this concept of universal brotherhood; its spirit
pervades the whole work and it is stated explicitly too, as by Conscience when he is describing Christ's life:

> And lawe lakked tho, for men loued nouȝt her enemys.
> And Cryst conseilleth thus and comaundeth bothe,
> Bothe to lered and to lewed, to louye owre enemys.
>
> xix 108-110

The 'tho' (then) in l. 108 refers to the time before Christ established
His New Law.

This universal charity is considered as a 'natural' quality and
whoever is unkind, in accord with the etymology of the word, is
unnatural, and grace is denied to 'alle vnkynde creatures' for, says
the Samaritan, 'vnkyndenesse' is a sin against the Holy Ghost.
The passage has already been quoted in which the Samaritan
claims that no penance or indulgence is of avail to anyone who is
ingratus to his 'kynde'. He continues:

> The holy goste hereth the nouȝt ne helpe may the by resoun;
> For vnkyndenesse quencheth hym that he can nouȝte shyne,
> Ne brenne ne blase clere for blowynge of vnkyndenesse.
>
> xvii 254-256

One might expect 'natural affection' of this kind to be likely to apply to that charity which 'begins at home', which is concerned and responsible for those with whom one has close ties, and indeed the expression 'kynde loue' may well be intended in this sense in Patience's enigmatic riddle. But this is not the kind of love which concerns Langland, and for him this 'natural' quality is fellow-feeling and good will to all men – a quality implanted in man's heart by God, regarded by the theologians as part of the natural law, an aspect of *synderesis*.[5] It is this love, part of man's instinct, about which Holy Church instructs the Dreamer in the *Visio*:

> And, for to knowe it kyndely, it comseth bi myght,
> And in the herte, there is the heuede and the heiȝ welle;
> For in kynde knowynge in herte, there a myȝte bigynneth.
>
> i 161-163

When this 'kynde loue' and conscience come together (iii 297), then lawyers will become honest workmen. And Conscience claims that it is impossible to completely extinguish this divine spark in man: 'The good wille of a wiȝte was neure bouȝte to the fulle'. (xiii 192.) The Samaritan's instruction of the Dreamer expands the same message:

> For vnkyndenesse is the contrarie of alkynnes resoun;
> For there nys syke ne sori, ne non so moche wrecche,
> That he ne may louye, and hym lyke, and lene of his herte
> Good wille and good worde, bothe wisshen and willen
> Alle manere men mercy and forȝifnesse,
> And louye hem liche hymself and his lyf amende.
>
> xvii 343-348

With the message that it is possible – in fact natural – to man, unless he distort his nature, to love all other men, we come a little closer to understanding Langland's concept of love.

III

The poem contains formal definitions of charity, because the Dreamer asks the question: what is charity? But these definitions in themselves do not provide a complete and coherent answer. For one thing, Langland puts statements and counter-statements into the mouth of a single character; for another, attempts to answer this question directly seem to degenerate into vague and copious wordiness. For example, the beginning of Anima's answer to this very question from the Dreamer:

'It is a ful trye tree,' quod he, 'trewly to telle.
Mercy is the more therof, the myddel stokke is Reuthe.
The leues ben Lele-Wordes, the lawe of Holycherche,
The blosmes beth Boxome-Speche and Benygne-Lokynge;
Pacience hatte the pure tre and pore symple of herte,
And so, thorw god and thorw good men, groweth the frute Charite.'

xvi 4-9

The impression this leaves on a modern reader is very vague and blurred, and it could not have been very precise for a medieval.[6]

As is apparent in literature of all ages, it is very much easier to define virtue by depicting its opposite, and Langland certainly found this so. It is true of the pictures of the Seven Deadly Sins and particularly so in the account of 'anti-charity' in Haukyn 'the actyf man'. Viewed in general terms, the character of Haukyn is little more than a compound of the Deadly Sins, but it is made vivid by the sharp observation of practical details from daily life: he is annoyed if anyone finds fault with him; if he gives to the poor he does it so as to boast about it; if he cannot get the upper-hand over anyone it makes him ill; his mind is always on gain, either by false witness or false measure; he is quite prepared to steal:

Ȝif I ȝede to the plow, I pynched so narwe,
That a fote-londe or a forwe fecchen I wolde,
Of my nexte neighbore nymen of his erthe;
And if I rope, ouer-reche, or ȝaf hem red that ropen,
To seise to me with her sykel that I ne sewe neure.

xiii 371-375

These details are readily appreciable by a modern reader, because the world has changed so little.

In Haukyn, Langland is dealing with practical matters and practicality is the key-note of his concept of charity. He is never really satisfied unless he is dealing with everyday living. When the Dreamer thanks Thouȝt for his instruction and help, he is still unsatisfied because what he really wants to know is 'How Dowel, Dobet, and Dobest don amonges the peple' (viii 109) and Thouȝt sends him off to Witte ('understanding' or 'intelligence'). Conscience is the first to mention Piers in the *Vitae*, where he is to appear as Christ, and the importance of his coming is that he will show what Dobest is, 'in dede' (xiii 132). Theory is easy but practice is more difficult, and Langland is suspicious of too much intellectualizing. As Anima says, the more good matter a man hears, unless he practises it, the more harm it does him.

The most obvious need stressed by Langland throughout the poem is practical generosity to the poor, and its importance is indicated by all the abstractions. Witte insists on it and so does Lewte:

> For owre ioye and owre hele Iesu Cryst of heuene,
> In a pore mannes apparaille pursueth vs euere,
> And loketh on vs in her liknesse, and that with louely chere,
> To knowen vs by owre kynde herte and castyng of owre eyen,
> Whether we loue the lordes here byfor owre lorde of blisse.
>
> xi 179-183

This is love of God expressed through generosity to His creatures. Ymagynatyf and others give the same message: love the poor and show your love by helping them. As Witte says, the Church should give the lead in this work:

> Foles that fauten Inwitte, I fynde that holicherche
> Shulde fynden hem that hem fauteth and faderelees children;
> And wydwes that han nou3te wherwith to wynnen hem her fode,
> Madde men, and maydenes that helplees were.
>
> ix 66-69

And the operation of this Welfare Church should be supplemented privately:

> Godfader and godmoder that sen her godchildren
> At myseise and at mischief and mowe hem amende,
> Shal haue penaunce in purgatorie but 3if thei hem helpe.
> For more bilongeth to the litel barne, ar he the lawe knowe,
> Than nempnyng of a name, and he neuere the wiser!
>
> ix 74-78

Modern civilisation has found no better pattern than this, except that in most cases the State has taken over from the Church, but what is so noteworthy in this fourteenth-century writer is his

overriding concern for practicality and 'humanism' in religion –
the Church should be concerned with the physical welfare of its
members, just as godparents should be concerned with the
physical well-being of their godchildren.

Langland's concept of love is possible and practicable because,
as we have already seen, it does not depend on liking but, as the
Samaritan says, on wishing people well and helping them if we
can. Everyone is capable of this because it is distinct from partiality
or sentimentality. Langland's own freedom from sentimentality is
readily apparent. A glance at his attitude to bringing up children
is enough to convince the reader of this. Resoun at Mede's trial
says that he will have no mercy until, among other things,
'childryn cherissyng be chastyng with ȝerdes' (iv 117), and then in
his sermon he

> bad Bette kut a bow other tweyne,
> And bete Betoun therwith but if she wolde worche.
>
> v 32-33

He goes on to advise merchants to discipline their children, for
'Whoso spareth the sprynge spilleth his children' (41). Love can
certainly operate better through concerned chastisement than
through flattery. It has nothing to do with the way Haukyn tried
to please men for:

> *Si hominibus placerem, Christi seruus non essem;*
> *Et alibi: nemo potest duobus dominis seruire.*
>
> xiii 313-314

And although Piers is concerned with the welfare of workmen who
refuse to work, there is nothing soft or sentimental in the way he
talks to them:

> 'Now, bi the peril of my soule!' quod Pieres al in pure tene,
> 'But ȝe arise the rather and rape ȝow to worche,
> Shal no greyne that groweth glade ȝow at nede;
> And though ȝe deye for dole the deuel haue that reccheth!'
>
> vi 119-122

Practical and possible though it may be, it is still difficult
to fully appreciate a concept of love which is independent of
sentimental attachment or partiality, leave alone practise it, and

Langland was very aware of this. Late in the poem, when the Dreamer is discoursing with Faith and Hope, he makes an understandable reaction to Hope's doctrine of love:

> 'It is ful harde for any man on Abraham byleue,
> And welawey worse ȝit for to loue a shrewe!
> It is liȝter to leue in thre louely persones
> Than for to louye and leue as wel lorelles as lele.
> Go thi gate,' quod I to *Spes*, 'so me god helpe!
> Tho that lerneth thi lawe wil litel while vsen it!'
>
> xvii 41-46

Langland is doing two things here: he is admitting the difficulty of practising the law of love, and, as the Dreamer, at this point traditionally naïve, he is deliberately misunderstanding *Spes* so that the reader, who has understood the reiterated message so much better, will identify with the instructor: it is by no means impossible to practise the virtue interpreted by Piers to his band of pilgrims, to treat one's neighbour as 'thow woldest he wrouȝte to thiselue'. (v 574.)

But this is not a complete answer to the difficulties a man has to face in the field of practical generosity. Since no man's resources are unlimited, he has to choose whom to help and whom to refuse, and he is more likely to reject those he dislikes, especially if they will not help themselves. Piers asks Hunger how to deal with wastrels; it is only famine and misery that have made them work, and now that these have gone and they will be able to sponge on others again, they will do so. How does one cope with these people? Piers realizes his responsibility to them because

> 'They are my blody bretheren,' quod Pieres, 'for god bouȝte vs alle;
> Treuthe tauȝte me ones to louye hem vchone,
> And to helpen hem of alle thinge ay as hem nedeth.'
>
> vi 210-212

Hunger gives a compromise answer which amounts to, keep wastrels just alive 'With houndes bred and hors bred' (217) and give all you can to those who are needy through no fault of their own. Modern humanistic thought might include the wastrels among the latter, too, and might postulate an explanation for their idleness in

terms of maladjustment to a society which is at least partly to
blame for it. And this is a relevant point, for Langland too seems
to doubt the reliability or validity of such personal judgments,
because he makes Hunger revert to a position which does not
really answer the question at all: take men at their face value and
let God judge them:

> And alle maner of men that thow my3te asspye
> That nedy ben, and nau3ty, helpe hem with thi godis,
> Loue hem and lakke hem nou3te, late god take the veniaunce;
> Theigh thei don yuel, late thow god yworthe:–
>   *Michi vindicatam, et ego retribuam.*
>
> vi 225-228

He even contrives to explain the notoriously difficult 'Make to
yourselves friends of the mammon of unrighteousness . . .' in this
context. Langland worries this problem – he returns to it, for
example, in the Pardon and again examines both sides, coming
down slightly on the side of 'let God judge'. But he feels, one
senses, that this is no practical answer because, since every man's
means are limited, he must choose.[7]

Charity is, naturally enough, against violence and killing. At the
trial of Lady Mede Conscience says that when he and 'kynde loue'
come together:

> Alle that bereth baslarde, brode swerde or launce,
> Axe other hachet or eny wepne ellis,
> Shal be demed to the deth but if he do it smythye
> Into sikul or to sithe, to schare or to kulter.
>
> iii 303-306

But again, this statement contains an inherent difficulty: vengeance
shall be taken on the man who carries a weapon – he shall be killed.
If charity is to be infinite, who is to take vengeance? Langland
returns to this consideration much later in the poem, in the discourse by the Samaritan (= Charity). To kill a man, body or soul,
is a sin against the Holy Ghost, and

> How my3te he axe mercy or any mercy hym helpe,
> That wykkedlich and willefullich wolde mercy anynte?
> Innocence is nexte god, and ny3te and day it crieth,
> 'Veniaunce, veniaunce, for3iue be it neuere,

> That shent vs and shadde owre blode, forshapte vs, as it were;
> *Vindica sanguinem iustorum!*'
> Thus 'veniaunce, veniaunce' verrey charite asketh.
>
> xvii 284-289

An *impasse* is indeed reached when charity itself cries out for vengeance. This is a point which will be considered later with Langland's thoughts on the extent of God's love for man. Obviously at times, Langland held the orthodox view that there were some sins that 'cried out to heaven for vengeance' and, presumably, got it.

For all his apparently excessive enthusiasm, it is remarkable how frequently moderation is advocated, and this again is part of the poet's practicality. As Pacience tells Haukyn, both dearth and over-plenty lead to evil; *caristia* (want, insufficiency) leads to 'vnkyndnesse' and 'ouer-plente' to pride, 'Ac mesure is so moche worth, it may nouȝte be to dere' (xiv 74). Moderation is again championed, by Nede, towards the end of the poem:

> So Nede, at grete nede, may nymen as for his owne,
> Wythoute conseille of Conscience or cardynale vertues,
> So that he suwe and saue *spiritus temperancie.*
>
> xx 20-22

He goes on to say that no virtue can compare with Moderation, not even justice or fortitude, because in excess even these Cardinal Virtues can lead to evil. Nede's speech corroborates and amplifies what Conscience has told the Dreamer, that he should have stolen rather than live in desolate poverty. As long as he can get it in no other way, and as long as he is ruled by Moderation, he is at liberty to steal food, drink and clothing to keep himself alive.

'To love is to give' we are told many times, but Langland does not neglect to consider how this works out in practice – in dealing with wastrels, for example. And elsewhere in the poem there are directives to be sensibly concerned about money; sense must temper generosity. The Dreamer asks Holy Church about money and she refers him to the Gospel text 'Render unto Caesar . . .',

> For riȝtful reson shulde rewle ȝow alle,
> And kynde witte be wardeyne ȝowre welthe to kepe,
> And tutour of ȝoure tresore and take it ȝow at nede;
> For housbonderye and hij holden togideres.
>
> i 54-57

Money is not to be despised or thrown away, because man must live. Even Lady Mede's self-defence has a certain cogency and, much as he may dislike them personally, Langland does not exclude the mercantile classes from the Pardon – as long as they use their gains well. Anima, in his discourse on charity, advises lords and ladies to think twice before they squander on worthless clergy the substance which should rightly go to their heirs. Langland's idealism does not blind him to a realization of the nature of man and his society and he does not advocate impossibilities. But man's heart must not reside in his treasure for, as Pacience tells Haukyn, all our labour is lost, 'But owre spences and spendynge sprynge of a trewe wille' (xiv 197).

Langland is certainly aware of man's lower nature. For the most part the identification of loving with giving is a concept of man's highest capability and Langland's ideal – a disinterested self-effacement purely for the glorification of God or the well-being of fellow-men. But when, at times, a sense of bargaining and self-interest enters, one feels that the purity is contaminated: the more generous one is, the more one gains from it. Again Langland shows his practical realization of what men are made of – since part of their nature is self-seeking, perhaps the best thing to do is channel the self-seeking element towards the bliss of heaven and achieve practical good in the process. This is by no means an uncommon attitude in the Middle Ages, and at least it is more acceptable than being counselled on 'How Mercy Encreeseth Temporal Goods'. Lewte says that if you entertain your friends you are rewarded by them, for they return your hospitality, but repayment for entertaining the poor is made by Christ:

> Ac for the pore I shal paye, and pure wel quyte her trauaille
> That ȝiueth hem mete or moneye and loueth hem for my sake.
>
> xi 189-190

Pacience's explanation to Haukyn of the essential equality and justice of God's creating some men rich and others poor is a straightforward balancing of joy on earth and joy in heaven: all created beings suffer a time of hardship or labour (in the case of animals, the winter) and a reward of happiness. The poor and wretched suffer their hardship on earth and have their reward of

happiness in the next life. The rich, on the other hand, take their
reward and happiness first, on earth, and then pay for it in the
world to come; the poor are the fortunate ones and the rich deserve
our sympathy – indeed! One should not take too seriously Langland's belief in this naïve equation because it tends to run counter
to his conviction of the limitlessness of God's loving-kindness and
mercy; the equality of the bargain is intended as an inducement to
the rich to be generous to the poor because they can, by so doing,
achieve the double reward of ease on earth and heaven as well. Not
many manage it but, according to Pacience, it is possible:

And as an hyne that hadde his hyre ar he bygonne,
And whan he hath done his deuor wel men doth hym other bounte,
ʒyueth hym a cote aboue his couenaunte, riʒte so Cryst ʒiueth heuene
Bothe to riche and to nouʒte riche that rewfullich lybbeth;
And alle that done her deuor wel han dowble hyre for her trauaille,
Here forʒyuenesse of her synnes and heuene blisse after.

xiv 149-154

Pacience is not the only one to point to this self-seeking motive in
charity: Anima tells the Dreamer that Charite 'Coueiteth . . . none
erthly good but heuene-riche blisse' (xv 170) and later in the poem
Conscience, talking of Christ's Passion, says that we may

se bi his sorwe that who so loueth Ioye,
To penaunce and to pouerte he moste putten hymseluen,
And moche wo in this worlde willen and suffren.

xix 62-64

It would be unjust to stress what one might feel to be the less
commendable side of practical charity in the poem, because it is
almost certainly there so as to canalize man's baser promptings
into action which is good in itself – and, in any case, it is far out-
weighed by the frequent exhortations to love God and men for their
own sake and not for what is to be gained from it. The emphasis
would be wrong, too, if it stressed Langland's insistence on the
practical manifestations of charity to the extent of obscuring his
realization of the importance of the spirit which prompts it. To
love is to give, but to give is not necessarily to love. As Anima says,
one can never recognize charity by appearances but only by knowing the heart, which only Christ can do. But before leaving

Langland's concern with the practicalities of life it is necessary to consider briefly his thoughts on contemporary society and its structure because these must affect his attitude to people and to practical charity.

IV

One of the dominant impressions gained from a reading of *Piers Plowman* is the poet's dislike, even hate, of worldly wealth and power and those who possess them, and wherever the book is opened one finds evidence of his sympathy with the poor and wretched. His most moving description is in the C-text and begins thus:

> The most needy aren oure neighebores, and we nyme good hede,
> As prisones in puttes and poure folke in cotes,
> Charged with children and chef lordes rente,
> That thei with spynnynge may spare, spenen hit in hous-hyre,
> Bothe in mylk and in mele to make with papelotes,
> To aglotye with here gurles that greden after fode.
> Also hemselue suffren muche hunger,
> And wo in winter-tyme with wakynge a nyghtes
> To ryse to the ruel, to rocke the cradel,
> Bothe to karde and to kembe, to clouten and to wasche,
> To rubbe and to rely, russhes to pilie,
> That reuthe is to rede othere in ryme shewe
> The wo of these women that wonyeth in cotes.
>
> C x 71-83

The world has changed very little for some people. It is no wonder the poet's heart goes out to what he can see and depict so vividly and that he promises them the compensation of heaven for their sufferings in this world. But apart from his expression of compassion, Langland is at pains to stress, through the mouths of most of his abstractions, the spiritual superiority of poverty to a life of riches and ease. He reminds us more than once of Christ's choosing earthly poverty – through Lewte, for instance:

> Iesu Cryste on a Iewes douȝter alyȝte, gentil woman though she were,
> Was a pure pore mayde and to a pore man wedded.
>
> xi 240-241

Langland here defers to the tradition, as old as the Apostolic Church, that Mary as well as Joseph was of 'gentil' lineage, but the

s

significance of the comment is in the stress on Christ's poverty.[8]
Ymagynatyf says that grace can flourish only among the poor and
humble and this is why Christ and those who wished to imitate
Him chose earthly poverty. One has to rely on the poor for
practical charity for, as Study says, if the poor were no more
generous than the rich, 'Mendinantz meteles miȝte go to bedde'
(x 65). There is a kind of inevitability about this because, as is said
in reference to Haukyn, *Vbi thesaurus tuus, ibi et cor tuum* (xiii 399).
The reason why Langland complains so often and so bitterly about
the clergy is that too few of them have their heart in the right place –
he starts in the *Visio* with the pardoner and parish priest in league,
dividing the spoils which should go to the poor, and with the friar
'absolving' Lady Mede for the sake of her contribution to a stained-
glass window; and so he continues.

It cannot surprise us, bearing in mind this attitude and the
background to which we are introduced at the very beginning of
the poem where

> Some putten hem to the plow, pleyed ful selde,
> In settyng and in sowyng swonken ful harde,
> And wonnen that wastours with glotonye destruyeth
>
> Prol. 20-22

that Langland at times expresses thoughts germane to social
revolution. Probably the most famous lines in the poem are the
couple expressing ultimate equality, when Piers tells the knight
that

> in charnel atte chirche cherles ben yuel to knowe,
> Or a kniȝte fram a knaue there, knowe this in thin herte.
>
> vi 50-51

Holy Church says that God commanded the earth to produce 'in
comune three thinges' (i 20), clothing, food and drink sufficient
for everyone if they are used in moderation. And later, Pacience
tells Haukyn that 'Crystene sholde ben in comune riche, none
coueitouse for hymselue'. (xiv 200.)

But although idealistic thoughts of goods held in common run
through the poet's mind, he is, as we know, a realist and very aware
of man's acquisitive nature. He does not seriously visualize anything other than the medieval hierarchical structure. And at the
end of the poem, when the friars are to be admitted to Vnyte,

significantly it is Enuye who advises them to go to the universities
and learn, among other things, to prove by Seneca 'That alle
thinges vnder heuene ouȝte to ben in comune' (xx 274). He
obviously believes here that this is merely doctrine preached by
those who hope to gain personally from it. Acceptance of the
established hierarchy is plain in the *Visio*, in Piers's instructions to
his pilgrims and in the Pardon, too. And no nineteenth-century
reactionary would exhibit a stronger sense of respect for inherited
nobility and dislike of the *nouveaux riches* than we find in the
famous autobiographical passage in the C-text:

> Hit bycometh for clerkus Crist for to seruen,
> And knaues vncrouned to cart and to worche.
> For shold no clerk be crouned bote yf he ycome were
> Of franklens and free men and of folke yweddede.
> Bondmen and bastardes and beggers children,
> Thuse bylongeth to labour; and lordes kyn to seruen
> Bothe god and good men, as here degree asketh:
> Some to synge masses other sitten and wryte,
> Rede and receyue that reson ouhte spende.
> Ac sith bondemenne barnes han be mad bisshopes,
> And barnes bastardes han ben archidekenes,
> And sopers and here sones for seluer han be knyghtes,
> And lordene sones here laborers and leid here rentes to wedde,
> For the ryght of this reame ryden aȝens oure enemys,
> In confort of the comune and the kynges worshep,
> And monkes and moniales that mendinauns sholden fynde,
> Han mad here kyn knyghtes and knyghtfees purchased,
> Popes and patrones poure gentil blod refuseth,
> And taken Symondes sone seyntewarie to kepe.

C vi 61-79

What concerns Langland most is that all orders should perform
properly the functions of the class into which they were born and
this applies to poor labourers as well as to nobles. The following
complaint about contemporary workmen occurs at the end of
passus vi of B:

> And but-if he be heighlich huyred, ellis wil he chyde,
> And that he was werkman wrouȝt waille the tyme,
> Aȝeines Catones conseille comseth he to Iangle:–
>   *Paupertatis onus paciencer ferre memento.*

> He greueth hym aȝeines god and gruccheth aȝeines resoun,
> And thanne curseth he the kynge and al his conseille after,
> Suche laws to loke laboreres to greue.
> Ac whiles Hunger was her maister there wolde none of hem chyde,
> Ne stryue aȝeines his statut, so sterneliche he loked.
>
> 314-321

And Langland's admonition of the rich does at times seem to spring from a genuine concern for their salvation; like so many others, he is convinced that wealth and power can corrupt a man irretrievably, and whereas a rich man who uses his wealth well will reap great rewards, he believes that such men are difficult to find. Pacience prays for these:

> And haue reuthe on thise riche men that rewarde nouȝte thi prisoneres
> Of the good that thow hem gyuest *ingrati* ben manye;
> Ac, god, of this goodnesse gyue hem grace to amende.
> For may no derth ben hem dere, drouth, ne weet,
> Ne noyther hete ne haille, haue thei here hele,
> Of that thei wilne and wolde wanteth hem nouȝt here.
>
> xiv 168-173

Langland is no anarchist. When we are first shown the 'felde ful of folke', law and order is established by 'The kynge and the comune and kynde witte the thridde' (Prol. 121) so that every man should know his place and function. And the conclusion of the Cat Belling episode, spoken by the wise mouse, is that irksome as the king's rule may be, this is better than the chaos which would result if there were no one to govern.

To medieval minds, life on earth reflected the pattern of life in heaven which according to the orthodox and general belief was hierarchical. The picture is made clear in the account by Ymagynatyf of the penitent thief's position in heaven:

> Ac though that thef had heuene, he hadde none heigh blisse,
> As seynt Iohan and other seyntes that asserued hadde bettere.
> Riȝt as sum man ȝeue me mete and sette me amydde the flore,
> Ich haue mete more than ynough, ac nouȝt so moche worship
> As tho that seten atte syde-table or with the souereignes of the halle,
> But sitte as a begger bordelees bi myself on the grounde.
>
> xii 196-201

And Ymagynatyf goes on to imply a similar hierarchy in hell. Just as the thief was the 'lowest' in heaven, so was Trajan only just inside hell, and that was why he was taken out so easily. The equation between the earthly and heavenly hierarchy is indicated by Holy Church when she speaks of the obligations of kings and knights. She is reminded of King David and his 'dubbed kniʒtes', and following this, how 'criste kingene kynge kniʒted ten' (i 105), the orders of angels.

It is relevant to our consideration of charity to realize that not only is the heavenly pattern of hierarchy mirrored on earth, but also that all the acts of kindness and courtesy practised on earth have their source in God and are themselves a mirror, or rather extension, of life in heaven. And this cosmic view of life tends to make more meaningful such acts of kindness, courtesy and politeness in social intercourse, acts which otherwise might seem merely arbitrary requirements of a particular society. Often in Middle English literature one finds the Christian way of life referred to as 'cortaysye'; not only this – life in heaven is also referred to as 'cortaysye', and so is grace, the transmission of the heavenly way of life into men's hearts.[9] These ideas and this phraseology are part of Langland's equipment. Pacience, for example, assures the rich who take pity on the poor that they will be comforted by 'Criste of his curteysie' (xiv 147) and the idea is implicit in the following comment by Anima:

> . . . charyte is goddis champioun and as a good chylde hende,
> And the meryest of mouth at mete where he sitteth.
> The loue that lith in his herte maketh hym lyʒte of speche,
> And is companable and confortatyf as Cryst bit hymselue.
>
> xv 210-213

His courtesy derives from the love in his heart which is natural to man and part of his heritage from heaven.

Langland's views on the ethical problems of wealth, inheritance and hierarchy are as mixed and complex as those of any twentieth-century liberally minded man. Although at times he had idealistic visions of community ownership with moderate provision for everyone, thus avoiding the evils occasioned by too much or too little, for the most part he would accept the structure of society as he knew it, provided that men used the wealth and power they had been given in what he considered the right way. I think he would accept this pattern as a mirror of the social structure in heaven and accept the fact of inherited wealth and power as the working of Providence. But although at one point, in the Pardon, there is suggestion of correlation between a man's position in the earthly hierarchy and his subsequent position in the world to come – good knights will join the patriarchs and prophets, good bishops the apostles, etc. – generally he would assume no such necessary correlation. On the contrary, the more wealth and power a man possesses in this world, the more difficult it is for him to achieve spiritual wealth. We all start with the same potential in the spiritual world, we are all equally 'gentil', made to belong to the same (noble) family through our spiritual rebirth in Christ's Redemption:

> For the best ben somme riche and somme beggers and pore.
> For alle are we Crystes creatures and of his coffres riche,
> And bretheren as of o blode, as wel beggares as erles.
> For on Caluarye of Crystes blode Crystenedome gan sprynge,
> And blody bretheren we bycome there, of o body ywonne,
> As *quasi modo geniti* and gentil men vche one,
> No beggere ne boye amonges vs but if it synne made.
>
> xi 191-197

v

God is charity – that is, love. So we are told frequently, as well as 'He that dwelleth in love, dwelleth in God and God in Him'. God the Father made His love intelligible to man by putting it on earth in the form of His Son; so Ymagynatyf:

> For the heihe holigoste heuene shal tocleue,
> And loue shal lepe out after into this lowe erthe,
> And clennesse shal cacchen it and clerkes shullen it fynde.
>
> xii 141-143

The poetry is at its most lyrical at these points, as, for example, in Holy Church's exposition of the same theme in the *Visio*:

> heuene my3te nou3te holden it [love], it was so heuy of hymself,
> Tyl it hadde of the erthe yeten his fylle,
> And whan it haued of this folde flesshe and blode taken,

Was neuere leef vpon lynde li3ter therafter,
And portatyf and persant as the poynt of a nedle,
That my3te non armure it lette ne none hei3 walles.

i 151-156

And because God is the source of charity, only He can recognize true charity, so Anima tells the Dreamer when he identifies Piers with Peter, with Christ, that is, the perfect man, God manifest. This is the mediator in human form that man must rely on; this is the love which links man with his source and its source. Its manifest action on earth is what man must copy, helped by the natural infusion of love which is every man's share of his creator. And Langland is concerned not only with discovering the pattern by which man should live, but also with the nature and extent of the source too – God's love for man.

One of the great problems in Langland's mind, even though it may not be explicitly stated, is this: if man is to aim at the ultimate expression of love, charity to his enemies, surely this must also apply to the source of all love, God Himself. And this concern is clearly implied in two distinct but not mutually exclusive questions: if God is the source of charity, how can He possibly have created a large part of mankind (non-Christians) to be destined to the unending torture of traditional perdition? And moving on from this, how can He allow the possibility of *any* man's suffering these perpetual torments? Here he comes very close to the position of Origenism which preaches (heretically) the ultimate salvation of all souls. The first of these problems has its centre usually in the possibility of salvation for the Jews, with somewhat less emphasis on the other group of non-Christians familiar to medieval Christendom, the Saracens. And the problem of God's dealings with the Jews is mixed up with the poet's own concern and charity for these people.

As one might expect, especially if it is to be questioned, the orthodox and generally accepted attitude is well represented in the poem: Christians should strive for the salvation of Jews and Saracens by converting them; a Christian's duty is to do good to all men, but the faithful come first (an extension of the concept of 'charity beginning at home'); the Jews' responsibility for the Crucifixion, the main stated cause for hating them, is mentioned several times, and very great attention is paid to the doctrine of the necessity of baptism for salvation. But then, at one point, we find resort to casuistry so as to mitigate the exclusiveness of this doctrine and so find 'a way out' for the Jews (and God). The Dreamer puts to Ymagynatyf the orthodox doctrine that no one can be saved without 'Crystendome', that is, baptism:

> '*Contra*,' quod Ymagynatyf tho, and comsed for to loure,
> And seyde, '*saluabitur vix iustus in die iudicij*.
> *Ergo saluabitur*,' quod he, and seyde namore Latyne.[10]
>
> xii 278-280

The just (heathen) shall be saved *vix.*, 'hardly, with difficulty', therefore he *shall* be saved. He goes on to cite the case of Trajan, the just heathen, who was taken to heaven from hell. There are three kinds of baptism – by water, by blood and 'thorugh fuire' which Ymagynatyf describes as 'ferme bileue' (283). This last, and most important in the context, is usually called baptism of desire. But *Piers Plowman* is not merely a disputation, and the 'feel' of the poem, the inclination of the poet's mind, makes it clear that Langland is far more 'liberal' in this dispute than most of his contemporaries – inevitably, since his one dominant message is love. Ymagynatyf moves away from argument depending on the force of the word *vix* to statement which is more convincingly an expression of Langland's belief in God's goodness and love: a man who lives according to the truth and the law as he understands it, and who considers his law to be the best, will certainly not be rejected by the God of truth. Another indication of Langland's doubt about the necessity of baptism for salvation is put into the mouth of Lewte, shortly after the passage asserting our 'gentility' through Christ's Redemption:

> For what euere clerkis carpe, of Crystenedome or elles,
> Cryst to a comune woman seyde, in comune at a feste,
> That *fides sua* shulde sauen hir and saluen hir of alle synnes.
>
> xi 210-212

This forms part of an injunction not to judge and criticize our neighbours, but the line 'what euere clerkis carpe, of Crystenedome or elles' seems somewhat gratuitous in the context and indicates Langland's preoccupation and the trend of his thought. Soon after this, and again apparently gratuitously, Lewte mentions that it was a 'Iewes douȝter' that Christ chose as his mother.

Langland seems to have thought highly of the Jews, particularly because of their practical charity; and because this is so important to him it serves to strengthen his conviction that the source of all charity would not condemn them to eternal damnation. One of Conscience's predictions in her sermon at Westminster, is that when he and 'kynde loue' come together, 'suche loue shal arise' and there will be such peace and 'perfit trewthe' among the people,

> That Iewes shal wene in here witte and waxen wonder glade,
> That Moises or Messie be come into this erthe,
> And haue wonder in here hertis that men beth so trewe.
>
> iii 300-302

The interesting point here is that the Jews would *rejoice* at this good – which must argue goodness in them. There is no doubt about why they should be so close to the poet's heart when he expresses the following opinion of them, through Wit: if Christian prelates did their duty, no one would go hungry:

> A Iuwe wolde nouȝte se a Iuwe go Iangelyng for defaute
> For alle the moebles on this molde, and he amende it miȝte.
> Allas! that a Cristene creature shal be vnkynde til an other,
> Sitthen Iuwes, that we Iugge Iudas felawes,
> Ayther of hem helpeth other of that that hym nedeth.
> Whi nel we Cristene of Cristes good be as kynde
> As Iuwes, that ben owre lores-men? shame to vs alle!
>
> ix 81-87

Compare this with the attitude expressed in Chaucer's *Prioress's Tale*. No wonder Langland should expect the Jews to be saved by the God of love when his impression of them is that, in spite of the imperfection of their law which did not include loving enemies, they do behave as Christ taught men to behave. At one point in his long discourse, Anima argues that faith alone can save the ignorant and that perhaps because of this many Jews and Saracens will be saved before Christians (of whom more will be expected) because

> ... Iewes lyuen in lele lawe, owre lorde wrote it hymselue,
> In stone, for it stydfast was and stonde sholde eure –
> *Dilige deum et proximum* is parfit Iewen lawe –

And toke it Moyses to teche men til Messye come;
And on that lawe thei lyuen 3it and leten it the beste.
xv 572-576

And this is the law Langland is concerned to preach. There is no
implication that he doubted the truth and rightness of Christianity,
and he thought too that every effort should be made to convert non-
Christians, but what is clear, to my mind, is that he believed that
God in His charity would not condemn people because they were
not baptized Christians. It is the occasional detail, as much as
anything, which builds up this impression of Langland's attitude.
When the Dreamer, for example, asks Faith if Jesus is going to
fight with the Jews or the Scribes, ' "Nay," quod he, "the foule
fende and Fals-dome and Deth." ' (xviii 28.) Now it seems to me
that the only reason for including this bit of dialogue is to emphasize Christ's fight against, and triumph over, evil principles rather
than specific races or people. And *Piers Plowman* is not a theological exercise in Latin, by a schoolman, but a fourteenth-century
poem in English, in alliterative metre, an area in which it is difficult
to find even lip service paid to the unique recommendation of the
Third Lateran Council that Jews should be tolerated on the
grounds of humanity. More than once the poet mentions that it
could only have been by God's will that certain men crucified
Christ, and this statement leads into consideration of the second
of Langland's great concerns in respect of God as the source of all
love: can the All-loving condemn any man to the eternal endurance
of such dreadful pains as hell is said to contain?

Langland is by no means a poet of hell and damnation – again a
claim which might not seem very apparent after only a superficial
reading, because this may well leave a general impression of harsh
condemnation of sin and warning of its penalties. But closer
examination, and particularly if one compares him with his contemporaries, shows Langland extremely tentative in his thoughts
about eternal damnation. There are, of course, the orthodox dicta
on this topic, but, again on balance, the inclination is towards
God's love and infinite mercy and its ultimate inability to punish
man with the traditional unceasing torments of hell. The tentative-
ness is often in the form of an 'escape clause' which can easily be

missed. When, for example, in the *Visio*, Piers comes forward to direct the pilgrims to Truth, that is God, he warns them against various hazards and says that if they consider themselves too much, they may lose God's love and never come into His presence, 'but grace thow haue' (v 626) – unless He should grant you His grace. He goes on to say that it will be very difficult for a person not related to any one of the seven sisters who serve eternal Truth (the virtues of abstinence, humility, etc.) to come to God's courts, 'but grace be the more' (638) – unless God's grace should outweigh the lack of virtue. Then Scripture, pleading for charity among men, warns against killing, for the Lord says, He will punish men for their sins in purgatory or the pit of hell, 'but mercy it lette' (x 371) – unless my mercy prevents my vengeance. Towards the end of the poem, when the 'brewere' says that he will not be ruled by Christ or any sense of justice, Conscience tells him that if this is so, the 'cursed wrecche' will certainly not be saved, 'but if the god helpe'. These parentheses might easily be missed, but they are present throughout the poem, and through them one senses Langland's feeling that if men are to act with charity and mercy, God ought to too.[11]

The impression to be stressed is that Langland had serious reservations about eternal damnation – there is no suggestion that he thought sin should go unpunished. His great belief is in purgatory, temporary punishment; and this is a state of suffering which need not be in a particular place, as is indicated in the Pardon when it deals with those afflicted on earth, who

> For loue of her lowe hertis, owre lorde hath hem graunted
> Here penaunce and her purgatorie here on this erthe.
>
> vii 104-105

The emphasis is on temporary rather than eternal punishment in the following statement about the fate of the evildoer:

> Ac Resoun shal rekne with hym and rebuken hym at the laste,
> And Conscience acounte with hym and casten hym in arrerage,
> And putten hym after in a prisone, in purgatorie to brenne,
> For his arrerages rewarden hym there to the daye of dome,
> But if Contricioun wol come and crye, bi his lyue,
> Mercy for his mysdedes with mouth or with herte.
>
> xi 126-131

The point to notice here is the reference to burning 'to the daye of dome', that is, the General Judgment, at the end of the world, but by implication, therefore, not necessarily *after* it. The continual mention of, and emphasis on, mercy even to those who opposed and tortured Christ is remarkable in the fourteenth century when the usual reference to them is to enemies who deserve no mercy. Langland's emphasis is indicated by Holy Church:

> the fader that formed vs alle,
> Loked on vs with loue and lete his sone deye
> Mekely for owre mysdedes to amende vs alle;
> And ȝet wolde he hem no woo that wrouȝte hym that peyne,
> But mekelich with mouthe mercy he bisouȝte
> To haue pite of that poeple that peyned hym to deth.
> Here myȝtow see ensamples, in hymselue one,
> That he was miȝtful and meke and mercy gan graunte
> To hem that hongen him an heiȝ and his herte thirled.
>
> i 164-172

And the Dreamer remembers, in his discussion with Scripture, that the repentant thief who died with Christ went 'Withouten any penaunce of purgatorie to perpetuel blisse' (x 421). God's mercy is supreme, we are told time and again, and it is love who assesses the penalties and pronounces judgment 'Vpon man for his mysdedes' (i 160). It is to infinite love that man must aspire.

Sin is, of course, to be deprecated and avoided at all costs, but much as it is preached against and to *be* preached against, the unavoidable impression is that Langland considered the worst man could achieve infinitesimally small compared with God's power of love and forgiveness. When Repentaunce is receiving the Seven Deadly Sins the scoundrel Coueytise is in danger of despair and, harsh as Repentaunce can be, he immediately reassures him with these words:

> Haue mercye in thi mynde and with thi mouth biseche it,
> For goddes mercye is more than alle hise other werkes;
>   *Misericordia eius super omnia opera eius etc.*
> And al the wikkednesse in this worlde that man myȝte worche or thynke,
> Ne is no more to the mercye of god than in the see a glede.
>
> v 288-291

Then in his prayer to God in the general absolution of the Sins he remembers the great Christian paradox, '*O felix culpa! o neces-sarium peccatum Ade!*' (v 491). If God had not allowed sin, Christ would not have been born to redeem mankind, and so sin is happy in that without it the world would have been denied Christ. Resoun, rebuking the Dreamer for his harsh criticism of his fellow-men, reminds him that since man is made of flesh he cannot help at times following the flesh, for '*nemo sine crimine viuit*'. (xi 394.) Man must rely on God's charity for his salvation; he cannot live without sinning, 'for sothest worde that euere god seyde was tho he sayde, *nemo bonus*'. (x 441.)

The one instance in the poem in which an argument is put into the mouth of one 'good' abstraction only to be proved absolutely wrong by another, is in the account of the Harrowing of Hell. Pees, associating herself with Loue and Mercy, tells Riȝtwisnesse that Christ is going to take Adam and Eve and others from hell; Riȝtwisnesse asks her if she is mad or drunk: because Adam and Eve rejected both God's law and His love, it is absolutely certain

> That her peyne be perpetuel and no preyere hem helpe.
> Forthi late hem chewe as thei chose, and chyde we nouȝt, sustres,
> For it is botelees bale, the bite that thei eten.

xviii 198-200

Pees then argues that people have to suffer in order to realize the opposite, bliss, and so it is with these:

> her foly and her synne
> Shall lere hem what langour is and lisse withouten ende.
> Wote no wighte what werre is there that pees regneth,
> Ne what is witterly wel til weyllowey hym teche.

224-227

Now Adam and Eve are representative of all mankind, and the interesting suggestion here is that when man sins, he does so in foolishness, realizing neither the enormity of the offence nor the reality of the punishment. And the further inevitable suggestion is that God would not punish foolishness with everlasting damnation. One of the chief constituents of a mortal sin is 'full knowledge' – and human understanding is certainly incapable of full knowledge in terms of infinity and God. An orthodox theologian might argue that *such* knowledge is not necessary, but the inclination of Lang-land's thought would seem to be that it is.

Man has to cope, not only with his own foolishness and lack of understanding, but also with the Devil and his guile. Lucifer argues that the souls in hell are his according to law and justice, because the Ruler of Heaven Himself said that if Adam ate the apple, all men should die and dwell with the devils in hell. But Satan points out to him that these souls were won through deceit and, says Gobelyn, 'We haue no trewe title to hem, for thorwgh tresoun were thei dampned' (291). This, indeed, is Christ's argument when He claims the souls:

> For the dede that thei dede, thi deceyte it made;
> With gyle thow hem gete agayne al resoun.
>
> 331-332

Then He claims that even according to the Old Law of strict justice, He can claim them because 'al that man hath mysdo I, man, wyl amende' (339). Note the *al*. His death shall release 'both quykke and quyte that queynte was thorw synne' (344). And as Adam and everyone else died spiritually because of a tree, so 'Adam and alle thorwe a tree shal torne aʒeine to lyue' (357). The section of Christ's speech following this is worth quoting more fully because, apart from its intrinsic beauty, it is, to my mind, the clearest indication that Langland thought of God's charity as ultimately extending to all men and taking them away from the Devil – a line of thought certainly not original to Langland, but remarkable in a fourteenth-century English poet, and certainly not orthodox. And note that these lines are spoken by Christ, so that their full weight cannot be doubted:

> For I, that am lorde of lyf, loue is my drynke,
> And for that drynke today I deyde vpon erthe.
> I fauʒte so, me threstes ʒet, for mannes soule sake;
> May no drynke me moiste ne my thruste slake,
> Tyl the vendage falle in the vale of Iosephath,
> That I drynke riʒte ripe must, *resureccio mortuorum*,
> And thanne shal I come as a kynge, crouned with angeles,
> And han out of helle alle mennes soules.
> Fendes and fendekynes bifor me shulle stande,
> And be at my biddynge where so eure me lyketh.

And to be merciable to man thanne, my kynde it asketh;
For we beth bretheren of blode, but nouȝte in baptesme alle.
Ac alle that beth myne hole bretheren, in blode and in baptesme,
Shal nouȝte be dampned to the deth that is withouten ende;
    Tibi soli peccaui, etc.

xviii 363-376

It is true that Langland is still concerned enough with baptism to
mention it, but notice the parenthesis, 'for we are blood-brothers,
though not all in baptism'; and surely the emphasis here is on
Christ's charity, as God and man, for all other men. He continues
by likening Himself to the king of a country coming upon the
scene of an execution and having the power to grant the condemned man life:

And I, that am kynge of kynges, shal come suche a tyme,
There dome to the deth dampneth al wikked;
And ȝif lawe wil I loke on hem, it lithe in my grace,
Whether thei deye or deye nouȝte for that thei deden ille.
Be it any thinge abouȝt, the boldenesse of her synnes,
I may do mercy thorw riȝtwisnesse and alle my wordes trewe.
And though holiwrit wil that I be wroke of hem that deden ille,
    Nullum malum inpunitum, etc.,
Thei shul be clensed clereliche and wasshen of her synnes
In my prisoun purgatorie til *parce* it hote,
And my mercy shal be shewed to manye of my bretheren.
For blode may suffre blode bothe hungry and akale,
Ac blode may nouȝt se blode blede, but hym rewe.

382-393

A man cannot see his kind bleed without pitying them. And then
follows the mysterious quotation from St Paul, II *Corinthians*, xii 4:
'and I heard secret words which it is not granted to man to utter'
which, in this context, Langland must intend to imply that after
the Final Judgment no soul will remain in hell. I should be an
unnatural king, Christ says, if I did not help my kindred, especially
in such need as they will be. And when Christ took human form,
He became kin to all mankind.

The poem as a whole would seem to reveal the mind of a man
whose inclinations led him towards Origenism. But he is unsure
and tends to draw back from the directly heretical statement. It

would seem that he believed in predestination; that ultimately every man was destined to eternal joy in heaven and, what is more, would attain it even though, in his foolishness, he might 'reject' God when he was living on earth. There would be 'rank' in heaven – in accordance with the orthodox view, degrees of appreciation of God and His joy, depending on one's behaviour on earth. The way one was to behave on earth was contained in the law, 'love God and man'; this is the pattern of existence in heaven, emanating from God who is infinite love and part of whose nature is present as the divine spark in every man's soul. No wonder Langland would consider such a God incapable of damning men eternally; the God who, at the beginning of the poem has, in the words of Holy Church, shown mercy even to the rebellious angels in their fall: they

> fellen out in fendes liknesse nyne dayes togideres,
> *Til god of his goodnesse* gan stable and stynte,
> And garte the heuene to stekye and stonden in quiete.
>
> i 119-121

Whether Langland was fully conscious of the implications of such a statement or whether he would be prepared to defend it must remain doubtful, but his overwhelming concept of a God of infinite love and mercy is unquestionable.

Satire in *Piers Plowman*

S. T. KNIGHT

The definition of the term 'satire' has always presented problems; everyone who writes on the topic begins with a bold definition but almost everyone else can find reason to question the definition and can find examples of satire which it excludes. In this essay I hope to avoid this danger by taking a course of action which may seem, from different viewpoints, either judicious or cowardly. I adopt a definition of 'satire' merely as a tool of exploration, a definition deliberately made in order to reveal certain complexities and subtleties in *Piers Plowman,* and the efficiency of this revelation is the only end of the definition. It may indeed be that other satirical works are susceptible to similar examination in similar terms, but the definition used here is conceived not as an absolute, having authority in all cases and leading in Platonic fashion to the centre of the idea of satire – rather it is a relative which has a specific value in a certain situation.

I would understand 'satire' as a literary mode in which, through a fiction of some sort, an author is critical of human affairs in relation to themselves. There are three elements here; first that the mode is a fiction: I use this word in the neo-Aristotelian sense, to include all written, or indeed spoken, emanations which are not factual.[1] Secondly, that satire is critical in its nature – this perhaps is the one thing on which definitions of satire agree, though they may argue over the variety of methods used to criticize. Thirdly, and perhaps most importantly, that satire deals with human affairs within their own terms: by this I mean that the satirist is concerned with a more adequate, sometimes a more nearly perfect, conducting of the world's affairs. It is certainly true that Christian satirists

T

almost always draw their authority from super-material sources, reflecting on human pettiness in the light of eternal rectitudes, but it seems to me that in *Piers Plowman* there is a marked difference in tone between material directed at the proper conduct of the world and material which looks forward to heaven.

Consequently it is the third element of this definition which makes it into a tool of exploration of *Piers Plowman*, for in terms of this poem I take it that central to the satiric mode are the passages where Langland talks about pardoners, merchants, bishops, friars and all the familiar topics of medieval corrective literature. I wish to exclude from the satirical mode the stretches of theological, emotional and intellectual writing where Langland explores the principles behind the Christian cosmology as he sees them. For this material I intend to use the term 'theological'; in place of the terms 'satirical' and 'theological' one could perhaps use 'tropological' and 'anagogical', for these terms would show more clearly that the one mode is a different and deeper understanding of the material discussed in the other mode, but there seems little virtue in using technical and obscure terminology when familiar language is at hand.

Although I have surrounded this definition with qualifications and do indeed regard it as relative to this case, I would not like to imply that it is quite worthless in other cases. Indeed, it may well be that this definition provides such a useful tool for investigating the overall literary effect of *Piers Plowman* that it may be useful with reference to other satires too. But such an argument would be an extension of the investigation that is made in this essay, and while I shall foreshadow such an extension, space does not permit it here. Perhaps the limitations of space are beneficial, for satire is so protean that a wider discussion of it may be dangerous, the danger lying in the fact that a search for a complex fact about many works might prevent us from apprehending a simple fact about a single work.

Consequently this essay sets out to explore the relation in *Piers Plowman* between the familiar satirical material of medieval tradition and the more adventurous material, perhaps equally familiar in other medieval traditions, of theological investigation. It would be wise, however, to say at the beginning that Langland, like most great writers, is ahead of his critic in this enquiry and when we have diligently separated the modes and have, in the examiners' jargon, compared and contrasted them, he finally shows us that they cannot be separated, that in his massive vision these literary modes stand related as does the whole creation and that their interrelation is the bold literary device by which the universe that is in his poem stands united.

Satire is, in the sense defined above, a familiar enough thing in medieval literature. The transmission of the classical satirists certainly faltered after the disintegration of the Roman Empire, but equally certainly it never failed entirely.[2] Although one can never assume that a medieval writer who refers to a text, or who even quotes a text, has ever had the text in front of him, there is ample evidence to show that the major Roman satirists were well enough known. Juvenal and Persius are solidly in the mainstream of what Curtius characterizes as the 'curriculum', the great tradition of ancient authors who were read in the 'grammar' studies of the monastic, cathedral and secular schools. Martial too was a curriculum author, though not a major one, and Horace was primarily known to the Middle Ages as a satirist for, in one of those curious quirks of cultural history, his odes were not well known.[3] It is true that grammar, as the Middle Ages understood it, fell out of favour in the developing universities, but by then the satirists had been absorbed into medieval Latin culture as a whole, had been taken in, to a good degree, to the corpus of cultural material that the church continually transmitted.[4]

These writers are hardly a major source of literary influence, however, and there is no question, in the Middle Ages, of imitating the classical satirists as later centuries were to do. The point is that, however tenuous the transmission, the classical satirists provided a firm basis of *auctoritee* for criticism of the state and, to some extent, a model of how to go about it, though not many Christian moralists needed much suggestion in how to criticize the follies of their ages. The writers of Latin moral poetry in the early Middle Ages keep alive the traditions of public criticism and the earliest Middle English poems show that the tradition is vigorous.

The Owl and the Nightingale, for example, is a satirical poem which reveals considerable point, in the persona of the owl[5]:

> Vor þane þu sittest on þine rise
> þu draȝst men to fleses luste,
> þat wlleþ þine songes luste;
> Al þu forlost þe murȝþe of houene,
> For þarto neuestu none steuene.

But it also reveals considerable delicacy, mostly through the persona of the Nightingale:

> 'Hule,' ho sede, 'seie me soþ,
> Wi dostu þat unwiȝtis doþ?
> þu singist a niȝt & noȝt a dai,
> & al þi song is "wailawai".'

Standing alone as it does, this poem shows that the spirit of literary satire is very much alive, that critical analysis of society can be written with a light touch.

There is, of course, a good deal of evidence that even at this early time English was relatively rich in poetry of moral criticism – *Poema Morale, Ormulum* and *Cursor Mundi* are an adequate testimony to the existence of the didactic spirit in the early Middle Ages. The extreme gravity of these poems and in particular the thinness of the fictional element in them might seem to exclude them from the satirical mode. John Peter found it easier to call poems like this 'complaints'[6], and one can see some point in doing this. Yet, as is plain in *Piers Plowman,* the fictional mode that we here call satire draws its material very largely from the literature of plain moral statement, and indeed at times all satirists seem to break the bonds of their fiction and to speak directly to their audience. The categories of satire and complaint are not discrete, as the reviewers of Peter's book pointed out,[7] and it is important to realize that, at least in the Christian environment, complaint and satire are closely interwoven.

The increasing evidence of satire in the fourteenth century may well be partly an indication that more manuscripts were surviving rather than that satire was growing in strength, but the increasing number of satirical lyrics in this period, both secular and religious, shows a lusty tradition[8] and the end of the century sees satire flourish wonderfully, as the quantity of manuscripts of *Piers Plowman* and *The Canterbury Tales* shows us. Satire marches on in the fifteenth century, not perhaps matching the previous century in quality but certainly outdoing it in bulk. Gower is a notable exponent of the genre, for apart from his satirical works in French and Latin the Prologue to the *Confessio Amantis* is almost entirely satirical. Dunbar and Henryson seem the best satirists of this century, and their work leads directly on to that of Skelton and Wyatt, whom we might loosely term the first of the Renaissance satirists in English.

There is no problem in seeing a general satiric tradition in this way, but when we look more closely at *Piers Plowman* in terms of time and place the poem seems, as it does in so many ways, rather enigmatic. *Winner and Waster* is generally thought to antedate the A-text, and it is a moral alliterative poem which displays some fine touches of imagination as it discusses a limited topic with considerable point, but this is really all we can find in the way of a satirical tradition which the author probably knew well.[9] There is a wider ambience to the poem which goes beyond literary satire, for a work like Trevisa's translation of Richard FitzRalph's attack on the friars[10] seems close to Langland's observations on the friars in some places; other evidence suggests that Langland may have had sympathies with Uthred de Boldon or even dealings with him.[11] It is certainly out of this sort of thinking and writing that *Piers Plowman* is born, but there seem no specific references in the poem to any earlier English literary work.

There are, of course, plenty of poems which to a greater or lesser extent seem to be given inspiration by Langland; *The Parlement of the Thre Ages, Mum and the Soothsegger, The Crowned King, Pierce the Plowman's Crede* and *Death and Liffe* are generally held to be examples of this.[12] It is rather hard to believe, though, that Langland's poem alone sparked off a revival of moral alliterative poetry, especially when so much alliterative poetry exists in other modes and when the *Gawain* group, culturally isolated though it seems to be, is so strongly moral. It is also hard to believe that 'In a somer sesoun whanne softe was the sonne' was the first line Langland ever wrote, but in neither case can one plead on negative evidence. Rather one must look internally in the poem and see how familiar

Langland's satirical method is in contemporary terms, for in his satire he is a powerful voice of his time. But it is when he extends the scope of contemporary satire that he most clearly states his position as a major poet. Before seeing just how Langland develops satire it is first necessary to establish the basic nature of the satire in the poem.

The Dreamer's initial visionary experience occupies the first five passus of the poem, and it announces itself as having a worldly concern:[13]

> Al the welthe of this worlde and the woo bothe,
> Wynkyng as it were, wyterly ich saw hyt,
> Of tryuthe and of tricherye, of tresoun and of gyle,
> Al ich saw slepynge as ich shal ʒow telle.
>
> i 10-13

This sounds very much like the opening of a formal satire on the foibles of the world, and the things that the Dreamer sees strengthen this impression. It is true, of course, that a preliminary part of this vision is one of symbolic right and wrong:

> Esteward ich byhulde, after the sonne,
> And sawe a toure, as ich trowede, truthe was therynne;
> Westwarde ich waitede in a whyle after,
> And sawe a deep dale; deth, as ich lyuede,
> Wonede in tho wones and wyckede spiritus.
>
> i 14-18

These lines arouse suggestions of meaning deeper than 'the welthe of this worlde and the woo bothe' and they are suggestions which Langland is to follow up later, but for the moment these observations stand in the context merely as if they give authority to the implicit judgments the author is making, because he goes on to reveal, in a familiar manner, the estates of medieval society. The Dreamer first sees the ploughmen who:

> ... putte hem to plow and pleiden ful seylde,
> In settyng and in sowyng swonken ful harde,
> And wonne that thuse wasters with glotenye destroyeth.
>
> i 22-24

The Dreamer's eye passes over other practisers of the active life until he comes to the second estate of the medieval world, the clergy:

> I fonde ther frerus, alle the foure ordres,
> Prechynge the peple for profit of the wombe,
> And glosynge the godspel as hem good lykede.
>
> i 56-58

and after a fierce revelation of the failings of the clerical life the satire passes on to the estate of nobility:

> Thanne cam ther a kyng, knyȝthod hym ladde,
> The muche myȝte of the men made hym to regne.
>
> i 139-140

This division has to some extent been obscured by the revisions which have made the first passus a rather ragged affair in C,[14] and another factor which obscures the simple satiric pattern is Langland's discursive style, for he deals with a number of types of people under each category. The inclusion of hermits under the ploughmen section might seem to upset the estate-satire system, but it seems clear that Langland is referring to those who were not born to clerical rank (as he feels you should be, see vi 63-79) but who undertake to worship God by simple actions, for they:

> ... for the loue of oure lorde lyueden ful harde,
> In hope to haue a gode ende and heuene-ryche blysse.
>
> i 28-29

In this first passus Langland asserts very strongly that he is a satirist, not only by what he states, but also by the vigour with which he states it. It is a densely packed vision of England, full of movement, of quickly changing scenes, and it comes to a fine confused climax:

> Kokes and here knaues crieden 'hote pyes, hote!
> Good goos and grys, go we dyne, gowe!'
> Tauerners – 'a tast for nouht' – tolden the same,
> 'Whit wyn of Oseye and of Gascoyne,
> Of the Ruele and of the Rochel wyn, the roste to defye.'
> Al this ich sauh slepynge and seuene sythes more.
>
> i 226-231

The extra alliteration we find here and the frequent use of extra syllables, especially in the first half-line, impress the whirling vigour of the scene on the reader; Langland is talking about the world and is talking with authority: the authority is his because he has the poetic power to create the clamour of the London streets and the confused, fast-moving picture of medieval England in his field full of folk. But the clamour of the ending and the pace of the whole passus do not fully conceal the careful satiric structure, that structure which represents the three estates of England. In order to suggest a microcosmic view of the country Langland uses the same satiric pattern that Gower uses in the Prologue to the *Confessio Amantis* and the same pattern that Chaucer suggests by having three immaculate men on his pilgrimage, men who are described ethically, with little or no physical detail – Parson, Knight and Ploughman.

If Langland had continued his poem in this vein then he would have a high place among English satirists; but his plan is different. His wish is to talk less about things and more about meanings:

> What the montayne bymeneth and the merke dale,
> And the feld ful of folke, ich shal zow fayre shewe.
>
> ii 1-2

The briefly-mentioned large symbols of the field, the tower and the dale are brought back into the focus of the poem and, just as would happen in a morality play, a figure of authority comes 'doun fro that castel' and addresses the representative of *humanum genus* who stands, puzzling, in the centre of the stage.[15] Lady Holy Church is a figure of great authority and she addresses the Dreamer now, but the nature of her address shows very clearly the scope of Langland's ambitions.

The early part of her speech seems to provide a gloss on the first passus,[16] but then she turns to a loftier topic; she closes with a message which states in ineffable simplicity the centre of the Christian mystery:

> Alle that worchen that wikkede ys wenden thei shulle
> After hure deth-day and dwelle ther wrong ys;
> And alle that han wel ywroght wenden they shulle
> Estwarde to heuene euere to abyde,

Ther treuthe is, the trone that trinite ynne sitteth.
Lere it thus lewede men, for lettrede hit knoweth,
Than treuthe and trewe loue ys no tresour bettere.

ii 130-136

This is reminiscent of the opening description of the symbolic field, and in a lesser writer this would be the end of the poem; the satire of the first passus has been topped off by a suitable interpretation. But Langland is a harder man to please than that: we still have a long way to go. This speech may state truths, but it does not explain them, and the Dreamer, 'Will', allegorically possessed only of volition, is naturally baffled. But Holy Church is not the person to undertake his education, it seems, for in a passage of unique power Langland ends the passus with a long series of images where Holy Church almost sings in honour of love. Here is some of Langland's finest poetry, here we find images of great delicacy:

Loue is the plonte of pees, and most preciouse of vertues;
For heuene holde hit ne myȝte, so heuy hit semede,
Til hit hadde on erthe ȝoten hymselue.
Was neuere lef vpon lynde lyghter therafter,
As whanne hit hadde of the folde flesche and blod ytake;
Tho was it portatyf and pershaunt as the poynt of a nelde,
May non armure hit lette nother hye walles.

ii 149-155

And here also we find images of great bluntness:

Thauh ȝe be trewe of ȝoure tonge and trewelich wynne,
And be as chast as a chyld that nother chit ne fyghteth,
Bote yf ȝe loue leelliche and lene the poure,
Of such good as god sent goodliche parte,
Ȝe haue no more meryt in masse ne in houres
Than Malkyn of hure maidenhod wham no man desireth.

ii 176-181

The passage ends in a crescendo of images:

So loue ys lech of lyue and lysse of alle peyne,
And the graffe of grace and graythest wey to heuene.

ii 200-201

and the effect is more like the lyrics of the school of Rolle than anything else.[17] Rather than explain, Holy Church celebrates the mystery of love in an almost liturgical fashion which is splendidly appropriate to her as an allegorical figure. In some sense Holy Church's speech throughout this passus is an epigraph to the whole poem, an epigraph which we will not understand until the very end of the poem when Holy Church appears again in a very different allegorical guise. She is the first allegorical figure the Dreamer meets and she will be the last, in passus xxiii, when he finally enters the edifice of Holy Church. Her early appearance here is something of a statement of intention by Langland: he is writing satire, it is true, but he is also writing theology. The ranking of the two modes seems at this stage self-evident, but this does not mean that satire is worthless, for once Holy Church has made her speech – a formal declaration that the allegory is open and is to be complex, as it were – the mode of the poem comes sharply back to that of the first passus. The start of the Dreamer's education is 'to knowe the false', and when Holy Church has effected the transition from her natural mode back to the mode of plain satire, she vanishes from the scene.

The level of the whole discussion of Meed is material satire and the misuse of worldly wealth is the first issue:

> Tomorwe worth Mede wedded to a mansed wrecche,
> To on Fals Faithles of the feendes kynne.
>
> iii 41-42

Throughout a passage of mounting speed the bad characteristics of Meed are set out until the criticism of Theology gives rise to the remarkable scene where Langland shows how Meed and her rout go into action:

> And ich myself Cyuyle and Symonye my felawe
> Wollen ryden vpon rectours and riche men deuoutours,
> And notories on persons that permuten ofte,
> And on poure prouysors and on apeles in the arches.
> Somenours and southdenes that *supersedeas* taketh
> On hem that louyeth lecherie lepeth vp and rydeth,
> On executores and suche men cometh softliche after.
> And let cople the comissarie, oure cart shal he drawe,
> And fecche forth oure vitailes of *fornicatores*.
> Maketh of Lyer a lang cart to lede alle these othere,
> As fobbes and faitours that on hure fet rennen.
>
> iii 183-193

Here Langland works brilliantly at the satirical level; the abstract figures of the personified allegory who have been condemned by the lofty agency of Theology are brought home firmly into fourteenth-century reality and, as before, a wild and somewhat comic confusion suggests the frenzied activity that is typical of the corrupt world.[18] This vigorous strain is maintained throughout the passus, and it reaches a fine climax at the end when the rout of Meed is dispersed – Liar, characteristically, gets away and begins a long and successful business career:

> Lyghtliche Lyere lep awey thennes,
> Lorkynge thorw lanes, to-logged of menye.
> He was nawher welcome for hus meny tales,
> Oueral houted out and yhote trusse,
> Til pardoners hadden pitte and pullede hym to house.
>
> iii 225-229

It is, of course, necessary to go outside the material world to find the standards by which to dismiss Meed and materialism; Langland shows us this skilfully by illustrating how Meed can controvert Conscience's arguments against her when they are materially based themselves. Her answer is so effective that the King observes.:

> ... by Cryst, at my knowynge,
> Mede ys worthy, me thynketh, the maistrye to haue.
>
> iv 285-286

Conscience answers this by making in the first place a very delicate distinction between the categories of reward, but then he goes on to raise the level of discussion and outlines the proper courses of the Christian:

> And man ys relatif rect yf he be ryht trewe;
> He acordeth with Crist in kynde, *uerbum caro factum est*;
> In case, *credere in ecclesia*, in holy kirke to byleyue;
> In numbre, rotie and aryse and remyssion to haue
> Of oure sory synnes, asoiled and clansed,
> And lyue, as oure crede ous kenneth, with Crist withouten ende.
>
> iv 357-362

This deepening of the discussion does not, however, indicate a shift in the nature of this dream – it is merely an appeal to a higher authority, for the dream goes on in its satirical way.

Langland maintains a sense of strict verisimilitude in the next passus, for before the case of Conscience *v.* Meed can 'get on', as the lawyers say, we hear an earlier case in the same court. The case of Peace *v.* Wrong deals very much with contemporary realities, for Peace here is the concept represented in 'the King's peace' or 'a breach of the peace'. Wrong 'rauyschede Rose, the riche wydewe' and has indulged in a whole catalogue of lively medieval crimes. The sense of medieval England and the struggles for power that went on in it is very strong here, and, when Meed steps in with an offer of settlement and Peace is happy enough, Langland shows with a deft stroke that this whole scene has not been one of the law's delays, but is directly relevant to the larger issues of the dream. But, says the King, 'for conscience's sake' Wrong will not get off so lightly; Meed shall not guide the course of law in any way.

Throughout scenes like this there is a passionate and detailed concern with the running of the country: Langland is agitated by the way in which the exchange of money can suppress true justice, can interfere with that deep-based natural law in which every Christian inevitably believes. Never a man to do things by half, Langland includes a good deal of precise exhortation – he attacks the people who buy what passes for absolution by building fine windows in churches:

> Ac god to alle good folke suche grauynge defendeth,
> To wryten in wyndowes of eny wel dedes,
> Leste prude by peyntid there and pompe of the worlde.
>
> iv 68-70

The prohibition is timely, for Meed has said about lechery:

> 'Hit ys synne as of seuene non soner relesed.
> Haue mercy,' quath Mede, 'on men that hit haunten,
> And ich shal keuery ȝoure kirke and ȝoure cloistre maken,
> Bothe wyndowes and wowes ich wolle amenden and glase'.
>
> iv 62-65

In a similar vein, Langland shows a remarkable passion for minutiae when he recommends a close check on the characters of

merchants, to avoid accidental deaths being caused when righteous
fire visits the houses of evil men:

> Forthy mayres that maken free men, me thynketh that thei ouhten
> For to spure and aspye, for eny speche of seluer,
> What manere mester other merchaundise he vsede,
> Er he were vnderfonge free and felawe in ʒoure rolles.
>
> iv 108-111

He talks on this level at the very end of the dream, practical to the
last, for even after Meed has been dismissed Reason makes a
curiously pragmatic final speech, urging that the King should free
himself of capitalistic pressures:

> And ich dar legge my lyf that Loue wol lene the suluer,
> To wage thyne, and helpe wynne that thow wilnest after,
> More than al thy marchauns other thy mytrede bisshopes,
> Other Lumbardes of Lukes that lyuen by lone as Iewes.
>
> v 191-194

It is an appropriate end for a dream which has very plainly dealt
with the proper running of the Christian commonwealth, with the
establishment of natural law in England. As in any Christian
political writing, reference must be made to the sources of that
natural law, the spiritual authorities must be referred to, but this
in no way alters the tone of the dream, which is one of political
satire.

The interesting bridge passage between the first two dreams in
the C-text provides the first suggestion that the poet is now to
move away from traditional satire as he has shown it in the first
dream. In this passage of waking allegory the poet appears to probe
his own motives and seems to provide his own justification for
being a poet:

> And ʒut fond ich neuere in faith, sytthen my frendes deyden,
> Lyf that my lyked, bote in thes longe clothes.
> Yf ich by laboure sholde luye and lyflode deseruen,
> That labour that ich lerned best, therwith luye ich sholde.
>
> vi 40-43

This scrutiny of his own life and the verification by Reason and
Conscience that he is doing the right thing set very firmly the tone

for the next dream. Satire is still, largely, the mode, but here the satire is directed towards the individual and his own needs and duties – the satire is no longer political in the widest sense.

The opening sequence of the dream is a massive sermon by Reason. This is set in the field of folk and Reason, supported by Conscience, stands before the King. One of the C-text's revisions is to make this scene more obviously follow on from the previous dream, and the sense is very strong that this is a new stage in the examination of life that the Dreamer began back in the first passus.[19] Reason now speaks to all, not just to the King:

> Ac ich shal seye as ich seih, slepynge as it were,
> How Reson radde al the reame ryght for to lyuen.
>
> vi 125-126

As Conscience did before, so Reason appeals to a high authority when he says:

> Ac зut shal come a kyng and confesse зow alle,
> And bete зow, as the byble telleth, for brekyng of зoure reule,
> And amende зow monkes, moniales and chanons,
> And putte зow to зoure penaunce, *ad pristinum statum ire*.
>
> vi 169-172

Although sixteenth-century men self-indulgently interpreted this as a foresight of their own reforming activities, it refers in fact to a defender of the faith greater than Henry VIII. The allegory is taking place in the light of heaven, yet so far that light is only used to look more clearly at earthly things.

The confession of the sins which follows is a directly personal sort of satire; often comical and often biting, here Langland sets out the typical failings of the medieval Christian. There is a strong grotesque element, of course, for satire commonly exaggerates, and many people find this to be the most potent sequence in the whole poem. Here Langland creates within the poem the vivid and often revolting world of the ordinary man:

> Tho Clement the cobelere cauhte hym by the mydel,
> For to lyfte hym on loft he leyde hym on hus knees;
> Ac Gloton was a gret cherl and gronyd in the liftynge,
> And couhed vp a caudel in Clementes lappe;
> Ys non so hongry hounde in Hertfordeshire

That thorst lappe of that leuynge, so vnloueliche hit smauhte.
   With al the wo of the worlde, hus wif and hus wenche
Bere hym to hus bedde and brouhte hym therynne;
And after al this excesse he hadde an accidie,
He slep Saterday and Sonday tyl sonne ʒede to reste.
Thenne awakyde he wel wan and wolde haue ydronke;
The ferst word that he spak was, 'ho halt the bolle?'

vii 409-420

It is important to recognize that Langland is not indulging in
unpleasantness just for the sake of it. To create in verse this sort of
scene is to give the poet an unshakeable hold on reality; the
ordinary life of ordinary people is embraced in the poem, for
Langland is filled with that human interest which Johnson found
lacking in *Paradise Lost*. This means that the satire is successfully
realized in the poem, and this is of great effect, for throughout this
whole dream Langland reveals a depth of understanding that
seems to qualify him very strongly to talk about all levels of society
There is not only the rather mordant insight that the confession of
the sins reveals, there are also passages which reveal a deep concern with ordinary people, and the finest of these deserves full
quotation:

The most needy aren oure neighebores, and we nyme good hede,
As prisones in puttes and poure folke in cotes,
Charged with children and chef lordes rente,
That thei with spynnynge may spare spenen hit in hous-hyre,
Bothe in mylk and in mele to make with papelotes,
To aglotye with here gurles that greden after fode.
Also hemselue suffren muche hunger,
And wo in winter-tyme, with wakynge a nyghtes
To ryse to the ruel to rocke the cradel,
Bothe to karde and to kembe, to clouten and to wasche,
To rubbe and to rely, russhes to pilie,
That reuthe is to rede othere in ryme shewe
The wo of these women that wonyeth in cotes;
And of meny other men that muche wo suffren,
Bothe afyngrede and afurst, to turne the fayre outwarde,
And beth abasshed for to begge, and wolle nat be aknowe
What hem needeth at here neihebores at non and at euen.

x 71-87

In poetry like this Langland creates, rather than states, a sense of charity and of passion in his poem; and it is from this source, from the fact that he both understands and feels for the ordinary people, that his examination of the duties of humanity draws so much of its conviction.

This examination is the main part of this dream, in fact, for once the seven deadly sins have confessed, the destructive criticism is over and we see the rather sad spectacle of humanity looking for a better part, casting around for constructive criticism:

> A thousand of men tho throngen togederes,
> Cryyng vpward to Crist and to hus clene moder,
> To haue grace to go to Treuthe; god leyue that thei mote!
> Ac ther was weye non so wys that the way thider couthe,
> Bote blostrede forth as bestes ouer baches and hulles.
>
> viii 155-159

It is Piers Plowman who helps these people out of their bestial confusion and who sets out the duties of the world. The constructive element of the satire is laid out strongly and clearly – each person has his particular duty and Piers is the arbiter. This whole long sequence is very much in terms of temporal duties, and it seems that things are being sorted out well. True, it is not easy to control Hunger, as Piers finds, but there is the promise of a pardon from Truth and the poem seems to be drawing to a satisfactory conclusion. We are, I feel, deliberately led into believing that the coming pardon will end all problems: so much stress is placed on each person's temporal duty that, by a kind of *suppressio veri*, we are led to believe that this is *all* their duty. Also the last passus of this second dream gives a very long account of those who will receive the pardon and those who will not – the validity of the pardon is an unspoken assumption throughout.[20] At one moment, even, Piers takes on an anagogical significance in this dream, as it is suggested that work alone will bring men to heaven:

> Atte hye pryme Peers let the plouh stonde,
> And ouer-seyh hem hymself; ho so best wrouhte,
> He sholde be hyred therafter when heruest-tyme come.
>
> ix 119-121

The first dream, we might recall at this point, told us truths, but not the complete truth, for it was necessary to go on and look at the Christian life of the individual after discussing the life of the state. And the same is true here: the pardon from Truth is, in a sense, illusory, for it merely suggests that the poem has not yet fully discovered what it is to do well.[21] In one of those enigmatic climaxes that Langland seems to enjoy, when things are found to be not what they seemed, Piers himself is baffled. The satirical mode, we find, has not given us the whole truth, for it has dealt in temporalities and in deeds. As the poem moves on into the Vision of Do Well (as it seems to be most reliably called[22]) the satiric mode no longer holds the centre of the poem. The poem changes to a more intellectual mode, to an attempt to find by cerebral means just what more is needed, just what the Christian life does entail as well as good deeds.

It is a highly dramatic change, of course, rather like the earlier moment when we found that Meed was not quite as simple as she seemed, but could do good things as well as bad.[23] This sort of climax seems to have appealed to a love of paradox in Langland's mind, and it is certainly effective in showing that we have all been taken in. The audience is made to experience the sudden turn of the argument, for with a shock we are shown that things are not nearly over – we are just getting down to the really difficult business.

And the forthcoming business of the poem is clearly not satirical, though satire is still used from time to time for various purposes. The satire is not set aside, but it is not a total answer. Those earlier moments, when the immaterial was used as brief authority, are now to grow into the central issues of the poem: the Christian's spiritual duty and the mechanics of salvation are the issues to be taken up now. One needs to realize, though, that in the very difficult passus which follow, the poet's credibility as an investigator depends on the force and fire with which he has characterized ordinary life in the preceding passus; the way in which he writes satire gives him the basis of reality from which he can move into much more difficult fields. The theology rises out of the satire and, as we shall see, deliberately refuses to lose contact with it.

At the beginning of *Dowel*, Thought rephrases much of the material of the first two dreams, as the Dreamer thinks over what

U

he has seen. But as soon as new faculties are applied to the problems at hand new sorts of answers are provided; Wit gives a much more cerebral analysis than any we have seen before:

> 'Syre dowel dwelleth,' quath Wit, 'nat a daye hennes,
> In a castle that Kynde made of foure kyne thynges;
> Of erthe, of aier yt is made, medled togederes,
> With wynd and water wittyliche enioyned.
> Kynde hath closed therynne craftilyche with alle
> A lemman that he loueth wel, lyke to hymselue.
> *Anima* hue hatte; to hure hath enuye
> A prout prikyere of Fraunce, *princeps huius mundi*.'
>
> xi 127-134

This sort of discussion is typical of what is to follow in the next few passus: to a certain extent they are the theoretical centre of the work, as Langland seeks to explain and justify positions which are essential to his whole poem. But this does not mean that the satiric mode is abandoned for the theological mode. Rather, the satiric mode continues in a subservient character, for Langland introduces a good deal of detailed material from everyday life both to supplement what he is saying in theory and also to retain artistic hold of that real world, to which the theory ultimately must apply or be worthless. Having spoken of *kynde*, that great natural force, at some length, Langland makes, by a rather awkward word-play, a transition to a much more mundane discussion:

> Ho so lyueth in lawe and in loue doth wel
> As these weddid men that this worlde susteynen?
> For of here kynde thei come, confessours and martyres,
> Patriarkes and prophetes, popes and maidenes.
>
> xi 202-205

This begins a long discussion of matrimony, of the proper times for conception and of contemporary vices connected with marriage. It is a passage which could well come from the second dream, but here it stands as a large counter-balance to the theoretical material that has been put forward. It does, though, stand rather clumsily in the passus, for the word-play which introduces the discussion is hardly convincing, and the transition back to the theoretical study of Dowel is even less skilfully done:

And thus ys Dowel, my frend, to do as lawe techeth,
To louye and to lowe the and no lyf to greue.
Ac to louye and to lene, leyf me, that is Dobet;
Ac to ȝeue and to ȝeme bothe ȝonge and olde,
Helen and helpen, is Dobest of all.

xi 304-308

Perhaps here, where Langland writes clumsily, his intention is most clear, for artistic smoothness has not obscured the sinews of his argument. It seems that he is very concerned to maintain a connexion with the real world of men and women that has been discussed in the first two dreams. Obviously a discussion as complex as that which is proceeding at this time must deal very much in pure theory, but the poet seems unwilling to be completely esoteric for a long period. The abstract unity of the passus might have been much improved by the absence of this discussion of marriage, but, clumsy as it is, it appears to suit Langland's purposes to include it, for in this way the real can subsist in the poem along with the theoretical.

The centre of this whole sequence of the poem is the growth of two ideas; the first is the questioning of the value of ratiocination, for substantial doubts are raised about the value of reason in the theological context. It is Study who says plainly:

Ac Theologie hath teened me ten score tymes,
The more ich muse theron, the mystiloker hit semeth,
And the deppere ich deuyne, the derker me thynketh hit.
Hit is no science sothliche, bote a sothfast byleuye;
Ac for hit lereth men to louye ich byleyue theron the bettere.

xii 129-133

And, arising from this argument, Langland, in another passage of paradox, shows that the apparently worthless characteristic of Recklessness can come very close to holiness, for it is this rather enigmatic figure who first broaches the issue of Patient Poverty, that important theme in the poem. Finally Ymagynatyf sums up this long sequence of argument; he accepts some of Recklessness's points but also shows that the reason has its value, provided it is within the framework of true faith – his words are the synthesis of the conflicting strands of argument that Langland has laid out before us:

So grace is a gyfte of god and kynde witt a chaunce,
And cleregye and connyng of kynde wittes techynge.
And ʒut is cleregie to comende, for Cristes loue, more
Than eny connynge of kynde witt, bote cleregie hit ruwele.

xv 33-36

But throughout this elevated conceptual discussion which quite self-consciously at times mirrors the *summa* of the medieval theologians, there is another strand working, that strand of simple material discussion which has here been called satire. In passus xiii there is a passage of pseudo-autobiography[24] before the long speech of Recklessness is sprung upon the reader. We hear how the Dreamer himself is led astray and in particular we hear how the friars have cordially assisted him in his errors:

By so thow riche were, haue thow no conscience
How that thow come to good; confesse the to som frere,
He shal asoile the thus sone, how so thow euere wynne hit.

xiii 5-7

A similar effect is created when Recklessness uses a very mundane image, illustrating the virtues of poverty by suggesting that a messenger can conduct his business much more quickly than a merchant and can also walk without fear of robbery; this illustrates how:

. . . the poure pacient purgatorye passeth
Rathere than the ryche, thauh thei renne at ones.

xiv 31-32

This is an extended exemplary metaphor in the manner of the sermon, and it performs in the poem all the services that the humble exemplum can perform for the preacher: it explains and clarifies and it keeps the audience in touch with the continuing argument.[25]

A function very similar to this is performed by the use of large images, indeed the image and the exemplum often merge together. The concrete imagery that Langland uses throughout the satirical parts of the poem has been discussed to some extent by Langland scholars, but it is interesting to see that the same vivid flair continues throughout a sequence of very different general tone.[26] Thus

an extended image concerning types of seeds is used in passus xiii
to illustrate the advantages of suffering:

> Ac seedes that been sowen and mowe suffre wyntres,
> Aren tydyour and tower to mannes byhofthe
> Than seedes that sowen beeth and mowe nouht with forstes,
> With wyndes ne with wederes, as in wynter-tyme;
> As lynne-seed and lik-seed and lente-seedes alle
> Aren nouht so worthy as whete, ne so wel mowen
> In the feld with the forst and hit freese longe.
> Ryght so, for sothe, that suffre may penaunces
> Worth alowed of oure lorde at here laste ende.
>
> xiii 186-194

And Langland says pithily of clerics who become greedy business-
men:

> Right as weodes wexen in wose and in donge,
> So of rychesse vpon richesse arisen al vices.
>
> xiii 229-230

Here the realistic touches, familiar in the satiric mode, add
weight to the theory, but perhaps more interesting are moments
when it seems that, after the theorization has beeen made, the issue
returns to satire. Thus at the end of Recklessness's very long
speech he assures the clergy that if they perform their jobs properly, they will not go hungry:

> . . . yf thay trauaile treweliche and tristen in god almyghty,
> Hem sholde neuere lackye lyflode, nother lynnen ne wollene.
> The title that ȝe taketh ȝoure ordres by telleth ȝe beth auaunced,
> And needeth nat to nyme seluer for masses that ȝe syngen;
> For he that tok ȝow title sholde take ȝow wages,
> Other the bisshop that blessed ȝow and enbaumede ȝoure fyngeres.
>
> xiv 102-107

The topic here is a very detailed and a very practical one; the poet
recognizes the reasonable concern of priests for a living wage. It is
very reminiscent of the attitude in the first dream, where Langland
had a practical eye to the ordering of the state. This is really the
first re-entry of the satiric mode into the centre of the poem for a
good while, and that it is no accident is shown by the end of
Ymagynatyf's speech. Here the Dreamer is being urged to accept

the world, not to question it too much (a lesson he has been given before, but has hardly heeded, see xiii 32 et seq.) and one of the issues he is to accept is the mysterious working of salvation:

> And where hit worth other nat worth, the byleyue is gret of treuthe,
> And hope hongeth ay theron to haue that treuthe deserueth;
> *Quia super pauca fidelis fuisti, supra multa te constituam.*
>
> xv 213-214

But the other issue is more mundane: he is to accept the ordering of life on earth, unjust as it may seem, for life on earth is ordered in the light of eternity:

> . . . the pokok and the popeiay, with here proude federes,
> Bytokneth ryght riche men that regnen here on erthe.
> For porsewe a pocok other a pohen to cacche,
> And haue hem in haste at thyn owene wil;
> For thei may nat fleo fer ne ful hye nother,
> For here fetheres that faire ben to fle fer hem letteth.
>
> xv 173-178

The reader must feel, on reading these passages, that the potent theology of these recent passus has not been set out merely for its own sake: the poem may seem to be a *summa* in parts, but not here; it is looking again like a poem about the world and the way people live in it, and this impression is greatly strengthened in the next major sequence of the poem, where Patient Poverty is confirmed as the only fit state of life for the ordinary Christian, where we discover, at last, what it is to Do Well – to live in a state of physical and spiritual humility.

The next dream is prefaced, as before, by a brief satirical glance at the corruption of the world, of the friars in particular,[27] and then Langland plunges into a long dream sequence where, to a large extent, the poet brings together his realistic mode and his theoretical mode into a single point. A barrage of concrete imagery introduces this structural theme as the Dreamer describes the dinner he attends:

> Cleregie calde after mete, and thenne cam Scripture,
> And seruede hem thus sone of sondrie metes menie,
> Of Austyn, of Ambrosie, of alle the foure euangelies.
>
> xvi 43-45

but the master friar cannot eat this food:

> Ac here sauce was ouere-soure and vnsauerliche grounde,
> In a morter, *post-mortem*, of meny bitere peynes,
>
> xvi 49-50

There is even contemporary satire here as the Dreamer says:

> 'Ich shal Iangly to thys Iordan . . .'
>
> xvi 92

The vivid opening to this dream leads into the important scene where Patience remonstrates with *Activa-Vita* (also called Haukyn in B). In this passage the poet condenses his two strands of thought, the satiric and the theological, into the one remarkable image of Patient Poverty: this is a state at once physical and spiritual, and it answers all man's needs. This concept is put in some of Langland's finest poetry, as Patience explains to *Activa-Vita*:

> For lent was ther neuere lyf bote lyflode were yshape,
> Wherof othere wherfore and wherwith to lyuen;
>   The worme that woneth vnder erthe, and in water fisshes,
> The crykett by kynde of fur, and corlew by the wynde,
> Bestes by gras and by greyn and by grene rotes.
> In menynge that alle men myghte the same
> Lyuen thorgh leell byleyue, as oure lord wittnesseth.
>
> xvi 240-246

In answer to Activa Vita's question 'Have you any of that food with you', Patience says:

> 'ȝe', quath Pacience, and hente oute of hus poke
> A pece of the pater-noster and profrede to vs alle.
>
> xvi 248-249

The whole series of food-images that Langland has used for Christian faith and doctrine comes here to a paradoxical climax: this is not really an image at all, for we are being told that this is, indeed, sustenance, a sustenance which obviates the need for physical food. The establishment of this issue is really the end of the problem that was raised in the second dream – what is Dowel? This is the sustenance which replaces worry about physical issues. The point is pressed home at great length in the following passus where Patience elaborates enormously the importance and the value of Patient Poverty. Again using a massive material image to create the spiritual world, and with that sense of the symbolism of the seasons that is so close to much medieval poetry,[28] Patience states the unity of the creation, physical, climactic and spiritual:

Muche myrthe is in May amonge wilde bestes,
And so forth whil somer lasteth heore solace dureth;
And muche myrthe amonge riche men is that han meoble ynow and
heele.
Ac beggers aboute Myd-somere, bredless thei soupe,
And ʒut is wynter for hem wors, for wet-shood thei gangen,
Afurst and afyngred and foule rebuked
Of these worlde-riche men that reuthe hit is to huyre.
Now, lord, send hem somer somtyme, to solace and to Ioye,
That al here lyf leden in lowenesse and in pouerte!

xvii 10-18

It is another of Langland's dramatic paradoxes that the wretched poor of the first two satirical dreams here move into the theological spotlight, as it were: theirs is the state of grace now, it is not just one of the modes of physical life.

This point is worth dallying on, for the stage is an important one. Langland has established to his own satisfaction what is the proper course of human life. And yet, as one so often has to say, he does not stop here. Problems have already been raised about the rationale of salvation, and the Dreamer has been told that it is a mystery which he should not presume to probe.[29] Langland, therefore, does not *probe* it, but rather he undertakes to elaborate and celebrate the motive force behind the concept of salvation, the basic force of charity. Langland is at his most precisely allegorical here, for although it is Conscience, Clergy and Reason who have brought the Dreamer so far, it is *Liberum Arbitrium*, free will, who leads the Dreamer on, for only the freely made choice can illuminate charity to the Christian – '*Credo ut intelligam*'.[30] The Dreamer says:

'Leue *Liberum Arbitrium*,' quath ich, 'ich leyue, as ich hope,
Thou couthest telle and teche me to Charity, ich leyue?'
xix 1-2

The slightly uncertain poetry here is not untypical of a good deal of the more conceptual passages of theology throughout this part of the poem; but although we must at times judge that Langland is not writing at his best, it is nevertheless easy enough to see what he is attempting to do, and perhaps one might suggest that the remarkable thing is that *any* of this difficult conceptual material rises to the level of good poetry, not that a good deal of it is rather lame. The attempt, indeed, is almost as confounding as the deed.

The poem had, for a while, picked up the satiric mode again as, in the large images of poverty and the humble life, the poet had stressed that the issues established theologically are to be lived in all the reality of the satiric world, but now *Liberum Arbitrium* moves on to more lofty theological issues. The immensely elaborate image of the tree of life introduces, and in its intricacy symbolizes, a complex passage of theological discussion: the life of Christ up to Palm Sunday is interspersed with encounters with Faith and Hope, the two spiritual attributes basic to the Christian life, and finally the Dreamer encounters the Samaritan, type of Christ and the embodiment of charity, the summit of Christian virtues. The climax of this sequence, and the true climax of the poem, is the magnificent passus which recounts the Crucifixion and the Harrowing of Hell.

Here Langland most clearly states his greatness as a poet, as his verse rises to heights it has only suggested before and gives us a sustained poetic celebration of the central mystery of the Christian faith. And indeed, it seems to me that the magnificence of the passus is central to its meaning. There is no specific rational need to tell this story – the worst-informed of the audience would have been familiar with the details – but the need is entirely poetic. The intensity of the concept of charity is created within the poem, it is not imported from outside, not accepted by hearsay; Langland recreates for us the very actions which bring charity and love into the world at their most intense. The passus is the keystone of the poem in every sense, for Langland's authority as a poet derives ultimately from the quality of passages like Christ's speech after the Harrowing, where we find that the alliterative line can achieve a remarkable height of style:

And now bygynneth thi gyle agayn on the turne,
And my grace to growe ay wydder and wydder.
The biternesse that thow hast browe, now brouk hit thyself;
That art doctour of deth, drynk that thow madest!
For ich that am lord of lyf, loue is my drynke,
And for that drynke todaye deyede, as hit semede;
Ac ich wol drynke of no dich, ne of no deop cleregie,
Bote of comune coppes, alle cristene soules;
Ac thi drynke worth deth and deop helle thy bolle.
Ich fauht so, me fursteth ȝut, for mannes soule sake;
   Sicio.
May no pyement ne pomade ne presiouse drynkes
Moyste me to the fulle, ne my thurst slake,
Til the vendage valle in the vale of Iosaphat,
And drynke ryght rype most, *resurreccio mortuorum.*

         xxi 402-415

This is the summit of the theological mode in the poem and, as one might expect, this mode at its highest is, for a Christian poet, more inspiring and more far-reaching than the satiric mode. The Dreamer is moved to prayer and the poem moves on into what the manuscripts call *Dobest.*

Then, however, the poem's tempo slackens, as the story of Christ's life after the Resurrection is told at an intensity rather less than we have heard before. It is something of a poetical anti-climax: this may well be partly due to the difficulty of sustaining highly powered poetry over a good period, but it does have a curiously successful pacing effect – the poem slows down here and it slows down suitably. For what is to follow is yet another dramatic turning about. It is the last turn-about Langland has for us, and it is quite the most effective as he descends from the transports of theological celebration to the tragically mundane level at which he shows the state of the church on earth. Satire comes back, and the rest of the poem is satire; the slowing of the poetical tempo in the first part of passus xxii seems to prepare us for the almost sickening anti-climax as we move from the exultation at the end of passus xxi to the revelation of the wretched state of human affairs.

It is in the moment when Grace itself begins to counsel Piers Plowman that the poem moves back to its mundane sphere:

For ich wolle dele today and diuyde grace
To alle kynne creatures that can hus fif wittes;
Tresour to lyue by to here lyues ende,
And wepne to fight with that wol neuere faille.
For Antecrist and hise shal al the worlde greue,
And encombry the, Conscience, bote yf Crist the helpe.
And fele false prophetes, flaterers and glosers
Shullen come, and be curatours ouer kynges and erles.
Thanne shal Pruyde be pope and pryns of holychurche,
Couetise and Vnkyndenesse cardinales hym to lede.

                                                xxii 215-224

It is the specific nature of grace on earth that is found important:

To somme men he ȝaf wit, with wordes to shewe,
To wynne with truthe that the worlde asketh,
As preostes and prechours and prentises of lawe,
Thei to lyue leelly by labour of tounge,
And by wit to wyssen other as Grace wolde hem teche.

                                                xxii 229-233

Langland, we see, has not forgotten 'what the world asketh'.
This is no mystical tract before us, it is a huge poem directed to
the proper ordering of the Christian life – how it should be ordered
and, above all, why it should be ordered in that way. Langland is
not content to deal out injunctions; he has set out, not so much to
justify the ways of God to man, but rather to explain them. And
having discussed the theoretical issues at such length and with
such force, it is now time for him to turn back to material issues, to
see just how human beings run their divinely organized world.
The potency of the world is great, for man's opportunities are
huge – in a superbly phrased conventional image Langland shows
this:

Grace gaf to Peers a teome of foure grete oxen;
That on was Luc, a large beest and a louh-chered,
Marc, and Matheu he thirde, myghty beestes bothe;
And Ioyned til hem on Iohan, most gentil of alle,
The prys neet of Peers plouh, passynge al othere.

                                                xxii 262-266

With such assistance the edifice of Holy Church is built, and the
allegory makes it a barn, continuing to follow the strand of animal

and vegetable imagery which has achieved the status of a major theme in the poem:

> Now is Peeres to the plouh; Pruyde hit aspide,
> And gadered hym a gret ost; greuen he thenketh
> Conscience, and all Cristene and cardinale uertues,
> To blowen hem doun and breken hem and bite a-two the rotes.
>
> xxii 337-340

An apocalyptic battle ensues, a psychomachia which moves across the sociology and the history of medieval Europe.[31] The forces of evil are described with rigorous satirical detail:

> The countrey is the corsedour ther cardinales cometh ynne;
> And ther thei liggen and lengen most lecherie ther regneth.
>
> xxii 419-420

During the hubbub the Dreamer himself enters the Church, but the end of his spiritual pilgrimage is far from the end of the poem: the battle rises to a crescendo and finally, with that love of detail that so characterizes Langland's best satire, we are shown how one apparently small fault can destroy the defences of Holy Church. Contrition lies exhausted by 'the plastres of the persoun' and so a friar provides a more soothing balm:

> He goth and gropeth Contrition and gaf hym a plastre
> Of 'a pryue payement and ich shal preye for 30w,
> And for hem that 3e aren holden to, al my lyf-tyme,
> And make 30w my lady, in masse and in matynes,
> As freres of oure fraternite for a litel seluer.'
> Thus he goth and gadereth and gloseth ther he shryueth,
> Til Contrition hadde clene for3ute to crie and wepe and wake
> For hus wickede werkes as he was woned byfore.
> For comfort of hus confessour contricion he lefte,
> That is the souereyne salue for alle kynne synnes.
>   Anon Sleuthe seih that and so dude Pruyde,
> And comen with a kene wil Conscience to assaile.
>
> xxiii 363-374

The poem has a gloomy end; here is no joyful ringing of bells and gathering of angels.[32] Rather, there is a deliberately unsentimental assessment of the state of Christianity. Conscience alone, the individual's sense of ultimate rightness, the voice of God in man, is left on the stage:

> 'By crist,' quath Conscience tho, 'ich wol bycome a pilgryme,
> And wenden as wide as the worlde regneth,
> To seke Peers the Plouhman that Pruyde myghte destruye.'
>
> xxiii 380-382

Conscience looks for that fit ecclesiastical authority symbolized by the ploughman, the man who approaches Christ and Peter most closely. But even these are not Langland's last words – with an astonishing sense for detail, for making each point conclusive, he makes Conscience continue:

> And that freres hadden a fyndynge that for neode flateren,
> And counterpleideth me, Conscience; nowe Kynde me avenge,
> And sende me hap and hele til ich haue Peers Plouhman!
>
> xxiii 383-385

Almost the last words of the poem point out that the real problem with the friars is an organizational one; they are forced to beg, and the transition is easy from a holy mendicancy to an occupational mendicancy. The rule of the order, Langland implies, imposes conditions too strict for ordinary men.[33] It is a charitable touch, perhaps even a very bold argument.[34] But above all it is deeply serious and deeply practical, and it is only if we grasp the minute practicality of Langland's work that we can grasp the totality that, with all its looseness and frequent errancy, *Piers Plowman* is. Langland is a poet, but he is using his poetry to enforce his conceptual standpoint: the world, basically perfect and divinely ordered, is being appallingly run by men.

Satire is thus the final mode of *Piers Plowman*, and in a sense the whole poem is truly a satire. But Langland has so completely expanded the satirical mode that he has made it almost a genre to itself. His huge ambition is to include, within his satire, the very moral concepts which give him the right to judge the standards by which the world he observes is errant. Of course, ambition alone cannot elect one to literary greatness, and there are many poetic qualities which create Langland's authority. His plain and colloquial language, his fluent and idiomatic metre and perhaps most particularly his flair for the humble but compelling image all create the style to enact the massive content.[35] And the style is basically the hard-hitting plain-spoken style of the satirist – this is the source of the poem's energy as poetry.

To outline his theological standards, to illuminate the backcloth against which the sad world is silhouetted, Langland leaves the topics of the satirist, but this only means that he returns to satire finally with all the more weight behind his condemnation. The contrast between the passionate triumph of passus xxi and the dismal confusion of passus xxiii is a very powerful one, and this fine crisis is achieved partly by the poetic imagination of passus xxi and partly by the determination with which the poet returns to the world, his insistence to tell not only the truth, but the appalling whole truth.

Piers Plowman is in totality a satire, then, but Langland has extended the nature of satire and has set a new standard. Satire provides the opening scenes of the poem, where it discusses politics. It also leads into the discussion of the Christian's duty, and when this discussion has moved out to the theoretical and conceptual plane in *Dowel* the satiric mode is referred to frequently and anchors the discussion in reality. Next the poem abandons satire altogether and moves into the fully theological, not to say liturgical, mood as it recreates the central acts of the Christian faith. At last satire comes back to its place in the centre of the poem but, because of the way the poem has developed, satire has been almost redefined by Langland's use of it – the vision of the world that satire finally reveals is filled with a consciousness of the immense spiritual forces at work in the Christian cosmos. The follies and vices that satire uncovers do not exist only in material terms, they also exist as tragic departures from the path of Christian duty that has been mapped out by Langland both at the temporal and at the spiritual level. The implications of the satire in the last two passus are thus made huge. The atttempt to discuss such topics in literature is in itself admirable; the fact that these topics are discussed with an authority that totally convinces the reader is the real mark of Langland's standing as a writer.

The greatness of Langland's ambition, and the extent to which it succeeds, place him in very rare company. In English only Milton can really be called the same sort of poet, and the comparison is by no means in Milton's favour. Of Dante alone can it be said that he writes with the same huge ambition and surpasses Langland in most of the areas of the genre: perhaps that is a large enough tribute to Langland, and one with which he would have been well content.

12

Chaucer's Contemporary

J. A. W. BENNETT

'None is greatest in the kingdom of heaven; and it is so in poetry.'
Blake's dictum should deter us from drawing up poetical balance
sheets or from using one author as a stick to beat another; and it
makes us regret the more that the artist who in more than one
sense drew Chaucer's pilgrims afresh – his cartoon must be read
alongside his estimates of the Canterbury travellers in his Advertise-
ment for it – evidently never came upon *Piers Plowman*: no edition
of Langland was published between 1651 and 1817; and when
Whitaker's bulky quarto appeared in that year it cost seven
guineas. Such references to Langland as appear in the interval –
like Byron's comment that 'obscene' Chaucer does not deserve his
celebrity as well as *Piers Plowman* – evidently depend on quotations
in The Muses' Library (1737) or Warton's *History* (1774-81). But
it was in a Westminster not greatly altered since Langland's day
that Blake learnt the secret of the Gothic spirit: in giving Love the
human form divine, Pity a human face, he was re-enacting the
supreme allegorical achievement of Langland's eighteenth passus:

> Loue, that is my lemman, suche lettres me sente
> That Mercy, my sustre, and I mankynde shulde saue;
> And that god hath forgyuen, and graunted me, Pees, and Mercy,
> To be mannes meynpernoure for eueremore after.

B xviii 180-183[1]

The dance of these damsels on Easter morning is a subject that
must have appealed to Blake's pen. As it was, it fell to his spiritual
descendant Edward Calvert to embody, in his memorable en-
graving of the Ploughman with 'hard as hurdle arms' urging his
team towards the light and the divine Pastor, that intensity and

integrity of vision which gives Langland his assured place in the kingdom of poetry. Calvert's inscription: 'seen in the Kingdom of Heaven by vision through Jesus Christ our Saviour',[2] bears the impress of Blake's belief in the identity of poetry and truth; and in the drawing itself the three Graces are transmuted into just such dancing maidens as Langland describes (xviii 424). True, Calvert's grand design is impregnated with the particularity of observation that critics associate with Chaucer rather than with the allegorist: the team of horses, the vines, the acres of wheat, seem a direct creation of the life-force that Chaucer called Kind. But the same critics fail to note that there is more in the *Canterbury Tales* about heaven's 'blisful regne' where every soul is replenished 'with the sight of the parfit knowing of god' than in the whole of *Piers Plowman*. The purpose of the present study is to resolve this paradox, to suggest that the attributes and assumptions common to these master-poets are more important than the qualities that appear to divide them. Lest I fail to disturb the traditional assumption that in the last analysis Langland remains a preacher, Chaucer a poet of creative imagination, be it remembered throughout that it is the allegorist who gives Ymaginatif a rôle dignified and dynamic, and who justifies the function of a 'makar' by indicating that poetry and song betoken man's highest bliss:

> Thanne piped Pees of poysye a note,
> '*Clarior est solito post maxima nebula phebus,*
> *Post inimicitias clarior est et amor.*'
>
> . . . .
>
> Treuth tromped tho, and songe '*Te deum laudamus*';
> And thanne luted Loue in a loude note.
>
> B xviii 406-408, 422-423

The first and fundamental affinity between the two poets lies in a quality that sophisticated criticism is loath to recognise or identify: their Englishness. To be sure, *Scrutiny* and Dr Leavis have given this quality a virtue which, because it supposedly resides in people in 'close contact with the soil and with traditional ways of living' is thought to be typified in the 'vital idiom' of *Piers Plowman* rather than in the cosmopolitan Chaucer. But twenty years earlier Edward Thomas had put his finger more precisely on

x

this source of Langland's appeal, when he described him as 'half-Londoner, half-Worcestershireman, and *all* Englishman'.³ It is this sense of England as a whole that distinguishes Langland, and later Chaucer, from all their predecessors. Anglo-Saxon poetry, in the nature of things, reveals no such consciousness; and even when it is local, it does not particularise: the Blackwater at ebb tide, as described in *Maldon*, is almost the only clearly visualised English scene in the whole corpus. In the thirteenth century the chronicle that goes by the name of Robert of Gloucester yields a panegyric and affixes an epithet that was to stay:

> England is right a merye lond: of alle other on with the best;
> iset in the on end of the worlde: as al in the west.
>
> .　.　.　.　.　.　.　.　.　.　.　.
>
> So clene a lond is Engelond: so clene withouten hore,
> the veireste men in the world therinne beth ybore.⁴

The same chronicle shows us town and gown at strife in Oxford streets in the riots of 1264; and *Havelok* gives us a glimpse of porters gathering daily on the Bridge at Lincoln, as they still did in the eighteenth century. But for the most part the early romances are not concerned with the recognisable scene but with fabled forest sides: *Athelston* is exceptional in specifying such details as the names of stopping-places on the road from Canterbury to Westminster.

For a Londoner, Chaucer gives us surprisingly little of the life of London city: the scene in *Troilus* when the warden of the gates bids folk drive in their cattle at evening (v 1177 ff), which has been cited as a sight which the poet 'witnessed nightly from his Aldgate tower', is in fact a straight transcript from Boccaccio. There remain the casual allusion to Jack Straw and his *meynee*, and the beginning of Roger the cook's tale of a Cheapside apprentice. When we meet the pilgrims they are already in Southwark: the Tabard (and the Bell) benefited from the traffic congestion on London Bridge that would prevent such a considerable company crossing to the south bank in the early morning. It is to Langland's fifth passus that we must turn for the daily life of Cockslane and Cheap, Tyburn and Garlickhythe. The third and fourth passus are set firmly in the Westminster of parliament and the lawcourts;

and the evidence for his knowledge of the purlieus of St Paul's and Cornhill (C vi, *ad init.*) is too well known to need quotation. It is more to the present purpose to recall that these scenes of urban life are juxtaposed with vistas of the fields and farms of Malvern and Herefordshire. This variety in itself gives a unique breadth to his poem; and it is constantly reinforced by allusions bespeaking a still wider familiarity with England east and west and south.

To balance such allusions as Chaucer's 'biside a toun men clepen Baldeswelle' with Langland's 'Frenche of the ferthest ende of Norfolke' would be a profitless pastime. But we should remark the limits of Chaucer's interest: Dartmouth, the shipman's conjectured home-port, is 'fer by weste'; Strother is 'fer in the north, I kan nat telle where'. His miller and his reeve give us an Oxford and a Cambridge that can be confirmed from contemporary records (though strangely enough the King's Hall at Cambridge is nowhere else, not even in the unpublished records, called 'the Soler Hall'): 'hende Nicholas' is one of those 'wanton chamberdekyns' whose morals caused the Oxford authorities to enact that 'all scholars should reside in a Hall or College [and] should battel with the same . . . or be cut off from the University by expulsion like a rotten limb'.[5] But it is Langland who shows us the university man disputing in good set terms:

> '*Contra*,' quod I as a clerke, and comsed to disputen,
> And seide hem sothli, '*sepcies in die cadit iustus*;
>
> . . . .
>
> And Dowel and Do-yuel mow nouȝt dwelle togideres.
> *Ergo* . . .'
>
> viii 20-25

The Shipman's tale requires some knowledge of the Low Countries but probably no more than Langland had (cf. xiii 392). Both poets assume that their readers are acquainted with pilgrimage routes and with places of pilgrimage at home and abroad. There is nothing to suggest that Langland ever crossed the Channel. Yet his sense of that Christendom of which he knew England to be but part is as evident as Chaucer's; being manifested no less in his references to trade with Prussia or Flanders than in his keen scrutiny of the Papal Curia whether resident at Rome or Avignon.

Topography, however, takes us only a little way in establishing similarity of response to the English scene. In attempting to characterise the older features of an English townscape, Mr Thomas Sharp fixed on the juxtaposition of the sublime and the ordinary, '. . . the harmonious groupings of dissimilar elements'.[6] No phrases could better describe the sudden changes of tone that distinguish Chaucer's work from its French or Italian counterparts, even at the points where he is following them most closely. These juxtapositions are to be found equally in his earliest work:

> 'And farewel, swete, my worldes blysse!
> I praye God youre sorwe lysse.
> To lytel while oure blysse lasteth!'
>   With that hir eyen up she casteth
> And saw noght. 'Allas!' quod she for sorwe,
> And deyede within the thridde morwe.
> But what she sayede more in that swow
> I may not telle yow as now;
> Hyt were to longe for to dwelle.

– and within a few lines the poet is pledging a feather-bed of the finest quality to Morpheus or to Juno if they will cure his insomnia (*Book of the Duchess*, 209 ff); whilst in *The Knight's Tale* Theseus's peroration, beginning with a high-toned statement of divine purpose, finishes with an offhand dismissal of useless grieving for the dead Arcite:

> 'Why grucchen heere his cosyn and his wyf
> Of his welfare, that loved hem so weel?
> Kan he hem thank? Nay, God woot, never a deel.'
>   *CT*, A 3062-3064

This down-to-earth tone has commended Chaucer to all classes and all ages. Yet it is unique only inasmuch as he is concerned more with the human than the divine. Langland keeps an equipoise, alternating between divine and human, sublime and ordinary, to much the same effect as Chaucer. Thus in the very first lyrical imaging-forth of the Incarnation, he transmutes Isaiah's messianic tender plant growing as a root out of dry ground (*Isaiah, c.* 53) into a plant of peace that in heaven yearns for its fill of earth and on earth becomes the perfect man who leads perfected men to heaven:

> And whan it haued of this folde flesshe and blode taken,
> Was neuere leef vpon lynde liȝter ther-after,
> And portatyf and persant as the poynt of a nedle,
> That myȝte non armure it lette ne none heiȝ walles.
>
> i 153-156

Then, without warning, we plunge to a street scene in London city:

> And a mene, *as the maire is*, bitwene the kyng and the comune.

We are suddenly in the world of the young Richard, Wat Tyler, and William Walworth. Forty lines later the doctrinal exposition finishes with similar abruptness. Holy Church's figure of *caritas* as the lock of love, the leech of life, 'the graith gate that goth in-to heuene', makes a sublime conclusion. But we are not to rest in sublimity:

> 'Now haue I tolde the what treuthe is, that no tresore is bettere,
> I may no lenger lenge the with, now loke the owre lorde!'

– as if to say that this is as much doctrine as a 'doted daffe' can absorb at one time; Holy Church has other business. This is the real 'Art of Sinking in Poetry', and it is just as difficult as the art of soaring. Chaucer and Langland are the first English poets to achieve it, and they do so in a peculiarly English way.

A like pattern can be traced in the larger canvases. The Knight's 'noble story' gives way to gusty fabliaux: in the one Arcite lies in his grave 'Allone, withouten any compaignye', in the other the same phrase describes the amorous Nicholas in his bachelor's bed. The miracle of the Prioress's tale is followed by the mirth of Sir Thopas. We take all this so much for granted that we fail to note that Langland had used the same technique of contrast years earlier: after Repentance's great prayer (v 488-513), the movement of the narrative begins afresh with the grotesque figure of a palmer laden with the signs and symbols of a smug profession.

From the Resurrection and Pentecost we pass at once to sharp and scathing satire on the friars.

One clue to this 'couple-coloured' effect lies in the very prayer of Repentance just referred to. After appealing to the verse *Verbum caro factum, est et habitauit in nobis*, he adds:

> And bi so moche, me semeth, the sikerere we mowe
> Bydde and biseche, if it be thi wille,
> That art owre fader and owre brother, be merciable to vs.
>
> v 509-511

As Auerbach discerned, the doctrine of the Incarnation was totally incompatible with the principle of the separation of styles: Christ had come not as a hero or a king but as a carpenter's son. It is easy enough to perceive the relevance of this truth to a homogeneous allegory like *Piers Plowman* (though Auerbach himself unaccountably passed this poem by), but it is equally applicable to the rich medley of the *Canterbury Tales* or the *omnium gatherum* of birds of divers orders and opinions in the *Parliament of Fowls*. For the whole of creation was redeemed by the Incarnation – which is why Dunbar enjoins 'fowlis in the are' to 'sing with your nottis upoun hicht' and flowers to:

> Revert yow upwart *naturaly*,
>
> . . . .
>
> In wirschip of that Prince wirthy
> *Qui nobis Puer natus est.*
> (*Rorate celi desuper*, 33 ff)

Inasmuch as this doctrine provides the impetus for every passus of *Piers Plowman*, it is in that poem that the fusion of styles is found at its most complete, and by the same token its doctrine of *caritas* makes for a breadth and wholeness of vision unsurpassed in Chaucer or even in Dante. Langland can credit the heathen Saracens with a 'lippe of owre byleue', since they all 'parfitly bileueth/In the holy grete god and his grace thei asken' (xv 492, 532), and can recognise in the Jews a kindness that puts Christians to shame. Conversely the imperialist war in France stirs him to his sharpest satire – voiced by a knight who anticipates Chaucer's knight, who likewise 'cam late fro biʒunde' (cf. iii 109): a sense of the wastefulness of that war permeates the latter's account of the domain of Mars, enlarging as it does on Boccaccio's details: 'The shepne brennynge with the blake smoke. . . A thousand slayn, and nat of qualm ystorve . . . The toun destroyed, ther was no thyng laft.' (*CT*, A 2000 ff.).

Both Chaucer (cf. *CT*, A 275) and Langland (cf. B v 200 and vii 20) associate trades and merchants with *covetise*. But it is the Langland who was nourished on ascetic spirituality who can yet justify commercial activities by the scholastic doctrine of the just price (. . . they shulde bugge boldely that hem best liked,/And sithenes selle it aȝein and saue the wynnynge.': vii 24-25). He sees the Holy Spirit Himself as sanctifying every form of living that contributes to the common weal – priest and ploughman, teacher and thatcher, monk and merchant, lawyer and labourer, knight and mathematician, artist, artisan, ascetic (xix 224-250).

Now if this array of vocations reminds us of anything besides the field full of folk 'worchyng and wandryng as the worlde asketh' in Langland's Prologue, it is surely of the very fellowship that Chaucer was to describe more minutely in *his* Prologue, with its own distinctive fusion of the actual and the ideal. Once we abandon the fruitless search for 'real life' originals, and the futile distinction between the allegorical and the actual, the likenesses can be seen as striking. Many years ago Nevill Coghill drew out the resemblance between the ploughman in both poems[7]; to his evidence we need add only the circumstance that both these countrymen have sufficient social and economic freedom to make a pilgrimage (it matters little that Piers's journey becomes purely spiritual). At the outset of both works the ploughman is the symbol of honest, selfless activity:

> In settyng and in sowyng swonken ful harde,
> And wonnen that wastours with glotonye destruyeth.
> Prol. 21-22. (cf. vi 26-27)

> A trewe swynkere and a good was he,
> Lyvynge in pees and parfit charitee.
>
> . . . .
>
> He wolde thresshe, and therto dyke and delve,
> For Cristes sake, for every povre wight.
> *CT* A 531-537

Piers, too, dikes and delves (v 552-553) and manures his fields with dung carried on a cart drawn by a mare – the mare that Chaucer's ploughman rides. And not only does he pay tithes 'of my corne and catel' (vi 94, cf. *CT* A 539-540), but he shows the same 'parfit charitee' to his neighbour: 'I shal lene hem lyflode but 3if the londe faille' (vi 17). One might dismiss some of these identities of phrase or function as inevitable, or as pointing to some lost common model in homiletic literature. Yet it remains noteworthy that no other character in either poem is represented as positively eager to fulfil all his duties to the church and to the poor in whose apparel 'Iesu Cryst of heuene . . . pursueth vs euere' (xi 179-180).

Both poets, again, view religious with the same eyes. If Chaucer's prioress is 'so pitous' that she would weep if she saw a mouse caught in a trap, Langland's abbess 'were leuere swowe or swelte than soeffre any peyne' (v 154: the alliterative phrase is recorded outside alliterative verse only in Chaucer). Chaucer's friar, familiar with the women of the town, easygoing in confession if the penitent contributed to his order, is a duplicate of the friar-confessor of that pliable maid Meed, who spoke 'ful softly' in shrift and promised heaven if she would meet the cost of the window in the friar's new church (iii 35-50). Chaucer's Oxford clerk embodies Langland's conception of Study – though that included 'alle the musouns in musike' as well. 'Yf thow coueite to be riche', says Dame Study, 'to Clergie comst thow neuere' (C xii 110), so Chaucer's student has 'but litel gold in cofre', spending on books all that his 'frendes' (kinsfolk?) gave him, and praying in return for their souls' weal; which is precisely what Langland's Dreamer describes himself as doing:

> 'Whanne ich 3ong was', quath ich, 'meny 3er hennes,
> My fader and my frendes founden me to scole.
>
> . . . .
>
> [Now] I synge for hure soules of suche as me helpen.'
>
> C vi 35-36, 48

That Chaucer's student is devout his very presence on the pilgrimage suggests: a threadbare Arts man with a passion for Aristotle (to whom Langland also gives due honour) would hardly leave his lectures and his books unless devotion impelled him. As for the parson, it is Chaucer who provides the exemplary figure, possessing every quality that Langland desiderates. As a conscientious priest teaching his flock the articles of the Creed ('Cristes loore and his apostles twelve'), he answers to Langland's Clergy who identifies himself with that Creed (x 230 ff). He cares for the poor 'in sickness and mischief' – those 'pore peple . . . in the put of myschief' for whom Patience prays (xiv 174). And as if in deliberate contrast to the chopchurches of Langland's prologue who

> . . haue a lycence and a leue at London to dwelle,
> And syngen theer for symonye, for siluer is swete.
> Prol. 85-86

and who stay in London even in Lent, when especially they should be preaching and hearing confession (Prol. 89-91), Chaucer's parson

> . . . sette *nat* his benefice to hyre
> And leet his sheep encombred in the myre
> And ran to Londoun unto Seinte Poules
> To seken hym a chaunterie for soules.
> *CT* A 507-510

Equally idealised is Chaucer's knight, who loves 'Trouthe and honour, fredom and curteisie' – and so mirrors the well-mannered Christian knight of *Piers Plowman*, passus vi. 'Courteously' is the very word used to characterise the tone in which Langland's knight addresses his fellow-pilgrim the ploughman (vi 34). In both poets the emphasis is on Christian duties and qualities rather than on silks and fine array. Just as Chaucer's knight had 'foughten for oure feith', so Langland's is to defend Holy Church 'For wastoures and fro wykked men that this worlde struyeth' (vi 29); and it is the 'spiritual' Langland who limns a lord's everyday life on his manor, doing justice to his tenants, journeying to Westminster, hunting and hawking – the favourite occupations of Chaucer's squire for which Langland provides the *rationale*: boars and foxes break down hedges, and falcons kill the wild fowl who crop the wheat (vi 30-33). The harmony of interest between Langland's knight and ploughman gives a certain piquancy to the formula of humility that Chaucer's knight chooses when he acknowledges that:

I have, God woot, a large feeld to ere,
And wayke been the oxen in my plough.

CT A 886-887

This goes a little out of the way of his usual rhetoric, and would catch the sympathetic ear of his humblest listener. There is, in fact, hardly a trade, occupation or character in Chaucer's Prologue or his tales of contemporary life that has no antecedent in *Piers Plowman*. Even the Wife of Bath is adumbrated in the wife of Avarice who was 'a webbe and wollen cloth made' (v 215), and in the scene where Helen flaunts her new coat at Sunday mass (v 110-111).

The general point was made long since – if a shade ambiguously – by that once-eminent Victorian writer Sir J. R. Seeley: 'Chaucer seized upon the happy idea of limiting each class [in Langland's Prologue] to a single individual, and the still happier idea of combining them into a company with a common object which allowed them to associate together on nearly equal terms.' But one may go further. For the idea of a company with a common object is already present in Langland:

Pilgrymes and palmers pliȝted hem togidere
To seke seynt Iames and seyntes in Rome.
Thei went forth in here wey with many wise tales,
And hadden leue to lye al here lyf after.

Prol. 46-49

In the face of this passage it is curious that modern scholars can still assert that 'the reason for Chaucer's choice of a pilgrimage as a setting for his stories is unknown'. There could be no plainer indication that when folk went on pilgrimage they went, as they still do, in a party, and agreed to beguile the time with storytelling. As the Host says – and it is practically the first thing he says:

'. . . *wel I woot*, as ye goon by the weye,
Ye shapen yow to *talen* and to pleye.'

CT A 771-772

He knows that they will be doing what everyone did. Whether or no Chaucer already had personal experience of such a pilgrimage when his 'happy idea' presented itself, Langland's lines would be likely to remind him of its literary potentialities. As it is, Langland's busy 'maze' recalls nothing so much as the last lines of the *House of Fame*: its wicker suburb

> Was ful of shipmen and pilgrimes,
> With scrippes bret-ful of lesinges,
> Entremedled with tydynges.
>
> . . . .
>
> O, many a thousand tymes twelve
> Saugh I eke of these pardoners,
> Currours, and eke messagers,
> Wit boystes crammed ful of lyes.
>
> 2122-2129

Langland, too, had seen 'A thousand of men thronging together' (v 517); but of his 'ribaudes' most set out to seek Truth, leaving behind only those professional liars, the pilgrim and the pardoner.

We can now scarcely avoid considering the probability of Chaucer's having actually seen a copy of *Piers Plowman* in the interval between its first publication (? c. 1370) and the beginnings of the Tales at least ten years later. The large number of surviving manuscripts points to frequent copyings before the turn of the century. Langland was certainly living in London or Westminster for part of this period; and they would be the easiest places in which copies might be commissioned, or found for sale. From a miniature in Cotton Tib. A viii we know exactly what a bookshop of the time would look like; but about fourteenth-century publishing we know little – except that there was a demand for portable bibles on the part of academics and men of Langland's own class. It is probable enough that bible publishers had already established themselves in the neighbourhood of St Paul's – the area they were to occupy for six hundred years. Certainly by 1353 John de Grafton had set up as a 'parchemener and stacionarius', and he was still there in 1356. St Paul's was the haunt, too, of chantry priests, like Langland himself perhaps, who had little to do but sing prayers, listen to sermons, and read. The sermons they heard at Paul's cross, as Langland certainly did (x 73): it was the recognized centre for theological disputation. Only Westminster could provide as good a market for new books. If Caxton set up his printing shop there, it was because he knew it as the place to catch not only the nobility but the well-to-do customers up from the country for a court case (like the group in Langland's second passus) or for a session of parliament (like that in his third); the third passus shows that Langland knew this area intimately, and since Malvern Priory was a sister house to Westminster Abbey itself it is possible that he lived there first on going to London.

We seem narrowed down, then, to a few London bookshops – some not far from Chaucer's house at Aldgate and close to Langland's own cottage on Cornhill; the others at Westminster, scene of much of Chaucer's official life (and not only as an M.P.), the place where he was first robbed, and where he died. Topographically and biographically speaking, no two English poets for two centuries so closely overlap. They must have passed each other in the street – medieval London if not as 'white and clean' as Morris thought, was certainly small – perhaps as Chaucer was hurrying back from the office via Paternoster Row with his second-hand torn copy of Macrobius (*Parliament of Fowls*, 110) or a remainder volume of the old-fashioned tail-rhyme romances that he was to parody in *Sir Thopas*; perhaps with *Piers Plowman* itself.

And how easily might it have caught Chaucer's eye! The opening lines evoke the soft sun of summer in the very phrase of his own *Parliament* (685). He too had roamed from field to field on the first morning of May, and 'mette a merueilouse sweuene':

> Whan I was layd, and hadde myn eyen hed,
> I fel aslepe withinne an hour or two.
> Me mette how I was in the medewe tho,
> And that I romede in that same gyse.
> *Legend of Good Women* G 102-105

– as Langland's Dreamer 'romed aboute/Al a somer sesoun' (viii 1-2). The hint of faery at the beginning of the Prologue, the lively Cheapside scene at the end, the brilliant opening sketch of Chaucer's *bête noire*, a pardoner raking in rings with his fake bull: all this, to say nothing of the topicality of the Cat and Rat fable or of the recognisable picture of the King's mistress in Lady Meed, would tempt Chaucer to buy. And if in turning the pages he saw that they had much to say about salvation and predestination, that would hardly displease the translator of Boethius and the deviser of Palamon's and Troilus's soliloquies on the same topics. Nor need we suppose that the city poet would be deterred by, or disdainful of, Langland's diction or metre. The vocabulary of *Piers Plowman* is far removed form the local and almost 'precious' diction of the *Gawain* poet: there is hardly a word in Langland's Prologue that Chaucer might not have used. The Parson's reference to 'rum, ram, ruf', which is so often invoked, merely implies that as a Southerner he is 'ill at those numbers', not that his fellow pilgrims cannot understand them. Indeed, the Host, a city-bred man if ever there was one, when dismissing tail-rhyme as 'drasty', begs Chaucer to give them something better, if not in prose then 'in geste' – which here and elsewhere may possibly mean 'in alliterative verse': the Parson says he cannot *geeste* 'by lettre'; Gavin Bone notes a similar use in *Knyghthode and Bataile* (*Medium Ævum*, vii, 226).

But how, it may be said, can the Chaucer 'that God of Loves servantz serve' sort with the poet of Dowel, Dobet, Dobest? The gap is not so great as appears at first sight (and Chaucer's descriptions of himself as lover are not necessarily to be taken at face-value). Both writers look critically at *mariages de convenance*, and for both true wedded love was prefigured in Paradise. So says the Parson, for whom it 'maketh the hertes al oon of hem that been ywedded, as wel as the bodies' (*CT* I 919); 'God maked it, as I have seyd, in paradys, and wolde hymself be born in mariage' (917), and so says Langland's Wit:

> And thus was wedloke ywrouȝt and god hym-self it made;
> In erthe the heuene is – hym-self was the witnesse.
>
> ix 116-117

And when Wit says that

> It is an oncomely couple, bi Cryst, as me thinketh,
> To ȝyuen a ȝonge wenche to an olde feble,
> Or wedden any widwe for welth of hir goodis,
> That neuere shal barne bere but if it be in armes!
>
> ix 160-163

he might well be commenting on the Merchant's Tale or the Wife of Bath's *apologia*. The fruit of mercenary marriages is 'Ialousye

Ioyeles and Ianglyng on bedde' (ix 165-166) – the complete anti-
thesis of the union of Emily and Palamon, in which 'nevere was
ther no word hem bitwene/Of jalousie or any oother teene' (*CT*
A 3105-3106). The very first definition of Dowel is 'trewe wedded
libbing folk' and it is to such that God grants 'Grace to go to hem
and agon her lyflode' (ix 106-107). Chaucer, who knew as well as
Langland that we are all 'pilgrymes, passynge to and fro' (*CT*
A 2848), has the Host of the Tabard commend the parson's
intention

> To shewe yow the wey, in this viage,
> Of thilke parfit glorious pilgrymage
> That highte Jerusalem celestial.
>
> *CT* I 49-51

with a phrase reminiscent of Langland: 'to do wel God sende yow
his grace'. The parson's final words point to humility as prerequisite for heavenly glory, and Chaucer concludes his lifework
with a prayer for 'grace of verray penitence'. Langland's Conscience – setting out anew at the close of his poem 'to seke Piers the
Plowman that *Pryde* may destruye' – 'gradde after grace'.

   In view of this cluster of common sympathies it is surely time to
dismiss for ever the false antithesis that represents Chaucer as new
and adventurous, Langland as traditional and conservative. Langland's development of the allegorical mode as a means of conveying
both external reality and spiritual self-knowledge is just as striking
in its way as Chaucer's philosophical enlargement of earlier poetic
themes. Whether or not we agree to call their sane and sanative
qualities peculiarly English, a recognition of their affinities will
surely lead us to a better understanding of English poetry in their
century.

Notes

1 E. T. Donaldson, *Piers Plowman, the C-Text and its Poet* (London, 1949) p. 23, note 1.

2 In this discussion of the text I am greatly indebted to the long and closely argued account of editorial procedure by Professor Kane in his Introduction to the Athlone Press A-text. Several aspects of the textual state of the poem as we have inherited it are also discussed, with far closer knowledge of the poem than I possess, by Professor Russell in the first essay in this book. In particular he deals with the distinction between authorial and editorial revision and the relationship between B and C.

3 E. T. Donaldson, 'MSS R and F in the B-Tradition of *Piers Plowman*', *Transactions of the Connecticut Academy of Arts and Sciences* xxxix (1955) 177-212.

4 G. H. Russell, 'The Salvation of the Heathen: The Exploration of a Theme in *Piers Plowman*', *Journal of the Warburg and Courtauld Institutes* xxix (1966) 101-116.

5 *Piers Plowman*, edited by Elizabeth Salter and Derek Perasall, York Medieval Texts (London, 1967).

6 E. Vasta, *The Spiritual Basis of Piers Plowman* (London, 1965).

7 G. Kane, *Piers Plowman, the Evidence for Authorship* (London, 1965).

8 D. C. Fowler, *Piers the Plowman, Literary Relations of the A and B Texts* (Seattle, 1961). I cannot agree with Professor Fowler that B, and possibly C, may have been written by John Trevisa.

9 M. L. Samuels, 'Some Applications of Middle English Dialectology', *English Studies* xliv (1963) 94.

10 C. W. Stubbs, *The Christ of English Poetry* (London, 1906) p. 77, cf. E. D. Hanscom: 'Langland sees but things; that larger observation which perceives relations is foreign to his genius. Hence it follows that his poem consists of a series of detached pictures, a collection of separate visions, a compilation of distinct arguments, of which the connection must be sought rather in the probable intention of the writer than in the structure of his work.' 'The Argument of the

Vision of Piers Plowman', *PMLA* ix (1894) 412, and Jusserand, quoted by Professor Elliott, below, p. 347.

11 W. P. Ker, *English Literature Medieval* (London, 1912, ed. of 1945) p. 146.

12 M. W. Bloomfield, *Piers Plowman as a Fourteenth-century Apocalypse* (New Brunswick, 1961).

13 D. W. Robertson and B. F. Huppé, *Piers Plowman and Scriptural Tradition* (Princeton, 1951) pp. 236-237; E. M. W. Tillyard, *The English Epic and its Background* (London, 1954) p. 166.

14 R. W. Frank, *Piers Plowman and the Scheme of Salvation* (London, 1957) ch. 2; S. S. Hussey, 'Langland, Hilton and the Three Lives', *RES* vii (1956) 132-150.

15 Frank, p. 15.

16 The point is well made by Bloomfield, pp. 106-107.

17 G. Owst, *Literature and Pulpit in Medieval England* (Cambridge, 1933) ch. 9 (cf. Donaldson, *Piers Plowman*, p. 143, note); E. Salter, *Piers Plowman: An Introduction* (Oxford, 1962) pp. 24-57; A. C. Spearing, *Criticism and Medieval Poetry* (London, 1964) ch. 4.

18 Spearing, p. 72.

19 J. A. Burrow, 'The Audience of *Piers Plowman'*, *Anglia* lxxv (1957) 373-384.

20 Burrow, *op. cit.* Cf. Bloomfield, pp. 34-41; Salter and Pearsall, pp. 51-58; S. S. Hussey, 'Langland's Reading of Alliterative Poetry', *MLR* lx (1965) 163-170.

21 As has been done, notably by Robertson and Huppé.

22 Dante, *Convivio* ii, ch. 1 (quoted by Coghill, 'The Pardon of Piers Plowman', *Proceedings of the British Academy* xxx (1944) 352), Hilton, *Scale of Perfection*, Book II, ch. 43.

23 Bloomfield, ch. 1.

24 Donne, Satyre III, *The Satires, Epigrams and Verse Letters*, ed. W. Milgate (Oxford, 1967).

CHAPTER I

1 The title of this paper is designedly tentative. What follows is an attempt to delineate the nature of the problem. Any full and conclusive discussion must await the appearance of the full statement of the textual situation of the poem. I would wish to acknowledge my debt to Professor George Kane with whom I have often discussed the

Piers Plowman textual problem, unfailingly with profit. For the views expressed in this essay, however, he bears no kind of responsibility. All quotations from the A-version are taken from George Kane, *Piers Plowman: the A-Version* (London, 1960): all quotations from the B- and C-versions (unless otherwise specified) are taken from W. W. Skeat, *The Vision of William Concerning Piers the Plowman*, Parts ii and iii. EETS 38 and 54 (1869 and 1873).

2 The statement of Skeat in *Parallel Extracts from Twenty-nine MSS of Piers the Plowman*, EETS 17 (1866) pp. 1-12 is still the statement of the orthodox position. The only substantial challenge to this view is found in G. Gornemann, *Zur Verfasserschaft und Entstehungsgeschichte von 'Piers the Plowman'* (Heidelberg, 1915).

3 A full account of the manuscript and the process of its compilation is given in G. H. Russell and Venetia Nathan, 'A *Piers Plowman* Manuscript in the Huntington Library', *Huntington Library Quarterly* xxvi, 2 (1963) 119 ff.

4 Now MS [S.L.] V. 88 in the library of the University of London.

5 C i 105-117. No other manuscript except Ilchester seriously dissents from this form.

6 For a full discussion see the introduction to Kane's edition, especially pp. 19 ff.

7 A convenient list of all manuscripts of the poem, arranged in their categories, is found in E. T. Donaldson, *Piers Plowman: the C-Text and its Poet* (New Haven, 1949) pp. 227 ff. To his lists some small alterations and additions have to be made, but these do not materially alter the picture.

8 Such manuscripts are listed in Donaldson, p. 229.

9 Detailed discussion of this process as it affects the A-version is found in Kane, pp. 19 ff.

10 See Kane, pp. 19 ff.

11 G. Kane, *Piers Plowman: The Evidence for Authorship* (London, 1965). The book contains reference to, and a summary of, the more important contributions to the debate.

12 For details, see the introduction to Kane's edition.

13 W. W. Skeat, *The Vision of William Concerning Piers the Plowman in Three Parallel Texts* (reprinted; London, 1954).

14 Obvious exceptions are C iv 315 ff, C vi 1 ff.

15 See G. Kane, '*Piers Plowman*: Problems and Methods of Editing the B-Text', *MLR* xliii (1948) 1-25.

16 Compare, however, the view of Skeat as expressed in his edition of the B-text, EETS 38, pp. vi ff and xxxix f.

Y

17 It is, perhaps, proper to suggest that the text of the C-version offered in Skeat's editions is not, at least in my judgment, fairly representative of the best manuscript tradition of the version. Better texts are offered by the traditions represented by manuscripts like MS Hm 143, which has recently been used by Elizabeth Salter and D. A. Pearsall as the base manuscript for their edition of selections from the C-version, *Piers Plowman* (London, 1967), or by BM Additional 35157 used by F. A. R. Carnegy, *An Attempt to Approach the C-Text of Piers the Plowman* (London, 1934). As from passus xiii, a valuable text is supplied by MS Trinity College Cambridge R.3.14, a conjoint manuscript which has already been used by Kane as the base text for his edition of the A-version. A useful comparison of the texts supplied by Hm 138, Hm 143 and BM Additional 35157 is given by R. W. Chambers, 'The Manuscripts of *Piers Plowman* in the Huntington Library, and Their Value for Fixing the Text of the Poem', *Huntington Library Bulletin* viii (1937) 1-27.

18 The evidence for this is perhaps most clearly established in those contexts in which the A- and C-versions appear in agreement against the B-version. While it is true that, in certain cases, an alternative explanation is possible, the weight of the evidence seems conclusively to suggest that A and C here preserve the original reading, while B is corrupt.

19 See Donaldson for a full discussion of this phenomenon.

20 It must be admitted that in some cases, the identification of a scribally induced corruption is not certain. In this, as in all editorial matters, an opinion based on an evaluation of possibilities must be formed in each case.

21 This situation poses an editorial problem. A reading originally scribal in origin is transformed by the fact of its admission by the C-reviser into a genuine reading of the C-version. It is, in my opinion, hazardous to edit these readings out of the C-version since we have no way of judging the motives which led to the retention. It may have been inadvertence: it may also have been a deliberate decision.

22 Compare, for example, C ii 74; v 137; vii 207; ix 32.

23 A large number of other instances could be cited. As examples one might take A ii 6, A iii 35 ff, A iv 14-15, A ix 18-19 and their corresponding B- and C-versions.

24 G. H. Russell, 'The Salvation of the Heathen: the Exploration of a Theme in *Piers Plowman*', *Journal of the Warburg and Courtauld Institutes* xxix (1966) 101-116.

CHAPTER 2

1 'The Pardon of Piers Plowman', *Proceedings of the British Academy* xxx (1944) 303-357.

2 '*Piers Plowman*: The Pardon Reconsidered', *MLR* xlv (1950) 449-458.

3 'The Pardon Scene in *Piers Plowman*', *Speculum* xxvi (1951) 317-331.

4 'Marchauntz in the margyne hadden many ʒeres' (line 18), i.e. it was written in the margin that merchants were given many years of remission of purgatory.

5 It has recently been stressed by Professor Przemyslaw Mroczkowski ('Piers and his Pardon. A Dynamic Analysis', *Studies in Language and Literature in honour of Margaret Schlauch* (Warsaw, 1966) pp. 273-291) that this disquisition on the contents of the pardon does not appear in the pardon itself when it is unfolded ('Al in two lynes it lay and nouʒt a leef more'), and from this he infers that it is Piers's own improvisation. That Piers, rather than the narrator, has been the speaker is an interesting but (despite line 16, 'this pardoun Piers sheweth') unlikely suggestion. It could of course be insisted that although the text of the pardon consisted of two lines only and not a word more, the margins of the document were crammed with commentary: this, however, would diminish the visual effect of the sudden sight of the pardon, and Langland is constantly willing to shift the literal level of the narrative in order to attain effects more important than that of simple consistency.

6 As Skeat points out, Langland seems to have confused Nebuchadnezzar's dream with Belshazzar's vision of the writing on the wall, also expounded by Daniel. Which of these two was uppermost in Langland's mind as he wrote makes no difference to our argument.

7 Macrobius, *Commentary on the Dream of Scipio*, trans. W. H. Stahl (New York, 1952) p. 90.

8 It could of course also mean a papal pardon, but, as we shall see, the allegory of God sending a pardon would have suggested the analogy of a royal pardon.

9 *The Scale of Perfection*, ed. E. Underhill (London, 1948) p. 246.

10 *Ancrene Wisse*, ed. G. Shepherd (London, 1959) p. 21.

11 *Religious Lyrics of the Fourteenth Century*, ed. Carleton Brown (Oxford, 1957) pp. 18-20.

12 *Works*, ed. F. N. Robinson (London, 1957) p. 618, lines 59-61.

13 For the text and an account of the development of the charter image

see M. C. Spalding, *The Middle English Charters of Christ* (Bryn Mawr College Monographs, 1914).

14 Spalding, pp. 28-30.

15 Spalding, pp. 100-102.

16 Ed. J. J. Stürzinger (Roxburghe Club, 1895) p. 83. 'I, Jesus, supreme lord of the heavens, to our lieutenant Michael and to all the assessors present for our judgment: greetings.'

17 Stürzinger, p. 84. 'By special grace I grant that those, who at the end have made confession of their sins, shall be freed from hell.'

18 The casket contains 'a bountiful sufficiency from the treasury of my Passion of which there remains so great abundance, from the merits of my Mother, to whom none may be compared, from the merits of all my saints of which great are the stores in heaven'. (Stürzinger, p. 85.) This allusion to the Treasury of Merit suggests that Guillaume in composing his literary imitation of a royal charter of pardon was reminded also of papal pardons.

19 On this see E. C. Perrow, 'The Last Will and Testament as a Form of Literature', *Transactions of the Wisconsin Academy of Sciences, Arts and Letters* xvii (1913).

20 EETS ES 72, p. xxix.

21 On Langland's continuous substitution of one allegory for another, see the illuminating article of John Burrow, 'The Action of Langland's Second Vision', *EC* xv (1965) 247-268.

22 A. E. Burn, *The Athanasian Creed and its Early Commentaries*, Texts and Studies iv (1896) p. 10.

23 *Summa Theologica*, II, ii, qu. 137, art. 2: 'The difficulty of persisting in a good work for a long time gives merit to perseverance.'

24 The parable is alluded to in Piers's first speech, v 559, 'He ne withhalt non hewe his hyre that he ne hath it at euen'.

25 cf. M. W. Bloomfield, *Piers Plowman as a Fourteenth-century Apocalypse* (New Brunswick, 1961) pp. 91-94, 212.

26 Ed. H. C. Hoskier (London, 1929) p. 1: 'The hour is very late and the times very wicked, let us keep watch. Behold threateningly near is the most high judge.'

27 EETS 209, p. 29; this reference is given by Frank, *Speculum* xxvi, 322.

28 This kind of distinction had been made by St Augustine in his comment in Psalm xxiv, 10: 'Et ideo universae viae Domini, duo adventus Filii Dei unus miserantis, alter judicantis.' *PL* 36, 185. ('"All the ways of the Lord" refers to the two comings of the Son of God, the one when He shows mercy, the other when He judges.')

29 Ibid. 1282. '. . . now is still the time for mercy: the future will be the time for judgement.'

30 *PL* 113, 1010. 'These two are always united in Him, but at different times different effects manifest themselves, mercy now, judgement in the future.' For the discussion of God's justice in relation to His mercy (as an introduction to the subject of the Last Judgment) in the *Sentences* and in Bonaventura's Commentary on this work, see Bonaventura, *Opera omnia* iv (Quaracchi, 1889) 955 and 964-965.

31 *The Macro Plays*, EETS ES 91, p. 149.

32 For an example see *Middle English Sermons*, EETS 209, pp. 86-89.

33 For the history of this theme see Hope Traver, *The Four Daughters of God* (Bryn Mawr College Monographs, 1907).

34 *Zephaniah* i, 14-15. 'The great day of the Lord is near, it is near and all too swift; the voice of the day of the Lord is bitter, there will the strong man be troubled. That day is a day of wrath, a day of trouble and distress, a day of disaster and wretchedness.'

35 For the texts of the responsory and the *Dies irae* see F. J. E. Raby, *A History of Christian-Latin Poetry* (Oxford, 1953) pp. 445-448.

36 Cf. 1 *Peter* iv, 18.

37 Raby, p. 446.

38 Raby, p. 448.

39 Raby, p. 448.

40 Ed. A. C. Cawley (Manchester, 1961) p. 3.

41 EETS ES 120, p. 174.

42 *Allegorical Imagery* (Princeton, 1966).

43 *The Golden Legend*, translated William Caxton, ed. F. S. Ellis (Temple Classics, 1900) I, p. 79.

44 *Vita Jesu Christi*, ed. L. M. Rigollot (Paris, 1878) iv, 97.

45 E. Mâle, *L'Art religieux du xiiie siècle en France* (Paris, 1948) pp. 191-192 and fig. 100.

CHAPTER 3

1 For convenience I shall refer to the second part of the poem as the *Vita* here. This is, however, strictly speaking, only the title of passus ix – end in the A-text. In B and C the word is dropped, and *Dowel, Dobet* and *Dobest* stand alone. See R. W. Frank, *Piers Plowman and the Scheme of Salvation* (London, 1957) p. 34. Curiously enough, the MSS titles are not included in George Kane's edition of the A-text (*Piers Plowman, the A Version*, London, 1960), where
Y*

passus ix follows viii without comment. They are, of course, recorded on pp. 1 ff as part of the descriptions of the MSS.

2 In 'Love, Law and *Lewté* in *Piers Plowman*,' *RES* xv (1964) pp. 241 ff. As the present paper is, in a sense, a continuation, I have had to refer the reader to this article rather frequently.

3 See, especially, below pp. 100 ff concerning the recurring theme of triads combined with a fourth. My analyses of such passages are necessarily tentative, as I have tried to indicate; light can be thrown on them, but definitive explanations are hardly possible.

4 Aristotle, *Nicomachean Ethics* (tr. W. D. Ross, Oxford, 1925) v, ii. 1130 b. See 'Love, Law and *Lewté*', p. 256.

5 See 'Love, Law and *Lewté*', pp. 257 ff.

6 'Love, Law and *Lewté*', p. 251.

7 'Love, Law and *Lewté*', p. 249 f. Langland's view of the primacy of love is not unlike that of St Bonaventura (for a discussion of St Bonaventura's view in relation to another theme which is of great importance to Langland, i.e. poverty, see G. Leff, *Heresy in the Later Middle Ages* (Manchester, 1967) I, pp. 84 ff).

8 All quotations are, unless otherwise stated, from the B-text.

9 In B xv 23 ff Langland uses a passage from the *Etymologies* of Isidore of Seville to define the mental faculties which appear as characters in Dowel. Thought is matched to *mens*: 'for that I can and knowe called am I *Mens*' (25). The meaning is thus 'the comprehension of ideas'; i.e. the understanding which the Dreamer lacked when he was awake is now available, and enables him to examine and elaborate given ideas.

10 Frank, p. 34. This chapter, besides an excellent discussion of the undoubted difficulties inherent in Langland's use of the formula, gives full references to other views, which I will not repeat here.

11 'Love, Law and *Lewté*', pp. 252, 258-259.

12 At xii 33 *lewté* is equated with Dowel. But this is a special case in which the Good Life (thought of as a whole) is discussed in terms of marriage, with a play on *lewté* (33), love (34) and law (35). On this passage see below pp. 83, 87.

13 See Frank, p. 36, for a discussion and references.

14 The very difficult allegory of the Tree really requires extended treatment. See Frank, pp. 86 ff for an interesting discussion with full references to other views.

15 *de Regimine Principum* i 15 (*Aquinas, Selected Political Writings*, ed. d'Entrèves, p. 80).

16 Frank, p. 34.

17 ix 94-97. The passage is, however, obscure, and the C-text substitutes one which is in accord with Thought's definitions and with Wit's own conclusion (C xi 185-192).

18 Note, especially, x 129-134 on the importance of Dowel as the basis of the Good Life and on Dobest as the force which acts on man. Also 187-188 on the importance of love in relation to all three members of the triad.

19 This, for example, is the sense of patience in the poem usually given that name in Cotton Nero A x. The Dreamer uses the word in an obviously more limited sense at xi 402: 'To se moche and suffre more, certes,' quod I, 'is Dowel.' The immediate retort is that if he had really suffered (i.e. in the wider sense) he would have learnt something.

20 cf. e.g. xviii 59, 363. An allied phrase expressing the same complex of ideas is 'leche of lyf' used of love (i 202-203).

21 For the incarnate Christ 'learning' (in this case leechcraft, from Piers Plowman) see xvi 103 ff.

22 For a contradictory view which does not seem to have found much acceptance see D. C. Fowler, *Piers the Plowman: Literary Relations of the A and B texts* (Seattle, 1961).

23 The importance of the prophetic passages in *Piers Plowman* (which are not by any means easy either to modern taste or modern understanding) has tended to be overlooked. M. W. Bloomfield's book, *Piers Plowman as a Fourteenth-century Apocalypse* (New Jersey, 1961), does the poem a good service by refocusing attention on the prophetic element.

24 For the doctrine of patient poverty in *Piers Plowman* and contemporary works see Frank, pp. 74 ff and the references there given; also Bloomfield, index, *sub* Poverty.

25 cf. 'Law, Love and *Lewté*', p. 257.

26 See below pp. 106-107.

27 Epistle, ii, 8. The whole chapter is of importance for Langland's conception of Dowel.

28 In C the King is crowned 'to culle with-oute synne' those who will not obey Dobest and 'to kepen ous alle/And reulen alle reaumes by here thre wittes'. (C xi 100-104.)

29 See 'Love, Law and *Lewté*', pp. 244 ff.

30 *Alchemical Studies* (Collected Works, xiii, London, 1967) p. 96.

31 See Berthelot, *Collection des anciens alchimistes grecs* (Paris, 1887-88) VI, v, 6.

32 It is likely that Langland was aware that such a Good King and

such a Good Pope were among the normal *personae* of apocalyptic visions. In these they are instrumental in bringing about the millennium on earth. On this whole question see Bloomfield. It does not seem to me that Langland uses the King and Pope in this sense here, though knowledge of a possible extension of their rôles might add another depth of meaning to the passage for a contemporary reader.

33 On this issue see D. Knowles, *The Religious Orders in England* (Cambridge, 1957) II, ch. vii, and Leff, especially I, part i.

34 The C reading suggests that Langland has no special allusion in mind, but merely chose 'Abingdon' as a place name which fitted the alliteration to stand for the Church in his own country, with whose reform he is, naturally, specially concerned.

35 For a recent authoritative account of Wycliffe's views see Leff, II, ch. vii, and the references there given.

36 For Cain standing in a general sense for the wicked see, e.g. ix 118 ff. Langland's apocalypticism hardly seems central to his plan. In passus xx, for example, his treatment of Antichrist is so general that it does not seem apocalyptic at all. He leads a war of vices against virtues which seems to indicate the normal difficulties of Christian life, rather than the institution of a new age. Here Langland may be influenced by Wycliffe for whom Antichrist can mean anyone opposed to Christ: 'Quod quicumque est Christo vel legi sue contrarius dicitur Antichristus', *de Potestate Pape*, 118 (see Leff, II, ch. vii). If so, he does not share Wycliffe's identification of Antichrist with the visible Church (although he may have known of his impolite identification of CAIM with the initial letters of the four orders).

37 Langland's position in relation to the various apocalyptic doctrines which were current in his day, stemming for the most part from the writings of Joachim of Fiore, is fully discussed by Bloomfield. Leff, I, part i, gives excellent accounts of individual, mainly continental contributors to the tradition. As I have indicated, I do not consider Langland's apocalypticism as far-reaching as Bloomfield does, although it is indubitably present in the poem.

38 Bloomfield, p. 100. It is not, however, quite true to say (p. 123) that Langland concentrates on the Harrowing of Hell at the expense of the Incarnation and Passion. I have elsewhere discussed his use of imagery associated with the Incarnation ('Langland on the Incarnation', *RES* xvi (1965) pp. 349 ff), and the passage we are about to consider is concerned with the life of Jesus on earth. The Passion is

given two separate treatments in *Dobet*; at full length in passus xviii, and summarily, as part of the account of the life in xix 136 ff.

39 Langland would seem to be deliberately manipulating the biblical source, *Matthew* ii, 11, in order to achieve this effect. He alters the order from gold, frankincense and myrrh, and does not appear to follow any of the usual glosses. In these myrrh, for example, is almost always associated with death. For a representative selection see the *Catena Aurea*, ed. P. A. Guarienti (Rome, 1953) on this verse.

40 *Opera Omnia* viii (Quaracchi, 1898). For a discussion of this work in relation to the poverty debate see Leff, I, 84 ff.

41 *Opera Omnia* ix, 238 a-b. See Leff, p. 85.

42 In viii 90, it is said of Dobet that he 'is ronne in-to Religioun and hath rendred the bible'. Skeat, in his note on the passage, *q.v.*, took this to mean 'translated the Bible', though he was puzzled by the fact that the A-text agrees, and is likely to have been written before the Wycliffian translations were made. But 'render' does not mean 'translate' in *Piers Plowman*. (In fact, the first instance of this sense noted by *OED* is dated 1610: see *Render* vv., I, 6.) It means 'to learn (by heart)', or 'to repeat something learned, recite' (*OED* sense I, 1), and these meanings fit the contexts which Skeat glosses by 'translate' (C xviii 322, of the heathen *learning* and repeating the Creed, not translating it into their own language; C vii 217, of learning, and repeating, a lesson in dishonesty). Dobet 'precheth to the poeple' (B viii 91) effectively because he has learnt the Bible by heart, completely learnt it. This passage has nothing to do with vernacular translation.

CHAPTER 4

1 See 'The Action of Langland's Second Vision', *EC* xv (1965) 247-268.

2 This process of the 'draining away' of inner virtue is recognized, according to A. C. Charity, in Old and New Testament history, and is counteracted there by typology: 'Typology in both Testaments does not exist to inhibit God's speaking any word but a word from a past grown rigid; it is used instead to allow the right hearing of a word which concerns the present and is new. It was thus that the call at the Exodus must have struck home to Israel, compared with the ancient "archetypes". But when the act of God at the Exodus lost

its precarious dependence on faith and became, or seemed to become, their possession, which nothing could shake or alter, and so itself only an "archetype", a "security", preventing the hearing of God's new word and the seeing of his new act, it was thus, in turn, that the word of a future was spoken, which would correspond to the past but transcend it. This is how genuine typology works in the Bible always,' *Events and their Afterlife* (Cambridge, 1966) pp. 157-158.

3 These lines contain the germ of the more famous passage of attempted self-exculpation in the C-text, vi 1-104.

4 Including the dream-within-the-dream which occupies passus xi.

5 See A ix 103, B x 146 and B x 217.

6 Skeat's B-text is faulty at this point (as a result of scribal eye-skip) and lacks the crucial phrase. I assume that the true B reading was something like that in A which I quote from Kane's text.

CHAPTER 5

1 I perhaps simplify Professor Frank's position which is stated in *Piers Plowman and the Scheme of Salvation* (New Haven, 1957) pp. 2-3, and explained more fully in 'The Art of Reading Medieval Personification-Allegory', *ELH* xx (1953) 237-250. However, his view of the status of an allegorical character is significantly different from my own.

2 References to *Piers Plowman* are to the B-text.

3 In the C-text the evil nature of Meed is emphasized and the distinction between just and unjust payment made more fully in the discussion of the terms *mede* and *mercede* (C iv 292-409).

4 Frank, *Piers Plowman*, pp. 19-33.

5 Quoted by Skeat in his note on C xxiii 359. The equivalent line in B is xx 357.

6 C. S. Lewis, *The Allegory of Love* (Oxford, 1936) pp. 47-48.

CHAPTER 6

1 B v 544.

2 *Matthew* xxii, 37-39. The new commandment is derived from two precepts found in the Old Testament; see *Deuteronomy* vi, 5 and *Leviticus* xix, 18.

3 Prayer, fasting and almsgiving are the traditional non-sacramental forms of penance.

4 B xvi 21.

5 B xix 177-330.

6 B xix 178-185, 328-329.

7 B xv 50.

8 B i 84.

9 B xii 31. For Imaginatyf see especially M. W. Bloomfield, *Piers Plowman as a Fourteenth-century Apocalypse* (New Brunswick, 1961) Appendix III.

10 For this recurrent theme see B v 572-574, x 357-358, xv 574, xvii 11.

11 *Speculum Charitatis* I, 3 (*PL* 195: 507).

12 B xv, 190.

13 B xviii 22-23. This idea is mentioned earlier in the poem, B v 508.

14 C xvi 129-152.

15 C xvi 34.

16 C xvii 337-339.

17 *The Revelations of Divine Love of Julian of Norwich*, tr. J. Walsh (London, 1961) chs. 51-53. The quotation is taken from ch. 51, and is found on pp. 138-139. Anselm's use of the metaphor comes in Eadmer, *De similitudinibus*, ch. lxxxiv (*PL* 159: 655-657).

18 Peter Lombard, *Sentences*, I iii, 22 (*PL* 192: 533).

19 *Summa Theologiae*, 1a, 93, art. 1, pp. 50, 51. All page references are to the Blackfriars edition, vol. xiii (1964) ed. and tr. E. Hill.

20 *Speculum Charitatis*, I, 4 (*PL* 195: 508)

21 *De diligendo deo*, x 28 (*PL* 182: 991).

22 *Sermo* 272 (*PL* 38: 1247).

23 *Sermo* 227 (*PL* 38: 1099).

24 *Confessions*, VII, x, 16 (*PL* 32: 742).

25 Augustine, *De Trinitate* XIV, xviii, 24 (*PL* 42: 1055).

26 *Summa Theologiae*, 1a, 93, art. 4, pp. 60, 61.

27 For the part played by *Dowel* in the structure of the poem see p. 165 and the discussion of the Dreamer on pp. 172 and 175.

28 Cf. the passage on the restoration of the three powers of the soul by the three members of the Trinity in the sermons of the fourteenth-century German Dominican, Eckhart, *Meister Eckhart*, ed. F. Pfeiffer, tr. C. de B. Evans (1947), I, 247.

29 *The Scale of Perfection*, tr. G. Sitwell (London, 1953), II, 1, p. 144. See also Bk. I, ch. 43, 45, 51, 86, 92 and *Meister Eckhart*, I, pp. 101, 117, 124, 144.

30 Augustine, *Sermo* 9, *De decem Chordis*, viii, 9 (*PL* 38: 82); Bede,

In Marci Evangelium Expositio, xii (*PL* 92: 253); Anselm, *Proslogion*, i, in F. S. Schmitt, *Opera Omnia*, I (1946), p. 100; Eadmer includes a comparison between a monk and a coin in the *De similitudinibus*, xc (*PL* 159: 659-660); *Summa Theologiae*, 1a, 93, art. 1, pp. 50, 51.

31 Cf. Eckhart, *Tractate* iv, in *Meister Eckhart*, I, p. 307.

32 C iv 354-364.

33 See p. 151.

34 Cf. Eckhart's image of the tree of the Godhead, whose flower is love, and which grows in the soul: *Meister Eckhart*, I, p. 154.

35 *Speculum Charitatis*, I, 8 (*PL* 195: 512).

36 Cf. C xxi 327-329.

37 *Epistola ad Fratres de Monte Dei*, II, iii, 15 (*PL* 184: 348).

38 *Sentences*, I, iii, 7 (*PL* 192: 531). St Augustine's definitions come in the *De Trinitate*, X, xi, 17 to xii, 19 and XIV, xii, 15 (*PL* 42: 982-984 and 1048).

39 *Speculum Charitatis*, I, 3 (*PL* 195: 507).

40 B vi 210.

41 *Galatians* iii, 13-18.

42 B xix 178-185.

43 B xviii 20.

44 Cf. Eckhart, Sermon xlvii, *Meister Eckhart*, I, p. 124.

45 D. W. Robertson and B. F. Huppé, *Piers Plowman and Scriptural Tradition* (Princeton, 1951), p. 76, note 9.

46 *Summa Theologiae*, 1a, 93, art. 1, pp. 50, 51. The doctrine of deification, used by Langland at this point in the poem, was fairly common in the Middle Ages. Its fullest expression is found in the writings of Eckhart, for instance Sermon lvii: 'Our Lord says to every loving soul, "I was made man for you, and if ye are not God for me ye wrong me".', *Meister Eckhart*, I, p. 144. In England, at an earlier date, we find Edmund Rich using the same idea in *The Mirror of Holy Church*: 'God became man to make man God according to his nature.' See E. Colledge, *The Mediaeval Mystics of England* (1962), p. 132.

47 *Summa Theologiae*, 1a, 93, art. 4, pp. 60, 61.

48 *De Trinitate*, XIV, xvii, 23 and XIV, xviii, 24 (*PL* 42: 1054-1055). Cf. I *Corinthians* xv, 49 and II *Corinthians* iii, 18.

49 The traditional conflict between wit and will is referred to in the description of the court of Truth, B v 596.

50 C vi 82-83.

51 C vi 2 and B xviii 426; C xxi 473.

52 B xi 5-109.

53 B xi 315-394.
54 Cf. Ailred, *Speculum Charitatis*, I, 4 (*PL* 195: 508).
55 *Speculum Charitatis*, I, 5 (*PL* 195: 509).
56 B xv 540-543, C xviii 262-266.
57 B xvi 225-229, C xix 241-245; B xvii 138-262, C xx 111-228.
58 B v 546, i 135.
59 *Speculum Charitatis*, II, 4 (*PL* 195: 549). 1 *John* ii, 16.
60 F. Proctor and C. Wordsworth, *The Sarum Breviary* I (1882), pp. cccclxxxiii – div.
61 J. Wickham Legg, *The Sarum Missal* (1916), p. 79.
62 *Sarum Breviary*, I, pp. dclxxxv-dccviii.
63 B xviii 7-9.
64 B xviii 425.
65 B xix 205.
66 See note 3.
67 B vii 13-17, v 607-609, v 602.
68 B xix 224-243.
69 B xix 373-374, 381-388.

CHAPTER 7

1 *Pearl* (Oxford, 1953) p. xiv.
2 See especially R. W. Chambers, '*Piers Plowman*: a comparative study', *Man's Unconquerable Mind* (London, 1939) and G. Kane, 'The Vision of Piers Plowman', *Middle English Literature* (London, 1951). Kane discusses the relationship between poet and Dreamer in *Piers Plowman: the Evidence for Authorship* (London, 1965) and states that 'the procedure of naming Will in *Piers Plowman* indicates that the poet was not merely publishing his own baptismal name but also implying that the Dreamer was – to some indeterminable extent – made in his own image'. (p. 65.)
3 For a useful survey, see E. T. Donaldson, *Piers Plowman, the C-Text and its Poet* (New Haven, 1949) pp. 199-226.
4 *Piers the Plowman: Literary Relations of the A and B Texts* (Seattle, 1961) pp. 185-186.
5 *Piers Plowman: An Essay in Criticism* (London, 1962) p. 233.
6 *A Preface to Chaucer* (Princeton, 1963) p. 34.
7 *Piers Plowman and Scriptural Tradition* (Princeton, 1951) p. 240.
8 '*Troilus and Criseyde*' in *Chaucer and Chaucerians*, ed. D. S. Brewer (London, 1966) p. 78.

9 *Criticism and Medieval Poetry* (London, 1964) p. 92.

10 *Piers Plowman as a Fourteenth-century Apocalypse* (New Brunswick, 1961) p. 6.

11 J. Burrow, 'The Audience of *Piers Plowman*', *Anglia* lxxv (1957) 383.

12 *Pearl*, p. xiv-xv.

13 It would be convenient to interpret *shepe* as 'shepherd' and to see the Dreamer's self-portrait in terms of the rôles of 'active' shepherd and 'contemplative' hermit, neither of which he fills. However, such a sense is unlikely – see *OED shep*, 'A shepherd'.

14 Robertson and Huppé, pp. 33-34.

15 T. A. Knott and D. C. Fowler, *Piers the Plowman: a critical edition of the A-version* (Baltimore, 1952) give as their note '*unholy of werkis*. That is, a false hermit, one that leaves his cell and wanders about'. (154.) Compare Robertson and Huppé, p. 34 or Skeat's similar note in his Clarendon Press edition of the *Visio* (Oxford, 1869).

16 N. A. Chadwick, *An Edition of 'Disce Mori': Introduction and Seven Deadly Sins* (unpublished M.A. dissertation, University of Liverpool, 1966) notes the usual interpretation of the phrase in *Piers* when considering its meaning in 'Whan þei come to cherche, þei appere in þe presence of þeire lorde god with voide handes, vnholy of werkes, no þinge offrynge whiche is ayenst his comandement: but in habit gretly displesing vnto hym.' (123) but notes (294) that in *Disce Mori* at this point it seems to mean 'being guilty only of sins of omission': i.e. not having done any good works. Such an interpretation fits the Dreamer's rôle as observer and gives point to his quest for Dowel. On the other hand, while absence of good works is to be condemned in a layman, the concept of 'good works' has less point in the contemplative life of a recluse.

17 Donaldson, ch. v, discusses the poet's preoccupation with particular groups of people in the Field.

18 Cf. the description of Arthur in *Sir Gawain and the Green Knight*, 85-106, on which L. D. Benson comments: 'He will not eat until he sees or hears of some adventure (*it is noteworthy that he wishes only to see or hear of, not take part in, some adventure*) because of the custom that he through "nobleness" has acquired.' (*Art and Tradition in 'Sir Gawain and the Green Knight'* (New Brunswick, 1965) p. 97; my italics.)

19 Critics are virtually unanimous in maintaining that progression does take place in the Dreamer's understanding.

20 Convenient accounts are: W. C. Curry, *Chaucer and the Medieval*

Sciences (New York, 1926) ch. viii and C. B. Hieatt, *The Realism of Dream Visions* (The Hague, 1967).

21 See particularly: Bloomfield, pp. 11-14; E. Salter, *Piers Plowman, an Introduction* (Oxford, 1962) pp. 58-64; E. Salter and D. Pearsall (ed.), *Piers Plowman* (London, 1967) pp. 37-41.

22 E. Vasta (*The Spiritual Basis of Piers Plowman* (The Hague, 1965) pp. 28-29) argues that in his dreams Will receives, through grace, 'truths that surpass man's natural knowledge'. See also Salter and Pearsall, pp. 37-39.

23 *Romans* vii, 7-25.

24 See especially Fowler, p. 45 *et passim*.

25 V. A. Kolve, *The Play Called Corpus Christi* (London, 1966) ch. v.

26 Kolve, p. 113.

27 Kolve, p. 123.

28 Robertson and Huppé, p. 93. For a full discussion of the pardon scene see R. W. Frank, 'The Pardon Scene in *Piers Plowman*', *Speculum* xxvi (1951) 317-331 (reprinted in *Middle English Survey, Critical Essays*, ed. E. Vasta (Notre Dame, 1965)). This is the basis of Frank's discussion of the scene in his *Piers Plowman and the Scheme of Salvation* (London, 1957) ch. iii.

29 Robertson and Huppé, p. 101, regard the Dreamer as misled by the priest.

30 See the analysis of this episode by Lawlor, pp. 25-26.

31 The episode can, of course, be interpreted in many ways simultaneously; see Frank's account of criticism in his *Speculum* article.

32 e.g. Robertson and Huppé, p. 121: 'It should again be noted that Wit is not Will's Wit. The allegorical faculties are the faculties as such; the generalizations may be applied to the individual, but are not themselves of the individual.'

33 Kolve, p. 102.

34 'The Action of Langland's Second Vision', *EC* xv (1965) 247-268.

35 S. Delany, ' "Phantom" and the *House of Fame*', *Chaucer Review* ii (1967) 73.

36 For a different approach to this passage see Ben H. Smith, *Traditional Imagery of Charity in 'Piers Plowman'* (The Hague, 1966) pp. 21-35.

37 See the discussion by Donaldson, pp. 181-192. For other discussions of this passage see M. W. Bloomfield, '*Piers Plowman* and the Three Grades of Chastity', *Anglia* lxxvi (1958) 227-253 and Smith, pp. 56-73.

38 Salter and Pearsall, p. 146.

39 It may be noted that the presentation of the Trinity as three props

is a theologically dangerous image, and the angry look with which Piers stops further questions from the logically-minded Dreamer may reflect the poet's awareness of the inadequacy.

40 See Robertson and Huppé, pp. 191-192.

41 T. P. Dunning, *Piers Plowman, an Interpretation of the A-text* (London, 1938) p. 115.

42 Burrow, 'Action of Second Vision', states 'Repentance speaks, in the manner of a confessor, of absolving the Sins individually ... but his actual absolution ... is of a purely general and supplicatory character. He simply prays that God may have mercy on them all.' (251.) The difficulty is resolved if the sins are regarded as incapable of change.

43 Lawlor's phrase; critics (e.g. Dunning, pp. 120-126) praise the accuracy of the account and see it as a prelude to a more detailed working-out of a particular aspect in the rest of the poem.

44 *English Literature, Medieval* (London, reset 1945) p. 145; compare Lawlor's objections, pp. 248 f.

45 E. Vasta, 'Truth, the Best Treasure, in *Piers Plowman*,' *PQ* xliv (1965) 17-29, treats, in a rather different way, the problem of the individual and finite versus the absolute and infinite: 'As applied to God, *treuthe* names what is fixed and absolute: as applied to man, *treuthe* names the quality in virtue of which man on earth is transmuted, not to an identity with God, but to a conformity with him – to being *a* god and *like* Christ'. (21.) Working out this approach in his *The Spiritual Basis of 'Piers Plowman'* (The Hague, 1965) Vasta can conclude: 'Will is able to see the deified Piers because he is now like Piers. He, himself, has achieved perfection, and at this moment [C xxii 5-14] he is experiencing contemplation.' (138.) I would argue rather that this potential identity is never achieved.

CHAPTER 8

1 S. S. Hussey, 'Langland, Hilton and the Three Lives', *RES* vii (1956) 132-150; T. P. Dunning, 'The Structure of the B-text of *Piers Plowman*', ibid., 225-237.

2 J. Lawlor, *Piers Plowman: an Essay in Criticism* (London, 1962) p. 301.

3 *Matthew* iv, 4. Cf. Bromyard, s.v. *Vita*, speaking about the *Vita gratiae*: 'Hanc autem vitam, quedam in nobis causant, quaedam ostendunt: quedam conservant. Primo in nobis hanc causant auditus verbi Dei, sicut cibus corporis causat bonam vitam corporis: ita iste

cibus bonam vitam anime. Proverb. 4. Fili mi ausculta sermones meos, & ad eloquia mea inclina aurem tuam. Vita enim sunt invenientibus ea. Deuteronom. 8. & Matth. 4. Non in solo pane vivit homo &c . . . (*Summa Prædicantium*, Venice 1586, ff. 436v-437r). Cf. also opening of Bishop Brinton's Sermon 76 (*The Sermons of Thomas Brinton, Bishop of Rochester (1373-1389)*, edited by Sister Mary Aquinas Devlin, O.P., Camden Society Third Series lxxxv-vi (1954) II, 346).

4 G. R. Owst, *Literature and Pulpit in Medieval England* (Cambridge, 1933) ch. ix.

5 'Now there is this difference between men and angels, according to Dionysius: an angel perceives truth by simple apprehension, but a man comes finally to gaze upon simple truth only by progressive steps. Consequently, the contemplative life has only one activity in which it finally terminates and from which it derives its unity, namely the contemplation of truth, but it has several activities by which it arrives at this final activity. Some of these have to do with the understanding of principles from which one proceeds to contemplation of truth; others with the deduction from those principles to the truth one seeks to know . . .', *Summa Theologiae* II-II, 180, 3 (Blackfriars ed. 1966, pp. 22-23). Compare various fourteenth-century translations of *The Mirror of St Edmund*, EETS OS 26, pp. 20-22, 50; OS 98, pp. 224-225, 231 ff, 269 ff. See a summary of St Bonaventura's teaching in the *Itinerarium Mentis in Deum* in Hilda Graef, *The Light and the Rainbow* (1959) pp. 227-232.

6 *PL* 95: 303-309; translated by Sister Rose de Lima in *Life of the Spirit*, Nov. 1953, pp. 215, 216-217.

7 *Summa Theologiae*, II-II, qu. 179-182. Published as a separate volume, vol. 46, in the Blackfriars translation, *Action and Contemplation*, ed. Jordan Aumann, O.P. In Appendix I, Father Aumann summarizes St Thomas's teaching as follows: 'From a theological viewpoint, we conclude that there are two types or aspects of life in every man. Man's life on earth is a journey towards a goal, but this requires in the first place a kind of vision of the goal which is sought (contemplative aspect) and then a movement towards that goal by the performance of human acts (active aspect). This division into contemplative and active is a complete division because it proceeds according to what is proper to man as intelligent, and because the division of intelligence into speculative and practical is complete and sufficient.' (p. 86.)

8 MS e Mus. 35 (Bodley), marked in pages: pp. 244-245. The quota-

tion is from a prose treatise in which a great amount of theological doctrine is linked with the seven petitions of the Lord's Prayer. The treatise also occurs in MS Rawl. A. 356. It is referred to in the Summary Catalogue as a prose rendering of the *Speculum Vitae*. However, this prose treatise is different from William of Nassington's verse work, and also differs in detail from Friar Lorens's *Somme*.

9 Summary given by W. A. Pantin, 'Two Treatises of Uthred of Boldon on the Monastic Life' in *Studies in Medieval History Presented to F. M. Powicke* (1948) p. 376.

10 Uthred sums up his teaching neatly in his conclusion: 'Primo constare poterit ex premissis in quo modo vivendi sit ponenda pro hac vita hominis perfeccio personalis, quia videlicet in vita virtuosa secundum istas tres virtutes theologicas, et pro quanto in illis est virtuosior, de tanto perfeccior est persona, ut superius est ostensum; 2°. quod perfeccio status sive perfeccio gradualis ecclesie militantis consistit in illa vita quadruplici varie prout oportunitas exegerit executa, quam Dominus noster Ihesus in persona propria exemplavit, Iohannes Baptista, apostoli et eorum successores inferioresque prelati diligencius exequebantur et adhuc singuli secundum quod eis competit exequuntur exequive deberent . . .' (Pantin, pp. 376-377).

11 *Summa Theologiae* II-II, 179, 2.

12 *Summa Theologiae* II-II, 184, 185.

13 *Meditations on the Life of Christ*, trans. Sister M. Emmanuel (1934) p. 224 (beginning of ch. xlvii).

14 *Meditations*, end of ch. xlv, p. 220. Bromyard, *Summa*, ff. 435v-436r. Langland could certainly have known and used Bromyard's encyclopaedic work; Dr A. B. Emden has shown that it is mentioned in a MS sermon of 1354 (*Biogr. Reg. of the Univ. of Oxford*, I, p. 278).

15 For convenience, I use the Bodley Catalogue title of this work in e Mus. 35 and Rawl. A. 356, although it is not precisely a prose rendering of the *Speculum Vitæ*.

16 *Meditations*, ch. xlv, p. 219.

17 Ed. W. Nelson Francis, EETS OS 217, pp. 220-221.

18 *Book of Virtues and Vices*, p. 376.

19 *Summa Theologiae* II-II, 184, aa. 4 & 5.

20 *Op. cit.* pp. 119-120.

21 Scripture's *multi multa sciunt, et seipsos nesciunt* are the opening lines of a well-known chapter of St Bernard's *Meditations*, and the vision following in passus xi (lines 4-61) is inspired by this chapter: see a

summary of the chapter which reads like a summary of the opening of passus xi in Sermon 16b of *Middle English Sermons*, ed. W. O. Ross, EETS OS 209, pp. 98-99.

22 From the prose *Mirror of St Edmund*, ed. Perry, EETS OS 26, p. 20.

23 Brinton, II, 347. Ross, Sermon 43, p. 285. Cf. *The Book of Virtues and Vices*, pp. 172-184.

24 MS Rawl. A. 356, f. 11v. Cf. Sermon 44 in MS Royal 18 B. xxiii, which brings together all three practices placed before Haukyn in passus xiv: 'And þer-fore ȝiff þat þou wilte haue God in þin herte, firste clense it with contricion fro all filth of synne'; 'Poverte is þat oþur þat helpeþ þer-to, to holde clennes in herte and to halowe God þer-in'; 'The thirde þinge is þis þat kepeþ an herte clene, a souerayne vertewe, þe wiche is mekenes'. (Ross, pp. 291-292.)

25 Ross, pp. 297-299.

26 Pantin, pp. 375-376.

27 Devlin, II, pp. 392, 393. In this sermon, Bishop Brinton attacks the pernicious practice of making confession to extraordinary confessors such as friars not canonically empowered by the bishop of the diocese.

28 Ross, Sermon 43, p. 288.

29 Cf. *The Book of Virtues and Vices*: 'Þe sixte bataile, þat is riȝt stronge, is aȝens þe schrewen þat ben in þis world, þat beþ membres of Antecrist, þat maken werre vpon goode men wiþ here strenkþe . . . Þe membres of þat beest schewen now ouer al in wikked lordes and in wikked prelates þat þurgh here grete couetise defoulen and streepen and freten here pore vunderlynges . . .' (p. 186).

30 See, in particular, Sermons 85, 86 and 99; Devlin, II.

31 *Middle English Sermons*, p. 285.

32 Uthred of Boldon, *De perfectione vivendi*. In his conclusion, Uthred sums up thus: 'Et quanto gradus vel status talis fuerit superior in ecclesia militante, de tanto est perfeccior iudicandus, et consequentur convenerit quod proficiendus in gradum vel statum talem foret excellencior in perfeccione hominis personali'. (Pantin, p. 377.)

33 See *Speculum Christiani*, passim, but especially pp. 170 ff, on obligations and defects of priests. Ed. Holmstedt, EETS OS 182.

CHAPTER 9

1 E. T. Donaldson, *Piers Plowman: The C-Text and Its Poet* (New Haven, 1949) ch. vi.

2 E. Suddaby, 'The Poem *Piers Plowman*', *JEGP* liv (1955) 103.
3 S. S. Hussey, 'Langland, Hilton, and the Three Lives', *RES* vii (1956) 150.
4 E. Zeeman, '*Piers Plowman* and the Pilgrimage to Truth', *Essays and Studies* xi (1958) 15-16.
5 M. W. Bloomfield, *Piers Plowman as a Fourteenth-century Apocalypse* (New Brunswick, 1961) p. vii.
6 J. Lawlor, *Piers Plowman: An Essay in Criticism* (London, 1962) p. 301.
7 E. Vasta, *The Spiritual Basis of Piers Plowman* (The Hague, 1965) p. 27.
8 C. Muscatine, 'Locus of Action in Medieval Narrative', *Romance Philology* xvii (1963) 120.
9 Lawlor, p. 9. The same word is used by E. Salter and D. Pearsall in their edition of *Piers Plowman* (London, 1967) p. 36.
10 I have elaborated this view in my forthcoming book *The Gawain Country: A Study of the Topography of 'Sir Gawain and the Green Knight'*.
11 R. Woolf, 'Some Non-Medieval Qualities of *Piers Plowman*', *EC* xii (1962) 117.
12 Lawlor, p. 9.
13 This theme is discussed rather more fully in my 'Landscape and Rhetoric in Middle English Alliterative Poetry', *Melbourne Critical Review* iv (1961) 65-76.
14 See A. H. Bright, *New Light on Piers Plowman* (London, 1928).
15 See B x 326, C vi 177; and the articles by N. Coghill in *MÆ* iv (1935) 83-89 and by G. D. G. Hall in *MÆ* xxviii (1959) 91-95.
16 See M. W. Bloomfield in *PQ* xxxv (1956) 60 ff.
17 Vasta, p. 26.
18 W. P. Ker, *English Literature Medieval* (London 1912, repr. 1945) p. 145.
19 Muscatine, p. 122.
20 J. Burrow, 'The Action of Langland's Second Vision', *EC* xv (1965) 267-268.
21 Cp. J. Martin, 'Wil as Fool and Wanderer in *Piers Plowman*', *Texas Studies in Literature and Language* iii (1962) 535-548, especially 543 ff, and Woolf, p. 118.
22 J. F. Adams, '*Piers Plowman* and the Three Ages of Man', *JEGP* lxi (1962) 39.
23 Zeeman, p. 8.

24 Langland repeats *faste* five times in less than twenty lines, but this is greatly modified in the C-text.

25 Woolf, p. 117.

26 J. A. Burrow, 'The Audience of *Piers Plowman*', *Anglia* lxxv (1957) 383.

27 T. P. Dunning, *Piers Plowman: An Interpretation of the A-text* (Dublin, 1937) p. 153.

28 From *Piers Plowman: The A-Version*, ed. G. Kane (London, 1960).

29 Lawlor, p. 113.

30 Martin, p. 541.

31 R. W. Frank argues for unity of place and time for the *Visio*, but this cannot be extended to the *Vita*. See his 'The Pardon Scene in *Piers Plowman*', *Speculum* xxvi (1951) 324.

32 S. J. Kahrl, 'Allegory in Practice: A Study of Narrative Styles in Medieval Exempla', *MP* lxiii (1965) 107.

33 Thus J. J. Jusserand in *Piers Plowman. A Contribution to the History of English Mysticism*, tr. M.E.R. (repr. New York, 1965) p. 155: 'There is therefore nothing prepared, artistically arranged, or skilfully contrived, in his poem. The deliberate hand of the man of the craft is nowhere to be seen. He obtains artistic effects, but without seeking for them; he never selects or co-ordinates.'

34 Recently, for example, by S. S. Hussey, 'Langland's Reading of Alliterative Poetry', *MLR* lx (1965) 164.

35 Burrow, 'Audience', pp. 377 ff.

36 Cp. A. C. Spearing, *Criticism and Medieval Poetry* (London, 1964) ch. iv.

37 R. E. Kaske, 'The Use of Simple Figures of Speech in *Piers Plowman* B: A Study in the Figurative Expression of Ideas and Opinions', *SP* xlviii (1951) 599.

38 Lawlor, p. 208.

39 D. Traversi, 'Langland's *Piers Plowman*', in *The Age of Chaucer*, ed. B. Ford (London, 1954) 143.

40 E. Salter, *Piers Plowman: An Introduction* (Oxford, 1962) p. 7.

41 Cp. J. P. Oakden, *Alliterative Poetry in Middle English. A Survey of the Traditions* (Manchester, 1935) pp. 389-391.

42 *MED* s.v. *grēt* (3), 2.

43 See A. H. Smith, *English Place-Name Elements*, English Place-Name Soc. xxvi II, 133 ff. s.v. *sōcn*.

44 *Sir Gawain and the Green Knight*, ed. J. R. R. Tolkien and E. V. Gordon; 2nd. ed. revised by N. Davis (Oxford, 1967) line 2098.

45 This is quite lost in the much tamer C-version.

46 Salter, p. 71.
47 *Piers the Plowman. A Critical Edition of the A-Version*, ed. T. A. Knott and D. C. Fowler (Baltimore, 1952).
48 Although some manuscripts read *balkes*, the word used in *Pearl* 62.
49 M. L. Samuels, 'Some Applications of Middle English Dialectology', *English Studies* xliv (1963) 81-94, especially p. 94.
50 Although it must be remembered that the C revision often achieves the opposite effect. Cp. Donaldson, pp. 51 ff.
51 *Pearl*, ed. E. V. Gordon (Oxford, 1953) line 65.
52 Woolf, p. 118.
53 Whose individuality at least and perhaps his identity also have been established beyond doubt by G. Kane's authoritative study, *Piers Plowman. The Evidence for Authorship* (London, 1965).
54 I wish to express my thanks to Miss Carolyn A. Angas for her assistance in the preparation of this essay.

CHAPTER 10

1 For extensive consideration of the relationship of *Piers Plowman* to medieval sermons see G. R. Owst, *Literature and Pulpit in Medieval England* (Cambridge, 1933) ch. ix; A. C. Spearing, *Criticism and Medieval Poetry* (London, 1964) ch. iv; E. Salter and D. Pearsall, *Piers Plowman* (London, 1967) pp. 48 ff.
2 See below p. 275.
3 All quotations are from the B-text unless otherwise stated.
4 See R. Quirk, 'Vis Imaginativa', *JEGP* liii (1954) 81-83 and M. W. Bloomfield, *Piers Plowman as a Fourteenth-century Apocalypse* (New Brunswick, 1961) Appendix III.
5 See *Catholic Encyclopaedia* XIV, pp. 384-385.
6 This, I believe, must be true, however familiar the reader might be with Langland's imagery. See B. H. Smith, *Traditional Imagery of Charity in Piers Plowman* (The Hague, 1966) pp. 56 ff.
7 The poet's concern with this problem is further evidenced by the differences in argument, expansion and contraction and arrangement of lines in the three texts. But the same tentative 'conclusion' is reached in C as in B. The differences have been analysed by E. T. Donaldson, *Piers Plowman: The C-Text and Its Poet* (New Haven, 1949) pp. 130 ff.
8 Immediately after this, Langland uses the Martha-Mary story, not

as the usual illustration of the superiority of contemplative life over active, but to elevate poverty.

9 See my '*Cortaysye* in Middle English', *Mediaeval Studies* xxix (1967) 143-157.

10 The poet's continuing concern with the problem of the necessity of baptism for salvation is indicated by the very heavy revision of such passages in the C-text. These have been examined in detail by G. H. Russell, 'The Salvation of the Heathen: the Exploration of a Theme in *Piers Plowman*', *Journal of the Warburg and Courtauld Institutes* xxix (1966) 101-116.

11 An interesting work, contemporary with the B-text of *Piers Plowman* and concerned with many of the same problems, is Wimbledon's Sermon (ed. I. K. Knight, Duquesne U.P., 1967) called by Millar Maclure 'the most famous sermon ever delivered at Paul's Cross'. This work shares similar attitudes with *Piers Plowman*, particularly in social matters, but when it promises eternal damnation for evil-doing, unlike *Piers Plowman* not once does it include an 'escape clause' to indicate the expectation, or even possibility, of God's ultimate mercy.

CHAPTER 11

1 See Northrop Frye's glossary under *Fictional*: 'Relating to literature in which there are internal characters, apart from the author and his audience.' *Anatomy of Criticism* (Princeton, 1957) p. 365.

2 Gilbert Highet's book *Juvenal the Satirist: A Study* (Oxford, 1954) devotes a long section to Juvenal's survival which may be taken as paradigmatic for the fortunes of Roman satire in the Middle Ages, see Part iii, especially pp. 180-205.

3 E. R. Curtius, *European Literature and the Latin Middle Ages*, trans. W. R. Trask (New York, 1953) pp. 49-50.

4 As Highet shows, pp. 191-203.

5 I quote from E. G. Stanley's edition (London, 1960), lines 894-898 and 217-220.

6 J. Peter, *Complaint and Satire in Early English Literature* (Oxford, 1956).

7 See the review by J. Kinsley and S. W. Dawson, *RES* ix (1958) 60-63 and that by Sears Jayne, *MP* lv (1957-58) 200-202.

8 A number of the lyrics in the Vernon MS have strong satirical elements, see Carleton Brown's *Religious Lyrics of the XIVth*

Century, 2nd. ed. revised by G. V. Smithers (Oxford, 1952) pp. 125-208. Many of the lyrics printed by R. H. Robbins in his edition of *Historical Poems of the XIVth and XVth Centuries* (New York, 1959) are satirical and there are a few satirical songs in his edition of *Secular Lyrics of the XIVth and XVth Centuries* (Oxford, 1952).

9 On this topic see S. S. Hussey, 'Langland's Reading of Alliterative Poetry', *MLR* lx (1965) 163-170 and E. Salter '*Piers Plowman* and *The Simonie*', *Archiv für das Studium der neueren Sprachen und Literaturen*, cciii (1967) 241-254.

10 *Defensio Curatorum* in EETS OS 167.

11 See G. H. Russell, 'The Salvation of the Heathen: The Exploration of a Theme in *Piers Plowman*', *Journal of the Warburg and Courtauld Institutes* xxix (1966) 101-116, especially pp. 112-116.

12 In his book *Alliterative Poetry in Middle English: A Survey of the Traditions* (Manchester, 1935), J. P. Oakden identifies these poems as being 'The *Piers Plowman* Group', though he considers *Richard the Redeles* and *Mum and the Soothsegger* to be separate poems; part II, p. 178.

13 I quote from Skeat's C-text for two reasons: firstly because until the new editions of B and C appear Skeat's C-text seems textually the more reliable, and secondly because it now seems possible to accept as a premise that this text is Langland's last word on his topic; see George Kane, *Piers Plowman: The Evidence for Authorship* (London, 1965) and G. H. Russell's article in this volume, pp. 27-49.

14 A only barely mentions the land-owning class (line 96 in Kane's edition), but although B and C discuss this estate at length the other additions they make tend to obscure this potentially greater clarity; the rats' fable has this effect, and C, which gives Conscience a good deal to say which was merely described in B and also includes the Ophni and Fineas passage in the speech (lines 103-124), is even more formless.

15 This is a mutation of the scene which is suggestively dream-like; it is hardly what is implied by the 'toure on a toft' in the first passus.

16 For a detailed exposition of this, see T. P. Dunning, *Piers Plowman: An Interpretation of the A-Text* (Dublin, 1937), especially pp. 31-51.

17 Carleton Brown, in *Religious Lyrics of the XIVth Century*, prints a number of lyrics of this sort: 'A lament over the Passion' (pp. 94-95), 'A Song of the Love of Jesus' (pp. 102-106) and 'A Salutation to Jesus' (pp. 106-107).

18 This is all reminiscent of some of the comic scenes in the medieval drama; the comedy of the vice in the morality plays is perhaps one

example, but closer analogues come from the miracle plays: see in particular V. A. Kolve's discussion in *The Play Called Corpus Christi* (Stanford, 1966) ch. vii.

19 In A Conscience preaches *with a crois*; in B Reason preaches *with a crosse*, but in C Reason preaches *reuested ryȝt as a pope* and *Conscience his crocer* stands before the king. C is thus more precisely referring back to the first dream.

20 This is particularly effective in C, where the discussion of those who will receive the pardon is greatly extended, see C x 186-281.

21 There now seems to be a general agreement on the meaning of the pardon scene, see Dunning, pp. 145-152, and for an authoritative analysis R. W. Frank, *Piers Plowman and the Scheme of Salvation* (New Haven, 1957) pp. 22-33. Of course, there is a curious omission here in the C-text, as if the A/B-version is too complicated and allusive, and so any study based on C has to be cautious in discussing the pardon. But it seems to me that the general effect in C is the same as A/B.

22 The A MSS which name this section of the poem all call it the *Vita* (see Kane's edition, pp. 1-18). The B- and C-versions seem to use the term *Visio* when they use a term at all. Many critics have spoken of the 'lives' of Do Wel, Bet and Best, but the B- and C-texts do not divide the manuscripts in this way. This does not mean, of course, that the poem is not divided in this way, though it might make it seem rather less likely. The exact connotation of the manuscript divisions in the continuation of the poem is a difficult problem and may well be an important one, but it is one that cannot really be discussed adequately until the new editions of B and C appear.

23 I have in mind Meed's speech against Conscience, iv 221-284.

24 In *The Autobiographical Fallacy in Chaucer and Langland Studies* (London, 1956) George Kane has effectively shown that we should use a term like pseudo-autobiography in a case like this.

25 The *locus classicus* is G. R. Owst, *Literature and Pulpit in Medieval England* (Cambridge, 1933), especially ch. iv, 'Fiction and Instruction in the Sermon *Exempla*'.

26 Langland's imagery has been discussed to some extent by Elizabeth Salter, *Piers Plowman: An Introduction* (Oxford, 1962), especially pp. 48-52. There have been other discussions of elements of the imagery, like E. T. Donaldson's examination of the minstrel images, *Piers Plowman: The C-Text and Its Poet* (New Haven, 1949), pp. 147-153, and R. E. Kaske, 'The Use of Simple Figures of Speech in *Piers Plowman* B: A Study in the Figurative Expression of Ideas and

z

Opinions', *SP* xlviii (1951) 571-600, but a full literary discussion, similar to Caroline Spurgeon's analyses of Shakespeare's imagery, would be very welcome.

27 xvi 9-12 discusses friars in detail; it is a short waking passage, for Will falls asleep at line 25.

28 There are obvious examples – *Sir Gawain and the Green Knight*, almost all of Chaucer's works, *The Testament of Cresseid* and so on – but it is also common in lyrics and ballads for the season and climate to set the tone for the action and feeling of the whole piece.

29 Ymagynatyf has said this, xiv 230-234, and Study has implied it, xii 129-133.

30 David Knowles finds this to be the basic concept of St Anselm's influential revitalizing of Augustinian material, *The Evolution of Medieval Thought* (London, 1962) especially pp. 98-106.

31 M. W. Bloomfield, in his stimulating book *Piers Plowman as a Fourteenth-century Apocalypse* (New Brunswick, 1961) gives a detailed analysis of this section of the poem, pp. 127-154.

32 In this respect *Piers Plowman* is unlike *The Pilgrim's Progress* and *The Divine Comedy*, and more like *Paradise Lost*; it is a point which casts a good deal of light on the poet's scheme as a whole.

33 In this implication, Langland's analysis rather agrees with the most authoritative modern historian, see David Knowles, *The Religious Orders in England*, I (Cambridge, 1948) especially ch. xi 'The Friars Minor', pp. 114-126, and ch. xv 'The Evolution of the Franciscan Ideal', pp. 171-179.

34 It is bold because such a questioning of an institution seems rare; even FitzRalph's attack is not so radical. Bloomfield discusses this issue, pp. 148-149, but even he can find little other evidence of arguments quite like Langland's; see also his ch. iii.

35 John Lawlor has discussed Langland's style at some length in *Piers Plowman: An Essay in Criticism* (London, 1962) pp. 189-239, and Bloomfield has some perceptive comments, pp. 34-41. But in general, Langland's diction and metrics, like his imagery, await a full critical discussion.

CHAPTER 12

1 All references to *Piers Plowman* are to the B-text unless stated otherwise, and the text of Chaucer is that of Robinson.

2 Reproduced on dust-cover. For Calvert's Ploughman see R. Lister, *Edward Calvert* (London, 1962), plate xvii and analysis pp. 66-73 and L. Binyon, *The Followers of William Blake* (London, 1925), plate 6.

3 Edward Thomas, *The Last Sheaf* (London, 1928), p. 101.

4 Robert of Gloucester, *Chronicle* ed. W. A. Wright (Rolls Series) lines 1-2, 180-181.

5 *Statua Antiqua Universitatis Oxoniensis*, ed. Strickland Gibson (Oxford, 1931) p. 208.

6 T. Sharp, *Oxford Replanned* (London, 1948), p. 20.

7 N. Coghill, 'Two Notes on *Piers Plowman*,' *MÆ* iv (1935) 92.

Index